Hilkhot Nashim

Halakhic Source Guides

Volume I

JOFA
JEWISH ORTHODOX FEMINIST ALLIANCE

מגיד
MAGGID

HALAKHIC SOURCE GUIDES

HILKHOT NASHIM

הלכות נשים

Volume I

Kaddish
Birkat Hagomel
Megillah

EDITED BY

Raḥel Berkovits

JOFA
Maggid Books

Hilkhot Nashim
Halakhic Source Guides
Volume I: Kaddish, Birkat Hagomel, Megillah

First Edition, 2018

Maggid Books
An imprint of Koren Publishers Jerusalem Ltd.

POB 8531, New Milford, CT 06776-8531, USA
& POB 4044, Jerusalem 9104001, Israel
www.maggidbooks.com

The publication of this book was made possible through
the generous support of *Torah Education in Israel.*

ISBN 978-1-59264-467-4, *hardcover*

A CIP catalogue record for this title is
available from the British Library.

Printed and bound in the United States

Contents

Dedication

This entire project is dedicated to my father, Jacques Censor (Ya'akov ben Moshe veTemerel), *a"h*. A diamond merchant all his adult life, he was a man of few pretensions but he was brilliant, innovative, and had a wry, wicked sense of humor. He was fluent in six languages and was widely read.

He knew vast sections of the Talmud by heart, but never made a display of his knowledge or capabilities. When I had a halakhic question during my internship and residency, I would simply call him on the phone from the hospital, tell him the problem and on the spot he would quote me a seemingly relevant piece of Gemara and explain how to deal with the issue. I was always a bit suspicious of his convenient Gemara "quotations" since the rabbis of his Talmud always seem to rule exactly as I had hoped. One day, however, as I was reading Rabbi Dr. Lord Imanuel Jacobovits's book on medical ethics, there was one of the Gemaras, exactly as Dad had quoted! I quickly called him and confessed to my previous doubts and apologized. I never could understand how he knew so much, since I knew he did not have the time to learn as we were growing up. He laughed and explained that he had learned with his mentor, Rabbi Berger, in Antwerp, Belgium, after work from age eighteen until he was twenty-six, when Rabbi Berger went on *aliya* to then Palestine. "I just remember it all," he said.

When I was growing up, the tradition was to send boys to *yeshivah* and girls to public school. However, I was sent to Ramaz along with my brother. My father's expectations were exactly the same for both of us. He studied Gemara and Ḥumash with me just as he did with my brother. In fact, his greatest pleasure later in life was to learn Gemara with my oldest child, a daughter, right up until the day he suffered his devastating stroke.

He died in 2005, unfortunately before this project was conceived. He would have loved these source guides. My father was a firm believer that the way we would be most likely to keep *halakhah* was if we understood the issues behind the rulings and made the determination for ourselves, rather than him telling us what we had to do.

He is sorely missed.

Monique ("Nicky") C. Katz, M.D.

Abbreviations

M.	Mishnah	*Meg.*	Megillah
B.T.	Babylonian Talmud	*Ḥag.*	Ḥagigah
J.T.	Jerusalem Talmud	*Yev.*	Yevamot
T.	Tosefta	*Ketub.*	Ketubbot
		Ned.	Nedarim
Sh. Ar.	*Shulḥan Arukh*	*Sot.*	Sotah
O.Ḥ.	*Oraḥ Hayyim*	*Git.*	Gittin
E.H.	*Even Ha'ezer*	*Kid.*	Kiddushin
Ḥ.M.	*Ḥoshen Mishpat*	*B. Kam.*	Bava Kamma
Y.D.	*Yoreh De'ah*	*B. Mets.*	Bava Metsia
		B. Bat.	Bava Batra
Ber.	Berakhot	*Sanh.*	Sanhedrin
Shab.	Shabbat	*Shevu.*	Shevuot
Eiruv.	Eiruvin	*Eduy.*	Eduyot
Pesaḥ.	Pesaḥim	*Avod. Zar.*	Avodah Zarah
Suk.	Sukkah	*Menaḥ.*	Menaḥot
Beits.	Beitsah	*Arakh.*	Arakhin
Rosh Hash.	Rosh Hashanah	*Nid.*	Niddah

Preface

גדול תלמוד שהתלמוד מביא לידי מעשה.

Great is Torah study for it leads to observance. (Sifrei Devarim 41)

This series presents an in-depth look at halakhic topics that affect a woman's obligation and involvement in Jewish ritual life. These essays aim to increase awareness of relevant halakhic issues among women and men so that they can make deliberate choices about their observance. We believe that placing great value on the Jewish tradition of learning and developing the skills needed to understand *halakhah* and its processes are crucial in maintaining a passionate and informed commitment to observance among Jews. One of the main goals of this series is to clarify what the texts actually say, with the hope that increased knowledge and a better understanding of the reasons behind common practice will lead to increased observance. The aim of an in-depth analysis of these sources is that the reader will learn not only what the normative *halakhah* is, but will understand how it developed; that under the surface of what is considered normative *halakhah* is a dialectic of multiple and valid attempts at understanding and interpreting our earliest halakhic literature.

In these essays, the rabbinic texts themselves are presented not as references but as the main focus of the discussion. All sources are explained and translated into English to enable the reader with a limited Hebrew language background to also work through the original texts. We invite you, the reader, to come and learn the relevant Talmudic, Geonic, medieval, and modern rabbinic texts; to become more knowledgeable about the rich halakhic discussion on each topic; and to find your place in the chain of the *masoret* – the tradition.

In this first volume of the series we focus on some of the rituals connected to the synagogue, where in the modern day, women first started to take a more active participatory role – reciting *kaddish* to mourn the loss of a loved one; blessing *hagomel* after a dangerous experience, childbirth, or illness; and reading *Megillat Ester* to publicize the Purim miracle. Besides learning the texts on your own, we encourage you to invite a friend to study the sources in a *ḥavruta* partnership or to organize a study group in your community. It is our wish that these essays bring fervor for a knowledge of the halakhic sources to communities, study groups, classes, and the individuals who learn them.

We dedicate this series to women who are committed to *halakhah* and are struggling to embrace more of our beautiful heritage, to better fulfill the *mitsvot* of *ahavat Hashem* (love of God) and *avodat Hashem* (service of God), and in doing so, enrich the entire Jewish community.

גל עיני ואביטה נפלאות מתורתך.

Open my eyes so I will see the wonders from Your Torah. (Psalms 119:18)

ACKNOWLEDGMENTS

With *shevakh* and *hoda'ah leHashem* on the printing of this first volume in the *Hilkhot Nashim* series, we would like to thank the following people for their expertise, creativity, and contributions to the series: Carol Newman, Robin Bodner, Adina Gerver, Adam Parker, Leslie Rubin, Miles B. Cohen, Jonathan Kremer, Dina Najman, Devorah Zlochower, and Debby Koren. The series would not be possible without the support and dedication of current and former JOFA professional staff. We would also like to thank the staff at Maggid Books, Gila Fine, Tomi Mager, Mikhael Reuven, Nechama Unterman, and Shira Finson, who devoted countless hours to turning the series into a printed reality.

Raḥel Berkovits, Halakhic Editor
Monique C. Katz, Patron
Gail A. Katz, Project Coordinator

A Daughter's Recitation: Women and Mourner's *Kaddish*

Raḥel Berkovits

INTRODUCTION

The emotionally charged recitation of mourner's *kaddish*[1] for a deceased loved one stands at the heart of the Jewish bereavement experience. A strong sense of parental honor and duty creates a feeling of obligation among Jews of all backgrounds and pulls them to the synagogue daily to recite the mourner's *kaddish*. Traditionally, this public testimony to bereavement and personal crisis has been seen as the job of the son; however, the possibility of a daughter reciting *kaddish* for a deceased parent is not purely a modern concept. The earliest texts in the halakhic literature on this topic deal with the situation in which there are no sons to recite *kaddish*. Many of the cases record that fathers, concerned with their lack of sons, willed or commanded their daughters to recite *kaddish* on their behalf and even arranged a structure for them to do so. These texts make up the basis for discussion in the modern sources when a daughter wishes to honor her deceased parents through the recitation of *kaddish*, regardless of the existence of male siblings. The halakhic literature discusses and analyzes this issue of *kaddish* by addressing the following questions:[2]

---

1. This chapter will use the accepted English expression "mourner's *kaddish*." However, it is important to note that this phrase is not an accurate translation of the Hebrew *kaddish yatom*, which literally means "orphan's *kaddish*." The reframing of the English translation to include all mourners and not just those who have lost their fathers (or parents) reflects a major shift in the evolution of the *kaddish* ritual itself, which will be discussed later in this chapter.
2. Many of the questions listed point in opposite directions. This oddity is an outgrowth of the complex issues involved in the topic and understanding of mourner's *kaddish* itself and will be explained in the course of this chapter.
   This topic also deals with another subset of interesting questions:
   - Are daughters considered halakhic offspring?
   - Should *ben/banim* be read exclusively to refer to son/sons or inclusively to refer to child/children?
   - Can women also bring *naḥat ruaḥ* (peace of spirit) to the deceased?
   - Are women obligated in *kiddush Hashem* (public sanctification of God's name)?
   - What is the interplay among social norms, custom, and law?

1. May a daughter recite mourner's *kaddish*?[3]
2. Is there a difference between a daughter reciting *kaddish* in the synagogue or in a private *minyan* (prayer quorum of ten) at her home?
3. May she recite *kaddish* from the women's section of the synagogue?
4. Must she recite *kaddish* from the women's section of the wsynagogue?
5. May she recite *kaddish* alone or must it be in conjunction with a man?
6. Must she recite *kaddish* aloud or only quietly?[4]

Clearly, women are obligated in the laws of mourning[5] and are required to honor their parents.[6] However, the ritual of *kaddish*, although strongly linked to these two halakhic categories,[7] does not fall clearly into either of them. To fully understand the issues surrounding women's recitation

3. Leon Wieseltier, in his book *Kaddish* (New York: Alfred A. Knopf, 1998), eloquently states on p. 178:

   > May a woman say *kaddish*? It is a controversial question. It sounds to some like a feminist provocation. But ask the question differently. May a daughter say *kaddish*? Suddenly the controversy disappears, at least for me. If you deny the *kaddish* to the daughter, then you do not understand the *kaddish*. The *kaddish* is not an obligation of gender. It is an obligation of descent. This is not about men, this is about sons. This is not about women, this is about daughters.

4. Does the *minyan* need to hear the words to respond and therefore she must say *kaddish* aloud or is there a prohibition against hearing a woman's voice in the synagogue and so she should recite it quietly? Is it sufficient for just other women, and not the men who constitute the *minyan*, to hear her recitation and respond to her *kaddish*?
5. See Rambam, *Sefer Hamitsvot* Positive Commandment 27 and *Mishneh Torah, Hilk. Avel* 2:1; *Sefer Haḥinnukh,* end of 264; *Mordekhai Mo'ed Katan,* end of 890; *Responsa Mahari Veil* 13; *Sh. Ar., Y.D.* 374:4 and 390:5; and *Be'ur Hagra, Y.D.* 390:7.
6. See Exod. 20:11; Deut. 5:15; Lev. 19:3, Rashi ad loc.; M. *Kid.* 1:7; T. *Kid.* 1:1; B.T. *Kid.* 29a and 30b–31a; Rambam, *Hilk. Mamrim* 6:6; *Tur, Y.D.* 240; *Sh. Ar., Y.D.* 240:17 and *Shakh* ad loc. 19.
7. The general idea that a child must honor his or her parents after their deaths is reflected in B.T. *Kid.* 31b; Rambam, *Hilk. Mamrim* 6:5; and *Sh. Ar., Y.D.* 240:9. See *Levush, Y.D.* 376:4, who permits a child to say *kaddish* for the mother while the father is still alive, as he conceptualizes *kaddish* as honoring the mother after her death.

of mourner's *kaddish,* the unique nature of this *kaddish* must be examined and its many complexities and nuances explained.

MOURNER'S *KADDISH*: A GENERAL OVERVIEW[8]

The general history and development of *kaddish* is unclear and its origins debated among scholars.[9] The term *kaddish* is never used in the Mishnah or Talmud. It is first mentioned in Tractate *Soferim.*[10]

1. *Tractate Soferim 10:6*	**מסכת סופרים פרק י הלכה ו**
And do not say *kaddish* and *barekhu* with fewer than ten.	ואין אומרין קדיש וברכו פחות מעשרה.

---

8. The length and breadth of this chapter does not permit a thorough discussion of the development of *kaddish* in general or even specifically of mourner's *kaddish.* The subject will be discussed only through its presentation in the rabbinic sources. No attempt will be made to specifically date the origin of mourner's *kaddish,* the location of its inception, or possible links to any particular historical phenomenon. This chapter will also not attempt to discuss the content and meaning of *kaddish* and why it was appropriated as part of the mourning ritual.
9. See David de Sola Pool, *The Kaddish* (New York: Union of Sephardic Congregations, Inc., 1964); Daniel Sperber, *Minhagei Yisra'el Mikorot Vetoladot* (Jerusalem: Mossad Harav Kook, 1989), ch. 6 (Sperber's first note lists many articles); Yisrael Ta Shma, "*Ketsat Inyanei Kaddish Yatom Uminhagav,*" *Tarbitz* 53 (1984): 559–568; Ismar Elbogen, *The Historical Development of Jewish Prayer* (English translation) (Philadelphia: Jewish Publication Society, 1993), 80–84; Shmuel Glick, *Or Le'avel: Lehitpatḥutam Shel Ikrei Minhagei Avelut Bemasoret Yisra'el Mile'aḥar Hakevurah Ad Tom Hashivah* (Israel: Keren Ori, 1991), 147–158; Leon Wieseltier, *Kaddish* (New York: Alfred A. Knopf, 1998); Andreas Lehnardt, "A New Book on the *Kaddish,*" *Jewish Studies Quarterly* 8 (2001): 190–203. For some traditional explanations and discussions of *kaddish,* see *Maḥzor Vitry* 87; Rambam *Seder Tefillot Nussaḥ Hakaddish; Responsa Harambam* 208; *Tur, O.Ḥ.* 56; *Arukh Hashulḥan, O.Ḥ.* 55:4; and *Responsa Mishpetei Uzziel,* Vol. 1, *O.Ḥ.* 2. For an article on women reciting *kaddish,* see David Golinkin, "*Teshuvah Be'inyan Amirat Kaddish Yatom Al Yedei Nashim,*" *Va'ad Hahalakhah,* Vol. 3 (1988-89), Schechter Institute of Jewish Studies, http://www.responsafortoday.com/vol3/6.pdf.
10. Written after the codification of the Talmud in the time period of the Savora'im, Tractate *Soferim* reworks M. *Meg.* 4:3, which lists the rituals that require a quorum of ten. M. *Meg.* does not mention *kaddish* even though it does mention other mourning and prayer rituals. See Tractate *Soferim* 16:9, 18:10, 19:9, and 21:5–6 for other references to *kaddish.*

Based on this source, rabbinic tradition requires a prayer quorum for all recitations of *kaddish*.[11] However, this text cannot actually refer to all the various forms of *kaddish* in the liturgy[12] today, as each type of *kaddish* has different historical origins and developed at a different time.[13]

The first mention of a *kaddish* linked to death is found in the period of the Ge'onim. *Kaddish* was recited by the *ḥazzan* (cantor) at the burial or following the eulogy upon the recitation of *tsidduk haddin*.[14] However, it is clear from the sources that this *kaddish* is said only in response to the Torah verses found in the prayer[15] and not as an expression of mourning.

---

11. See, for example, *Sh. Ar., O.Ḥ.* 55:1, *Taz* ad loc., and *Mishnah Berurah* 55:2.
12. There are five different types of *kaddish*:
    - Complete *kaddish* קדיש שלם
      It includes "תתקבל צלותהון" ("may their prayer be accepted") with "יהא שלמא רבא" ("may great peace"). This *kaddish* is recited at the end of the service.
    - Half *kaddish* חצי קדיש
      It ends with the words "דאמירן בעלמא ואמרו אמן" ("which are said in the world and we say Amen").
    - Mourner's *kaddish* קדיש יתום
      It is the complete *kaddish* minus the sentence "תתקבל צלותהון" ("may their prayer be accepted").
    - Rabbinic *kaddish* קדיש דרבנן
      It adds "על ישראל" ("For Israel") before יהא שלמא רבה ("may great peace"). This *kaddish* is recited after learning *halakhah* or Mishnah with *Aggadah*. (Rambam thinks it is recited only after learning *Aggadah*.) It is recited by mourners.
    - *Kaddish gadol* קדיש גדול (Also known as *kaddish teḥiyyat hameitim*.)
      It is said after finishing a tractate or after *tsidduk haddin* at a burial. Its content deals with belief in resurrection of the dead.
13. The phrase יהא שמיה רבה מברך לעלם ולעלמי עלמיא seems to be the earliest fragment of *kaddish*. It is based on Ps. 113:2 and Dan. 2:20 and mentioned in B.T. *Ber.* 3a and 57a and B.T. *Shab.* 119b as bringing merit to those who proclaim it. See also *Sifrei Devarim* 306; *Targum Yerushalmi* Gen. 49:1 and Deut. 6:4. In the Talmudic period, the phrase was said following a public sermon. See B.T. *Sot.* 49a and Rashi ad loc. s.v. *akiddusha desiddra*.
14. *Tsidduk haddin* weaves together numerous verses to declare an acceptance of God's decree. It is based on the verses uttered by R. Ḥaninah b. Teradyon and his family upon their deaths, as cited in B.T. *Avod. Zar.* 18a.
15. See *Responsa Rashi* 189:2:
    ובשעת הקבורה היו שם מוחים ואומרים שלא לומר צידוק הדין מפני המועד ואף לא **קדיש מפני שהקדיש לא בא אלא בשביל הפסוקין של צידוק הדין.**

2. *Otsar Ge'onim*
Mashkin (Mo'ed Katan)
#139, p. 49

אוצר גאונים
משקין (מועד קטן)
סימן קלט, עמוד מט

R. Natronai Ga'on, Sura, Babylonia (ninth century)

And that which you asked: One who has died, and one year later, his relatives brought his bones [for reburial], do they recite *tsidduk haddin* and *kaddish* on him or not?

וששאלתם מי שמת ולאחר שנה הביאו קרוביו עצמותיו אומרין עָליו צידוק הדין וקדיש או לא?

Know that *kaddish*, i.e., *yitgadal*, we have found its purpose is not for the dead; rather, it is to follow the eulogy or to follow *tsidduk haddin*. For anywhere that there are words of Torah, we respond afterward, "*Amen yehei shemeih rabba*." So, similarly, with eulogy and *tsidduk haddin*. All of this is if within the twelve months [the body] was brought and the skeleton is still extant, then it is appropriate to eulogize him and afterward we recite *kaddish*, and so it is appropriate to do.... We learn from this that it is inappropriate to eulogize him after twelve months and since there is neither eulogy nor *tsidduk haddin*, there is no place for *kaddish*.

הוי יודע כי קדיש שהוא יתגדל לא מצאנו לו עיקר על המת אלא לאחר המספד או לאחר צידוק הדין שכל מקום שיש שם דברי תורה עונין אחריהם אמן יהא שמיה רבא, וכן הספד וכן צידוק הדין. וזה אם [בתוך] י"ב חדשים הובא ושלדו קיימת ראוי להספידו ולאחר ההספד אומרין· קדיש וכן ראוי לעשות.... למדנו ממנו שאינו ראוי להספידו לאחר שנים עשר חדש וכיון שאין הספד ולא צידוק הדין אין דרך לקדיש.

See also *Orḥot Ḥayyim Hilk. Avel* 11 and *Beit Yosef, Y.D.* 401:6.

Maḥzor Vitry, a compilation of the traditions of Rashi, is the first legal source to link *kaddish* to mourners. The text cites a *midrash*[16] about R. Akiva[17] to explain this practice.

3. *Maḥzor Vitry* #144 s.v. *nimtsa bisfarim*

R. Simḥah of Vitry, France (d. 1105)

מחזור ויטרי סימן קמד ד"ה נמצא בספרים

A story of R. Akiva who was walking on a path in a cemetery and met a man who was naked, black as coal, and carrying a large load of thorns on his head. R. Akiva, thinking he was alive, ran like a horse, shouting at him, and stopped him. He [R. Akiva] said to him: Why is this man doing such hard work? If you are a slave, and your master treats you like this, I will redeem you from his control. And if you are poor and people are playing tricks on you, I will make you rich. He [the man] said to him: Please, do not delay me lest those who are appointed over me become angry with me. He [R. Akiva] said to him: What is this and what is your work? He [the man] said to him: This man [himself] has died and every day they send me out to chop wood. He [R. Akiva] said to him: My son, what was your work in the world from which you came? He said: I was a tax collector and I showed favor to the rich and killed

מעשה בר׳ עקיבא שהיה מהלך בבית הקברות בדרך ופגע באדם אחד שהיה ערום ושחור כפחם והיה טעום [טעון] משאוי גדול של קוצים על ראשו. כסבור עליו ר׳ עקיבא שהוא חי והיה רץ כסוס. גזר עליו ר׳ עקיבא והעמידו. אמר לו מה לאותו האיש לעשות עבודה קשה כזאת. אם עבד אתה [ואדונך] עושה לך [כך] אני אפדה אותך מידו. ואם עני עתה ובני אדם באים עליך בעקיפין אני מעשיר אותך. אמר לו בבקשה ממך אל תעכביני שמא ירגזו בי הממונין עלי. אמר לו מה זו ומה מעשיך. אמר לו אותו האיש מת. ובכל יום שולחים אותי לחטוב עצים. אמר לו בני מה היה מלאכתך בעולם שבאתה ממנו. אמר לו גבאי

16. The story appears in a number of different versions in such texts as Tractate *Kallah Rabbati* 2:9, *Seder Eliyahu Zuta* 17, and *Otsar Midrashim* pp. 351, 450, and 458. For a full list of citations and versions, see de Sola Pool (*Kaddish*, 102n3), Glick (*Or Le'avel*, 157n110), and Ta Shma (*Tarbitz* 53, 559n1).

17. *Seder Eliyahu Zuta*, which some scholars think is the most correct version, has Rabban Yoḥanan b. Zakkai as the main protagonist, instead.

המכס הייתי. והייתי נושא פנים לעשירים והורג את העניים. אמר לו כלום שמעת מאותם הממונין עליך לפורענות איזו דבר שיש לו תקנה. אמר בבקשה ממך אל תעכביני שמא ירגזו עלי בעלי פורענות שאותו האיש אין לו תקנה. אלא שמעתי מהם דבר שלא היה יכול להיות. שאלמלא היה לו לעני זה בן שהוא עומד בקהל ואומר ברכו את ה' המבורך והם עונין אחריו ויהא שמיה רבה מברך מיד מתירין אותו מן הפורענות. ואותו האיש לא היה לו בן מעולם. והניח את אשתו מעוברת. ואיני יודע אם ילדה זכר. ואם ילדה זכר מי מלמדו תורה שאין לאותו האיש אוהב

the poor. He [R. Akiva] said to him: Have you heard from those who oversee your punishment something that you can do as repair? He said: Please do not delay me lest those who oversee my punishment become angry with me for this man [himself] cannot repair. But I have heard from them something that is impossible. If, perhaps, this poor man [himself] had a son who would stand in the congregation and recite *"Barekhu et Hashem hamevorakh"*[18] and they [the congregation] will respond after him, *"Vihei shemeih rabbah mevarakh,"*[19] immediately they will release him from the punishment. Now this man [himself] had never had a son, and [when he died] he left behind a pregnant wife, and I do not know if she gave birth to a male. And if she did give birth to a male child, who would have taught him Torah? For this man has never

18. The earlier versions of this story, like that quoted here in *Maḥzor Vitry*, do not mention *kaddish* explicitly, unlike what will appear in the sources below. See also n19 below.
19. At the end of this particular text, the congregation responds with the usual response of *"barukh Hashem hamevorakh."* However, based on other versions and texts, some scholars suggest that *"vihei shemeih rabbah mevarakh"* was an earlier response to *barekhu* than what is recited today. Others claim that, originally, *barekhu* and *kaddish* were one inseparable liturgical unit.

    Ta Shma, *Tarbitz* 53, p. 559 states:

    > וכבר העיר גינצבורג... וכל הקטע מדבר באמירת 'ברכו' ובעניית הקהלת שלא נוסחה אז כבימינו. ואף על פי שספר אור זרוע ביקש ללמוד מכאן על עצם מקורו של קדיש-יתום, אין הדבר כך לפי רוב הנוסחאות שבידינו.

    pp. 563–564:

    > נראה לי, כי יש מקום לחלוק על תפיסתו של גינצבורג. לדעתי, אין כוונת המעשה הזה לאמירת 'ברכו' בניגוד לקדיש דווקא, אלא משתקפת בו תפיסת 'ברכו' והקדיש כיחידה ליטורגית אחת, וכפי שאכן היו פני הדברים אליבא דאמת בימים מקדם. קרוב לוודאי, כי מתחילה היה 'ברכו' צמוד תמיד לקדיש, כחלק הסיום הקבוע שלו.

    See also the articles mentioned in n16.

had a friend. Immediately, R. Akiva pledged to go and find out if a male son had been born to him in order to teach him Torah and stand him before the congregation. He [R. Akiva] said to him: What is your name? He said to him: Akiva. And your wife's name? He said to him: Shoshniva. And the name of your city? Ludkeya [possibly the city Laodicea]. Immediately, R. Akiva became extremely distressed and went and inquired about him. When he reached the city, he asked about the man. They told him: May the bones of that man be ground up! He [R. Akiva] asked about his wife. They said: May her memory be blotted out from the world! He asked about his son. They said: He is uncircumcised. Even the commandment of circumcision we did not do for him. Immediately, R. Akiva went and circumcised him and sat him with a book before him, but he [the son] could not receive the Torah until he [R. Akiva] had sat forty days in fasting. A heavenly voice came out and said to him: For this one you fast?! He [R. Akiva] said: Master of the universe, have I not set him before You? God immediately opened his [the son's] heart and he [R. Akiva] taught him Torah, the recitation of *shema*, and Grace after Meals. And he [R. Akiva] stood him before the congregation and he [the son] recited *barekhu* and they responded after him, "*Barukh Hashem hamevorakh.*" At that moment, they released him [the father] from punishment. Immediately the man came to R. Akiva in a dream

מעולם. מיד קיבל עליו ר' עקיבא לילך לחפש אם הוליד לו בן זכר כדי ללמדו תורה ויעמידנו לפני הציבור. אמר לו מה שמך. אמר לו עקיבא. ושם אשתך. אמר לו שושניבא. ושם עירך לודקייא. מיד נצטער ר' עקיבא צער גדול והלך ושאל עליו. כיון שבא לאותו מקום שאל עליו. אמרו לו ישחקו עצמותיו של אותו האיש. שאל על אשתו. אמרו לו ימחה זכרה מן העולם. שאל על בנו. אמרו לו הרי ערל הוא. אפילו מצות מילה לא עיסקנו בו. מיד מלו ר' עקיבא. והושיבו בספר לפניו ולא היה מקבל התורה עד שישב (א') [מ'] יום בתענית. יצתה בת קול ואמרה לו לזה אתה מתענה. אמר לפניו רבונו של עולם והלא לפניך ערכתי אותו. מיד פתח הק' [הקדוש ברוך הוא] את לבו ולמדו תורה. וק"ש [וקריאת שמע] וברכת המזון. והעמידו לפני הקהל ואומר ברכו. והם ענו אחריו ברוך ה' המבורך. באותה שעה התירו אותו מן הפורענות. מיד בא אותו האיש לר' עקיבא בחלום. ואמר יהי רצון מלפניך הקב"ה [הקדוש ברוך הוא] שתנוח דעתך בגן עדן שהצלת אותי מדינה של גהינם. מיד פתח ר' עקיבא ואמר (תהלים קל"ה:י"ג) י"י שמך לעולם י"י זכרך לדור

and said: May it be the will before You, the Holy One, Blessed be He, that your soul rest in the garden of Eden for you have saved me from the punishment of Gehenna. Immediately, R. Akiva opened and said (Ps. 135:13): "God, Your name is forever, God, Your remembrance is from generation to generation." **And therefore, it is customary on Saturday night to have a person who has no father or mother lead the prayer service [lit., pass before the ark] to say *barekhu* or *kaddish*.**	ודור: **ועל כן נהגו לעבור לפני התיבה במוצאי שבת אדם שאין לו אב או אם לומר ברכו או קדיש.**

Although *Maḥzor Vitry* quotes a version of this *midrash* that does not mention explicitly that the son recited *kaddish*,[20] the text concludes that this story is the source of the custom for an orphan to lead the prayers on *motsa'ei Shabbat* (Saturday night) so that, as the leader, he may recite *kaddish* or *barekhu*. This jump is understandable as *kaddish* and *barekhu* serve the same liturgical purpose, inviting the congregation to bless God's name. *Maḥzor Vitry* explains that just as the son in this story was able to release his deceased father from the torments of Gehenna through the merit of his actions, so, too, any individual may do the same by acting similarly. *Maḥzor Vitry* states explicitly that the orphan's recitation takes place on *motsa'ei Shabbat*. The reason for this custom is the belief that during Shabbat, souls receive a reprieve and respite from Gehenna[21] and only return there to be tormented at Shabbat's conclusion.[22] *Maḥzor Vitry* also specifies that the orphan is to act as *sheliaḥ tsibbur* (prayer leader) and, in that capacity, lead the community

20. See n18 and n19 above.

21. See *Bereishit Rabbah*, 11, s.v. *vayevarekh Elohim*.

22. *Sefer Or Zarua*, Vol. 2, *Hilk. Motsa'ei Shabbat* 89:10 expands on this theme and explains further what the prayer leader can do:

כתב מורי ה״ר אלעזר מוורמש במוצ״ש [לאחר שאומרים] והוא רחום יכפר עון גו׳ ה׳ הושיעה המלך כו׳ מיד חזן או׳ ברכו במשך גדול מפני שהנשמות חוזרות לגיהנם לאחר מיכן ובעוד שמושך אינם חוזרים...

in the evening prayer service.[23] The orphan recites *kaddish* a number of times that are part of the daily evening liturgy. *Maḥzor Vitry* makes no reference to an additional *kaddish* specifically for mourners.

Or Zarua, a century later, cites the same *midrash*[24] and explains that this source is the basis of the custom for minors to recite an additional *kaddish* for a deceased father.

4. *Sefer Or Zarua*
Vol. 2, Laws of Shabbat #50

ספר אור זרוע
חלק ב הלכות שבת סימן נ

R. Yitsḥak ben R. Moshe, Vienna (ca. 1180–ca. 1250)

Our custom in the land of Canaan[25] and, similarly, the custom in the Rhineland is that after the congregation says *ein keloheinu,* the orphan stands and says *kaddish....* And our custom is logically [the correct one] because of an event that happened, the story of R. Akiva[26].... **And so found my teacher, R. Eliezer of Worms, in *Tanna Devei Eliyahu Rabbah***

מנהגנו בארץ כנען וכן מנהג בני רינוס לאחר שיאמרו הצבור אין כאלהינו עומד היתום ואומר קדיש.... וכמנהגנו מסתברא משום מעשה שהיה דמעשה בר"ע.... **וכן מצא מורי ה"ר אלעזר מוורמשא דתנא דבי אליהו רבא דקטן האומר יתגדל מציל אביו מן הפורענות.**

23. This custom to have an orphaned *sheliaḥ tsibbur* became so prevalent that at a certain point (around the fourteenth and fifteenth centuries) rabbinic authorities had to specifically state that it was permissible for an individual with living parents to lead the service on *motsa'ei Shabbat.* See *Leket Yosher,* Vol. 1, *O.Ḥ.* p. 56, #3:

פ"א במוצאי שבת לא היה בביה"כ שלו [של ר' ישראל איסרליין] חזן שאין לו אב ואם, ואמר לי עמוד והתפלל אע"פ שיש לך אב שאין איסור בדבר, כי תפלת ערבית לא נתקן ליתומים.

He continues to state that the same applies to the recitation of mourner's *kaddish,* which can also be said by others. See also *Responsa Maharil* 64 and *Sefer Ha'agur Hilk. Tefillat Arvit,* the end of 334.

24. There are some slight variations.

25. In his introduction to *Piskei Or Zarua,* R. Moshe Yehudah Hakohen Blau explains that *Or Zarua* was born in Bohemia (in what is currently the Czech Republic), which was called "the land of Canaan."

26. Though the story is quoted in full, it has been omitted here for the sake of brevity. *Or Zarua*'s version contains slight variations from the *Maḥzor Vitry* version and does explicitly mention *kaddish*:

"יאמר יתגדל ועונין אחריו יש"ר מברך מיד מתירין אותו האיש מן הפורענות".

**that a minor who says *yitgadal* [*kaddish*]
saves his father from punishment.**

This text is the first to mention the custom of a mourner reciting a specific *kaddish* at the end of the service in addition to those that the prayer leader recites. *Or Zarua* states that the story of R. Akiva is the basis for this practice. The content and description of the boy in the *midrash* implies that the son was a youngster without specifically stating his age. However, *Or Zarua*'s teacher, R. Eliezer of Worms (Germany, 1140–1225), known as Roke'aḥ, rules from the parallel version of the text found in *Tanna Devei Eliyahu Rabbah*,[27] which states that the son was five years old, that this *kaddish* is recited by a minor[28] to save his father.

It is clear from both *Maḥzor Vitry* and *Or Zarua* that mourner's *kaddish* developed as a custom of practice and is not an obligatory commandment. Originally, it was recited by young children who had not

---

27. *Eliyahu Zuta* (*Ish Shalom*), #17 states:

    אמר ר׳ יוחנן בן זכאי פעם אחת הייתי מהלך בדרך מצאתי אדם אחד שהוא מלקט עצים, דברתי לו [דבר] ולא החזיר לי (דבר), ואחר כך בא אלי ואמר לי אני מת ולא חי, אמרתי לו אם מת אתה עצים למה לך, אמר לי רבי האזין לי עד שאומר לך דבר אחד, כשהייתי חי [אני] וחבירי בפלטרי היינו עוסקים, כשבאנו כאן גזרו עלינו גזר דין שריפה, כשאני מלקט עצים שורפין את חברי, וכשהוא מלקט עצים שורפין אותי, אמרתי לו דינכם עד מתי, אמר לי כשבאתי לכאן הנחתי אשתי מעוברת ויודע אני שזכר הוא, בבקשה ממך הוי זהיר בו משעה שנולד עד שיהיה **בן חמש שנים**, הוליכהו לבית רבו למקרא, בשעה שהוא אומר ברכו את ה׳ המבורך מעלין אותי מדינה של גיהנם.

    See also *Perushei Siddur Hatefillah Leroke'aḥ* 77 where he cites the *midrash* to explain why the orphan recites *kaddish*.

28. Interestingly, at some point the custom of having a mourner lead services on *motsa'ei Shabbat* and the custom of having a minor recite *kaddish* merged. R. Yosef Caro in *Beit Yosef, O.Ḥ.* 53:6 (b) s.v. *vekatav hakolbo* speaks out strongly against this practice.

    ומדברי רבינו ודברי המפרשים שכתבתי משמע בהדיא שקטן אינו רשאי לירד לפני התיבה אפילו באקראי בעלמא ויש לתמוה על מה שנהגו שקטן יורד לפני התיבה במוצאי שבתות להתפלל תפלת ערבית...ושמעתי שהרב ה״ר יוסף אבודרהם קרא תגר על מנהג זה שנהגו הקטנים לירד לפני התיבה במוצאי שבתות והסכים על ידו הרב הגדול מה״ר יצחק די ליאון ז״ל לבטל...

    Further on, he does offer a number of fascinating explanations to justify the behavior and in *Sh. Ar., O.Ḥ.* 53:10 he codifies as follows (with Rema's note attached):

    יש ללמוד זכות על מקומות שנוהגים שהקטנים יורדין לפני התיבה להתפלל תפלת ערבית במוצאי שבתות. הגה: ובמקומות שלא נהגו כן, אין לקטן לעבור לפני התיבה אפילו בתפלת ערבית.

yet reached the age of obligation in *mitsvot*.[29] Although Roke'aḥ based his practice of minors reciting mourner's *kaddish* on the text of the *midrash* itself, over a century later, Maharil was asked to legally justify why a minor is halakhically permitted to recite a portion of the liturgy that requires a *minyan*.[30]

5. Responsa Maharil Haḥadashot #28

R. Ya'akov Moellin, Germany (1360–1427)

שו"ת מהרי"ל החדשות סימן כח

The great one of the generation, my teacher Rabbi Ya'akov Moellin, was asked... What is the reason it is called the "orphan's *kaddish*" and why do minors say this *kaddish*, since it is a *davar shebikdushah* [which requires a *minyan*]?

נשאל גדול הדור מוהר"ר יעקב מולין... הטעם למה נקרא קדיש יתום. ולמה הקטנים אומרים זה הקדיש הואיל והוא דבר שבקדושה.

Answer.... And it is the orphans who say it because they cannot say *barekhu* until they become adults, for all who are not obligated in the matter [*mitsvah* act] cannot fulfill the obligation on behalf of others. And all forms of *kaddish* are generally rabbinic decrees, but this *kaddish* is not obligatory, therefore, minors can say it. And in the story of R. Akiva, "*yehei shemeih rabba*" is also mentioned... as this *kaddish* is an addition

תשובה.... והיתומים שאומרים אותו לפי שאין יכולים לומר ברכו אלא א"כ [אם כן] נעשו גדול, דכל מי שאינו מחוייב בדבר אינו מוציא אחרים ידי חובתן, וכולהו קדישי דעלמא תקנתא דרבנן נינהו אבל קדיש זה לאו דבר שבחובה הוא הילכך יכולין קטנים לאומרו ובעובדא דר' עקיבא הוזכר ג"כ [גם כן]

29. Possibly, the fact that *kaddish* is not formulated in Hebrew and does not contain God's name nor the normative blessing formula made it a part of the liturgy that a minor could recite. See *Responsa Iggerot Moshe, Y.D.* Vol. 1, #258, where he discusses a leniency with *kaddish* due to these factors.

30. See also *Sefer Ha'agur Hilk. Tefillat Arvit* 334 and *Mishnah Berurah* 132:10. See also *Ḥikrei Lev, O.Ḥ.*, toward the end of 45, who offers a different reason why one should allow minors to recite *kaddish*.

and not obligatory... and all these are not rabbinic decree but rather custom.[31]	יהא שמי[ה] רבא... משום דקדיש זה הוי תוספת ולא חובה... וכל הני גופייהו לאו תקנתא דרבנן נינהו אלא מנהג.

R. Moellin states that mourner's *kaddish* is a ritual addition, and not obligatory.[32] Thus, it is different from all other forms of *kaddish*, which must be recited by an adult who is obligated in *mitsvot*. Adult mourners would lead the prayer services and the congregation would praise God's name by responding to *barekhu* (as was the custom stated in *Maḥzor Vitry*), but a minor is barred from leading the service.[33] Consequently, an extra *kaddish* that was not instituted by the rabbis was added for the minor to recite.[34] It is specifically because of the status of mourner's *kaddish* as a custom and not an obligation that minors are permitted to recite it.

The custom of mourner's *kaddish* is not codified in any of the major codes; Rambam, *Tur*, and *Shulḥan Arukh* do not mention the

---

31. Maharil states the following at the end of this text:

ומה שכתבת במקום שאין יתומים אם יתבטל קדיש יתום, חלילה וחס אלא לעולם אחר הדרשות והפסוקים חייבין להקדיש כמו שכתב המיימוני בהדיא אפי' קדיש דרבנן היו אומרים אלא שנתבטל דלא רגילי בהו אינשי ומ"מ אינ' חובה ותקנת' דרבנן כמה הני קדישי דתפילה דבמה מדליקי' וכל הני גופייהו לאו תקנתא דרבנן נינהו אלא מנהג. והא ודאי פשיטא דאין להם לירא לאות' שהוריהן בחיים מלומר קדיש או להתפלל במוצאי שבת, ואדרבא שפיר קעבדי וקורת רוח למתים בארכת ברכו במ"ש כמו שכתב א"ז מיהו אם אביו ואמו מקפידין ישמע להם כמו שכתוב בתשבץ [ושלו' על ישר']. ושלום הק' הלוי.

See n23 for a similar statement. See also Rema's gloss on *Sh. Ar., O.Ḥ.* 132:2, in a case where there are no orphans present.

32. *Shulḥan Arukh Harav, O.Ḥ.* 55:5 states a practical application of this concept when discussing using a minor as the *senif le'asarah* (an adjunct to the tenth to complete the *minyan*).

ומכל מקום לא יאמרו אלא ברכו וקדיש שהוא חיוב **אבל לא קדיש שאחר עלינו שאינו אלא מנהג.**

33. Further on in the responsum, Maharil does suggest an alternative method open to minors that would enable them to recite *barekhu*.

ומהר"ז רונקיל ז"ל אמר לנערים יתומים קטנים להרבות בהפטרות כדי לומר ברכו...

34. See *Sefer Maharil (Customs) Hilk. Tefillah,* s.v. [14] *sha'alu* where he states that if the child is very young, one should read *kaddish* aloud and have him repeat it word for word afterward.

practice. However, in one of his longest notes[35] on *Shulḥan Arukh,* Rema outlines many of the particulars of this ritual. Five centuries after it is first mentioned by *Or Zarua,* Rema describes mourner's *kaddish.* Note some of the differences and changes that have already occurred by Rema's time. Rema's depiction of this *kaddish* is useful for understanding key concepts relevant to the discussion of women reciting *kaddish,* which will arise later on.

6. Rema ***Yoreh De'ah 376:4*** R. Moshe Isserles, Poland (1525–1572)	**רמ"א** **יורה דעה סימן שעו סעיף ד**
Gloss: We find in various *midrashim* that one says *kaddish* for one's father (*Kol Bo* and Rivash in the name of *Tanhuma* and *Sifrei,* Baḥya in the name of Tractate *Kallah, Beit Yosef* in the name of the *Zohar,* and in *Or Zarua* in the name of *Tanna Devei Eliyahu Rabbah*); thus, they had a custom to say the final *kaddish* for one's father and mother for twelve months[36] and, similarly, they had a custom to read the *haftarah* from the Prophets, and to pray [as the leader] the evening service on *motsa'ei Shabbatot,* which is the time that the souls return to Gehenna. And when the son prays and sanctifies God's name in public, he redeems his father and mother from Gehenna (*Kol Bo* in the name of *Haggahot*). And we have the custom of reciting *kaddish* for the mother even when the father is still alive, [a father] cannot prevent his son from	הגה: ונמצא במדרשות לומר קדיש על אב (כל בו וריב"ש בשם תנחומא וספרי, ובחיי בשם מסכת כלה, וב"י [ובית יוסף] בשם הזוהר, ובא"ז [ובאור זרוע] בשם תנא דבי אליהו רבא); ע"כ [על כן] נהגו לומר על אב ואם קדיש בתרא י"ב חדש, וכן נהגו להפטיר בנביא, ולהתפלל ערבית במוצאי שבתות שהוא הזמן שחוזרין הנשמות לגיהנם, וכשהבן מתפלל ומקדש ברבים, פודה אביו ואמו מן הגיהנם (כל בו בשם הגהות). ונהגו לומר קדיש על האם אע"פ [אף על פי] שהאב חי עדיין, אינו בידו למחות לבנו שלא יאמר קדיש על אמו (סברת הב"י [הבית יוסף] ע"פ [על פי] המנהג)....

35. For the ease of the reader, selections from the full text are presented here in a number of shorter sections.

36. See also *Darkhei Moshe* on *Tur, Y.D.* 376:9.

reciting *kaddish* for the mother. (*Beit Yosef*'s opinion, based on the custom.) .... There is only room for this *kaddish* for one's father and mother alone, but not for other relatives (*Or Zarua*).	ואין מקום לקדיש זו אלא על אב ואם בלבד, אבל לא בשאר קרובים (בא"ז [באור זרוע]).

Rema begins by noting that the various midrashic sources prescribe the recitation of *kaddish* for one's father. However, it is clear from his gloss that in his time period, it is already the accepted norm to recite *kaddish* for one's mother as well.[37] Rema states that *kaddish* is recited exclusively for one's parents and not for other relatives.

Rema's notion that mourner's *kaddish* is only for children to recite for parents and not for any other relatives is based on the following statement in the Babylonian Talmud.

7. Babylonian Talmud Sanhedrin 104a	**תלמוד בבלי מסכת סנהדרין דף קד.**
The son can [earn] merit for the father, the father cannot [earn] merit for the son: as it is written (Deut. 32:39): "And from My hand there is no rescuer." Avraham cannot save Yishma'el, Yitsḥak cannot save Esav...[38]	ברא מזכי אבא, אבא לא מזכי ברא, דכתיב (דברים ל"ב:ל"ט) ואין מידי מציל, אין אברהם מציל את ישמעאל, אין יצחק מציל את עשו...

Referring to this passage, Rashba explains (*Responsa Harashba*, Vol. 5, #49) that since parents bring children, who are their flesh and blood, into this world and educate them to serve God, parents live on physically after death through their offspring and children's good deeds reflect meritoriously upon the parents. However, the reverse relationship

37. See *Responsa Harivash* 115 and *Levush, Y.D.* 376:4. *Torah Temimah* notes on Deut. 32, note 86 explains:

    אבל ברא מזכי אבא, ולכאורה צ"ע לפי הפסוק ואין מידי מציל למה ברא מזכי אבא, וי"ל בטעם הדבר משום דעפ"י רוב חנוך הבן תלי באב, וא"כ מכיון שהבן הגיע למדרגה שראוי לזכות בודאי גרים האב לזה, ולכן ראוי הוא ליהנות מזכותו, ולפי"ז נראה דגם את האם מזכה הבן, כי מתעודת האשה לחנך את הבנים, וא"כ גם לה חלק במעלותיו וכשרון נפשו.

38. See also *Sifrei Devarim* 329, s.v. *ve'ein miyadi.*

cannot be said to be true;[39] the parent is not made from the child and so the parent's actions cannot bring merit to the child. When a child causes the congregation to bless God's name, the parent is redeemed from Gehenna, since parents leave a part of themselves behind to live a life that blesses God. Because of this genetic gift to the world by the parent, mourner's *kaddish* cannot be effective with anyone other than children reciting it for their parents.[40]

Rema also discusses the logistics of the original custom of reciting mourner's *kaddish*: one mourner alone functioned as the prayer leader and led the congregation in the ritual.[41] For if the child's actions were to bring merit to their loved one, it had to be their act alone that caused the congregation to respond in praise of God and, thus, brought merit to the deceased parent. Because *kaddish* was recited by one per-

---

39. Rashba explains:

    תשובה: דע... והאב מוליד לבנים, והבן חלק מהאב בגוף: הבשר, והגידין, והעצמות. והאם נותנת אודם שבפנים.... אבל מה שאמרו: ברא מזכה אבא, ואבא לא מזכה ברא; הוא בעולם הנשמות. והוא, כי הבן עם היות גופו לבד חלק מחלקי האב ולא נפשו, כמו שאמרנו, מ"מ הרי הוא מסובב מן האב. ועל כן הבן מצווה בכבוד האב ובמוראו, ואין האב מוזהר כן כבן. שהמסובב לעולם חייב להמסבב לכבודו, ואף על פי שהוא מסובב מאליו הכרחי, לא רצוני. **וע"כ כשהוא מוליד בן צדיק עובד אלהים, נראה כאילו מסיבובו הוא עובד אלהים**, שהוא הביאו לעולם להיות צדיק, מושל בבית אלהים ועובד תחתיו...כי זהו תכלית כל שכר האדם, שישאר ממנו בעולם הגשמי עובד אלהים. **ואז נראה לו, כאלו הוא בעצמו העובד, ואינו מת אלא חי, שהוא הוליד מי שעובד להש"י** [להשם יתברך]. **וע"כ ראוי באמת שיזכה האב בזכות הבן**. אבל האב, למה יזכה את הבן בנפש, **והאב אינו חלק מן הבן**, ולא מסובב ממנו: לא בגוף ולא בנפש. א"כ מה יועיל זכות האב, לבן?

    He also states that *zekhut avot* (merit of the forefathers) only works to bring merit to children in this world and not in the world to come. See also B.T. *Sot.* 10b, *Tosafot* s.v. *deatai lealma deati* and the end of *Torah Temimah* notes on Deut. 32, note 86.
40. Rema, further on in his note, does mention a few customs that would lead to the practice today that *kaddish* may be recited for other relatives, although some understand Rema to be speaking exclusively about grandsons reciting for grandparents (see source #20).

    ואם אין בב"ה אבל על אביו ואמו, אומר אותו קדיש מי שאין לו אב ואם, בעד כל מתי ישראל. ויש מקומות שנהגו ששאר קרובים אומרים קדיש על קרוביהם כשאין אבלים על אביהם ואמם, ויש מקומות שאפילו יש אבלים על אביהם ואמם, אומרים שאר קרובים, אלא שעושים פשרה ביניהם שאין אומרים כל כך קדישים כמו האבלים על אב ואם (מהרי"ק שורש מ"ד:ל'); והולכין בכל זה אחר המנהג, ובלבד שיהא מנהג קבוע בעיר...
41. This practice is still the custom today in some congregations, particularly those that follow German traditions.

son, Rema goes on to discuss how to apportion the recitation of *kaddish* when more than one mourner is present.

8. Rema
Yoreh De'ah 376:4
R. Moshe Isserles, Poland (1525–1572)

רמ"א
יורה דעה סימן שעו סעיף ד

If there are three brothers and one foreign man [a non-relative] [present], the three brothers take the three recitations of *kaddish* [one for each brother] and the stranger takes one. They have a custom that on the anniversary of the death of one's parents [*yahrtseit*], one always recites mourner's *kaddish* and one who is capable of praying the whole prayer [service as leader] prays. And if there are other mourners, they have a custom that mourners within *shivah* take precedence and he [the one observing a *yahrtseit*] does not have a *kaddish* at all; [if mourners] in *sheloshim* [are present], he [the one observing a *yahrtseit*] has one *kaddish*; [if mourners] after *sheloshim* [within the first year][are present], all [recitations of] *kaddish* for that day are his [the one observing a *yahrtseit*]. And we count the seven and thirty [days of mourning] from the day of burial, even if the mourner did not hear [of the death immediately] (Maharil). As to whether a stranger is counted as a citizen of the town for the purposes of reciting this *kaddish*, we follow the custom [of that place] (*Agur*). There is only room for this *kaddish* for one's father and mother alone, but not for other relatives (*Or Zarua*).

שלשה אחין ואיש נכרי, השלשה אחין נוטלין השלשה קדישין והאחר נוטל קדיש אחד. ונהגו שאם מגיע לאדם יום שמת בו אביו ואמו, שאומרים עליהם קדיש יתום לעולם, ומי שיודע להתפלל כל התפלה, מתפלל; ואם יש אבלים אחרים, נהגו שתוך שבעה לאבלם הם קודמים, ואין לו קדיש כלל; תוך שלשים, יש לו קדיש אחד; לאחר ל', כל הקדישים של אותו היום הם שלו. ומונין שבעה ול' מיום הקבורה, אע"פ [אף על פי] שלא שמע האבל מיד (במהרי"ל). ואם נכרי הוא כאחד מבני העיר לענין קדיש זו, הולכים אחר המנהג (אגור). ואין מקום לקדיש זו אלא על אב ואם בלבד, אבל לא בשאר קרובים (בא"ז [באור זרוע]).

Rema outlines a clear hierarchy of who has priority in reciting *kaddish* among mourners who are still in *shivah* (the first seven days after burial), mourners in the following thirty-day period, and *yahrtseit* (the anniversary of death) observers, as well as among residents and visitors.[42]

In summary, various versions of the *midrash* of R. Akiva are the basis for the custom of an individual young son inviting the *minyan* to respond and praise God's name so as to ease the deceased father's torment in Gehenna. The son, even a minor, recited mourner's *kaddish* according to a set prioritization order and hierarchy within the community of other mourners. This non-obligatory custom of reciting mourner's *kaddish* took root in about the late twelfth century and, by the sixteenth century, had already become a central part of the bereavement process.

THE EVOLVING CUSTOMS OF MOURNER'S *KADDISH*

As *kaddish* developed and evolved as a ritual, so did the customs surrounding its practice. Unlike obligatory *mitsvot* that originate in Torah or rabbinic sources and, to a greater or lesser extent, have been observed with some uniformity throughout the ages, the rules and regulations for the recital of mourner's *kaddish* today are significantly different from years past. The customs of reciting *kaddish* have changed from one place or generation to the next.

An extreme illustration of this phenomenon is found in the writings of R. Avraham bar Ḥiyya Hanasi, who regards the whole notion of a ritual that brings merit to one who has died as ludicrous and unfounded in Jewish tradition.[43]

---

42. *Magen Avraham* 132:2 expands on this process with a new set of numerous rules for how to run a lottery to divide the various recitations of *kaddish* amongst the different individual mourners.

43. A century later, Rashba discusses a similar question quoting from the period of the Ge'onim. See *Responsa Harashba*, Vol. 7, #539 and also Vol. 5, #49. See also R. Menaḥem Kasher, *Torah Sheleimah*, Vol. 16, #19, an article titled "*Kapparah Lemetim*," pp. 257–259 (in the additions in the back), for an overview of the issue of whether the living can affect the dead. He specifically discusses the views of Roke'aḥ, *Shibbolei Haleket*, and Rav Hai Ga'on, who hold that the living can have only a limited effect on the dead and cannot bring them merit.

9. *Higgayon Hanefesh*, p. 32a — **הגיון הנפש דף לב.**

R. Avraham bar Ḥiyya Hanasi, Spain (c. twelfth century)

And so anyone who thinks that the actions of his sons and members of his people, done on his behalf after his death, and praying on his behalf, are of benefit to him, these are ludicrous thoughts and for naught in the eyes of all the sages and all men of knowledge. For the Torah and the rabbis did not speak of them...and we find no source in the Torah from which we could understand that the actions of those living in this world will merit the dead, with one exception.... This is [to return] stolen [property] that the deceased did not return during his lifetime and for which he will be punished in the world to come. And if the stolen [property] is returned to its owner after his [the thief's] death, it is appropriate to stop the [thief's] punishment in the world to come.... There is but one thing, according to the words of the rabbis,[44] that brings merit, and that is the study of Torah in this world, which brings merit to him who teaches it [the Torah] [even] after his death, as long as it [the Torah] continues to be taught after him.

וכן כל החושב על מעשי בניו ובני עמו שהם עושים בגללו אחרי מותו ומתפללים בעדו שהם מועילים לו, מחשבות בדויות הוא ותוחלת שוא בעיני כל החכמים וכל אנשי מדע, כי לא דברה תורה ולא דברו חכמים עליהם... ולא מצאנו בתורה מקום שנוכל להבין ממנו שמעשה החי בעולם הזה יהיה מזכה את המתים, כי אם דבר אחד.... והוא הגזלה אשר לא השיב המת בחייו יהיה נענש עליה לעוה"ב [לעולם הבא], ואם השיב הגזלה לבעליה אחרי מותו ראוי הוא לפסוק העונש ממנו בעוה"ב [בעולם הבא].... ויש דבר אחד לדברי החכמים שהוא מלמד זכות, והוא תלמוד תורה בעוה"ז [בעולם הזה] הוא מלמד זכותם על המלמד אותה אחרי מותו כל זמן שהיא מלמדת אחריו.

In R. Avraham bar Ḥiyya Hanasi's view, neither the Torah nor the rabbis[45] ever declared that acts of the deceased's descendants could bring merit to the deceased. The only beneficial act would be to study the

44. See *Bereishit Rabbah* (Theodor Albeck edition) 49:19, s.v. *lema'an hevi*.

45. It seems clear that either he was not aware of the obscure sources that cite the R. Akiva *midrash* or he did not see that aggadic story as reflecting a theological reality.

Torah taught by the deceased. The principle upon which the ritual of mourner's *kaddish* is based is unfounded in his view and would never have been instituted as a custom at all in his community.

As such, around the same time period, there existed Jewish communities where *kaddish* that is known today as mourner's *kaddish* was not recited specifically by mourners, but by young boys with living parents.[46]

10. Sefer Or Zarua ***Vol. 2, Laws of Shabbat #50*** R. Yitsḥak ben R. Moshe, Vienna (1180–1250)	**ספר אור זרוע** **חלק ב הלכות שבת סימן נ**
It is our custom: ... that after the congregation says *ein keloheinu* the orphan stands and says *kaddish*, but, in France, I saw that they are not strict about who says *kaddish*, if it is a young orphan or if it is a young boy who has a father and mother.	מנהגנו... לאחר שיאמרו הצבור אין כאלהינו עומד היתום ואומר קדיש אבל בצרפת ראיתי שאינם מקפידים על כך מי שיאמר קדיש אם נער יתום או נער שיש לו אב ואם.

Or Zarua, in the first legal text to link this specific *kaddish* to mourners, also acknowledges in the same text that customs differed regarding who recited this *kaddish*. The custom cited by *Or Zarua* was not the practice everywhere. In France, for example, the *kaddish* at the conclusion of morning prayers was not said by a mourner, but rather by any young boy, even one with living parents.[47]

On the other hand, in many communities it became much more common specifically for orphaned minors to recite this *kaddish*. Maharil, who explained above how minors can halakhically recite *kaddish*, addresses, in the same responsum, the question of whether an adult should say this *kaddish* as well.

46. Such an act would be unheard of today.

47. See n52 below.

11. *Responsa Maharil Haḥadashot #28*

R. Ya'akov Moellin, Germany (1360–1427)

שו"ת מהרי"ל החדשות סימן כח

Answer: ... And the orphans who say it [do so] because they cannot say *barekhu* until they become adults... and for this reason also it seems to me that even adults care about *kaddish yatom* [more] than other recitations of *kaddish* and *barekhu* as this *kaddish* is an addition and not obligatory, and they think it brings more peace of spirit to their [deceased] parents than with the other ones. And my opinion does not agree with them about this; on the contrary, greater is the one who is obligated and does [than the one who is not obligated and does, and thus, it is preferable to lead the prayers than to say mourner's *kaddish*].

תשובה:... והיתומים שאומרים אותו לפי שאין יכולים לומר ברכו אלא א"כ [אם כן] נעשו גדול... ומהאי טעמא נמי נ"ל [נראה לי] דאפילו הגדולים קפדי טפי אקדיש דיתום [יותר] משאר קדישות וברכו משום דקדיש זה הוי תוספת ולא חובה, וסברי דעבדי טפי קורות רוח להוריהם מבאחרים. ואין דעתי מסכמת עמהם בזה דאדרבה גדול המצוה ועושה.

Maharil is concerned about adults who place too great an emphasis on reciting mourner's *kaddish*.[48] The additional *kaddish* was a good solution for minors. However, Maharil believes that it is preferable for an adult who can lead the prayer services to do so rather than recite mourner's *kaddish*, for it is more meritorious to perform obligatory commandments than to perform optional ones. His view certainly differs from the current accepted practice of adults reciting mourner's *kaddish* even when they are not serving as prayer leaders.[49]

---

48. See also *Sefer Ha'agur Hilk. Tefillat Arvit* 334. Rema, toward the end of *Y.D.* 376:4, states:

    ...אבל לא נהגו להתפלל בשבת וי"ט, אף על פי שאין איסור בדבר, אבל בימות החול, מי שיודע להתפלל, **יתפלל ויותר מועיל מקדיש יתום שלא נתקן אלא לקטנים**; ומי שאינו יודע להתפלל כל התפלה, יתפלל למנצח ובא לציון וכו'...

49. See *Mishnah Berurah* 132:10, where he mentions that it would be better for adults to lead the services. However, he concludes that the mourner's *kaddish* is for minors and adults alike.

Maharil mentions another custom, which is quite different from the custom today.

12. Sefer Maharil (Customs) ***Laws of Celebrations, s.v. [23] beleil*** R. Ya'akov Moellin, Germany (1360–1427)	**ספר מהרי״ל (מנהגים)** **הלכות שמחות ד״ה [כג] בליל**
…and the custom in Mainz [is] that we do not say *kaddish yatom* every day; only three times on Shabbat…[50]	…ומנהג במגנצא שאין אומרים קדיש יתום בכל יום רק ג׳ פעמים בשבת…

The practice of reciting *kaddish* on Shabbat might be linked to the belief that souls are reprieved from Gehenna on Shabbat and return to suffer on *motsa'ei Shabbat*. Alternatively, this difference in practice can be attributed to other liturgical changes such as those mentioned in the following passage.

13. Minhagei Maharash Mineustadt ***#90 s.v. [2] ve'amar*** R. Shalom ben R. Yitsḥak, Austria (fourteenth century)	**מנהגי מהר״ש מנוישטט** **סימן צ ד״ה [ב] ואמר**
…those places in the Rhineland that do not say *kaddish yatom* on weekdays, this is because they do not say "as it is written in your Torah" after *aleinu leshabe'aḥ*, and so there is no *kaddish* on the verses.	…שאותן מקומות שברינוס שאין אומרין קדיש יתום בחול, היינו משום שאין אומרין ככתוב בתורתך אחר עלינו לשבח, ואז לא הוי קדיש על פסוקים.

50. *Responsa Maharil* 36, s.v. *vezeikher ledavar*:
ובאושטריי״ך נוהגים לומר קדיש יתום תדיר אף בחול ושמא מתוך כך אינם מקפידים.
Also, see all of *Responsa Maharil Haḥadashot* 28:
ומה שנוהגין ביש מקומות לומר תדיר קדיש יתום, מעת שנתרבה שעת הזעם בעולם לא היו מסתפקין [מספיקין] בשבתות וי״ט, והגדולים ג״כ אין כולם רגילין לעבור לפני התיבה, וגם ראיתי שמוחין בהן [שלא] להתפלל כדי שלא יתפללו שאינו ראוי׳ לכך.

Seemingly, on weekdays, a shorter version of *aleinu* was recited, which ended before reaching the verses of Torah[51] that require the recitation of *kaddish* and so mourners did not recite *kaddish*.

Over time, the number of times mourner's *kaddish* was recited increased as mourner's *kaddish* was recited during the week and on holidays as well.[52] The number of times *kaddish* was recited during each prayer service increased and additional recitations of *kaddish* were added to the liturgy[53] so that each individual mourner could recite one.

---

51. The *aleinu* prayer recited today is still shorter than that found in *mussaf* of Rosh Hashanah and does not include all ten verses found there.
52. R. Menaḥem ben R. Yosef ben R. Yehudah Ḥazzan, who compiled rulings of Rashi and his students, states in *Seder Troyes* 2:

    זמן קדיש אב ואם שהיא במקום קדיש לנער אין אומ׳ אותו בחנוכה בפורים ומוצאי י״ה ולא בחה״מ מפני זלזול מצות י״ט, אך כי יש מדרש שאומ׳ שהנשמות אינן שובתי׳ רק בר״ח ובשבת.

    Seder Troyes seems to be unique in its use of the term *kaddish lena'ar*, which he uses throughout his work to describe the *kaddish* known today as *kaddish yatom*. This text seems to reflect the same transition cited above in *Or Zarua* (source #10) of a *kaddish* set aside for youth that then became the mourner's *kaddish*. Maharil above (source #5) offers an explanation as to why young orphans would be given a *kaddish* to recite as they could not lead the prayer service. However, if the actual order was reversed and it *originated* as a *kaddish lena'ar* it is difficult to understand for what purpose children would be reciting it. *Maḥzor Vitry*, similarly reflecting the traditions of Rashi, also does not use the term *kaddish yatom* but, instead, in a number of places (#93, 157, 193, and 212) says something similar to "ועומד הנער לומר קדיש." In #101, the text explains:

    יעמוד הנער ואומר קדיש בלא תתקבל. וקדיש זה אינו אלא לחנך את התינוקות. ואינו בכלל שבע ביום הללתיך.

    Possibly, these texts reflect a tradition that links youngsters to the recitation of *kaddish* not as mourners but as an educational tool for preparing them to lead the prayer service, much the same way that today, they lead *anim zemirot* or *adon olam*. Interestingly, as shown above, *Maḥzor Vitry* 144 (source #3) quotes the story of R. Akiva not to show that a youngster should recite *kaddish* but, rather, that adult mourners should lead the evening prayers on Saturday night and *Or Zarua* mentions that, in France, youngsters with living parents recited the *kaddish*.
53. *Arukh Hashulḥan Hilk. Birkhot Hashaḥar* 55:4 explains:

    הקדמונים לא אמרו רק שבעה קדישים בכל יום, ג׳ בשחרית אחד אחר ישתבח והשני אחר תחנון והשלישי אחר ובא לציון גואל, ושנים במנחה אחד אחר אשרי והשני אחר תחנון, ושנים בערבית אחד קודם שמ״ע והשני אחר שמ״ע על שם שבע ביום הללתיך. ואח״כ הוסיפו עוד ג׳ היינו בכל תפילה לאחר עלינו וכתבו שכל איש צריך לקיים בכל יום אותיות צדי״ק והיינו צדיק אמנין ד׳ קדושות י׳ קדישים ק׳ ברכות. ותקנו קדיש לאחר

Mourners began reciting *kaddish* for eleven months instead of twelve months.[54] Although Rema said that *kaddish* was originally said only for fathers, he acknowledges that children began saying *kaddish* for their mothers as well. It is now customary to recite mourner's *kaddish* for many different relatives and even to hire a non-relative to recite mourner's *kaddish*.[55] Because *kaddish* evolved as a custom, and not as an obligatory ritual, traditions surrounding its practice are continuously developing and changing. Nowhere is this more apparent than in the movement from the hierarchical custom of a single mourner who recites *kaddish* (as mentioned above in Rema) to one in which all mourners present recite *kaddish* together.[56]

This change caused heated debate. R. Jacob Ettlinger refers to a dispute he had on this matter with his colleague, R. Baer Oppenheim of Eibenschitz, in which R. Oppenheim permits the community of mourners to recite *kaddish* in unison and R. Ettlinger strongly opposes the practice.[57] R. Oppenheim responds to the needs of one town in which they were building one large synagogue for all members and thus replacing a number of smaller, separate services. The community agreed that there would only be one service in town and that all mourners, no matter at what point in the mourning process they were (*shivah, sheloshim,* or *yahrtseit*), would recite *kaddish* together. A number of people

---

עלינו מפני היתומים שלא יוכלו להתפלל לפני העמוד וקראו לזה קדיש יתום. וביום קריאת התורה עוד קדיש לאחר קרה"ת ויותר אין מקום לקדישים. ועכ"ז הוסיפו עוד אחד אחר שיר של יום מפני היתומים המרובים אבל יותר מזה חלילה להוסיף.

54. See Rema, *Y.D.* 376:4, where he mentions both customs, at the beginning stating that *kaddish* is recited for twelve months and, at the end, adding:

ונהגו שאין אומרים קדיש ותפלה רק י"א חדשים, כדי שלא יעשו אביהם ואמם רשעים,
כי משפט רשע י"ב חדש.

See M. *Eduy.* 2:10 and B.T. *Rosh Hash.* 17a, where it states that a sinner remains in Gehenna for twelve months.

55. See *Iggerot Moshe, Y.D.* Vol. 1, #254.

56. One of the earliest mentions of more than one person reciting *kaddish* dates back to the seventeenth century, although from the texts that follow, one sees that this was clearly not the accepted norm in Ashkenaz at the time. See *Responsa Hilk. Ketanot,* Vol. 2, #48 and *Pitḥei Teshuvah, Y.D.* 376:6.

57. See also *Responsa Ḥatam Sofer, O.Ḥ.* 159, s.v. *od ani,* where he questions the efficacy of saying *kaddish* in unison, since no one specific person then causes the community to praise God's name.

protested this innovation, citing the preordained hierarchy laid out by Rema (source #8) and *Magen Avraham* (n42). However, the community felt that reverting to the old custom would cause continuous fighting, since there would be many fewer opportunities to recite the mourner's *kaddish*. They asked R. Oppenheim if they had acted correctly.

14. Responsa Binyan Tsiyyon #122 (R. Jacob Ettlinger)

שו"ת בנין ציון סימן קכב

R. Baer Oppenheim Eibenschitz, Moravia (1760–1849)

I responded to them, a great and correct reform I saw here [by their actions]. For the matter of mourner's *kaddish* we have not found in the two Talmuds, nor in Rambam or *Tur*. Only *Beit Yosef* in *Y.D.* (#376) brought in the name of *Kol Bo* that copied these words...of one who gathered wood [the story of R. Akiva]. But in *Shulḥan Arukh*, [he] does not bring this custom at all, the one that orphans say *kaddish*. Only the Rema brought it, and made it succeed, and established it. And in truth, the body of the story that the holy *Zohar* brings has no explanation. And possibly it came as thus to somebody in a dream.... Even though the Rema brought generally [without reference], and, after him, the *Magen Avraham* brought many laws [regarding] who has precedence in the matter of *kaddish*, they only said [this] for a town in which there are many synagogues and houses of study, and then it would be possible to fulfill their rulings and divisions in the manner of the priorities [of mourners in the] thirty [day period] and [the mourners on] *yahrtseits*. But in a town

והשבתי להם תקנה גדולה וישרה ראיתי כאן דהנה ענין קדיש יתום לא מצאנו לא בשתי תלמודיים גם לא ברמב"ם ובטור רק הב"י ביו"ד (סי' שע"ו) הביא בשם הכלבו שהעתיק דברי הזה... באחד שהיה מקושש עצים וכו' אבל בש"ע לא הביא כלל מנהג הלז דיתומים יאמרו קדיש. רק הרמ"א הביאו ועשה חיל וקים בזה ובאמת גוף המעשה שהביא הזה"ק אין לו פירוש ואפשר שבא כן לאחד בחלום.... אמנם אף שהרמ"א הביא סתם ואחריו המג"א הביא כמה וכמה דינים מי שיש לו קדימה בענין הקדיש לא אמרו רק בעיר שיש להם הרבה בתי כנסיות ובהמ"ד [ובתי המדרש] ואז נוכל לקיים פסקיהם וחלוקיהם בענין הקדימה שלשים ויא"צ [ויארצייט]. אבל בעיר שאין להם רק ביהכ"נ [בית הכנסת] אחת ובכל יום ויום שם אבלים שלשים ויא"צ

which only has one synagogue, and every day there are many mourners present both [in their] thirty days and *yahrtseits,* so as to minimize disputes, it is good for all of them to say [*kaddish*] at once [together] to broker peace. And regarding that which the critics claim, that one should not nullify the custom because every custom has its gate in heaven and its foundation in the holy heights, from the words of the *Magen Avraham* in *O.Ḥ.* #61, I say, to quiet a fight one can nullify [a custom], and already the rabbis said there, that which was written in holiness will be erased so as to bring peace between husband and wife,[58] so much the more so in the case here [one can erase a custom for the sake of peace].

[ויארצייט] הרבה כדי למעט במחלוקות טוב שיאמרו כולם בב"א [בבת אחת] כדי לתווך השלום. ומה שהמערערים טוענים שלא לבטל המנהג כי כל מנהג יש לו שער בשמים ויסודתם בהררי קודש מדברי המג"א בא"ח סי' ס"א אמר אני להשקיט הריב נוכל לבטל וכבר אמרו חז"ל [חכמינו זכרונם לברכה] שם שנכתב בקדושה נמחק כדי לעשות שלום בין איש לאשתו מכ"ש [מכל שכן] בנדון זה.

R. Oppenheim rules that it would be permissible for all mourners to recite *kaddish* together based on two main factors. First, mourner's *kaddish* is a mere custom with no source in the two Talmuds or in the codes of Rambam, *Tur*, or *Shulḥan Arukh.* Only Rema chooses to codify the rules regarding who should recite *kaddish.* R. Oppenheim goes so far as to suggest that the original story of R. Akiva mentioned in the *Zohar* possibly originated as a dream. He then surmises that Rema's ruling applied only in a situation where many prayer services existed. Secondly, he notes that it is permissible to uproot a custom for the greater good of peace if it will put an end to conflict, as it is permitted to erase God's name in the ritual of *sotah,* the suspected adulterous woman, to bring peace between couples.

R. Ettlinger responds with shock and outrage at R. Oppenheim's willingness to change the established custom.

58. Num. 5:23 and see *Bemidbar Rabbah* 9:36; *Mishnat R. Eliezer* 4, p. 75; and *Otsar Hamidrashim Meir,* p. 227.

15. *Responsa Binyan Tsiyyon, #122*

R. Jacob Ettlinger, Germany (1798–1871)

שו"ת בנין ציון סימן קכב

About this I will reply – I am generally shocked how the honorable rabbi, may his light shine, called [it] "a great and correct reform" to change a custom of Israel that they have practiced in all of the communities of Ashkenaz and Poland for more than three hundred years, with the mourner's *kaddish*, that each one should say it individually, and [instead] to walk in the footsteps of the innovators of our time who have changed the matters of liturgy and have also practiced this custom that the mourners should say *kaddish* together.... Therefore there is nothing better than to follow the way that [our] forefathers instituted, and to grant each one individually to say the *kaddish* that he is entitled to according to precedence as taught by the legal decisors (*posekim*).

על זה אשיב - תמהתי דרך כלל איך קרא מעכ"ת [מעלת כבוד תורתו] נ"י [נרו יאיר] תקנה גדולה וישרה לשנות מנהג ישראל אשר נהגו בכל מדינות אשכנז ופולין זה יותר משלש מאות שנה בקדיש יתום שיאמר כל אחד לבדו ולילך בעקבות המתחדשים בזמננו ששינו עניני התפלה והנהיגו גם המנהג הזה שיאמרו האבלים קדיש יחד.... לכן אין טוב רק לשמור דרך ארחות חיים אשר גבלו ראשונים ולזכות כל אחד לבדו בקדיש אשר יאות לו ע"פ [על פי] התורה אשר הורו הפוסקים למי הקדימה.

R. Ettlinger seeks to preserve three hundred years of tradition. He likens R. Oppenheim to the innovators and reformers of the day and urges that everything must be done to guard the life of the past.

R. Ettlinger lost the battle in this particular case and the practice of communal recitation of *kaddish* spread to the majority of synagogues,[59] even when more than one prayer service existed in the vicinity. The custom of reciting *kaddish* has evolved from the single mourner reciting *kaddish* to bestow merit on a deceased father a limited number of times on Shabbat based upon a strict rotation of turns, to relatives of any

59. Synagogues following the German custom still only have a single individual reciting *kaddish*.

type reciting *kaddish* multiple times a day[60] for eleven months. Many of these changes undermine the original purpose and understanding of *kaddish,* which is that a deceased's child directly causes the congregation to sanctify God's name, thus redeeming the parent with that action. Understanding the continuously changing customs with regard to reciting *kaddish* is extremely important in evaluating the sources concerning women's recitation of *kaddish* and will be returned to at the conclusion of this chapter.

HOW *KADDISH* DIFFERS FROM OTHER WOMEN'S ISSUES

Because of the unusual nature of mourner's *kaddish,* the issues at play in the halakhic discussion of whether a woman may recite *kaddish* are different from the question of equal obligation that appears in many other topics concerning women's participation in ritual.[61] Both men and women are obligated in the commandments to honor their parents in life[62] and mourn them at the time of their death.[63] However, as explained above, there exists no actual halakhic obligation[64] for either men or women to recite *kaddish* for deceased parents and, therefore, no one is acting as an agent for another as in other *mitsvot.*[65] Instead, a number of unique aspects directly related to the ritual of *kaddish* shape

60. See *Iggerot Moshe, Y.D.* Vol. 1, #254, s.v. *aval yode'a* where, in discussing hiring someone to recite *kaddish,* R. Feinstein emphasizes that once a day is sufficient. See also *Iggerot Moshe, Y.D.* Vol. 3, #42 where he states "ואין צורך להרבות בקדישים" unless others know that one is a mourner and so out of honor to one's parents one should recite *kaddish* in any situation. *Mishnah Berurah* 55:1 states:

    אומרים וכו' - כאשר טוב למעט בברכות כך טוב למעט בקדישים ועיין באחרונים שקראו תגר ע"ז שנאספים עשרה ב"א ואומרים כמה קדישים על פסוקי תורה או משנה או גמרא.

61. See, for example, the issues at play in "Women and Megillah: Part of the Miracle" below.
62. See n6 above.
63. See n5 above.
64. The colloquial expression, "I have a *ḥiyyuv,*" is a reflection of the emotional obligation that the child feels.
65. *Kaddish* is most certainly not a positive commandment caused by time. As explained above, it is neither a positive commandment (but rather a custom) nor is the need to say it caused by a change in time but rather by the unfortunate passing of a parent. See Rochelle L. Millen, "Women and Kaddish: Reflections on Responsa," *Modern Judaism* 10 (1990): 191–203, and Rochelle L. Millen, "The Female Voice of Kaddish,"

the discussion of women's participation. Even when the sources do not refer to them directly, these issues always exist in the background of the discussion.

Kaddish must be recited in the presence of a *minyan.*[66] Since mourner's *kaddish* originated as a prayer for minors to recite, one derives that those reciting *kaddish* do not necessarily need to be counted as part of the *minyan*. However, those reciting *kaddish* must be in the presence of the prayer group so that the quorum may respond. This law posed a problem for women reciting *kaddish,* since for many generations, synagogue architecture was such that the women's section of the synagogue was distinctly separate from the men's area; halakhically it was considered a distinct and separate domain disconnected from the *minyan*. Even as late as the turn of the twentieth century, *Arukh Hashulḥan* explains the following in reference to men standing in the women's section:

16. *Arukh Hashulḥan*
Oraḥ Ḥayyim 55:20
R. Yeḥiel Mikhl Epstein, Lithuania (1829–1908)

ערוך השולחן
אורח חיים סימן נה סעיף כ

Nevertheless, certainly those standing in the women's section do not join with those standing in the *beit hakenesset* [i.e., the men's section] even though there are windows from the women's section to the *beit hakenesset* and they even see the faces of those [in the men's section]. Since the divisions are complete, they comprise two [separate] domains.

מיהו זה ודאי העומדים בעזרת הנשים לא יצטרפו עם העומדים בבהכ"נ [בבית הכנסת] אף שיש חלונות מעזרת נשים להבהכ"נ [לבבית הכנסת] ורואים אלו פניהם של אלו כיון שמחיצות גמורות הן הוויין שתי רשויות.

Consequently, in order to recite *kaddish* in the presence of a *minyan,* a woman would either be required to enter the men's section of the

---

Jewish Legal Writings by Women, eds. Micah Halperin and Chana Safrai (Urim Publications, 1998), 179–201, where Millen wonders why the sources regarding women and *kaddish* do not mention this term.

66. *Sh. Ar., O.Ḥ.* 55:1. See source #1 and n11 above.

synagogue or form a private *minyan* in her home. Both of these solutions at times provoked opposition for different reasons, as will be examined in the sources that follow. Compounding the difficulty of a woman entering the men's section of the synagogue is the tradition mentioned above[67] that originally only one individual recited *kaddish,* and that person was determined based on a complex system of hierarchy in relation to how much time had passed since the death of the loved one. For a woman to outrank male members of the community and function as the sole person reciting *kaddish* also met with opposition. And so, in many of the sources that discuss women's participation in *kaddish,* the question of whether a woman may legally recite *kaddish* will not be debated because that is answered in the affirmative quite early on. Rather, these surrounding issues of tradition, culture, and social and physical reality will be at play.

RISHONIM

The earliest text that cites a custom distinguishing between the desired behaviors of sons versus daughters in relation to the loss of a parent makes no reference to *kaddish,* but, rather, refers to prayer itself.

17. *Responsa Mahari Veil* #13 — **שו"ת מהר"י ווייל סימן יג**

R. Ya'akov ben Yehudah Weil, Germany (d. before 1456)

For you asked, one whose father or mother passed away is there a *mitsvah* to notify them within thirty [days]? In *Mordekhai,* at the end of the laws of *Semaḥot,* he wrote explicitly that there is no need to notify one even about the death of a father and mother. Nevertheless, they have a custom to notify male children so that they can pray, since the deceased has peace of spirit from this, but for daughters there is no such custom.

ששאלת מי שמת אביו או אמו אם מצוה להודיעו תוך ל'? במרדכי בשלהי הלכות שמחות כתב בהדיא דאין צריך להודיעו אפילו על אב ואם. מ"מ [מכל מקום] נהגו להודיע לבנים הזכרים כדי שיתפללו, כיון דאית ליה להמת נחת רוח בזה, אבל לבנות אין מנהג בזה.

67. See source #8 above.

As shown above, R. Weil's teacher, Maharil, ruled that the proper practice for an adult mourning the loss of a parent was to lead the prayer service. Thus, there is value in notifying a son so that he may bring peace to his deceased parent in his role as prayer leader. There seemed to be no particular custom to notify the daughters, as they would not have had the opportunity to function in the same capacity.

R. Yosef Caro[68] dictates that one is not required to notify an individual in the case of death. However, R. Moshe Isserles (Rema), following the tradition of Ashkenaz, rules differently.

18. *Shulḥan Arukh*
Yoreh De'ah 402:12
Rema ad loc.

שולחן ערוך
יורה דעה סימן תב סעיף יב
רמ"א שם

R. Yosef Caro, Spain and Israel (1488–1575)
R. Moshe Isserles, Poland (1525-1572)

One who had [a relative] die and they did not inform him, there is no obligation to tell him, even [regarding the death] of his father or mother.

מי שמת לו מת ולא נודע לו, אינו חובה שיאמרו לו; ואפילו באביו ואמו;

Gloss [Rema]: Nevertheless, with male children we have a custom to inform so that they can recite *kaddish*; but with daughters there is no custom whatsoever to notify them (*Mahari Veil* #13).[69]

הגה [רמ"א]: ומכל מקום בבנים זכרים, נהגו להודיע, כדי שיאמרו קדיש; אבל בבנות, אין מנהג כלל להודיעם (מהרי"ו סי' י"ג).

---

68. R. Yosef Caro in the *Shulḥan Arukh* does not mention the mourner's *kaddish* at all and so does not make any statements about women's participation. However, in his commentary to the *Tur*, *Beit Yosef*, *Y.D.* 403:10, he quotes:

ואחת היתה זקנה שנח נפשה בעיר **ולא עזבה בן ולא בת** וקרוביה שכרו אחד שיאמר קדיש עבור נפשה...

From his mention of both "a son or a daughter" it might be possible to infer that had a daughter existed the relatives would not have needed to hire an outsider to recite *kaddish* on the old woman's behalf.

R. Moshe Isserles (Rema) in *Darkhei Moshe*, *Y.D.* 376:9 quotes *Beit Yosef*, but there it just reads "ולא עזבה בן."

69. See also *Levush*, *Y.D.* 402:12 and n140 below.

Rema codifies R. Weil's statements above concerning notifying the deceased's sons as law but changes the words "so that they can pray" to "so that they can recite *kaddish*." He preserves intact the end of R. Weil's view that no custom exists to inform daughters. The gender distinction is explained through understanding that the ruling of Rema originates with R. Weil's original statement. Even with this understanding, it is still assumed that the synagogue is not the domain of women in general nor daughters in mourning specifically.[70]

EARLY AḤARONIM

The first explicit discussion of a daughter reciting *kaddish* appears in the second half of the seventeenth century. R. Ya'ir Bacharach, writing in Germany, discusses a case that occurred in Amsterdam.

***19. Responsa Ḥavvot Ya'ir* #222** R. Ya'ir Bacharach, Germany (1639–1702)	**שו"ת חוות יאיר** **סימן רכב**
Question: A strange thing was done in Amsterdam and made known there. That one died without a son and commanded before his death that ten [men] would study[71] every day throughout the twelve months[72]	שאלה: דבר זר נעשה באמשטרדם ומפורסם שם. שאחד נעדר בלי בן וצוה לפני פטירתו שילמדו עשרה כל יום תוך י"ב חודש בביתו בשכרם

70. De Sola Pool (*Kaddish*, p. 104) quotes R. Abraham Hurwitz (1559–1615) from this time period, and cites the reference as p. 35 of the introduction of *Yesh Nohalim*. However, this author could not find the quote in the original. De Sola Pool quotes: האב יצוה לבניו להחזיק באיזה מצוה ואם מקיימין אותו נחשב יותר מן הקדיש. ואם כך אפילו יש לו בת יש לו תקנה זו. דקדיש זה אינו תפלה שיתפלל הבן על האב לפני ה' שיעלהו משאול אלא זכות ומצוה הוא למת כשבנו מקדש השם יתברך ברבים והקהל יענה אחריו אמן יהא שמיה רבא במרך.

71. Interestingly, the father did not organize a prayer *minyan* for his daughter but, rather, a regular study session (presumably also in his memory) for her to recite *kaddish*. The question of whether women may recite *kaddish* in other situations, such as a regular *siyyum* not in memory of a loved one, is linked to this discussion but beyond the scope of this chapter.

72. Originally, there existed a custom to recite *kaddish* for twelve months without fear that in doing so one was implying that the deceased was a *rasha* (sinner). See Rema,

in his house, for pay, and after the study the daughter[73] would say *kaddish*; and the sages and leaders of the community did not prohibit her [from doing so]. And even though there is no [halakhic] evidence to contradict the act, since a woman is also commanded to sanctify God's name, [and] there is also a *minyan* of men who are called *benei Yisra'el*, and even though the story of R. Akiva, which is the source for orphans reciting *kaddish*, occurred with a male child, in any event, it is logical that a daughter also provides benefit and peace of spirit to the soul [of the departed] since she is his offspring.

ואחר הלימוד תאמר הבת קדיש; ולא מיחו בידה חכמי הקהילה והפרנסים. ואף כי אין ראיה לסתור הדבר כי גם אשה מצוות על קידוש השם, גם יש מנין זכרים מקרי בני ישראל, ואף כי מעשה דר"ע [רבי עקיבא] שממנו מקור אמירת יתומים קדיש בבן זכר היה מ"מ [מכל מקום] יש סברא דגם בבת יש תועלת ונחת רוח לנפש כי זרעו היא.

Nevertheless, one should be concerned that, because of this [act], they will weaken the power of the customs of the children of Israel which are also Torah, and each one will build an altar for himself according to his own logic, and the words of the rabbis would be seen as laughter and a joke[74] and they will come to mock them....[75] And

מ"מ [מכל מקום] יש לחוש שע"י [שעל ידי] כך יחלשו כח המנהגים של בני ישראל, שג"כ [שגם כן] תורה הם, ויהיה כל אחד בונה במה לעצמו ע"פ [על פי] סברתו ומחזי מילי דרבנן כחוכא ואטלול' [ה] ויבואו לזלזל בו.... ולכן בנדון זה שיש אסיפה

Y.D. 376:4 where he mentions both customs and Glick (*Or Le'avel* 147n75).

73. It seems that the daughter was still living in her father's home and therefore possibly not yet of marriageable age. This scenario would fit with *kaddish* being said by minors.

74. See the notes of *Beit Leḥem Yehudah* to *Sh. Ar., Y.D.* 376:4, who disregards *Ḥavvot Ya'ir*'s legal argument and just focuses on his concern:

ואין לבת בקדיש לא דין ודת ואין זה אלא שטות, כי הוא כחוכא ואיטלולא.

See *Pitḥei Teshuvah, Y.D.* 376:3, who cites both parts of his argument.

75. In the section skipped, R. Bacharach compares the case of a woman reciting *kaddish* to a person who chooses to add extra bows in prayer. He explains that in B.T. *Ber.* 34a, the rabbis only state that one should teach an individual not to bow and *Tosafot* explain that it was a matter of personal conceit to be stringent and disregard the words of the rabbis. However, in R. Bacharach's view, the case of *kaddish* is different

therefore in this case which has a gathering [of people] and publicity, it should be prevented. And I write this according to my humble opinion – Ya'ir Ḥayyim Bacharach.	ופרסום יש למחות. והנלפענ"ד [והנה לפי עניות דעתי] כתבתי יאיר חיים בכרך.

In his responsum, R. Ya'ir Bacharach, *Ḥavvot Ya'ir*, simultaneously brings the most cogent legal argument supporting a daughter reciting *kaddish*, and, at the same time, he sets the precedent to deter the practice. He cites a case that occurred in Amsterdam where a father who had no sons arranged, before his death, a framework in which his daughter would be able to recite *kaddish* on his behalf. One can deduce a number of things from the description of the case itself. The father's desire for his daughter to say *kaddish* indicates that he believed that the religious value associated with the recitation could be fulfilled by a daughter. He also understood that under normal circumstances she would not do so, neither in the synagogue nor in a private *minyan*, so he arranged to hire a *minyan* of men to come to his home to ensure his wishes would come to fruition. Although this appears to be a novel suggestion, R. Bacharach clearly states that both the communal leaders and the rabbinic authorities[76] in

---

as people might actually learn from this practice and act in a similar manner, and therefore it cannot just be thought of as a personal case of misbehavior that does not need a strong reaction. R. Bacharach fears that a custom such as *kaddish*, which is not an actual rabbinic decree but based on tradition, needs even more support and protection and therefore he chooses to speak out against this individual case in Amsterdam.

76. R. Shimon Frankfurter, in his work *Sefer Haḥayyim* (a manual for women on religious life and behavior published shortly afterward in Amsterdam in 1703), 50, p. 49a, strongly disagrees with and disapproves of a woman reciting *kaddish*. He uses every legal concept that he can think of to protest such behavior. He mentions that a woman's hair is *ervah* (nakedness), that women are not permitted to be called to the Torah because of the dignity of the congregation, that a woman's voice is *ervah*, and that men do not use women to serve them. Even though on the last point, R. Frankfurter concedes that according to *Tosafot* (B.T. *Kid.* 82a, s.v. *hakol leshem shamayim*) nowadays we rely on the fact that everything is for the sake of heaven and so using the services of women is permitted, he still feels that such behavior is an ugly thing ("דבר מכוער"). On this line of reasoning, he continues by stating:
ואפילו הכי דבר מכוער הוא מכל שכן שתבא אשה בין אנשים ותהיה ראוי לקדיש וברכו להוציאם...

Amsterdam did not oppose her recitation of *kaddish* and accepted, without protest, the arrangement orchestrated by her father.

R. Bacharach opens his response by outlining three legal arguments in support of a daughter reciting *kaddish*. First, he explains that women are also commanded to sanctify God's name,[77] which is the centerpiece of the *kaddish* text. Second, God's name is sanctified in the presence of the sons of Israel and the ten hired men create that quorum. Last, while the midrashic story with R. Akiva involves a son, not a daughter, it is logical that a daughter can bring merit and peace to the soul of the deceased as she is also his offspring. It seems to be based on this logic that the rabbinic authorities of Amsterdam permitted the daughter to recite mourner's *kaddish* for her father. It is important to note that in the scenario under discussion, the daughter is the only individual reciting *kaddish* in this *minyan*. Neither the rabbis in Amsterdam who permitted the practice nor R. Bacharach who prohibited the act mention being concerned by a woman leading the *kaddish* prayer and chanting *kaddish* by herself in the presence of ten males.

Although R. Bacharach explicitly states that he cannot find any halakhic proof to contradict the legality of a daughter reciting *kaddish*, he unequivocally speaks out against such a practice. He worries that the customs of Israel, which are equivalent to Torah, will be weakened and the words of the rabbis will be mocked. The questions are: what exactly does he fear and what specific tradition[78] is he worried will be

R. Frankfurter also tries to bring support for his position from the midrashic story of R. Akiva and the son. He concludes his comments with a very strong statement against a daughter reciting *kaddish*:

כי אין לבת בקדיש לא דין ולא דת ואין זה אלא שטות חסידים אף שיש לו לשון למודים כי הוא כחוכה וטלולא...

77. See B.T. *Sanh.* 74a–b; Rif *Sanh.* 17b; Rambam *Sefer Hamitsvot*, positive commandment 9 and *Siyyum Mitsvot Aseih* (where he lists which of the sixty main *mitsvot* women are obligated in); Rambam, *Hilk. Yesodei Hatorah* 5:1; *Sefer Haḥinnukh*, positive commandment 296; *Urah Shaḥar Kedushah Ot Kuf* #6; *Margaliyot Hayam Sanh.* 74b #27; *Responsa Yaḥel Yisra'el*, Vol. 1, #21 (published 5751) or *Responsa Yaḥel Yisra'el* #39 (published 5763); and *Responsa Yabbia Omer*, Vol. 4, *O.Ḥ.* #9, end of first section. See also R. Aryeh A. Frimer, "Women and *Minyan*," *Tradition*, 23:4 (Summer 1988): 74n56 for more sources.

78. The large influx of crypto-Jews who fled Spain and Portugal and came to Amsterdam

endangered?[79] The simplest reading is that he opposes a woman taking on a role traditionally held by men of saying *kaddish* and he is worried about such a practice spreading. However, when one examines his language more closely, it is possible that something else is at stake. As has been shown above, there is no explicit rabbinic injunction against a woman's recitation of *kaddish*[80] and so what words of the rabbis will be mocked and disregarded? In stating his concerns, he mentions his anxiety about each person going out and building an altar according to his own reasoning. It is possible that R. Bacharach is less concerned with the specifics of a daughter reciting *kaddish,* per se, and is more focused on the implications of the father's act for other situations. The father realized that his personal needs would not be met in the traditional synagogue structure and so created his own arrangement separate from the community. One could imagine other male mourners, worried about their priority in the explicit hierarchical rules laid out by tradition, organizing their own *minyanim* to serve their own personal desires to have *kaddish* recited on their behalf,[81] or any group for that matter breaking away from

brought with them many new customs, and so R. Bacharach might have been particularly wary of any new practice.

79. R. Ḥayyim David Halevi, in his work *Aseih Lekha Rav* 5:33, asks this very question: וגם במקורם אין הדברים ברורים די הצורך. כי אם אמנם אמת הוא שזה דבר חדש וזר ואלה שלא ראוהו מעולם. אך למה דבר זה יגרום להחלשת מנהגי ישראל. ואם כונת הרב שעל כל נפטר יעשו מנין בבית והבנות יאמרו קדיש ולא הבנים, וזו כונתו להחלשת המנהגים. זו באמת תימה כמבואר בפשיטות למעיין. ולמה ייראו דברי חכמים כחוכא ואיטלולא אם תאמר הבת קדיש במנין שבבית, ולמה קשה להסביר שגם בתו היא יוצאת חלציו, וכשמ־קדשת שם שמים במנין שבבית עושה נחת רוח לנשמת הוריה ממש כמו אמירת קדיש ע״י הבן וכמו שנבאר להלן, אלא שאין מקום לזה כשיש בנים ועושים זה בבית-הכנסת. ולמה ייראה זה כחוכא ואיטלולא?

80. R. Bacharach, himself, does not read the R. Akiva story as making any kind of statement about the exclusion of females. Possibly, he is just speaking about the rabbis' statements of gender roles in general (as R. Frankfurter above in n76 seems to assume). However, that is a more difficult read.

81. The father in Amsterdam had *kaddish* recited on his behalf every day, a sum total many times larger than if he had had a son who only got to recite *kaddish* according to his turn in the hierarchy of the synagogue. Once other people noticed this fact, they might have wanted to do the same.

the community[82] to institute their own practices and traditions,[83] thus weakening the prevalent community rules and customs. Possibly this threat of the creation of new worship groups or personal "altars," each according to an individual's desire, motivates R. Bacharach to speak out so strongly against the precedent set in Amsterdam.

R. Bacharach's *pesak* (ruling) was addressed to a specific community and a specific situation. However, since he was so careful to distinguish between the legal aspects, which permit a woman to recite *kaddish,* and the "public policy" decision, appropriate to this case, that led him to prohibit the practice, that *posekim* (halakhic decisors) who followed him sometimes made different decisions and drew different conclusions for their own communities and times.

Contemporaneous with R. Bacharach's response to the events in Amsterdam, R. Ya'akov Reischer in Prague also deals with a case of a daughter reciting *kaddish.* In this case as well, the father dies without sons and stipulates that his daughter recite *kaddish* for him. However, interestingly, in this instance the father assumes his wishes will be met without the need to specifically hire a group of men to carry them out. Indeed, the questioner and R. Reischer both take it as a given that the daughter will recite *kaddish* during the prayer service. In fact, the whole focus of the responsum is not about the daughter's recitation at all but rather about the desire of her grandfather, the deceased's father, to also recite *kaddish* for his son in the synagogue with the rest of the mourners.

20. Responsa Shevut Ya'akov Vol. 2, #93

שו"ת שבות יעקב
חלק ב סימן צג

R. Ya'akov Reischer, Prague (1670?–1733)

In the question [asked] of me: A man passed away here with only two small

בשאלתי כאן נפטר איש אחד ולא היה לו כי אם שתי בנות

82. Although "breakaway *minyanim*" are a common practice today, in the small, close-knit communities of medieval Europe, they were potentially dangerous to the fabric of the community. See also M. *Avot* 2:5.

83. That fact that, at the end of his responsum (see n75), R. Bacharach brings support proof for protesting the Amsterdam case from an example of synagogue practice (extra bowing) might support this understanding of his concerns.

daughters, the oldest of whom is four years old. At the time of his illness, he commanded me that I would give him halakhic permission for his oldest daughter to recite *kaddish*, [although] not in the synagogue at all. Now, the father of the deceased has come to recite *kaddish* for his son in the synagogue with the rest of the mourners [who are reciting *kaddish*] for their parents. Although Rema wrote in #376 in the gloss, "If there are [other] mourners, etc., the rest of the relatives [can] say [*kaddish*], only they [must] make a compromise between them [and split up the recitations of *kaddish* for each] and [the rest of the relatives can recite] only if there is such an established custom in the city."[84] And his [Rema's] intention was specifically [for] grandsons. This is also the case in Maharik.[85] For it is the root and source of the law, for how could one think that the father recites *kaddish*? The son brings merit to the father, but not the opposite…

קטנות, והגדולה שבהן היא בת ארבע שנים, ובשעת חוליו צוה אלי שאתן לו התרה שבתו הגדולה תאמר קדיש, ולא בבה"כ [בבית הכנסת] כלל. ועתה בא אביו של הנפטר לומר קדיש על בנו בבה"כ עם שאר אבילים על אביו ואמו, אף דכתב רמ"א בסי'[מן] שע"ו בהגה שאם יש אבילים וכו' אומרים שאר קרובים אלא שעושין פשרה ביניהם ובלבד שיש מנהג קבוע בעיר עכ"ל [עד כאן לשונו] כוונתו דוקא בני בנים וכן הוא במהרי"ק שהוא שורש ומקור דין דמהיכי תיתי יעלה על הדעת שאביו יאמר קדיש ברא מזכה אבא אבל לא להיפך...

Answer: …And if so, on the face of it, it would appear that the father has [the right] to recite *kaddish* only under the condition that Rema stipulated,[86] [which is] specifically in a place where there is

תשובה:... וא"כ [ואם כן] לכאורה היה נראה דיש לאביו לומר קדיש אך ורק כיון שהתנה רמ"א דוקא במקום שיש מנהג קבוע בעיר ובלאו

84. His quote is actually a paraphrase of Rema's actual words in *Y.D.* 376:4.

85. *Responsa Maharik* 7.

86. In the full responsum, R. Reischer discusses that he disagrees with the questioner's understanding of Rema and he thinks that Rema was indeed referring to all relatives and not just grandsons. He also explains that in a case where there is no evil behavior, a father could bring merit to his son.

an established custom [to do such] in the town; without such [an established custom], he should not recite *kaddish* for his son where there are other mourners present. One should not move from his [Rema's] words where there is no known custom.... Nevertheless, to appease the mind of those who die, God forbid, without sons etc. [one might allow a father rights in the synagogue]. But, in the case before us, he already left a daughter who recites *kaddish* in the house with a *minyan* (because in the synagogue surely we do not let her say *kaddish* at all). If so, he [the deceased] already had peace of mind in this regard. And it appears that also with the regard to the matter of the prayer, his [the deceased's] father should only pray at the house with the *minyan* where the daughter is saying *kaddish*,[87] but in all the other prayers and [recitations of] *kaddish* they [fathers] do not have a right. So it appears to me. Ya'akov the insignificant	הכי לא יאמר קדיש על בנו במקום שאר אבלים ואין לזוז מדבריו היכא דליכא מנהג ידוע.... ומכל מקום כדי להפיס דעת המתים חס ושלום בלא בנים וכו' אבל בנדון שלפנינו שכבר הניח בת שאומרת קדיש בבית אצל מנין (כי בבה"כ [בבית הכנסת] בודאי אין להניח לה לומר קדיש כלל) א"כ [אם כן] כבר יש לו פיוס דעת בזה. ונראה דגם לענין התפלה יש לאביו להתפלל רק בבית אצל המנין שאומרת הבת קדיש אבל בשאר תפלות וקדישים אין להם זכות נ"ל [נראה לי]. הקטן יעקב

The questioner, a student of *Shevut Ya'akov* and the *av beit din* of the community of Greiznach, accepts with ease that the four-year-old[88] daughter will recite mourner's *kaddish* for her father and permits her to do so. However, he struggles with the father's desire to recite mourner's *kaddish* for his son, since that belies the original idea that *kaddish* is meant for children to bring merit to their parents and not the other way around. All the more so, the questioner is troubled by his understanding of the

87. In this case, unlike the one cited by *Ḥavvot Ya'ir*, the daughter recites *kaddish* as part of the regular prayer service and it seems that *Shevut Ya'akov* is not bothered by the family creating a separate, private *minyan*.

88. As stated above, *kaddish* was originally instituted for young children to recite.

law, as cited by Rema, that "relatives other than children" who may recite mourner's *kaddish* refers only to grandsons and they only do so if that is a custom in their town.

Shevut Ya'akov responds that one must uphold Rema in this case. This father should be allowed to say *kaddish* only if this is the custom in the town; if it is not (which seems to be the case from the tone of the questioner), then the father should not be granted a turn. *Shevut Ya'akov* concedes that one might need to soothe and appease a dying person who has no sons by appointing other relatives, such as a father, to recite mourner's *kaddish*. However, since in this case, the deceased has left a daughter to say *kaddish* at home with a *minyan*, the deceased is appeased and so his father has no right to recite mourner's *kaddish* in the synagogue, since his son's needs are being taken care of by his daughter. In fact, *Shevut Ya'akov* suggests that the father should pray and presumably lead the services as a mourner in the *minyan* where his granddaughter recites mourner's *kaddish*, as he has no right to anywhere else.

It is clear that *Shevut Ya'akov* maintains that it is completely permissible for a daughter to recite mourner's *kaddish* and that her recitation brings peace to the spirit of her parent. From his language and legal view regarding the inappropriateness of a father reciting *kaddish*, it is clear that the daughter recites *kaddish* alone. Therefore, his emphasis on her inability to recite mourner's *kaddish* in the synagogue does not seem to stem from a concern for her being the sole person and voice heard by and representing the male *minyan*, as all those aspects exist in the home setting in which he permits her to recite *kaddish*. From his concern with and allegiance to the rules set up by Rema regarding the order of mourners reciting *kaddish* in the synagogue and established custom in a community, it seems that since tradition had not yet made room for a daughter's right to represent her father within that synagogue-based hierarchy, *Shevut Ya'akov* was not willing to even consider her doing so and usurping the rules of order. Possibly the logistics of how a woman would enter into the men's section[89] to be in the presence of the *minyan* could have been a deterrent as well.

---

89. Presumably, in this case as well as the one mentioned by *Ḥavvot Ya'ir*, there would

Shevut Ya'akov's acceptance, in this case, of a daughter's recitation of mourner's *kaddish* is viewed later on by R. Ḥayyim David Halevi as representative of a larger normative communal practice and attitude.

21. *Aseih Lekha Rav* Vol. 5, #33

עשה לך רב
חלק ה סימן לג

R. Ḥayyim David Halevi, Israel (1924–1998)

The Rabbi "*Shevut Ya'akov*" was not asked if a daughter could recite *kaddish* or not, and wrote it [her recitation] as the most obvious thing according to that which the rabbi who asked the question ruled. And also the rabbi who asked the question ruled simply to permit the daughter to say *kaddish* without any halakhic discussion of the essential issue. And it is understood from this that the recitation of *kaddish* by a daughter was to them permissible, clearly and simply, and it appears that is how they practiced in their communities. Therefore, the responsum of the Rabbi "*Shevut Ya'akov*" is not a lone [opinion][90] against those who disagree. Rather, [it is] trustworthy testimony that this was the custom in those communities. Examine it and you will find it clear.

הרב שבות יעקב לא נשאל אם בת יכולה לומר קדיש או לאו, וכתב זה כדבר פשוט ביותר על פי מה שהורה הרב השואל. וגם הרב השואל הורה בפשיטות להתיר לבת לומר קדיש ללא כל דיון הלכתי בעצם העניין. ומשמע מזה שאמירת קדיש ע״י [על ידי] הבת היה להם היתר פשוט וברור וכנראה שכך נהגו בקהלותיהם ולכן תשובת הרב שבות יעקב איננה יחידאה לגבי סברת החולקים אלא עדות מהימנה שאכן כך נהגו באותן קהלות ודו״ק [ודייק ותמצא קל].

not have been a *meḥitsah* in the home. Further on, sources #32 and #48, for example, will have no problem with a woman entering the men's section to recite *kaddish*.

90. See *Sedei Ḥemed Hashalem*, Vol. 5, *Aseifat Dinim, Avelut*, #160, who believes that *Shevut Ya'akov* is a lone opinion and see, for example, *Sha'arei Teshuvah, O.Ḥ.* 132:5 who quotes *Shevut Ya'akov* as proof that a daughter is permitted to recite *kaddish* in her home.

R. Ḥayyim David Halevi explains that *Shevut Ya'akov*'s view is not a lone opinion but rather represents an established tradition of practice in which daughters recited *kaddish* in those communities.[91]

R. Katzenellenbogen, author of *Kenesset Yeḥezkel,* struggling to understand the difficult statement in the Gemara that God is filled with wrath for anyone who does not leave a son to inherit him,[92] takes the strict position of *Ḥavvot Ya'ir* even further.

22. *Responsa Kenesset Yeḥezkel* / שו"ת כנסת יחזקאל
End of *Yoreh De'ah* / סוף יורה דעה

R. Yeḥezkel Katzenellenbogen, Hamburg, Germany (1668–1749)

In my humble opinion, it is known from the story of R. Akiva…that the recitation of *kaddish* by the son nullifies the decree on his father. And that which God said, [that God is] "filled with wrath," the interpretation is that God judges him with strict justice in Gehenna, and when it said "to inherit him," the interpretation is that if he has a [grand]son from his son, he has the law of an inheritor and inherits with sons, and then he [the grandson] recites [mourner's] *kaddish.* However, if he has a daughter, she does not recite [mourner's] *kaddish* as *Ḥavvot Ya'ir* #226[93] wrote that no female says *kaddish,* and so, too, a [grand]son from a daughter, does not recite [mourner's] *kaddish,* and thus it says in the Jerusalem Talmud, "sons of

לענ"ד [לעניות דעתי] ידוע מעשה דר"ע [דרבי עקיבא]... דאמירת הבן קדיש מבטל הדין מעל אביו. וז"ש [וזה שאמר] הקב"ה [הקדוש ברוך הוא] מלא עברה פ'[ירוש] שדן אותו במידת הדין בגיהנם ודקדק וכאמר ליורשו פי'[רוש] שאם יש לו בן הבן דין יורש יש לו ויורש עם הבנים ואז הוא אומר קדיש אבל אם יש לו בת אינה אומרת קדיש כמ"כ [כמו שכתב] חות יאיר ס' רכ"ו שאין אומר'[ים] קדיש שום נקיבה וכן בן הבת ג"כ [גם כן] אינו אומר קדיש וז"ש [וזה שאמר] הירושלמי בני בנות אין כבנים וק"ל [וקל להבין]....

91. R. Ḥayyim David Halevi discusses a number of other interesting points in his full responsum, which will be examined later on in this chapter. See source #33.

92. B.T. *B. Bat.* 116a:

אמר רבי יוחנן משום ר' שמעון בן יוחאי: כל שאינו מניח בן ליורשו - הקדוש ברוך הוא מלא עליו עברה.

93. This text cites #226 but in the responsum of *Ḥavvot Ya'ir,* the correct number is #222.

daughters are not like sons."[94] And it is easy to understand....

What arises from our statements, [is that] there is only a place for the [grand]son from a son to recite *kaddish* if he did not leave [behind] sons and even this is a compromise.... For the [grand]son from a son, if there are a lot of mourners [for their parents], the [grand]son from the son should say [*kaddish*] just once as opposed to the two times another mourner should recite it. Indeed, the [grand]son from a daughter and all the more so a daughter [herself] do not have [the right to say] *kaddish* at all in the synagogue.[95] And if they want to make a [separate] *minyan*, it is permissible for the [grand]son from the daughter or for whoever wants to say *kaddish* for the sake of the deceased but, for the female [to say *kaddish*], not at all [can one make a *minyan*].[96]

העולה מדברינו שאין מקום לאמרת קדיש כ"א [כי אם] בן הבן אם לא הניח בנים ואף זה דרך פשר.... לבן הבן ואם הרבה אבילי'[ם] יגיד בן הבן רק פ"א [פעם אחד] נגד ב' פעמים שיאמר אבל א'[חר] אמנם בן הבת וכ"ש [וכל שכן] לבת אין להם קדיש כלל בבה"כ [בבית הכנסת] ואם רוצים לעשות מנין רשות לבן הבת או למי שרוצה לומר קדיש בגין המת ולנקבה כלל לא.

94. J.T. *Yev.* 6:6 (7c).

95. With the limited number of recitations of *kaddish* in the synagogue service, they do not merit one according to the hierarchy.

96. R. Yehudah Ashkenazi, in his eighteenth-century commentary to the *Shulḥan Arukh, Ba'er Heitev* to *O.Ḥ.* 132:5, appears to misquote *Kenesset Yeḥezkel* as saying the following:

> ובתשובת כנסת יחזקאל כתב דדוקא בן הבן אבל בן הבת לא יאמר קדיש וכ"ש [וכל שכן] לבת אין לה קדיש כלל בבהכ"נ [בבית הכנסת] ואם רוצים לעשות לה מנין רשות בידם ע"ש [עיין שם] סוף חלק י"ד [יורה דעה].

Either he did not have the wording of *Kenesset Yeḥezkel* in front of him at the time of writing or, more likely, it is a scribal or printing error and instead of לו or להם, the word לה appears. (Possibly it was just abbreviated as 'ל at one time.) It is clear that *Kenesset Yeḥezkel* did not sanction making a private *minyan* at home for a daughter to recite *kaddish*.

Kenesset Yeḥezkel's main focus is on interpreting a difficult passage in the Gemara and he uses the story of R. Akiva as his key. The wrath is that which God would inflict after death, if one did not have a son to say *kaddish* and thus grant reprieve. Because the text of the Gemara specifically uses the term "to inherit," *Kenesset Yeḥezkel* expands the scope a little from just the son and includes grandsons from sons. He then distinguishes between grandsons from sons and those from daughters. As grandsons from sons may inherit according to Jewish law when there are no sons alive, they are consequently considered descendants who can bring merit to the deceased with their recitation of mourner's *kaddish.*[97] However, contrary to normative *halakhah,*[98] he cites the Jerusalem Talmud's position that grandsons from daughters do not inherit and are not legally descendants of the deceased, and therefore do not take a place in the synagogue hierarchy to recite mourner's *kaddish.*[99] However, they, or any other male for that matter[100] may form a private *minyan* in order to recite mourner's *kaddish* if they so desire.

R. Katzenellenbogen states emphatically that a daughter does not recite *kaddish* in any location and he attributes this ruling to *Ḥavvot Ya'ir*. He does not explain the reasoning behind the prohibition and does not mention the concern cited by *Ḥavvot Ya'ir* of weakening the customs of Israel. On the one hand, his responsum deals with the issue of who is a legal heir. However, it would be difficult to explain that *Kenesset Yeḥezkel* opposes the practice on legal grounds that daughters are not halakhic heirs,[101] since from the time of the children of Israel's wanderings in the

97. See source #27 and n128 below for a view that does not allow even sons of sons to recite *kaddish.*

98. See Rambam, *Hilk. Neḥalot* 1:3; *Tur, Ḥ.M.* 276; and *Sh. Ar., Ḥ.M.* 276:1 who all explicitly state that offspring of a daughter can inherit if the daughter is no longer alive.

99. Clearly, this is another example of a *minhag* that has changed in today's synagogue practice.

100. As he does not consider grandsons from daughters relatives of the deceased, they are no different from any man who wants to recite *kaddish*, family or not.

101. Although his connective language (in source #22) seems to imply as such:

שאין אומר'[ים] קדיש שום נקיבה וכן בן הבת ג"כ [גם כן] אינו אומר קדיש וז"ש [וזה שאמר] הירושלמי בני בנות אין כבנים וק"ל.

desert, daughters have legally inherited from their fathers in the absence of sons, in response to the protests of the daughters of Tselofḥad.[102] That seems to be the simple reading of his statements, since he reads the R. Akiva story to be the way to avert God's wrath though the recitation of *kaddish*. That capability is granted to sons and, in a more limited fashion, to sons of sons. He reads the original *midrash* in light of his interpretation of the Gemara, to the exclusion of daughters. Despite the fact that he quotes *Ḥavvot Ya'ir* as his source for the tradition that daughters do not recite *kaddish*, it seems that he was not familiar with the content of the responsum[103] and did not know that *Ḥavvot Ya'ir* reads the R. Akiva story to include daughters as offspring who could bring reprieve to the deceased through the recitation of *kaddish*. R. Katzenellenbogen categorically rejects[104] the possibility that a daughter could aid her deceased father with the recitation of *kaddish* and so she does not have any rights in the synagogue. He prohibits her from forming a private *minyan* as well.

Within a similar period of time in Amsterdam, Prague, and Germany, questions concerning daughters' recitation of mourner's *kaddish* begin to appear. It was dying fathers and the communities that supported them who brought the question to the table. In those communities where fathers ordered and arranged for their daughters to say *kaddish* in a private *minyan*, rabbinic authorities accepted the practice without hesitation. In Germany, rabbinic leaders responded upon hearing of these cases with hesitation and opposition. They either acknowledged the rationale for the practice in Jewish law, but condemned it due to the disruption of customs, or rejected the premise outright. These initial views will be echoed and re-echoed throughout the generations and sources.

And his statement regarding grandsons from a daughter explicitly contradicts the normative accepted *halakhah*.

102. See Num. 27:1–11, 36:1–12; Josh. 17:3–6; M. *B. Bat.* 8:2; B.T. *B. Bat.* 115a and 119b; Rambam, *Hilk. Neḥalot* 1:3; *Tur, Ḥ.M.* 276; *Beit Yosef, Ḥ.M.* 276:1–2; and *Sh. Ar., Ḥ.M.* 276:1.

103. He misquotes the source reference of *Ḥavvot Ya'ir* (see n93 above) and at no point mentions any of the content of *Ḥavvot Ya'ir*'s ruling except to state that he prohibits the act.

104. See also *Responsa Meishiv Halakhah* 469.

LATER AḤARONIM

R. Elazar ben David Fleckeles,[105] writing a few generations after *Shevut Ya'akov* in Prague, testifies to the longstanding tradition of young daughters reciting *kaddish*.

23. Teshuvah Me'ahavah, Vol. 2 Oraḥ Ḥayyim 229:10

תשובה מאהבה חלק ב או"ח סימן רכט סעיף י

R. Elazar ben David Fleckeles, Prague (1754–1826)

It is true that *kaddish* is for honoring the father, as was written above in the name of Mahari Mintz,[106] and it is written [concerning the commandment to honor one's parents]: "So that your days may be long" [Exod. 20:11]. Do men need [long] life but women do not need [long] life?![107] Is it enough for them [women] just to adorn themselves? If so, how will they merit, etc. [the world to come]?[108]

הן אמת דהקדיש הוא מפאת כבוד אב כמ"ש [כמו שכתוב] לעיל בשם מהר"מ מינץ וכתיב "למען יאריכון ימיך" וכי גברי בעי חיי ונשי לא בעי חיי? יען די להן לקשוט את עצמן דאז להני נשי במאי קא זכיין וכו' [לעלמא דאתי]?

But I saw in the holy community of Prague a correct tradition of old. In the courtyard of the Kloizen synagogue, there sat old men and women, people who are blind or lame, from morning until afternoon, and they recite the entire book of Psalms daily. And they have the custom that one who has not left after him sons but rather young

אבל ראיתי בק"ק [בקהלת קודש] פראג מנהג יפה מקדמוני'[ם] בעזרת בה"כ [בית הכנסת] קלויזן שם ישבו זקנים וזקנות עורים ופסחים בשחרית עד עת צהרים ואומרים בכל יום כל ספר תהלים ונוהגים מי שלא הניח אחריו בנים כ"א [כי אם]

---

105. He was the main student of R. Yeḥezkel Landau, *Noda Biyehudah*, served under him as head of the rabbinical court, and succeeded him as chief rabbi of Prague.

106. Most of R. Yehudah (Mahari) Mintz's responsa were lost and only sixteen remain.

107. This turn of phrase is a play off B.T. *Kid.* 34a stated in reference to the *mitsvah* of *mezuzah*:

ונקיש מזוזה לתלמוד תורה! לא סלקא דעתך, דכתיב: (דברים יא) למען ירבו ימיכם, גברי בעי חיי, נשי לא בעי חיי?

108. See B.T. *Ber.* 17a and *Yalkut Shimoni Yeshayahu* 434.

daughters, five or six years old, they [the daughters] say[109] *kaddish*[110] there.	בנות קטנות בנות חמש ושש שנים אומרים שם הקדיש.

Teshuvah Me'ahavah approaches the issue of a daughter reciting *kaddish* from a new angle. Instead of focusing on the merit that the recitation will bring to the deceased, he looks at the situation from the perspective of the daughter. He sees *kaddish* as a way for the child to fulfill the commandment to honor her parents, which the Torah states will merit a long-lasting life. Basing himself on a statement made by the rabbis, R. Fleckeles proclaims that there exists no gender distinction when it comes to the basic need for long life, and how else will women attain it if not by reciting *kaddish* as an act of honoring their parents? Based on this logic, he praises the established custom of old in Prague of young, orphaned daughters reciting *kaddish* in the synagogue courtyard.

However, R. Fleckeles does not support daughters reciting *kaddish* inside the synagogue and condemns the appearance of any female, young or old, in the men's section of the synagogue.

24. *Teshuvah Me'ahavah, Vol. 2 Oraḥ Ḥayyim 229:10*	**תשובה מאהבה חלק ב או"ח סימן רכט סעיף י**
R. Elazar ben David Fleckeles, Prague (1754–1826)	
But in the synagogue, which is designated for prayer, I have never seen such a thing and it is not proper that any woman, young or old, should come to the men's house of prayer.[111] For according to the *Zohar* and the kabbalists [lit., sages of truth], *z"l*, a woman in the house of God is like placing	אבל בבהכ"נ [בבית הכנסת] המיוחד לתפלה לא ראיתי כזה מעולם ואינו נכון שתבא אשה כלל קטנה או גדולה לבית תפלת האנשים אשר לדעת הזוהר וחכמי אמת ז"ל האשה בבית ה' כהעמדת פסל שם ומה

109. R. Fleckeles does not mention whether there was a *minyan* present in the courtyard, although presumably one must have existed.

110. In this case, similar to the one cited by *Ḥavvot Ya'ir*, the daughters recite *kaddish* after learning.

111. In Europe, the women's section and men's section of the synagogue were so architecturally distinct that many sources refer to them in terms of separate buildings: the men's synagogue and the women's synagogue.

an idol there.[112] And it makes no difference to me if she is a minor or an adult. And it is not proper, the actions of those men who bring their young girls to synagogue, because just as one is commanded to say that which will be heard, etc. [so it is commanded upon a person not to speak that which will not be heard].[113]	לי קטן או גדול ולא יאות הן עבדי אותן האנשים המביאים בנותיהן הקטנות לבהכ"נ [לבית הכנסת] יען כשם שמצוה לומר דבר הנשמע וכו' [כך מצוה על אדם שלא לומר דבר שאינו נשמע].

R. Fleckeles even speaks out against fathers who bring their young daughters to synagogue with them in general. Once again, the comparison between that which he permits and that which he forbids gives insight into what exactly disturbs him from a legal perspective. It is not the daughter's recitation of *kaddish* per se that is problematic. In fact, he lauds such practice as long as it happens outside the synagogue. The concern in the synagogue does not seem to be an issue of hearing her voice for, as the sole person reciting *kaddish* in the public courtyard, surely the group present hears her! On the other hand, in the synagogue, he is equally disturbed by the presence of silent non-*kaddish*-reciting young girls. As his quote in the name of the *Zohar*, comparing a woman to an idol, reflects, *Teshuvah Me'ahavah* is disturbed by the idea of a female, no matter how young, entering into the male domain of the synagogue, a place where she does not belong and stands out like a foreign, enticing object. It seems that his concern is that the physical distraction of any female in the defined sex-segregated synagogue group might pull men away from focused worship. However, where a woman could be in the presence of a *minyan* without transgressing a male-only domain,[114] *Teshuvah Me'ahavah* finds a daughter's recitation of *kaddish* not only permissible but also personally beneficial and commendable.

Taking a much stronger stance against any possible impropri-

112. The author was unable to find this source reference even after speaking with academic scholars of the *Zohar*.

113. See B.T. *Yev.* 65b.

114. He explicitly states that in the courtyard there were both men and women reciting Psalms.

ety between the sexes, R. Efrayim Margoliyot rejects the notion of any daughter reciting mourner's *kaddish* anywhere. He first states his ruling in his code *Matteih Efrayim* and then explains and elaborates upon it in his notes, *Elef Lammatteh*, that follow immediately afterward in the same volume.

25. *Matteih Efrayim*
Laws of Mourner's Kaddish 4:8

מטה אפרים דיני קדיש יתום
שער ד׳ סימן ח

R. Efrayim Zalman Margoliyot, Brody, Galicia (1762–1828)

One who has no sons, just a daughter, and commanded before his death that ten [men] shall be paid to study in his home and, following the learning, the daughter will recite *kaddish* – one may not listen to him [his request] and one should prevent this from being done. All the more so, one should not permit [a woman] to recite the *kaddish* of prayer. And even if she is single it is prohibited, and all the more so if she is married, Heaven forbid to make her voice heard publicly with the recitation of *kaddish*, whether in the synagogue or a *minyan* [at home]. Rather, if she wishes to bring merit to her father, she should be careful [to attend] all times of prayer at a synagogue or *minyan* and listen carefully for the recitation of *kaddish* and respond "Amen" with proper concentration. [God] who knows all thoughts will consider it as if she fulfilled the command of her father.

מי שאין לו בנים רק בת וצוה לפני פטירתו שילמדו עשרה בביתו בשכרם ואחר הלימוד תאמר הבת קדיש אין לשמוע לו ויש למחות שלא לעשות כן ומכ״ש [ומכל שכן] שאין להניח שתאמר קדיש של תפלה ואפילו אם היא פנוי׳[ה] אסורה ומכ״ש [ומכל שכן] א״א [אשת איש] חלילה להשמיע קולה לרבים באמירת קדיש בין בבהכ״נ [בבית הכנסת] בין במנין אלא אם תרצה לזכות את אביה תהי׳[ה] זהירה בכל עתות התפלה בין בבה״כ [בבית הכנסת] בין במנין להטות אזנה באמירת קדישים לענות אמן בכוונה רצוי׳[ה] ויודע מחשבו׳[ת] יחשוב לה כאלו אמרה וקיימה מצות אביה.

R. Margoliyot quotes the case scenario cited in *Ḥavvot Ya'ir* but mentions only that the daughter should be prevented from reciting *kaddish* and does not address the logical legality of the issue. Unlike those who came before him, R. Margoliyot is unwilling, under any circumstance, whether in the synagogue or in the home, during prayer or even after learning, to allow a female voice to be heard by the male public. He suggests that if a daughter wishes to bring merit to her deceased father, she should attend all the prayer services, listen intently to others' recitation of *kaddish*, and answer "Amen," and this will count as if she herself said *kaddish* for her father.

In his notes, R. Margoliyot elaborates and clarifies his opposition to hearing a woman's voice.

26. *Elef Lammatteh, ad loc.*[115] — **אלף למטה שם**

R. Efrayim Zalman Margoliyot, Brody, Galicia (1762–1828)

And in my humble opinion, in our days, when promiscuity is common, one should not do thus, that a daughter recite *kaddish* even in a *minyan* in the house and even following learning. While there is no prohibition of *kol ishah* [woman's voice], as explained in *O.Ḥ.* #75[116] and *E.H.* #21[117] and in Magen Avraham[118] and *Beit Shemuel,*[119] nevertheless, it is most likely that her voice will be pleasant. And they	ולפע"ד [ולפי עניות דעתי] דבזמן הזה דשכיח פריצותא אין לעשות כן שתאמר הבת קדיש אפילו במנין בביתו ואפי'[לו] אחר הלימוד ואף על פי שאין בזה משום קול באשה ערוה כמבואר בא"ח [באורח חיים] סימן ע"ה ובאה"ע [ואבן העזר] סימן כ"א ע"ש [עיין שם] במ"א [במגן אברהם] וב"ש

115. In an earlier section, he references *Ḥavvot Ya'ir*'s concerns of weakening of the customs, everyone building their own altars, and if it is done in public it must be prevented. He also cites *Shevut Ya'akov*'s ruling that a daughter may recite *kaddish* even in prayer at a private *minyan* at home.

116. Rema, *O.Ḥ.* 75:3 explains that there exists no prohibition on hearing a woman's speaking voice:

    יש ליזהר משמיעת קול זמר אשה בשעת קריאת שמע. הגה: ואפי' באשתו, אבל קול הרגיל בו אינו ערוה.

117. The first section lists the rules to distance men from *ervah*. In it, it states: "ואסור לשמוע קול ערוה." This phrase is explained by *Beit Shemuel* below in n119.

118. *Magen Avraham* 75:6 emphasizes that a woman's speaking voice is not prohibited. He bases himself on *Beit Shemuel*'s ruling that is cited below in n119:

    זמר אשה - אפי' פנויה (ב"ש) וע' בא"ע סימן כ"א דקול זמר א"א לעולם אסור לשמוע אבל קול דבור' שרי (ל"ח):

119. *Beit Shemuel, E.H.* 21:4 explains it is only a singing voice that is prohibited:

    קול ערוה - אבל קול פנויה או קול אשתו מותר אלא בעת תפלה אסור כמ"ש בא"ח ועיין

say[120] [when] women sing and men answer, it is licentiousness. And look in *Eliyah Rabbah* #75[121] who wrote in the name of *Be'er Sheva*,[122] it is appropriate and correct for every proper God-fearing [woman], whether single or married, that she should not make her voice heard when there is a man [present], only her lips should move and her voice should not be heard at all for maybe a man who hears it will come to have immoral thoughts and immoral thoughts are worse than transgressions. So she needs to be careful to not cause people to fail by her hand....[123] And nevertheless it is obvious that this should not be done and it is likely that "the reward goes out with the loss" that, instead of what she thought, to merit God's name by her hand in public, it becomes a stumbling block to the masses. And also from our days we have not seen it. And to bring merit to

[ובית שמואל] מ"מ [מכל מקום] קרוב שהיא תכוון לבסומי קלא ואמרי'[נן] זמרן נשי ועניין גברי פריצותא ועיין בא"ר [באליה רבה] סימן ע"ה [סוף ס"ק ה] כתב בשם באר שבע ראוי ונכון לכל כשרה יראת ה' בין פנויה בין נשואה שלא תשמיע קולה כשיש איש רק שפתי'[ה] נעות וקולה לא ישמע כלל שאולי יבא האיש השומע לידי הרהור והרהורי עבירה קשין מעבירה כי צריכה ליזהר שלא יכשלו ב"א [בני אדם] ע"י [על ידה].... ועכ"פ [ועל כל פנים] בזה פשיטא שאין לעשות כן, שקרוב הדבר שיצא שכרה בהפסידה, שבמקום אשר חשבה לזכות שם שמים על ידה ברבים, בא מכשול לרבים. וגם מימינו לא ראינו כך. וכדי לזכות לאביה תהיה זהירה לילך לבית

בפרישה מ"ש בשם מהרש"ל ודוק' קול ערוה אסור אבל קול דיבור שלה מותר וא"ל מש"ס קידושין דף ע' דאיתא שם קול ערוה אפילו בשאלת שלומ' אסור תירץ הרשב"א קול דבור מה שהוא משיב על שאלת שלומה גרע טפי ב"ה:

120. B.T. *Sot.* 48a states:

אמר רב יוסף: זמרי גברי ועני נשי - פריצותא, זמרי נשי ועני גברי - כאש בנעורת. למאי נפקא מינה? לבטולי הא מקמי האי.

121. Written by Eliyahu ben Binyamin Wolf Shapira, who died in Prague in 1712, as a commentary to *Oraḥ Ḥayyim*.

122. Written by Yissakhar Ber Eilenburg (1570–1623, Poland) and published in 1614 in Venice. In *Sefer Be'er Mayyim Ḥayyim* 3 (end), p. 119, he speaks out against mixed *zemirot* on Shabbat, specifically when men and women sing at same table.

123. In the section skipped, he explains that one cannot deduce that public singing is permitted from the case of Devorah as it is different in two ways. The first is that God placed her in that role, and the second is that the text does not mention that men were present to hear her singing. See *Responsa Tsits Eliezer* 14:7 who, in prohibiting a daughter's recitation of *kaddish*, relies heavily on this reasoning of *Matteih Efrayim*.

her father she should be careful to go to synagogue at the times of prayer and to listen to the recitation of *kaddish* and to respond "Amen," for the one who responds "Amen" is greater than the one who blesses. And the one who knows thoughts [God], knows the content of her heart that if she was male she would sanctify [God's name] in public. And the one who thought to do and was forced and did not do – it goes up [counts] as if he [or she] did it.[124]	הכנסת בעתות התפלה ולהטות אוזן לאמירת הקדיש, ולענות אמן, שגדול העונה אמן יותר מהמברך. ויודע מחשבות יודע תוכן לבה, שאלו הייתה זכר הייתה מקדשת ברבים. וחישב לעשות ונאנס ולא עשה - מעלה כאלו עשה.

R. Margoliyot explains that although technically her *kaddish* recitation is not a violation of *kol ishah* (the halakhic principle that a woman's voice is licentiousness), as this prohibition does not apply to a woman's speaking voice, a woman speaking with men listening and responding is still problematic. The Talmud warns that a musical, responsive interplay between men and women leads to *peritsut* (sexual impropriety). R. Margoliyot worries that in his time, impropriety is common and so he bans a female from reciting *kaddish* even in her home and even after Torah study. He cites the ruling of *Be'er Sheva,* which was originally made in response to men and women actually singing Shabbat *zemirot* together,[125] that when men are present, a woman should not let her voice be heard but rather should just move her lips, as she does not want to lead a man to inappropriate thoughts. Were she to recite *kaddish,* instead of being a meritorious act of sanctifying God's name in public, she would do just the opposite of her intention, causing others to stumble and thereby presumably damaging her father's soul. Such behavior will not bring merit to her father and so she should just listen intently and respond to the *kaddish* of others, as it is greater to answer "Amen" than to be the one who blesses. God knows the intention of her heart, which is that if she were male she would have recited *kaddish* publicly and it is only due to

124. See B.T. *Ber.* 6a, *Shab.* 63a, and *Kid.* 40a.

125. See *Responsa Seridei Esh,* Vol. 2, #8, which permits boys and girls to sing *zemirot* together.

the circumstances of birth that she does not. R. Margoliyot compares the plight of the daughter to one who intends to do a *mitsvah* and only due to duress, in the end does not. Such an individual receives merit as if he or she had completed the act.

Unlike the approach of R. Margoliyot and *Kenesset Yeḥezkel* cited above, R. Avraham Glick allows the daughter to recite *kaddish* and even prefers that she do so rather than her son, the deceased's grandson.

27. *Responsa Yad Yitsḥak* Vol. 3, *Yoreh De'ah* #340

R. Avraham Glick, Hungary (1814–1909)

שו"ת יד יצחק חלק ג יורה דעה סימן שמ

Regarding his question of one who passed away, Heaven help us, and he did not leave a son, just a daughter, and she wishes to recite *kaddish* after him [her father]. And it arose in the mind of his eminence that since this daughter has a son, it would be preferable for this son to recite *kaddish* for his grandfather, as *Magen Avraham* 132:2 wrote.[126] Until here are his [the questioner's] words. If we follow the principle of the law, it would seem to me that it is preferable for the daughter to recite kaddish rather than the son of the daughter, according to that which was written in *Ḥavvot Ya'ir* #222 and brought in *Pitḥei Teshuvah* [*Y.D.*] #376,[127] that on halakhic grounds the daughter should recite *kaddish* as this, too, brings benefit to

אודות שאלתו באחד ששבק חיים ר"ל [רחמנא לצלן] ולא הניח בן זכר רק בת ורוצית לומר קדיש אחריו ועלה בדעת מעל'[תו] כיון שיש לזו הבת בן טוב יותר שזה הבן יאמר קדיש אחר זקנו כמ"ש [כמו שכתב] המג"א [המגן אברהם] סי'[מן] קל"ב ס"ק [סעיף קטן] ב' עכ"ד [עד כאן דבריו]. הנה אם נלך אחר עיקר הדין נ"ל [נראה לי] דיותר טוב שתאמר הבת קדיש מבן הבת לפמ"ש [לפי מה שכתב] בשו"ת [בשאלות ותשובות] חו"י [חוות יאיר] סי'[מן] רכ"ב והובא בפת"ש [בפתחי תשובה] סי'[מן] שע"ו דמדינא יש להבת לומר קדיש

126. *Magen Avraham* does not specifically mention whether a daughter should recite *kaddish* or not. He just rules, based on Rema, that in the case where no son exists, one may give a grandson one of the recitations of *kaddish*:

ובתשובת רמ"א דאם אין לו בן ראוי ליתן ג"כ לבן בנו קדיש אך שאר האבלים יאמרו ב' קדישים והוא קדיש אחד.

127. It seems clear from his misquote of *Ḥavvot Ya'ir* and his mention that it is found in

דגם בזה יש תועלת לנפש אבל אמירת בן הבן או בן הבת מפקפק הד"מ [הדרכי משה] שם סי'[מן] שע"ו בשם תשו' ב"ז [תשובת בנימין זאב] יע"ש [יעין שם].... אכן החו"י [החוות יאיר] מסיק דלא נכון שהבת תאמר קדיש בפרסום ומשמע אבל בצינעא כגון בביתה במנין מיוחד יש מקום שתאמר קדיש. וראיתי שגם השבו"י [השבות יעקב]... כ'[תב] כן לומר בביתה.... ומה טוב אם יש ביכולת הבת לשכור בן תורה שילמוד משניות ודאי טוב ויפה לנשמת הנפטר כנודע כי משנה אותיות נשמה וא"ל [ואין להאריך] יותר.

the soul of the deceased, but the recitation of a [grand]son from a son or a [grand] son from a daughter, the *Darkhei Moshe* #376 in the name of *Teshuvot Binyamin Ze'ev* doubts[128] [whether it benefits the deceased]. See there.... Yet, *Ḥavvot Ya'ir* concludes that it is improper for the daughter to recite *kaddish* publicly, and meaning that, in private, such as in her home in a special *minyan*, there is room [to say] that she could recite *kaddish*. And I saw that also *Shevut Ya'akov*... wrote that she should say it in her home.... And how much better, if the daughter has the [financial] capabilities, to hire a Torah student to study Mishnah. Surely, this will be good and pleasant for the soul of the deceased as it is known that the [word] *mishnah* [has the same] letters [as the word] *neshamah* (soul) and there is [no need] to say [lit., lengthen] more.

This case seems to be the first time that a daughter is recorded as desiring to recite *kaddish* of her own accord and not as a result of her father's wishes. In this case, it is a grown woman with a child of her own who wishes to recite *kaddish* for her father. Halakhically, R. Glick hesitates

another book that R. Glick did not see the responsum in the original. One can see how from the limited information that *Pitḥei Teshuvah* 3 quotes (and combined with *Shevut Ya'akov*), R. Glick could have assumed that a private *minyan* is permissible. קדיש - עי' בתשו' חות יאיר סי' רכ"ב שכתב במי שנעדר בלא בן וצוה שבתו תאמר קדיש. מדינא יש לה לומר דגם בבת יש תועלת ונחת רוח לנפש מ"מ יש לחוש שעי"ז יתחלשו כח המנהגים של ישראל וכיון דאיכא פרסום יש למחות ע"ש.

128. Rema does quote *Teshuvot Binyamin Ze'ev* 201 and 202 as saying "דאין מקום לקדיש זו רק על אביו ואמו," however, he quotes an even stronger statement against grandsons reciting *kaddish* in the name of Maharik *Shoresh* 44: בן הבן אינו חייב לומר קדיש על זקינו דקדיש הוא משום כבוד אב ואם ואין בן הבן חייב בכבוד זקינו ולכן אינו חייב לומר קדיש.

to have the grandson recite *kaddish* and, instead, prefers the daughter since, as the deceased's child, she surely brings merit to the soul of her father, which might not be the case with a grandson. R. Glick misquotes *Ḥavvot Ya'ir* as only opposing a daughter's public recitation of *kaddish*, but permitting it in a private *minyan*. He correctly cites *Shevut Ya'akov* as ruling likewise. Despite the above reasoning and ruling, R. Glick concludes by suggesting a better alternative to the daughter reciting *kaddish*. She should hire a learned man to study *mishnayot* in her father's memory for the merit of his soul. He does not explain if he makes this alternative suggestion because he questions the power of *kaddish* to help the deceased and finds this a better method in general, or if there is still something troubling him about a daughter's recitation in particular, despite his legal support for the practice in private.[129]

R. Ḥayyim Ḥizkiyah Medini opposed the idea of a daughter reciting *kaddish*, which he perceives to be an innovation. As chief rabbi of Karasu-Bazar in Crimea, R. Medini worked to increase Sephardic influence there.

28. Sedei Ḥemed Hashalem	**שדי חמד השלם**
Vol. 5, Aseifat Dinim	**חלק ה אסיפת דינים**
Mourning 160	**מערכת אבלות אות קס**

R. Ḥayyim Ḥizkiyah Medini, Crimea and Israel (1832–1904)

One should prevent the daughter from saying *kaddish* with ten after the death of her father who had commanded her [to do] so, for it [the recitation] is a new and strange thing in the eyes of the rabbis....[130] And, behold, recently, I was asked from a neighboring town by one of the Krymchaks[131] who wanted the	יש למחות בבת האומרת קדיש בעשרה אחרי מות אביה כי כן ציוה עליה כי הוא דבר חדש וזר בעיני הרבים.... והנה מקרוב נשאלתי מעיר הסמוכה שרצה אחד מהקרימצאקים שתאמר הבת קדיש על אביה שמת בלא בנים זכרים

129. He does not assume that the daughter could or would learn the *mishnayot* herself, so perhaps he is worried about her ability to say *kaddish*.

130. In the section skipped, he summarizes the views of many who came before him, such as *Ḥavvot Ya'ir*, *Shevut Ya'akov*, and *Kenesset Yeḥezkel*.

131. This Jewish ethnic and linguistic community lived in Crimea. Originally, they called

daughter to recite *kaddish* for her father who passed away without male children, and the questioner has stopped this from happening until my reply comes. And I responded to them that we are not permitted to change and do something innovative in the land. And even if there exists such a custom amongst the *Ashkenazim*, here amongst the *Sefaradim* such a thing has never been heard of anywhere and its absence is good. And this is the rule: it is preferable to refrain and not do anything. They received my response and she was prevented from saying *kaddish* for her father.	והשואל עכב בידו עד בא תשובתי והשבתי להם שאין רשאים לשנות ולעשות חדשה בארץ ואף אם יש מנהג זה בין האשכנזים הנה בין הספרדים לא נשמע דבר זה בשום מקום והעדר טוב וזה כלל שב ואל תעשה עדיף וקבלו תשובתי ותמנע היתה מלומר קדיש על אביה.

R. Medini disapproves of innovating new customs despite the interest of one from his community in doing so. He has never heard of a daughter reciting *kaddish* in the Sephardic community,[132] and he prevents her from acting against tradition. Interestingly, he may consider a daughter saying *kaddish* to be an Ashkenazic practice.[133]

---

themselves *Yehudi* or *Srel Balalary* (sons of Israel). At the beginning of the twentieth century, they switched to *Kirymchakh* from the Russian *Krymchak*. The name *Krymchaks* (Crimean Jews) distinguished them from other local Jewish populations such as Karaites and *Ashkenazim*, who also lived in the region.

132. See *Torah Lishmah, O.Ḥ.* 27; *Responsa Mishpetei Uzziel, O.Ḥ.* 3:13 (cited later in this chapter, source #31); *Responsa Piskei Uzziel Bishe'elot Hazeman* 3; *Aseih Lekha Rav* 5:33 (cited later in this chapter in source #33); and R. Ovadiah Yosef's statements (cited later in this guide in source #36) for other Sephardic responsa. R. Yehuda H. Henkin (*Equality Lost: Essays in Torah Commentary, Halacha, and Jewish Thought* [Urim Publications, 1999], pp. 46–47) mentions that the status of Ashkenazic women differed from their Sephardic sisters. Many Sephardic synagogues, even today, do not have a women's section. He cites R. Shalom Mashash (in his n26) saying that in Morocco, women did not go to synagogue even on Yom Kippur and few synagogues had designated spaces for them. See *Responsa Shemesh Umagen* 55:4 and 72:3.

133. As was shown above, all of the earliest cases dealing with a daughter's recitation of *kaddish* arose in Europe.

A reading of R. Eliezer Zalman Grayevsky's book *Kaddish Le'alam*, published at the end of the nineteenth century, would seem to back R. Medini's assumptions about Ashkenazic custom, as it presents a lengthy and detailed argument to support a daughter's recitation of *kaddish*. R. Grayevsky even presents some new arguments that had not been raised until this point.[134]

29. *Sefer Kaddish Le'alam* 11a–b

ספר קדיש לעלם דף יא.-יא:

R. Eliezer Zalman Grayevsky, Eastern Europe, England, and Israel (1843–1899)

According to what we have said above, there is no practical difference if the orphan is male or female. Even though there in the aggadic story it was a male child, in any event there is no difference to the soul of the deceased if also a daughter recites *kaddish* (for she is also called offspring regarding inheritance and the fulfillment of [the *mitsvah* of] procreation), and since this is his offspring, there is benefit and peace of spirit for the deceased, as we have written above. For *kaddish* is not a prayer; rather, it is great praise of God, may God be blessed, that God's name be sanctified and uplifted, and the entire congregation responds to this "Amen." And therefore, what difference would it make who the reciter is, if it is a son or daughter who says it? We have also found stated explicitly that a woman[135] may also pray on behalf of the

ולפי דברינו דלעיל אין נ"מ [נפקא מינה] אם היתום הוא בן או בת, ואף דשם באגדה המעשה היה בבן זכר מ"מ [מכל מקום] אין נ"מ [נפקא מינה] לנפש המת אם גם הבת יאמר קדיש (דגם היא מתקריא זרע לענין ירושה ולענין פ"ו [פרו ורבו]) דכיון דזרעו הוא יש גם בזה תועלת ונחת רוח להמת כמו שכתבנו לעיל דהקדיש הוא איננו תפלה רק שבח גדול להשי"ת [להשם יתברך] שיתקדש ויתעלה שמו וכל הקהל עונים ע"ז [על זה] אמן וא"כ [ואם כן] מאי נ"מ [נפקא מינה] לן מי הוא האומר אם הבן או הבת יאמר זאת, ומצינו בפירוש דגם אשה תוכל להתפלל עבור המתים כדמצינו

---

134. R. Shemuel Salant, then Ashkenazic chief rabbi of Jerusalem, gave his written approval of the entire text at the beginning of the book.

135. Here, in his notes to the text, R. Grayevsky mentions that *Ḥavvot Ya'ir* must not have seen the Jerusalem Talmud source as he opposes a daughter's recitation and he postulates that *Ḥavvot Ya'ir* must have only been referring to an adult woman and

dead, as we found in the Jerusalem Talmud, Chapter *Ḥelek* (*halakhah* 5) [in reference to Ḥannah praying]....[136] Look there. And from there is a definitive proof that a woman can also say *kaddish* to save the soul of the deceased and to raise him up.	בירושלמי פ׳[רק] חלק (הלכה ה׳)...ע״ש [עיין שם] ומזה הוכחה גמורה שגם אשה יכולה לומר קדיש להציל נפש המת ולהעלותו למעלה:
And do not say that from the words of the Jerusalem Talmud there is no proof and that we cannot learn from her [Ḥannah] since she was a prophetess; for one cannot say such, since all the laws of prayer we learn from her, as it is brought in the Gemara, "How many laws etc. can be learned from her" (B.T. *Ber.* 31a), look there. And also the entire issue of the greatness of *kaddish* stems from "And I will be sanctified among the children of Israel" (*venikdashti betokh benei Yisra'el*) (Lev. 22:32), and in *kiddush Hashem* (sanctifying God's name) women are also commanded. Thus, women may also recite *kaddish* for their fathers. Even though for adult women, it is possible that they disallowed it because of strong [male sexual] desires, but a minor daughter is permitted to recite *kaddish* without a doubt...	ואין לומר דמדברי הירושלמי אין ראיה ולא נוכל ללמוד ממנה יען שהיתה נביאה; דלא נוכל לומר כן דהלא כל דיני תפלה אנו למידין ממנה כדאיתא בגמ׳[רא] כמה הלכתא כו׳ איכא למשמע מינה (ברכות דף ל״א) ע״ש [עיין שם], ומה גם דכל ענין גדולת הקדיש הוא משום ונקדשתי בתוך ב״י [בני ישראל] כו׳ ועל קידוש השם נשים גם כן מצוות ולכן גם נשים יוכלו לומר קדיש על אביהם, אך בגדלות יוכל להיות דבטלום משום דתקיפא יצרא, אבל לא בקטנה בלי ספק תוכל לומר קדיש...

could have been concerned with *peritsut*, as in the case of *zimmun*. R. Grayevsky then continues and analyzes the question of whether *peritsut* is even a concern in times of mourning.

136. He writes:

> תני ריב״ב אומר ממשמע שנאמר תעיתי כשה אובד בקש עבדך, מה אבדה האמורה להלן סופה להתבקש אף אבדה האמורה בכאן סופה להתבקש, מי התפלל עליהן, ריב״ל אומר חנה התפללה עליהן דעדת קרח היתה שוקעת ויורדות עד שעמדה חנה והתפללה עליהן עכ״ל.

This text appears in J.T. *Sanh.* 10:4 (29c) with very slight variations.

R. Grayevsky believes that there is no distinction between a son and a daughter reciting *kaddish*. He makes a point similar to that of *Ḥavvot Ya'ir*, that even though the *aggadah* about R. Akiva refers to a son, the deceased would not mind[137] if a daughter recited *kaddish* instead of a son, as she is also considered legal offspring and brings peace of spirit to the deceased parent. R. Grayevsky emphasizes that *kaddish* is not a prayer but rather a vehicle to cause the community to respond with praise for God. It does not matter whether a male or female is the catalyst, as long as the desired outcome occurs.

R. Grayevsky is the first rabbinic authority to expand the scope of the discussion and state that a woman, and not just a daughter, may recite *kaddish*. He makes this point unequivocally. He cites the Jerusalem Talmud, which states that Ḥannah prayed for the dead. R. Grayevsky claims that this is a convincing proof as so many laws regarding prayer are learned from Ḥannah.[138] R. Grayevsky further explains that *kaddish* comes from the idea of sanctifying God's name and since women are also obligated in the commandment to sanctify God's name,[139] they may recite *kaddish*. R. Grayevsky suggests that those who prevented adult women from reciting *kaddish* may have done so because of a fear of men who are present becoming sexually aroused, although he has no doubt that a minor girl could recite *kaddish* in the presence of men without a problem. It is unclear which aspect of a woman's recitation would be provocative and R. Grayevsky does not elaborate. It even seems from his language of "it is possible that they disallowed it" that he, himself, is trying to figure out why others would have forbidden the practice and not that he, himself, would agree with such stringencies.

After offering these strong proofs in favor of women reciting *kaddish*, R. Grayevsky goes on to further support his position, quoting the details of the case brought by *Shevut Ya'akov* and continuing his argument.

137. His assumption about human nature appears to be true. As seen above, many of the cases cited are of fathers who demanded that their daughters recite *kaddish* on their behalf.

138. See B.T. *Ber*. 29a–31b.

139. See n77 above for source citations.

30. Sefer Kaddish Le'alam 11b–12a[140]

ספר קדיש לעלם דף יא:-יב.

R. Eliezer Zalman Grayevsky, Eastern Europe, England, and Israel (1843–1899)

And it is clear from his [*Shevut Ya'akov*'s] words that a daughter may also recite *kaddish*. Even more than this, we find in the responsa of *Mahari Veil* in the name of R. Yoḥanan of Travish (found also in *Tur Y.D.*[141]), that this is also the rule in the case of one who passed away in a town and hired someone to recite *kaddish* for him, that this person may recite *kaddish* for the deceased who hired him to say for him and the other mourners cannot push him aside, etc. See there. Therefore, how much more so, may a daughter recite *kaddish* for him, for she is preferable to another man that he hires to say *kaddish* for she is his seed in all matters. And also according to the words of the *Yam Shel Shelomo* on the first chapter of *Kiddushin*,[142] which I cited above, in which he refers to the custom of *kaddish* as words of the scribes[143] [rabbinic law]. And it does not help the father's prevention of the son's recitation of *kaddish* for the mother during the lifetime of the father, as

ומוכח מדבריו בהדיא דהבת תוכל ג"כ [גם כן] לומר קדיש, גדולה מזה מצינו בשו"ת מהרי"ו [בשאלות ותשובות מהר"י וייל] בשם ר' יוחנן מטרוויש (הובא ג"כ [גם כן] בטור יו"ד [יורה דיעה]) דה"ה [דהוא הדין] מי שמת בעיר והשכיר לו אחד שיאמר קדיש עבורו, שיוכל לומר קדיש אחרי המת ששכרו אותו לומר עבורו ולא יוכלו שארי אבילים לדחותו כו' ע"ש [עיין שם], וא"כ [אם כן] מכש"כ [מכל שכן] דבתו תוכל לומר קדיש עבורו דהיא עדיף מאיש אחר ששכרו לומר קדיש דזרעו היא לכל דבר, וגם לפי דברי היש"ש [הים של שלמה] פ"ק [פרק קמא] דקדושין שהבאתי לעיל דקרי למנהג קדיש דברי (כ)[ס]ופרים ולא מהני מחאת האב לבנו לבל יאמר קדיש על אמו בחייו בודאי לא נוכל לבטל

140. In the section skipped, R. Grayevsky suggests that Rema's opinion that one is only required to notify sons and not daughters at the time of a parent's death (source #18 above) is only a lone opinion.

141. See end of *Beit Yosef*, *Y.D.* 403:10 and *Responsa Ḥatam Sofer*, Vol. 2 (*Y.D.*), #345, s.v. *ulevarer hadevarim*.

142. *Yam Shel Shelomo Kid.* 1:63.

143. The printed text here says כופרים, but when one checks his earlier reference to *Yam Shel Shelomo* on page 10a and in *Yam Shel Shelomo* itself, the text clearly reads סופרים, which makes significantly more sense.

surely one cannot nullify a rabbinic law for a mere custom. What emerges from all this is that when it comes to reciting *kaddish* for the father, there is no distinction between a son or a daughter, for a child brings merit to the father, and all that their sons or daughters do [is a] *mitsvah* in this world so that there will be *naḥat ruaḥ* (peace of spirit) for their deceased father and surely it is good and saves him from the punishment of Gehenna.[144]

דבר מדברי סופרים בשביל מנהג בעלמא, ויוצא לנו מכל דברינו דלעיל דלענין לומר קדיש על אביהם אין נ"מ [נפקא מינה] בין בת או בן יען כי ברא מזכה אבא וכל מה שבניהם או בנותיהם עושים מצוה בזה העולם למען שיהיה נחת רוח לאביהם המת ודאי טוב הוא ומצילו מעונש גיהנם.

R. Grayevsky brings a new line of argument for a daughter's being permitted to recite *kaddish*. He explains that just as one could hire a non-relative to say *kaddish* and this person would have the right to *kaddish* that the other mourners could not challenge, all the more so, a daughter should be able to say *kaddish* as she is the deceased's offspring and preferable to a non-relative. R. Grayevsky goes on to state in the name of *Yam Shel Shelomo* that the customs of *kaddish* have become as strong as rabbinic law. Because of this, a living father cannot prevent his son from reciting *kaddish* for his deceased mother. R. Grayevsky builds on this premise and states that, as such, a woman should not be prevented from reciting *kaddish* just on the basis of a custom for women not to do so. Interestingly, to a certain extent, the words of *Ḥavvot Ya'ir* have been flipped on their head. *Ḥavvot Ya'ir* was worried that allowing a woman to recite *kaddish* would mock the words of the rabbis and now R. Grayevsky argues that to prevent her from doing so challenges the power of rabbinic law.

With R. Grayevsky's comparison to the non-relative reciting *kaddish*, one can now better understand his earlier statement about an adult woman being prevented from reciting *kaddish*. It seems that he is arguing that a woman should legally have rights in the synagogue

144. R. Grayevsky ends his statements by quoting *Sefer Hasidim*, that if the father commanded his offspring to cleave to a certain commandment then the fulfillment of that would benefit the father even more than the recitation of kaddish.

rotation just as a son would. He will not accept custom as a sufficient answer for why she would be prevented from actualizing her given role and so he postulates that perhaps it is an issue of sexual arousal in the synagogue[145] that has caused the rabbis to prevent an adult woman from reciting *kaddish,* as legally there is no practical difference between a son and a daughter. Both can bring peace of spirit and save their parent from Gehenna.

MODERN RESPONSES IN ISRAEL: FIRST HALF OF THE TWENTIETH CENTURY

Interestingly, R. Ben Tsiyyon Uzziel, the first Sephardic chief rabbi of Israel, in a 1942 discussion of the issue of a daughter saying *kaddish,* addresses a number of the same issues raised by R. Grayevsky. However, he comes to drastically different conclusions and follows the Sephardic custom to prohibit outright a daughter's recitation of *kaddish.*

31. *Responsa Piskei Uzziel Bishe'elot Hazeman* #3[146]

שו"ת פסקי עוזיאל בשאלות הזמן סימן ג

R. Ben Tsiyyon Meir Ḥai Uzziel, Jerusalem and Tel Aviv-Jaffa (1880–1953)

Recitation of *kaddish* by daughters for elevating the souls of their parents who did not merit to have sons

אמירת קדיש מפי הבנות לע"נ [לעילוי נשמת] הוריהן שלא זכו לבנים

...I will answer his request to inform him of my opinion regarding the question that stood before him: Is it pleasant and proper for daughters to recite *kaddish* in the synagogue or the mourning house for elevating the souls of parents who did not merit to have sons in their lifetime?

... הנני נענה לבקשתו להודיע חות דעתי בשאלה שעמדה לפניו אם נאה ויאה שהבנות יאמרו קדיש בביהכ"נ [בבית הכנסת] או בבית האבל לע"נ [לעילוי נשמת] הוריהן שלא זכו לבנים בחייהם.

145. He does not clarify if her presence alone would be problematic or if it is also an issue of hearing her voice.

146. See also *Responsa Mishpetei Uzziel,* Vol. 1, *O.Ḥ.* 2; Vol. 3, *O.Ḥ.* 13; and end of 23.

Behold, the questioner [lit. His honorable Torah scholar], in his all-encompassing knowledge and his incisive understanding, sought and found in all the words of the Rishonim and commented and explained their words and, after establishing both the negative and positive sides, ruled that it is not appropriate nor befitting for daughters to recite *kaddish* for their parents even in the house of mourning, and how much more so [it is inappropriate] in the synagogue. This is the advice he advised, that a person should teach his friend's son Torah and he [the friend's son] will be as his own son and he shall recite *kaddish* for him.… Regarding your question.... From the words of the Rishonim, their *midrashim* and *derashot*, the esoterica of the Torah and their *halakhot*, it is clear that all matters of *kaddish* are a tradition from the rabbis and as such we should not add to their words or innovate ideas from our [own] minds to explain the reasons of the tradition. For even for those who believe they can seek out the rationale for the written Torah [the *mitsvot*],[147] they do not seek out the rationale for received tradition for its entire essence and holiness stem from its esoteric nature that our minds cannot begin to understand its reasons and secrets. Thus, we should neither add to their words nor subtract from them based on our own views, and therefore, one should

והנה מעכ"ת [מעלת כבוד תורתו] בבקיאותו המקיפה ותבונתו החודרת חפש ומצא בכל דברי הראשונים ופרש והסביר דבריהם, ואחרי העמידו את צדדי השלילה והחיוב העלה להלכה שלא נאה ולא אריך שהבנות תאמרנה קדיש על הוריהן אפילו בבית האבלות, ואין צריך לומר בבית הכנסת, וזאת העצה היעוצה שילמד את בן חברו תורה והרי הוא כאלו ילדו והוא יאמר עליו קדיש.... באשר לשאלת מעכ"ת [מעלת כבוד תורתו].... מתוך דברי הראשונים במדרשיהם ודרושיהם, רזי תורה והלכותיהם מתברר שכל ענין הקדיש הוא קבלה מדברי רז"ל [רבותינו זכרונם לברכה], וכיון שכן אין לנו להוסיף על דבריהם ולחדש סברות מדעתנו בדרוש טעמי הקבלה, כי אף למאן דדריש טעמא דקרא, לא דריש טעמי קבלה, שכל עצמה וקדושיותה היא הרזיות ומסתורין שבה שאין שכלנו מגיע להבנת טעמיה וסודותיה. ולכן אין להו להוסיף על דבריהם ולא לגרע מהם מדעתנו, הלכך אין לחדש מנהג זה של הגדת הקדיש מפי הבנות.

147. The Babylonian Talmud associates this belief with the view of R. Shimon. See, for example, B.T. *Sanh.* 21a and *B. Mets.* 115a.

not innovate this custom of recitation of *kaddish* by daughters.

Do not think this is because daughters cannot bring merit to their fathers, for even more so we found [that] they [women] bring merit to the entire nation as mothers and prophets of Israel whose memory and merit shall never cease from the midst of Israel. How much greater the promise that God promised to women and in the merit of righteous women Israel was redeemed from Egypt. But since in these matters [the recitation of *kaddish*] we only have what was received from our predecessors, we proceed in their light.

ואל יעלה על הדעת שזה הוא מפני שאין הבנות מזכות את אביהם, שיותר מזה מצאנו, שהן מזכות את כל העם כאמהות ונביאות ישראל שזכרן וזכותן לא יסוף לנצח מקרב עם ישראל, וגדולה הבטחה שהבטיח הקב"ה [הקדוש ברוך הוא] לנשים ובזכות נשים צדקניות נגאלו ישראל ממצרים. אלא מפני שאין לנו בענינים כאלה אלא מה שקבלנו מפי קדמונינו שלאורם אנו הולכים.

Although, even though we do not grasp esoteric matters, one can find a reason for this matter [of daughters not reciting *kaddish*] based on the statement of the rabbis: "The son brings merit to the father." And the meaning of those words is thus: A son is the physical continuation of his father's being in his deeds and words, and fills his place in the congregation. He brings merit to his father in the world of souls, the eternal world that shines its revealed light as if from within a cloud to our world.... And our prayer with the recitation of *kaddish* – [both] "*yitgadal veyitkadash shemeih rabbah*" and "*yehei shemeih rabba mevarakh*" – correspond to the sanctification of God's name, may God be blessed and be raised up in God's world and [God's] creations through Israel who sanctify God's name

ואולם אעפ"י [אף על פי] שאין לנו יד בנסתרות, יש למצוא טעם בדבר, על יסוד מה שאמרו רז"ל [רבותינו זכרונם לברכה]: ברא מזכה אבא. ופירושם של דברים אלה הוא: שהבן שהוא המשך צורתו האישית של האב במעשיו ודבורו ובמלוי מקומו בקרב הצבור, הוא מזכה את אביו בעולם הנשמות הוא עולם הנצח שנגהו נגלה, כמתוך הענן, בעולם הזה.... ותפלתנו באמירת קדיש - יתגדל ויתקדש שמיה רבה, ויהא שמיה רבא מברך - היא מכוונת לקדוש שם ה' יתברך ויתעלה בעולמו ובריותיו על ידי ישראל מקדשי שמו בבתי כנסיות ובתי המדרש ובמעשי

in the synagogues and study houses and through *mitsvot* performed publicly through which God's holiness is made more manifest. As it states: "And I will be sanctified among the children of Israel."[148] From here, our rabbis learned that sanctification occurs only in the presence of ten, for with ten God's *Shekhinah* [presence] is manifest. This is the secret of *kaddish* itself and this is also the reason for its recitation by one's sons, for they continue his form and deeds, and fill his place in the holy community of the holy nation.

מצוות שנעשות בצבור שבהם ניכרת הקדושה יותר, כאמור: ונקדשתי בתוך בני ישראל. ממנו למדו רז"ל [רבותינו זכרונם לברכה] שאין קדושה אלא בעשרה, לפי שבעשרה קדמה שכינה ואתיא, זהו סודו של הקדיש עצמו, וזהו גם טעמו של אמירת הקדיש על ידי בניו שהם ממשיכים את צורתו ופעולותיו וממלאים את מקומו בעדת קדושים של עם קדוש.

And this thing [taking the father's place in the *minyan*] obviously can be fulfilled only by sons, who join the congregation of Israel, and not by daughters. Thus, they [daughters] do not recite *kaddish* in public, but they are commanded to honor their fathers by continuing to do the good deeds and charity of their parents and to increase their own [deeds]...[as] I wrote (*O.Ḥ.* #13, second edition).

דבר זה כמובן אינו מתמלא אלא על ידי הבנים שהם מצטרפים לעדה מישראל ולא על ידי הבנות. ולכן אינן אומרות קדיש בצבור, אבל הן מצוות לכבד את אביהן בהמשיכן מעשי חסד וצדקה של הוריהן ובהרבות משלהן... כתבתי (שם מהדורא תנינא, אורח חיים סימן י"ג).

R. Uzziel was asked whether it is appropriate for a daughter to recite *kaddish*[149] in a situation where the parents did not have sons. He responds that it is not appropriate behavior, not in the house of mourning and most certainly not in the synagogue. He states and then repeats (at the end of the text not shown here[150]) that it would be best to teach one's

148. Lev. 22:32.

149. The questioner's phrasing is interesting. From his language, one might assume the questioner thinks it is halakhically permissible.

150. He also advises that if a man does not merit sons, he should connect his name with a place of Torah and have other people study on his behalf.

friend's son Torah so that the boy then could act as one's offspring and recite *kaddish.*[151]

R. Uzziel's view is that since *kaddish* is a received, esoteric tradition, one cannot analyze the reasoning for it. Traditions must not be changed and one cannot innovate that daughters may recite *kaddish*. R. Uzziel makes it clear that women can bring merit to their parents just as they did for the nation in Egypt,[152] but not through the recitation of *kaddish*, as there is no precedent for this practice. Interestingly, after strongly stating that one should not try to offer reasons for received traditions, R. Uzziel suggests an innovative and new explanation for why daughters cannot recite *kaddish* that had not been voiced in the sources that preceded him. He understands the rabbinic statement that "the son brings merit to the father" (B.T. *Sanh.* 104a) to mean that the son is a continuation of the father's personal form through actions and words.[153] *Kaddish* is a means of sanctifying God's name publicly in the congregation, a quorum of ten.[154] This public sanctification of God's name is the essence of the mourner's *kaddish* ritual and the reason, in R. Uzziel's view, that the recitation is done only by a son. By replacing his father in the congregation, a son becomes his father's continuation in this world. As only sons count in the *minyan*, daughters may not recite *kaddish*[155] in any location or circumstance, although they may bring merit to their parents through good deeds.[156]

---

151. This advice is clearly being given to a man without sons well in advance of his demise so that it would be possible to implement.
152. See B.T. *Sot.* 11b and *Shemot Rabbah* 1:12.
153. See also *Responsa Mishpetei Uzziel*, Vol. 1, *O.Ḥ.* 2:2, s.v. *bera mezakeh abba.*
154. See B.T. *Meg.* 23b and B.T. *Sanh.* 64a–64b.
155. R. Hershel Schachter, in his book *Be'ikvei Hatson* (Jerusalem: Beit Hamidrash De-Flatbush, 1997), p. 24, suggests a similar thought process, although he acknowledges that his teacher, R. Soloveitchik, disagrees. (See end of n237.)

    ומה"ט יש לפקפק קצת ע"ד התשו' חו"' (הו"ד בפתחי תשובה ליו:ד ס' שע"ו סק"ג) שכתב, שמדינא יכולה הבת לומר קדיש, אלא שע"י כן יתחלשו כח המנהגים של ישראל וכו'. דיש לטעון ולומר, כיסוד הפרמ"ג הנ"ל [או"ח ס'נה א"א סק"ד], דמי שאינו מצטרף למנין עשרה, אינו יכול לשמש כש"ץ להזמין לדבר שבקדושה, וא"כ אולי מדינא אין הבת יכולה לומר קדיש, ויש לחלק.
156. See also *Responsa Yaḥel Yisra'el*, Vol. 2, #90 (published 5751) or *Responsa Yaḥel Yisra'el* #84 (published 5763), where R. Lau quotes his argument.

This view is difficult to understand. According to R. Uzziel's reasoning, it would not make sense for a son to recite *kaddish* for his mother. His ruling represents a clear break from prior texts on two counts. As was cited above in *Responsa Maharil*, by R. Ya'akov Moellin (source #5), mourner's *kaddish* originated specifically for minors to recite,[157] despite the fact that they could not count in a *minyan*. To argue that daughters cannot recite *kaddish* because they are not part of the *minyan* is inconsistent with prior tradition.[158] Secondly, *Ḥavvot Ya'ir*, who prohibited a daughter's recitation of *kaddish* for other reasons, and *Shevut Ya'akov*, who permitted it, both assumed that it was halakhically permissible for the daughter to recite *kaddish* even though it required the presence of a *minyan*. None of the sources up until this point maintain that the one reciting *kaddish* must count in the *minyan*[159] that is responding to the *kaddish*.[160]

R. Yeḥiel Mikhl Tukachinsky, in his treatise on the laws of mourning, *Gesher Haḥayyim*, published in 1947, simply lays out a number of different customs regarding a daughter reciting *kaddish* that reflect those very sources not addressed by R. Uzziel. He seems to continue the Ashkenazic tradition of the land of Israel presented by R. Grayevsky above in *Sefer Kaddish Le'alam*, which supports a daughter's right to recite *kaddish*.

157. In his long discussion on mourner's *kaddish* in general (*Responsa Mishpetei Uzziel*, Vol. 1, *O.Ḥ.* 2), R. Uzziel discusses his discomfort with minors reciting *kaddish*.

158. In fact, as will be seen again in the next source, many of the sources deal with a minor and a daughter combined.

159. R. Uzziel's reason is difficult on another count. A number of the sources cited above in n77 actually hold that women do count in the *minyan* for *kiddush Hashem* (although not in the *minyan* for prayer).

160. See also R. Yehuda Henkin, *Benei Banim* 2:10, where he brings proof from the fact that women can receive *aliyot* to the Torah despite the fact that they do not count in the *minyan* required for public Torah reading:

> ורק מה שצדד במאמרו שאשה לא תאמר קדיש כיון שאינה מצטרפת למנין עשרה אינו נכון כי היתה עולה אף לתורה קודם התקנה וגם אחריה בעיר שכולה כהנים לדעת מהר"ם ב"ב... ובפרט בקדיש יתום קיל טפי מפני שאינו חובת הצבור שלבן קטן אומר קדיש כמו שכתב בספר האגור סימן של"ד בשם מהרי"ל והוא בשו"ת מהרי"ל.

32. *Gesher Haḥayyim* Vol. 1, Chapter 30:8, #5

גשר החיים חלק א פרק ל:ח סעיף ה

R. Yeḥiel Mikhl Tukachinsky, Israel (1874–1955)

The main benefit of *kaddish* is for the son to say for his father and mother (as is told in the story of R. Akiva that was brought earlier in section three as it was said [B.T. *Sanh.* 104a], "the son brings merit to the father"). And if he did not leave a son, only a daughter, if she is a minor (less than twelve [years old]), there are many places that permit her to recite *kaddish* in the synagogue after *aleinu* and after *shir shel yom* or before *barukh she'amar*. And there are those that permit her to recite *kaddish* even after *ein keloheinu* but the *barekhu* is said by a man. And there are places that do not permit her to recite in the synagogue at all.... [161] Only if there is a *minyan* in her house can she recite *kaddish,* and they do not permit an adult daughter under any circumstances to recite *kaddish* in the synagogue.[162]

עיקר תועלת הקדיש הוא באמירת הבן על או״א [אביו ואמו] (כמסופר בהמעשה דר״ע [דרבי עקיבא] המובא לעיל סעי[ף] ג׳ וכדאז״ל [וכדאמרו זכרונם לברכה] (סנהדרין ק״ד.) ברא מזכי אבא). ואם לא השאיר בן אלא בת אם היא קטנה (פחות מי״ב [משתים עשרה]) יש מקומות הרבה שמרשים לה לומר קדיש בבית הכנסת אחר עלינו ואחר שיר של יום או קודם ברוך שאמר. ויש מרשים לה לומר אפילו הקדיש אחר אין כאלוקינו, אלא שהברכו אומר גבר. ויש מקומות שאין מרשים לה כלל לומר בביה״כ [בבית הכנסת].... בלתי אם יש מנין בביתה תוכל לומר שם הקדיש, ובת גדולה לא מרשים בכל אופן לומר קדיש בביהכ״נ [בבית הכנסת].

R. Tukachinsky summarizes a variety of practices regarding a daughter's recitation of mourner's *kaddish.* There are many places that allow a minor daughter to recite *kaddish* in the synagogue prior to or at the conclusion of *shaḥarit.* Others even permit it after *ein keloheinu,* although the *barekhu* must be said by a man, and there are those places that only allow the daughter to say *kaddish* in a private *minyan* in her house. R. Tukachinsky states that an adult woman is not permitted to recite *kad-*

---

161. He references *Kenesset Yeḥezkel, Ḥavvot Ya'ir,* and *Sedei Ḥemed.*

162. See *Kitsur Sh. Ar.* 26:20 and see *Sefer Hakaddish* of R. David Asaf, p. 171.

dish in the synagogue under any circumstances, though she may recite it in her home. Although he does not explicitly explain the reasoning differentiating between a minor and adult daughter, the concern seems to be about an adult woman entering into the men's section of the synagogue and that men hearing her voice is not the issue, as that would certainly occur in the context of a private *minyan*.[163] R. Tukachinsky summarizes the issue succinctly based on the practices of his day.[164] It is permissible for a daughter to recite *kaddish*. There is disagreement about whether it is appropriate, as a minor, for her to enter into the men's section of the synagogue to do so, or if she must only be in the presence of men in her home where seemingly it would be less distracting. The view that objects to a daughter reciting *kaddish* outright in any circumstances, even in her home, is not mentioned[165] at all.

MODERN RESPONSES IN ISRAEL: SECOND HALF OF THE TWENTIETH CENTURY–PRESENT

Unlike the Ashkenazic customs presented by R. Tukachinsky in *Gesher Haḥayyim*, R. Ḥayyim David Halevi continues to reflect the more

163. Although it is possible that issues of *peritsut*, including hearing her voice, are considered less glaring in a private space.

164. R. Neriyah Gutel, in his article "*Kaddish Yetomah – Teguvah*," *Tzohar* 8 (Fall 5762): p. 24, maintains that there was specifically a custom in Jerusalem for daughters to recite *kaddish*.

> אף למעשה, ואף אצל "אנשי ירושלים" מצאנו כמה וכמה הכרעות, אשר עקרונית הקילו בדבר...ובספר חזון למועד (כד, ד - עמ' סג) כתב ברבח"ז גרוסברג זצ"ל כי "יש נהגו שבתו הקטנה אומרת קדיש כשאין בן, וכן נהגו אצל מו"ח ז"ל" וכוונתו [כפי שביאר לי הרב אליהו גרוסברג-יבלחטו"א] לרה"צ ר' נטע וייס זצ"ל [ה'מגיד הירושלמי' שקדם לרב"צ יאדלר זצ"ל] אשר היו לו חתנים תלמידי חכמים חשובים ביותר, ועם זאת הורה שלא הם אלא הן, בנותיו, יאמרו את הקדיש; וכן ציין ר"נ סטפנסקי, בספרו 'ועלהו לא יבול': מהנהגותיו והדרכותיו של הגרש"ז אויערבאך זצ"ל (ח"א עמ' ק"ט) כי הגרשז"א סיפר על "ר' שרגא פייבל פרנק [בן אחיו של הרב צבי פסח פרנק זצ"ל ורבה של ימין משה] היו לו רק בנות, והדריך אותן...ושיגידו קדיש אחריו [לאחר מותו]" ואם כי הגרשז"א עצמו הוסיף והעיר כי "זאת היתה הדרכה מיוחדת שלו, ואצל אחרים לא ראינו שנהגו כמותו", ומ"מ שוב ראינו הנהגה 'ירושלמית' כזו הלכה למעשה.

165. Possibly, since R. Tukachinsky references *Ḥavvot Ya'ir* as quoted by *Pitḥei Teshuvah*, *Y.D.* 376:3, he did not realize the situation under discussion was actually in the home. Or possibly the communities whose customs he is summarizing did not agree with *Ḥavvot Ya'ir*'s public policy decision.

conservative stance held by Sephardic *posekim* with regard to a daughter's recitation of *kaddish*. However, unlike his teacher and mentor R. Uzziel, he does not forbid the practice outright as not being applicable to daughters but, rather, severely limits the scope of when they may be permitted to recite *kaddish*. He presents his view in his work, *Aseih Lekha Rav*, which was published in the 1970s.

33. *Aseih Lekha Rav* 5:33

R. Ḥayyim David Halevi, Israel (1924–1998)

עשה לך רב
חלק ה סימן לג

And according to this,[166] it is very clear that the same rule and reason apply to a daughter, for all that is said in reference to the son as the offspring of his loins is also, in reality, appropriate for the daughter....

ולפי זה פשוט ביותר שהוא הדין והוא הטעם גם בבת, שכל האמור לגבי בן כיוצא חלציו, שייך ממש גם בבת....

Rather, the son is obligated in *mitsvot* and he is the one who participates in communal prayer about which is said, "And I will be sanctified among the children of Israel,"[167] and therefore it is obvious that he sanctifies the name of Heaven in public with the recitation of *kaddish* and not the daughter. But when a person does not merit to leave a son after him and he has a daughter, why withhold from him that peace of spirit and elevation of the soul that her recitation of *kaddish* could benefit him? And particularly when he, himself, commanded and requested before his death [that she

אלא שבן הוא חייב במצוות, והוא המשתתף בתפילת ציבור שעליה נאמר: ונקדשתי בתוך בני ישראל, ולכן פשוט שהוא המקדש שם שמים ברבים באמירת הקדיש ולא הבת. אבל כאשר לא זכה אדם להשאיר אחריו בן ויש לו בת, למה נמנע ממנו אותו נחת-רוח ועילוי נשמה שיכולה אמירת קדיש על ידה להועיל לו. וביחוד כאשר הוא עצמו צוה ובקש לפני מותו, ויש בזה גם משום מצוה לקיים דברי המת....

166. See source #21 above, where R. Halevi discusses *Shevut Ya'akov*'s position, and n79, where he is cited trying to understand which traditions of the rabbis concerned *Ḥavvot Ya'ir*.

167. Lev. 22:32.

should recite *kaddish*] and there is also in this a *mitsvah* to fulfill the words of the deceased....

And, on the contrary, we have found in the language of the Torah that *ben* [son] also includes *bat* [daughter]. As is said with the matter of levirate marriage, "If brothers dwell together, and one of them dies, and he does not have a *ben*."[168] And, as it is known,[169] a daughter also exempts [from having to do] the levirate marriage because it [*ben* in the verse] includes both a son and a daughter.... It is clear, however, that also in the language of people, a daughter is included in the category of *banim* [sons/children].... And the reason [for forbidding the practice of daughters reciting *kaddish*] is very clear that one would never intend to deal with holy things and in a holy place in a form and manner that are liable to cause impure [sexual] thoughts, even the most minor, and in synagogue all different kinds of people are found [there], as is self-evident.

ואדרבא מצאנו בלשון תורה שבן כולל גם בת. כאמור בעניין יבום, כי ישבו אחים יחדיו ומת אחד מהם ובן אין לו, וכידוע גם בת פוטרת מהיבום כי בכלל בן וגם בת.... מבואר איפוא שגם בלשון בני אדם, בת היא בכלל הבנים.... והטעם פשוט ביותר שלא יתכן לעסוק בדברי קדושה ובמקום קדוש בצורה ובדרך העלולים לגרום הרהור עבירה אפילו קל שבקלים, ובבית הכנסת מצויים כל מיני בני אדם כמובן מאליו.

And for this reason, I did not permit in our case for a daughter to recite *kaddish* in the cemetery,[170] for also there many men are found and it is not the way of modesty.

ומטעם זה לא התרתי בנדון דידן לבת לומר קדיש בבית הקברות, כי גם שם מצויים אנשים רבים ואין זה מדרך

168. Deut. 25:5.

169. See, for example, Rambam, *Hilk. Yibbum Vaḥalitsah* 1:3 and *Tur* and *Sh. Ar., E.H.* 156:2.

170. See n192 where R. Eliezer Silver not only allows a daughter to recite *kaddish* at the grave but also permits ten women to make up the *minyan* for that purpose.

And also in the home, I only permitted in a *minyan* [composed] solely of family members. And not at a time when many come to pray with the community as is the custom in houses of mourning, as [then] returns the worry similar to the synagogue, and a *mitsvah* does not come through a transgression.[171] …[172]	הצניעות. וגם בבית לא התרתי אלא במנין של חוג בני המשפחה בלבד. ולא בשעה שבאים רבים להתפלל בצבור כנהוג בבתי אבלים, שאז חוזר החשש כמו בבית-הכנסת, ואין מצוה באה בעבירה....
And, therefore, I limited the permission to a *minyan* of solely family members, to cause peace of spirit to the deceased soul, and also to fulfill the words of his will. May it be [God's] will that the children of Israel will not come to this and will fulfill the verse that is written "and see children for your children, peace be on Israel."[173]	ולכן הגבלתי ההיתר למנין של חוג המשפחה בלבד, כדי לגרום נחת רוח לנשמת הנפטר, וגם לקיים דברי צוואתו. ויהי רצון שלא יבואו בני ישראל לידי כך, ויתקיים מקרא שכתוב וראה בנים לבניך שלום על ישראל.

R. Halevi believes that the core premise of the ritual of *kaddish*, that offspring can bring merit to the deceased, may be achieved by the daughter's recitation. He spends time analyzing and emphasizing the fact that daughters are considered offspring. He asserts that the Hebrew word *ben* is not gender-specific and therefore includes daughters. He cites the example of levirate marriage where the Torah uses the word *ben* but the halakhic understanding of that commandment refers to both sons and daughters. R. Halevi takes very seriously the specific request of the deceased for his daughter to recite *kaddish* and believes that there is a *mitsvah* to fulfill that command. However, he is extremely concerned by issues of modesty and inappropriate sexual

171. See B.T. *Ber.* 47b, *Suk.* 30a, and *B. Kam.* 94a, where this phrase is first used in the Talmud.

172. In the section skipped, R. Halevi cites B.T. *Suk.* 52a, which discusses that, at a *hesped* (eulogy), men and women should be separate as the [sexual] inclination still exists even in such situations.

173. Ps. 128:6.

thoughts and behaviors. He fears that in the presence of males who do not know the woman, her recitation might cause impure thoughts and he does not want to desecrate the holy space of the synagogue with even the most minor infraction. As he does not know what type of male might be at a public gathering like the synagogue, cemetery, or even a crowded house of mourning, R. Halevi prohibits a daughter from reciting *kaddish* in those locations. He fears that it will be a *mitsvah* which comes at the expense of doing a transgression and, as such, totally undermines the purpose of reciting *kaddish* in the first place. However, because of his strong desire to fulfill the request of the parent, R. Halevi does permit her to recite *kaddish* in the home in the presence of a male *minyan* made up solely of family members for whom there will be no issue of sexual thoughts. In this manner, he expresses his views that it is halakhically permissible for a daughter to recite *kaddish*, while at the same time solving his social concerns regarding male behavior.

Eretz Hemdah – Institute for Advanced Jewish Studies in Jerusalem responds to legal questions from all around the world in its published responsa *Bemareh Habbazak* and does not have any social concerns regarding a daughter reciting *kaddish*. The initial answers presented below were prepared by those studying in the institution with the guidance of the heads of the *kollel*, Rabbis Moshe Ehrenreich and Yosef Carmel, and then were approved for final publication by the founder, R. Shaul Israeli. They addressed two different questions concerning a woman reciting *kaddish*, both of which originated in South America.

34. Responsa Bemareh Habbazak ***Vol. 1, Question 4***	**שו"ת במראה הבזק** **חלק א שאלה ד**
R. Yosef Carmel, R. Moshe Ehrenreich, R. Shaul Israeli, Israel (twentieth–twenty-first centuries)	
Recitation of *kaddish* by a woman Cali, Colombia, *Adar* 1990	**אמירת קדיש על ידי אשה** קאלי, קולומביה, אדר תש"ן
Question: A woman who wants to recite *kaddish* quietly in the women's section of	שאלה: אישה הרוצה לומר קדיש בשקט, בעזרת הנשים של

the synagogue for her deceased husband as there are no sons to recite *kaddish* for him. Is she permitted?

בית הכנסת על בעלה שנפטר, כשאין בנים לומר עליו קדיש. הרשאית?

Answer: There are a number of reasons to obligate the mourner to recite *kaddish*:

תשובה: ישנם כמה טעמים לחיוב האבל בקדיש:

1) Through his recitation, he sanctifies God's great name in the worlds and thus atones for the sins of the deceased and saves him from punishment and even raises the deceased from one level to another in the garden of Eden.

א. ע"י [על ידי] אמירתו, מתקדש שמו הגדול בעולמות, ועי"כ [ועל ידי כך] מתכפרים עוונות הנפטר, ומציל אותו מן הפורענות, ואף שמעלה את הנפטר מדרגה לדרגה בגן עדן.

2) There is, in *kaddish*, a justification of the decree, that he accepts the rule of the kingdom of heaven, that all of God's judgments are true and just.

ב. יש בקדיש צידוק הדין שמקבל דין מלכות שמים, שכל משפטיו אמת וצדק.

And, seemingly, these reasons are also applicable even to a woman and, therefore, there was room to permit a woman to recite *kaddish*. However, the consensus of the Aḥaronim is not to permit a woman to recite *kaddish* in the synagogue. There are those who permitted a woman to recite *kaddish* in her home; however, the *posekim* who disagreed with this view increased, and they forbade [it] because of the weakening of the customs.

ולכאורה, טעמים אלו שייכים אף באישה, ולכן, היה מקום להתיר לאישה לאמר קדיש. אך, הסכמת האחרונים, שאין להתיר לאישה לאמר קדיש בבית הכנסת. יש שהתירו לאישה לאמר קדיש בביתה, אך רבו הפוסקים שחלקו על דעה זו, ואסרו משום היחלשות המנהגים.

In our case, if the woman recites *kaddish* in a regular voice from the women's section, there is room to permit. And there is no weakening of the customs. (So it seems, that

בנדון דידן, אם האישה תאמר קדיש בקול רגיל בעזרת נשים, יש מקום להתיר. ואין בזה משום החלשות המנהגים. (כך

in the women's section there is no [issue] of weakening the customs, even according to *Ḥavvot Ya'ir.*[174]) With this, it is worthwhile to point out that there is a simpler option and that is that the woman may hire a man who will recite *kaddish.*	נראה, שבעזרת נשים אין בזה משום היחלשות המנהגים, אף לחוות יאיר.) עם זאת, כדאי לציין שישנה אפשרות יותר פשוטה והיא, שהאישה תשכור אדם שיאמר קדיש.

This responsum is the first to address the question of a wife reciting *kaddish* for her husband. In this case, there are no sons and presumably no daughters as well. The responder states two purposes for the recitation of *kaddish* – to save the deceased from punishment and as a statement of acceptance of divine decree – both of which he believes are applicable to women. Unlike R. Halevi, above, who needed to prove that daughters were also legally considered offspring so as to establish their right to recite *kaddish,* this text reflects an accepted change in the modern world that *kaddish* may be recited by any relative and not just children. Although he succinctly summarizes the halakhic history of the issue, acknowledging that many Aḥaronim did not permit a woman to recite *kaddish* in the synagogue or even in her home due to the weakening of the customs, *Bemareh Habbazak* responds positively and permits the wife to recite *kaddish* from the women's section of the synagogue. Interestingly, he states that a woman's recitation from the women's section does not weaken rabbinic custom even according to the view of *Ḥavvot Ya'ir.*[175] It is important to note that the questioner explained that the woman wanted to recite *kaddish* quietly and the answer clearly

174. This line appears as a footnote in the responsum on the word *home,* in the previous paragraph. This issue of a daughter reciting *kaddish* from the women's section will be discussed and analyzed in depth in the next section of this chapter.

175. He does not explain his thought process on this point. One could suggest a number of ideas. Either he assumes that *Ḥavvot Ya'ir*'s opposition stemmed from the establishment of a separate *minyan,* as was suggested earlier in this chapter or from the prioritization system of only one person reciting *kaddish* which no longer exists, or that somehow his worry was linked to traditions of modesty that are lessened when the woman is in the women's section. See R. Y.H. Henkin in source #42 to follow, who makes a similar claim about *Ḥavvot Ya'ir.*

states that she must use her regular voice, presumably so that the *minyan* will hear her recitation and respond.[176]

The next question addresses the situation where there is no women's section from which a woman can recite *kaddish*.

35. Responsa Bemareh Habbazak Vol. 3, Question 28

שו"ת במראה הבזק חלק ג שאלה כח

R. Yosef Carmel, R. Moshe Ehrenreich, R. Shaul Israeli, Israel (twentieth–twenty-first centuries)

A *meḥitsah* [divider] for a woman reciting *kaddish* in the synagogue
Montevideo, Uruguay
Tammuz 1994

מחיצה לאשה האומרת קדיש בבית הכנסת
מונטוידאו, אורוגואי
תמוז תשנ"ד

Question: A few weeks ago the *shamash* [caretaker] of the synagogue passed away. His only daughter requested to recite *kaddish* and she comes every day to the synagogue. The synagogue in which we pray on weekdays is a small *beit midrash* without a specific women's section. This woman sits outside the synagogue, next to the opening of the entrance, at this stage without a *meḥitsah*.

שאלה: לפני מספר שבועות נפטר השמש של בית כנסת. בתו היחידה בקשה לומר קדיש והיא באה יום יום לבית הכנסת. בית הכנסת בו אנו מתפללים בימות החול הוא בית מדרש קטן ללא עזרת נשים מיוחדת. גברת זו יושבת מחוץ לבית כנסת, ליד פתח הכניסה, בשלב זה ללא מחיצה.

Is there a need for a *meḥitsah* if the woman sits outside the synagogue? One should note that the faces of the community [men] are not facing the entrance where the woman sits.

האם יש צורך במחיצה אם האשה יושבת מחוץ לבית כנסת? יש לציין שפני הציבור אינם כלפי הפתח היכן שיושבת האשה.

176. See end of source #36 below where the same legal requirement is stated and the lengthy discussion in the following section concerning R. Y.H. Henkin's statement (in source #44) that women should recite *kaddish* quietly.

Answer: There is room to permit the daughter to recite *kaddish* for her father in the entrance of the synagogue, in a place where there is no women's section. (See *Mishnah Berurah* 55:50, 51, 59. From his words, it follows that it is preferable to stand in the entrance of the synagogue for there she surely joins [with the *minyan*] for the recitation of *kaddish*.[177])	תשובה: יש מקום להתיר לבת לומר קדיש על אביה בפתח בית הכנסת, במקום שאין עזרת נשים. (עיין משנה ברורה סי' נ"ה ס"ק נ', נ"א, נ"ט. מדבריו יוצא שעדיף לעמוד בפתח בית-הכנסת, ששם היא בוודאי מצטרפת לאמירת קדיש.)

In this case, the daughter requested to recite *kaddish* and shows her dedication by attending *minyan* every day. However, in the small *beit midrash* in which the community prays on weekdays there is no women's section and so she sits outside the entrance and recites *kaddish* from there with no *meḥitsah*. *Bemareh Habbazak* permits the daughter's recitation of *kaddish* without a *meḥitsah* and states that she should specifically stand in the entrance of the synagogue so that she is in the presence of the *minyan*.

Besides his extensively published responsa, R. Ovadiah Yosef would respond to online halakhic questions with answers posted on the Internet by his staff. Although he takes a conservative stance as compared to the responsa in *Bemareh Habbazak*, his view on a daughter reciting *kaddish* is the most lenient when compared to the Sephardic *posekim* who came before him.

177. This line appears as a footnote in the responsum on the word *entrance* of the synagogue.

36. *Halacha Yomit*, **הלכה יומית**

1/31/2010 **16 שבט 5770**

http://www.halachayomit.co.il/DisplayRead.asp?readID=1302

R. Ovadiah Yosef, Israel (1920–2013)

Is the daughter allowed to recite *kaddish*?

האם הבת רשאית לומר קדיש?

Question: One who died without sons, is the daughter allowed to recite *kaddish* to elevate his soul?

שאלה: מי שמת בלא בנים, האם רשאית בתו לומר קדיש לעלוי נשמתו?

Answer: Behold the essence of the recitation of *kaddish* is a great virtue and benefit that cannot be estimated in honor of the soul of the father or mother who passed away from the world. For if punishments were decreed on them, through the recitation of *kaddish* they lighten the punishments from them and sometimes cancel the punishment completely. And so, if it was decreed that their lot should be in the garden of Eden, behold through the recitation of *kaddish* they go up and rise increasingly from strength to strength. And therefore, surely it is incumbent upon us to see when a person passes away from the world without sons, if it is possible that his daughters can recite *kaddish* for the elevation of his soul or not.

תשובה: הנה עצם אמירת הקדיש היא מעלה גדולה ותועלת שלא ניתן לשערה לכבוד נשמת האב או האם שנפטרו מן העולם. שאם נגזרו עליהם עונשים, על ידי אמירת הקדיש מיקלים מעליהם את עונשם, ולפעמים מבטלים מהם את העונש לגמרי. וכן אם נגזר עליהם שיהיה חלקם בגן עדן, הרי על ידי אמירת הקדיש הם עולים ומתעלים עוד ועוד מחיל אל חיל. ועל כן בודאי שמוטל עלינו לראות, כאשר נפטר אדם מן העולם בלא בנים, האם אפשר שבנותיו יאמרו קדיש לעלוי נשמתו, אם לאו.

And surely there is no possibility that the daughter can say *kaddish* in the presence of ten women of Israel,[178] for behold it is

ובודאי שאין כל אפשרות שהבנות תאמרנה קדיש בנוכחות עשרה נשים מישראל,

178. See n192 where R. Silver seems to permit such a thing at the cemetery.

known that *kaddish* is in the category of *devarim shebikdushah* [sanctified acts] that are forbidden to recite if there are not ten men from Israel, like the law of reciting "*barekhu et Hashem hamevorakh,*" and, therefore, the question turns to the manner in which the daughter comes to recite *kaddish* in front of ten men from Israel, and one should determine if there is a concern of prohibition.... [179]

כי הנה ידוע, שהקדיש הוא בכלל הדברים שבקדושה שאסור לאמרם אם אין שם עשרה אנשים מישראל, וכדין אמירת "ברכו את ה' המבורך", ועל כן נדון השאלה נסוב על אופן שהבת באה לומר קדיש בפני עשרה אנשים מישראל, ויש לדון אם אין בזה איזה חשש איסור....

And therefore, it is clear from the words of the *Teshuvah Me'ahavah* that, as law, one should not permit the recitation of *kaddish* by women in the synagogue, since this thing is liable to bring great violations and the sages of the Torah in general opposed such a custom. But in a different place, such as the home, or in an organized [gathering] in the women's section and the like, one should permit the recitation of *kaddish* by daughters of those deceased who have not left sons in this world. And the correct ruling is like the words of the *Teshuvah Me'ahavah*. And so ruled our teacher R. Ovadiah Yosef, may he live for many good days.

ועל כן מבואר מדברי התשובה מאהבה, שלהלכה אין להתיר אמירת קדיש על ידי נשים בבית הכנסת, הואיל ודבר זה עלול להביא לקלקולים גדולים, וחכמי התורה התנגדו בדרך כלל למנהג שכזה. אבל במקום אחר, וכגון בבית, או בהתארגנות בעזרת הנשים וכדומה, יש להתיר אמירת קדיש על ידי בנות הנפטרים, שלא השאירו בנים בעולם הזה. והעיקר להלכה כדברי התשובה מאהבה. וכן פסק מרן הרב עובדיה יוסף שליט"א [שיחיה לארך ימים טובים אמן].

179. R. Yosef then summarizes the views of *Shevut Ya'akov, Teshuvah Me'ahavah,* and *Ḥavvot Ya'ir*. He offers his understanding of *Ḥavvot Ya'ir*'s concern of the weakening of the customs but defines it in light of the modern situation of Jewish denominationalism today.

משום שעל ידי הנהגת דבר חדש שכזה, יבאו לפרוץ פרצות בישראל, כמו שאנו רואים במעשיהם של ראשוני הרפורמים, שהתחילו בשינויים שאינם נוגדים את עיקרי הדת, ולבסוף יצאו עוקרים את כל גופי התורה. לכן למעשה כתב שאין לאפשר אמירת קדיש על ידי הבת.

See source #53, where R. Ahron Soloveichik also addresses the issue of denominationalism today, but raises it as a reason to permit the daughter's recitation of *kaddish*.

Therefore, in conclusion: One who passed away from this world and did not leave sons after him to recite *kaddish* to elevate his soul, and merited[180] to have righteous daughters who want to recite *kaddish* for the elevation of his soul, one should permit them to recite *kaddish* when they gather with a *minyan* of men in the house to say words of Torah or after the reading of Psalms in whatever place it may be. However, in the main sanctuary of the synagogue, one should not conduct the recitation of *kaddish* by a woman.

לכן לסיכום: מי שנפטר מן העולם ולא השאיר אחריו בנים לאמירת קדיש לעלוי נשמתו, וזכה שיש לו בנות צדקניות הרוצות לומר קדיש לעלוי נשמתו, יש לאפשר להן לומר קדיש כאשר מתאספים מנין אנשים בבית לאמירת דברי תורה, או לאחר קריאת תהלים באיזה מקום שיהיה. אבל באולם הגדול של בית הכנסת, אין להנהיג אמירת קדיש על ידי אשה.

Note: Can she recite *kaddish* alone and aloud or in the background of men reciting *kaddish* aloud?... A woman who recites *kaddish* and they [the *minyan*] do not hear her, apparently there is no benefit [to the parents] in the recitation of the *kaddish*. But one needs to consider the issue.[181]

הג"ה: האם היא יכולה לומר קדיש לבד בקול רם או ברקע הגברים שאומרים קדיש בקול רם?... אשה שתאמר קדיש ולא ישמעו אותה, לכאורה אין תועלת באמירת הקדיש. אך יש לדון בדבר.

---

180. This text is the first to use the term "merited" in reference to having daughters. Usually the term is used with regard to those parents who did not "merit" to have sons. See, for example, the title of R. Uzziel's responsum in source #31.

181. This is one of the questions and answers that the "*Halacha Yomit*" (daily *halakhah*) staff added at the end of R. Yosef's responsum, in addition to these others:

האם אשה או אמא יכולה לומר קדיש?
למה אשה אינה יכולה לומר קדיש בבית הכנסת אם היא אומרת ברכת הגומל?
....האם אשה יכולה לומר דברי תורה בפני משפחתה או חברים?
....אשה או אמא יכולה לומר קדיש, אך עיקר התועלת היא בזרעו של האדם, ובתו נקראת זרעו. לכן לא רצו הפוסקים להקל אלא בזרעו דוקא. ואם אין לו זרע, עדיף יותר שישכרו בתשלום, איש אחד, שיאמר קדיש בכוונה לעלוי נשמת הנפטר.
ברכת הגומל נהגו בכל תפוצות ישראל לברך, ואין בזה שום חשש מצד מקלקלי הדת, שיש לחוש לדרכיהם בענין גדול כזה של קדיש.
אשה יכולה לומר דברי תורה בפני משפחתה.

R. Yosef believes that the benefits that *kaddish* brings to the soul of the deceased are so important and beneficial that he must examine the possibility of a daughter reciting it. He emphasizes that surely she is unable to do so in the presence of ten women and that it is with regard to her reciting *kaddish* in front of ten men that he must determine if it is permitted. R. Yosef uses the ruling of *Teshuvah Me'ahavah* (source #23) as his precedent, particularly his example of girls reciting *kaddish* in the courtyard in Prague. Like *Teshuvah Me'ahavah* and R. Halevi (source #33) he does not allow the daughter to recite *kaddish* in the synagogue for fear of both the sanctity of the space and that the sages before him did not accept such a custom. However, unlike the earlier Sephardic *posekim* (*Sedei Ḥemed,* R. Uzziel, and R. Halevi), R. Yosef permits daughters to recite *kaddish* in the presence of a general male *minyan* at home or in any other gathering such as for the recitation of Psalms, in the women's section, or any other place as long as it is not in the main sanctuary of the synagogue.

All the cases brought in modern Israel were of families in which the deceased had no sons. At times, the parent requested before death that his daughter recite *kaddish* and, in the more recent responsa, the wife or daughter herself desired to do so. It seems that in all the situations where the woman was permitted to recite *kaddish,* she did so alone and in a manner in which the *minyan* could hear her. It was not specified anywhere that she must recite *kaddish* simultaneously with a male, and the addendum to R. Yosef's responsum specifically mentions that a quiet recitation seems problematic. This practice to permit a daughter's recitation of *kaddish* will also be a trend in the United States, although the question of whether she may recite it alone will be one significant difference from the modern Israeli responsa.

See n211 for the view of R. Yitsḥak Yosef, R. Yosef's son, on a daughter's recitation of *kaddish.*

MODERN RESPONSES IN AMERICA: SECOND HALF OF THE TWENTIETH CENTURY

Rabbi Yosef Eliyahu Henkin

A short article published in 1963 by R. Yosef Eliyahu Henkin shaped much of the modern-day discussion, especially in the United States, surrounding the issue of a daughter reciting *kaddish*. His statements generated much argument and debate and, to a significant extent, framed the way this issue has been viewed ever since.

37. Hapardes, Year 38	**הפרדס שנה לח**
Booklet 6 (February 1963)	**חוברת ו (אדר תשכ"ג)**
#44, pp. 5–6	**סימן מד, עמוד 5–6**

R. Yosef Eliyahu Henkin, Eastern Europe and United States (1880–1973)

Recitation of *Kaddish* by the Daughter. I was driven to write an essay with this title due to a letter in the printed circular signed in the name of R. Moshe Leib Blair[182]	**אמירת קדיש ע"י [על ידי] הבת.** נתעוררתי לכתוב מאמר בשם זה ע"י [על ידי] המכתב-נדפס החוזר, חתום בשם הרב משה

182. R. Blair (see Appendix A for the complete text of his responsum) addresses the question of whether a daughter is obligated to recite *kaddish*, as he sees the ritual of *kaddish* as part of the laws of mourning in which women are obligated. He explains that they are obligated to sanctify God's name and can bring peace of spirit to the deceased and so a daughter should be obligated to recite *kaddish* as well. He brings a number of different arguments to support his view, such as *kaddish* is a prayer and women are obligated in prayer; the rabbis in Amsterdam allowed it; and, in many cases in *halakhah*, the word *ben/banim* includes *bat/banot* unless explicitly noted. In an interesting read of *Ḥavvot Ya'ir*, R. Blair suggests that his opposition was to a daughter reciting *kaddish* specifically after learning and not to a daughter reciting *kaddish* during prayer.

דבריו האחרונים של החות יאיר צריכין באור. הוא מדבר שהאב צוה שילמדו עשרה אנשים תורה בביתו י"ב חודש ואח"כ תאמר הבת קדיש. זה הוא באמת בונה במה לעצמו ומבטל מנהג ישראל, כי גם בב"כ רק אנשים אומרים קדיש אחר הלמוד ולא נשים - אבל הוא אינו מדבר אודות הקדיש של הי"א חודש שהאשה אומרת בעזרת נשים או אפילו בעת שבעה בביתה כשמתפללים עשרה אנשים. על זה בודאי לא שייך לומר ומחזי מילא דרבנן כחוכא וטלולא. הנה כבר אנו רואים בזמננו בב"כ ארטודוקסיים שנשים עומדות אחרי עלינו וה"סיום", ואומרות קדיש ואין אנו מזלזלים באמירתן. אדרבה, אנו מביטים על זה בכבוד ולא ח"ו בזלזול.

of Chicago regarding the recitation of [mourner's] *kaddish* by a daughter in order to bring peace of spirit to the deceased. I proposed to explain the issue of *kaddish*, in what manner it brings peace [to the deceased], as well as explaining *kaddish* and its customs....

ליב בלייער משיקאגו, ע״י [על ידי] אמירת קדיש ע״י [על ידי] הבת בכדי להביא קורת רוח להנפטר. וראיתי לבאר ענין קדיש ובאיזה אופן הוא מביא קורת רוח. גם ביאור הקדיש ומנהגיו....

And let us move on to discuss the issue that was suggested of kaddish [recited] by a daughter. If the daughter comes to pray in the women's section and affirms her actions with sanctifying the Shabbat, *kashrut* [observance] and purity and modesty, all of which are essential, and she desires to also say kaddish in front of the women, at the time that they are saying kaddish in the men's synagogue [section], it is possible that there is no objection [i.e., it is halakhically permissible]. However, if she comes [in] to the men's synagogue [section] even in modest dress and all the more so in American dress, which is the opposite of holiness, the essence of which is to separate from lewdness and its accoutrements, which are voice,

ונבא לענין ההצעה של קדיש לבת. אם הבת תבוא להתפלל בעזרת נשים ותכשיר מעשיה בקדושת שבת, כשרות וטהרה וצניעות שכ״ז [שכל זה] הם עיקרים ותחפוץ לומר גם קדיש בפני הנשים, בזמן שאומרים קדיש בביהכנ״ס [בבית הכנסת] של האנשים, אפשר שאין קפידא. אבל אם תבוא לביהכ״נ [לבבית הכנסת] של אנשים אפילו בלבושי צניעות ומכ״ש [ומה כל שכן] בלבושי אמריקה שהם היפך הקדושה שעיקרה פרישה מהעריות ואביזריהו שהם קול ומראה ופריצות המלבושים כ״ז [כל זה] הוא היפך מקידוש ש״ש [שם שמים],

---

R. Blair states that even if there are not ten women in the women's section to answer her, this situation is fine as she is saying *kaddish* word for word with the men and so their response covers her. (This statement is a bit difficult to understand legally, for it sounds as if he assumes that ten women answering would be halakhically acceptable.) R. Blair decries the phenomenon of hiring someone else to recite *kaddish* and calls out to other rabbis to encourage the daughter to do so herself. He ends with a strong statement of bringing women closer to the Jewish community through the recitation:

> ומה אנו רואים עתה? שהקדיש נכלל בכלל אבלות וחשוב לה כמו מצוה דאורייתא. הקדיש הביא הרבה בני ישראל לבה״כ וקרב אותם ליהדות, וככה יקרה גם לבנות ישראל, אנו נקרב אותן ליהדות ולתורתנו הקדושה.

ומה יהא צער להנפטרים ולא קורת רוח כלל ואף שכ"ז [שכל זה] אסור גם מחוץ לביהכ"נ [לבבית הכנסת], אבל הביהכ"נ [הבית הכנסת] הוא המבצר האחרון ששמירתו נותנת תקוה לקדושה בכלל, אבל בהריסת הקדושה בו, הכל אבד ח"ו [חס ושלום]. והי"ת [והשם יתברך] יעזרנו לקדש ולהתקדש עם כל ישראל.

appearance, and licentious dress, all this is the opposite of sanctifying the name of Heaven, and will pain the deceased and will not bring peace at all. While all this is prohibited also outside the synagogue, the synagogue is the last fortress whose defense gives hope for holiness in general.[183] However, with the destruction of the holiness within it, all is lost, God forbid. And God, who is blessed, should help us to sanctify and be sanctified with all of Israel.

Although heralded by some as the revolutionary responsum that allows women to recite *kaddish* in the synagogue, R. Henkin's position actually reflects the more conservative view seen in the sources up to now and adds a number of new stringencies and conditions to a daughter's recitation that had not been the norm in the other responsa that permitted a daughter to recite *kaddish.* To a certain extent, R. Henkin follows in the footsteps of those who were concerned about women entering into the men's section to recite *kaddish.* It is clear that he believes that her presence in the men's section will jeopardize the sanctity of the space, even if she dresses modestly. Where R. Henkin differs from those who came before him is that, instead of saying "the daughter has no place in the synagogue," he permits her to recite *kaddish* from the women's section at the time the men are reciting *kaddish.*[184] He also notes, in a reflection of the modern-day trend, that the daughter might desire[185] to say *kaddish* and not that her father has stipulated as such. R. Henkin

183. See *Sefer Hakaddish* of R. David Asaf, p. 172, who cites R. Henkin word for word.

184. Here, it is unclear whether R. Henkin means that she must say *kaddish* in unison with a man or whether he is just explaining that she says *kaddish* in the women's section at the appropriate time in the service to do so. This issue will be clarified and discussed in depth later on in this chapter.

185. His responsum was written before the responsa in Israel that are cited in the previous section, which mention the woman's desire and also that she recited *kaddish* from the women's section.

stresses that she must affirm her actions with the observance of other commandments.[186]

R. Henkin first discussed the issue almost twenty years earlier in a responsum republished by his grandson, and there, also, he mentions that the daughter may recite *kaddish* from the women's section, although this time he offers a specific rationale of why one should allow this practice and prevent any other.

38. *Responsum Manuscript 1946 Printed in Sefer Teshuvot Ibra Vol. 2, #4, section (2) and Responsa Benei Banim Vol. 2, #7 ** (Note)*	**תשובת הגמו"ז כת"י משנת תש"ז נדפסה בתשובות איברא חלק ב סימן ד (2) ובשו"ת בני בנים חלק ב סימן ז.**(הג"ה)**

R. Yosef Eliyahu Henkin, Eastern Europe and United States (1880–1973)

On the subject of *kaddish*, if a young girl can recite *kaddish* in the synagogue, here already the Aharonim have spoken about it. And nonetheless I remember that in my youth, a young girl recited *kaddish*	ע"ד [על דבר] קדיש אם נערה יכולה לאמר קדיש בביהכ"נ [בבית הכנסת], הנה כבר דברו בזה האחרונים. ובכ"ז [ובכל זאת] זכרוני שבילדותי אמרה

186. This stipulation fits directly with R. Henkin's statements at the beginning of this text (source #37), which were not quoted above, in which he downplays the importance of reciting *kaddish* in its own right for anyone, men or women, and emphasizes, instead, the importance of good deeds:

שלמעלה אין קורת רוח אלא ע"י מעשים טובים, שעושים הבנים שברא מזכה אבא, וכן אחרים כשעושים מצוות בגרמת הנפטר, וצאצאיו, ועל כן צריך להיות הקדיש מקושר עם תשובה תפלה וצדקה, ולפי שיפור המעשים, באה למעלה המנוחה וקורת רוח להנפטר. ומבואר בפוסקים שאמירת הרבה פעמים קדיש הוא חסרון, וקרא על זה מקרא "תשתפכנה אבני קדש בראש כל חוצות", כי לבד שאין זה כבוד שמים "והקריבהו נא לפחתך", הנה זה מורה שרוצה לפטור עצמו רק באמירת קדיש. והקדיש אצלם כעין לחש בלי כונה והבנה. ובאמת הקדיש הוא רק טפל למעשים טובים. ומה שסומכים על הנאמר בתקוני זהר "שהקדיש פוטר שעה וחצי בגיהנם" הכונה על אמירת קדיש בכלל, ולא על כל קדיש וקדיש, והחשבון של שעה וחצי, הוא בא להורות שלא לפטור עצמו רק בקדיש, כי לשאר היום צריך אומץ בתשובה תפלה וצדקה.... ועכ"פ זהו מקור שלא לפטור עצמו בקדיש אלא להרבות במעש"ט, ולא להרבות בקדישים....וממילא אין הגון שכ"א יאמר כמה קדישים, ואפילו "יארצייט" די לו בקדיש אחד... ותחת להרבות בקדישים ירבה בלמוד ובצדקה, באופן זה זכה בן את הוריו ויהי להם קורת רוח, אבל אם יזניח את העיקר - תורה ומעש"ט ויתפוס רק בטפל אין כאן קורת רוח לנפטרים כלל.

in front of the men in a community of righteous and [God-]fearing [people]. And you know, his honor [referring to the questioner], that even *kaddish* [recited] by men, if they are not fit to be prayer leaders, one should have great hesitation [to permit them to recite it] as anyone who recites *kaddish* in the congregation, he is a quasi prayer leader – and a prayer leader has to be worthy. And despite that we consider *kaddish* to be a worthy act, as it is known that were it not for *kaddish*, many would refrain from teaching their sons prayer and would not come to synagogue. And when they come because of *kaddish*, they come a bit closer to Judaism also the rest of the year, and for this reason itself, one should also not rebuff the young girls – since it [saying *kaddish*] causes closeness to Judaism – and, indeed, it is proper that she should stand behind the *meḥitsah* and there she should pray and also there she should recite *kaddish*, and if she should push and enter in front of the *meḥitsah* at the time of *kaddish*, since undoubtedly also others are saying [*kaddish*] according to the current custom that many say *kaddish* [together], it does not bother us.

נערה קדיש לפני האנשים בקהלה של חסידים ויראים. וידע כת״ר [כבוד תורתו] שאף קדיש של האנשים, אם אינם ראויים להיות ש״ץ [שליח ציבור] יש לפקפק בו הרבה, שהרי כל האומר קדיש בציבור הוא מעין ש״ץ [שליח ציבור] - וש״ץ [ושליח ציבור] צריך שיהא הגון. ובכ״ז [ובכל זאת] מחזיקין ענין הקדיש לדבר הגון, שידוע שאילולא הקדיש היו נמנעים הרבה מללמד את בניהם תפילה, ולא היו באים לביהכ״נ [לבית הכנסת] וכשבאים בגלל קדיש מתקרבים מעט ליהדות גם בשאר השנה, ומטעם זה גופא אין לדחות גם את הנערות - מכיון שזה גורם התקרבות ליהדות - ואמנם ראוי שתעמוד מאחורי המחיצה ושם תתפלל וגם שם תאמר קדיש, ואם תדחוף ותכנס לפנים מהמחיצה בשעת קדיש מכיון שמסתמא גם אחרים אומרים כפי המנהג עכשיו שרבים אומרים קדיש לא איכפת לן.

And in the days of the Aḥaronim who discussed this, it was the custom that one person would say *kaddish* – and therefore the young girl should not lead [lit., stand before the ark] the recitation of *kaddish* – for such was the way of the Rishonim, that

ובימי האחרונים שדברו בזה היה המנהג שאחד היה אומר קדיש - וע״כ [ועל כן] אין לה לנערה לעמוד לפני התיבה לאמר קדיש - כי כך היה דרך הראשונים שהאחד

the one reciting *kaddish* would say it before the ark [as the prayer leader] and it certainly is not proper to allow the young girl to come before the ark as a prayer leader even for *kaddish* alone. But now that everyone says [*kaddish*] in his own place, and there are many who recite [*kaddish*], do not push this away with two hands; and I have already written that it is correct [that she] should stand behind the *meḥitsah*.	האומר קדיש היה אומר זה לפני התיבה ובודאי שאין ראוי להניח לנערה לבוא לפני התיבה בתור ש"ץ [שליח ציבור] אפילו בעד קדיש לבד. אבל עכשיו שכ"א [שכל אחד] אומר במקומו ורבים הם האומרים אין לדחות זה בשתי ידים וכבר כתבתי שנכון שתעמוד אחורי מחיצה.

R. Henkin states that he remembers that in his youth[187] he saw a young girl[188] recite *kaddish* in the men's synagogue; however, he, himself, is troubled by this practice. In general, even for men, R. Henkin is concerned with the character of the person reciting *kaddish*, since he functions as a quasi prayer leader. He is willing to be lenient in this regard as he realizes that many people, who otherwise would not be, are drawn to the synagogue and to Judaism because of the need to recite *kaddish*. It is for this reason that one should not discourage women and prevent them from reciting *kaddish* as they, too, may be drawn closer to observance by reciting *kaddish*.

At this point, R. Henkin's statements become slightly more difficult to understand. R. Henkin expresses, as he did in both texts, that it would be appropriate for her to stand behind the *meḥitsah*; however,

---

187. R. Henkin was born in Klimavichy, Belarus, and studied at the Slutzker Yeshiva.

188. R. Yehuda Henkin makes it clear that his grandfather did not mean that only young girls could recite *kaddish*. After quoting his grandfather's text, he goes on to explain:

> מה שנקט נערה הוא לאו דוקא דזיל בתר טעמא וכן שמעתי מכמה רבנים שבתו של גדול אחד אמרה קדיש על פי הוראת הגמו"ז והיא הייתה מבוגרת, אלא אורחא דמילתא נקט נערה כי לנשואות אין פנאי לאמר קדיש. וכן במאמר ב"פרדס" כתב בסתם שבת יכולה לאמר קדיש ולא חילק. ורק המעשה בקהילה של חסידים ויראים בודאי היה בנערה דוקא כי אמרה קדיש בתוך עזרת הגברים מה שאין כן בעזרת הנשים אין חילוק בין נערה לנשואה...

And, in *Equality Lost* (48n11), he states: "The term '*na'arah*' refers to a girl before marriage; however, my grandfather permitted married women as well to recite the *kaddish*."

he adds that if she were to push her way into the men's section,[189] it would not matter as many people say *kaddish* together. He explains that, originally, the custom was for only one person to recite *kaddish*, and in that scenario, it would be inappropriate for a young girl to stand before the ark, the place of the prayer leader, even if only to recite *kaddish*. Now that all those reciting *kaddish* remain in their places (i.e., do not stand before the ark) and recite *kaddish* together, one should not bar her entirely, albeit it would be much preferred for her to remain behind the *meḥitsah*.

It seems that R. Henkin's position is as follows. He does not feel comfortable with a young daughter reciting *kaddish* in the men's section on two counts. In the case when there is only one person reciting *kaddish*, he does not want her to act as a prayer leader standing before God and the community as their representative,[190] and, in general, he feels that there is something more modest and appropriate about having a young girl remain behind the *meḥitsah*. It is only because customs have changed and *kaddish* is now recited by many together from their own seats that it is permissible for a daughter to recite *kaddish*. If she does enter the men's section, she should not be pushed away but it would certainly be more correct for her to remain in the women's section and to recite *kaddish* from there.

It is hard to extrapolate from these two short sources, but it would seem that R. Henkin would not allow a woman to recite *kaddish* alone in a *minyan* in her own home as she would be functioning as the sole

---

189. It is unclear why a woman would behave as such unless she knew the sources that up until now only allowed *kaddish* to be recited in the presence of a *minyan* in the men's section. See also *Responsa Torah Lishmah O.Ḥ.* 27 who voices a similar concern; he, however, feels this worry would be reason to prevent her from reciting *kaddish* at all.

גם יש לחוש הואיל והיא רוצה לומר קדיש בעבור אביה תכנס לפנים ממחיצתה ותאמר קדיש של תפלה ג"כ לכן צריך למחות בידה.

190. It is clear that R. Henkin feels that a woman acting in this manner is "just not done." However, he does not actually articulate what exactly is the legal problem with this scenario. The woman is not actually fulfilling anyone's obligation, which is the usual legal problem when defining who can act as leader. His grandson later on reads it that he fears that people will get confused and think that a woman could act as prayer leader in other situations.

prayer leader. Nor does it seem that he would allow a woman to recite *kaddish* alone from the women's section, for the same would be true.[191] If this analysis is correct, then R. Henkin actually holds one of the more stringent views on this issue in direct opposition to those sources cited above who permitted a woman to recite *kaddish* alone.

Upon the publication of his article in *Hapardes*, R. Henkin was challenged by other rabbinic authorities, all of whom shared the same concern: How was it possible for a woman to recite *kaddish* from the women's section? One such response, voiced by R. Shlomo Wahrman (published later in 1981), outlines his concerns with R. Henkin's ruling. After a thorough review of many of the sources on a daughter saying *kaddish*, R. Wahrman writes:

39. *Sefer She'erit Yosef*
Vol. 2, #60
Recitation of Kaddish by a Daughter

R. Shlomo Wahrman, New York (1926–2013)

ספר שארית יוסף
חלק ב סימן ס
אמירת קדיש על ידי בת

And in my humble and weak opinion I did not merit to understand his words... as one does not say *kaddish* with fewer than ten males, and it is clear that one does not include a woman in the ten.... And according to this, since a woman does not join for any *davar shebikdushah*, again when she says *kaddish* in the women's section in the presence of the women, behold, she does not say it in the presence of ten as the women's section is a domain unto itself and there is no joining [with the men's section]. (See *Arukh Hashulḥan* 55:20 that

ולענ"ד [ולעניות דעתי] הקלושה לא זכיתי להבין את דבריו...דאין אומרים קדיש בפחות מעשרה זכרים, ומבואר דאין לצרף אשה לעשרה.... ולפי"ז [ולפי זה] כיון דאין אשה מצטרפת לכל דבר שבקדושה שוב כשאומרת קדיש בעזרת נשים בפני הנשים הרי אומרת שלא בפני עשרה דהרי עזרת נשים היא רשות בפ"ע [בפני עצמה] וליכא צירוף. (ועי' [ועיין] בערוך השלחן בסי' [סימן] נ"ה אות כ' דבודאי העומדים

191. R. Yehuda Henkin, in defending his grandfather, will stress just this point. Possibly, though, the fact that she is not standing before the ark might reduce his actual concerns. Additionally, in a *minyan* in her home, the very fact that the space is removed from the synagogue setting will possibly mitigate the concern that she will be confused with an actual prayer leader.

certainly those standing in the women's section do not join with those standing in the *beit hakenesset* [i.e., the men's section] even though there are windows from the women's section to the *beit hakenesset* and they even see the faces of those [in the men's section]. Since the divisions are complete, they comprise two [separate] domains.) And it is clear that if someone lives next to the synagogue and hears *kaddish* that is said in the synagogue when he is alone in his house, it is forbidden to recite *kaddish* as behold his house is a separate domain and does not join [with the *minyan*] and once again, there are not here [the presence of] ten. Except for this, even though I am dust under the feet of the *ga'on* R. Yosef Eliyahu [Henkin], *ztsk"l*, nevertheless, in my humble opinion, I am worried that if we permit the recitation of *kaddish* by daughters according to the ruling of the *ga'on* R. Yosef Eliyahu, again the assimilators of our time (that all their intentions are to innovate a new Torah and to change the received [tradition], God forbid, and they search with lights [for] a Torah scholar [lit., a great tree] to hang on him their absurdities [lit., empty bottles]) will learn from this to join [count in the ten] a woman for every *davar shebikdushah* and they will say that the strict adherents to the law [*perushim*] already permitted it. And you should know that when I presented my words before my teacher and rabbi, the exceptional *ga'on*, our teacher the Rav R. Eliezer Silver, *zts"l*, he agreed with what

בעזרת נשים לא יצטרפו עם העומדים בביהכ"נ [בבית הכנסת] אף שיש חלונות מעזרת נשים לביהכ"נ [לבית הכנסת] ורואים אלו פניהם של אלו דכיון דמחיצות גמורות הן הויין ב' [שתי] רשויות). וברור דאם מישהו דר סמוך לביהכ"נ [לבית הכנסת] ושומע קדיש שנאמר בביהכ"נ [בבית הכנסת] כשהוא לבדו בביתו דאסור לו לומר קדיש דהרי ביתו הוא רשות בפ"ע [בפני עצמו] ואינו מצטרף ושוב אי"כ [אין כאן] עשרה. ובר מן דין אף שעפר אני תחת כפות רגליו של הגרי"א [הגאון רב יוסף אליהו] זצוק"ל [זכר צדיק וקדוש לברכה] מ"מ [מכל מקום] לענ"ד [לעניות דעתי] חושש אני שאם נתיר אמירת קדיש של בנות כפי הוראתו של הגרי"א [הגאון רב יוסף אליהו] שוב מתבוללי זמננו (שכל כונתם לחדש תורה חדשה ולשנות את המקובל ח"ו [חס ושלום] ומחפשים בנרות אילן גדול לתלות עליו בוקי סריקי) ילמדו מזה לצרף אשה לכל דבר שבקדושה ויאמרו כבר התירו פרושים את הדבר. ות"ל [ותדע לך] שכשהצעתי את דברינו לפני מו"ר [מורי רבי] הגאון האדיר מוהר"ר [מורינו הרב רבי] אליעזר זילבער זצ"ל [זכר צדיק לברכה] הסכים עם מש"כ [מה שכתוב כאן] ואדרבא אמר לי שכבר הביע לפני הגרי"א

is written here. As a matter of fact, he told me that he had already expressed to the *ga'on* R. Yosef Eliyahu his opposition to his ruling.[192]	[הגאון רב יוסף אליהו] התנגדותו להוראתו...

R. Wahrman[193] has two main concerns with R. Henkin's ruling: one halakhic and one linked to public policy. R. Wahrman believes, like all the sources before him, that the women's section is a distinct domain,

---

192. Interestingly, R. Shlomo Riskin in a post to the Women's Tefillah Network listserv (October 7, 2002, Digest #1099), states that R. Eliezer Silver permits ten women to constitute a *minyan* at the grave site, presumably because he infers that there is a difference between mourner's *kaddish* in the synagogue and in other situations:

> I would also mention that at a memorial service for a departed individual, if there are ten women and even if there is not a *minyan* of men it is possible for a woman to recite *kaddish* which is expressly for the purpose of mourning and thereby fulfilling the *mitsvah* of *kibbud av va'em* which applies to women as well as to men.
>
> The basis for this is an incident which I heard from Rav Soloveitchik concerning Rav Eliezer Silver, which I later heard from Rav David Silver, Rav Eliezer Silver's son, himself and which was confirmed by Rav David Silver in writing in a letter sent to Dr. Joel Wolowelsky; the content of the letter is:
>
>> Dear Sir,
>>
>> Please pardon my handwriting; I recently reached the age of 90. It is true. My father *zts"l* did tell me a number of times that at one occasion in Cincinati [sic], where funeral general services took place at funeral homes, some people went to the funeral services and did not go to the burials. It once happened when the funeral took place, it was noted that not a full *minyan* were present at the burial, the daughters broke out in tears. My father *z"l* noted that there were more than a *minyan* of women there. He separated the women from the men and allowed the daughters to say *kaddish* after their father.
>>
>> Respectfully, David Silver.

See *Responsa Yeḥavveh Da'at*, Vol. 6, #5 who definitely states that a male *minyan* is needed at a grave as *kaddish* is a regular *davar shebikdushah*. See R. Hershel Schachter, in his book *Be'ikvei Hatson* (24n5), where he opposes this practice:

> ובפשוטו הי' נראה שמה שאמרו בשם ת"ח מהדור הקדום, שאם יש עשר נשים בביה"ק, אע"פ שאין שם עשרה אנשים שאשה רשאה לומר קדיש, עפ"י פשוטו אין דבר זה נכון כלל וכלל לדינא ופשוט.

Apparently, R. Shuki Reich permits the students at Midreshet Lindenbaum in Jerusalem to form a *minyan* of women for the recitation of *kaddish* after a *siyyum*.

193. His language in the section quoted is similar to that of R. Shalom Yeḥezkel Shraga

separate from the men's section, and therefore how then could R. Henkin allow a woman to recite *kaddish* from the women's section, since there is no *minyan* present there? Furthermore, R. Wahrman is concerned that permitting a daughter to recite *kaddish* will lend credibility to those reformers who wish to argue based on this ruling that it is permissible to count a woman in a *minyan* in general.[194]

R. Avraham Zilberberg expresses similar concerns in a responsum[195] regarding a daughter reciting *kaddish* for her mother.

Rubin-Halberstam, the *Admor* of Tzieshnov from Brooklyn, New York, in *Hapardes*, Year 38, Booklet 1, 4:6, "On the Topic of a Daughter Reciting *Kaddish* in Her House or Even in the Women's Section," who also adds:

> והנה עיקר הלימוד שצריכין עשרה לקדיש ולתפלה הוא מונקדשתי בתוך בנ"י, וכבר ארז"ל בכל מקום שאתה מוצא גדר ערוה אתה מוצא קדושה, ומכלל הן אתה שומע לאו שבמקום שפורצין גדר ערוה ח"ו ומחללין קדושת ביהכ"נ בזה שנשים או בתולות באות לתוכה ועוד אומרות קדיש בזה מגרשין הקדושה. ובמקום לעשות טובה לנשמת הוריהם עוד יורדים אותם לבאר שחת ר"ל....וגם שתאמר בעזרת נשים לא נכון שתאמר מטעמים הנ"ל רק כפי פסקי הגאונים הקדמונים שתענה אי"ר וגם תזכה הרבים במצות ומעש"ט כארז"ל נשים במה קא זכיין שתשתדל בעד הפצת לימוד התורה לבני' ואצל בני העניים וזהו יהי' זכות גדול להורי' יותר מהכל.

Responding to a letter from R. Halberstam, R. Yitsḥak Weiss, in *Responsa Minḥat Yitsḥak*, Vol. 4, #30 also agrees with these same concerns and adds another example:

> ואף דראיתי באחרונים, שחקרו על המנהג בכמה מקומות, שיש הרבה אבלים, ובפרט ביום היא"צ [היארצייט] [יום הזכרון] מקדושים שלנו, שכמעט כל הקהל אומרים קדיש, ואין שם ט' שיענו אמן, וצדדו מטעם דרק הקדישים שבתפילה, דבא להוציא הרבים, צריך ט' שיענו כמו בתפילה, לא בקדיש יתום, דהוי רשות ולא בא להוציא רבים, ויהדרו שעכ"פ יענו שנים, כמו דאיתא במחצית השקל (סוס"י ו') בברכת השחר עיי"ש, [אבל לא עלה על הדעת, לומר קדיש, אף שאין שם עשרה אנשים,] והוא פשוט.

194. See *Responsa Yaḥel Yisra'el*, Vol. 2, #90 (published 5751) or *Responsa Yaḥel Yisra'el* #84 (published 5763), where R. Lau has a similar worry:

> ולהלכה נראה שאין לסמוך על היתרו של הגרי"א הנקין, ובמיוחד בימינו יש לחשוש לסברת החוות [יאיר והמשנת] בנימין שעלולים לבוא מתקנים למיניהם וילמדו מכאן להתיר לנשים לעבור לפני התיבה ועלולה לצאת תקלה מתחת ידינו, על כן אין להתיר לנשים לומר קדיש בכל אופן.

See also *Responsa Torah Lishmah O.Ḥ.* 27:

> וצריך למחות בידה יען כי איכא בזה חשש תקלה דהשתא ילמדו בזה שתאמר קדיש גם בתפלה שהוא קדיש דחיובא ותפטור את האנשים השומעין...אבל הכא גבי קדיש דצריך צירוף הנה הרואה אותה אומרת קדיש חושב שהיא משלמת לעשרה ג"כ ומצטרפת עמהם וא"כ יחשוב דהיא שייכה בקדיש וממילא מוציאה האנשים גם בחיוב קדיש דתפלה.

195. The book was published in 1948. The responsum itself does not have a date on it.

40. Responsa Mishnat Binyamin #34 / שו"ת משנת בנימין סימן לד

R. Avraham Binyamin Zilberberg, Poland and United States (d. 1962)

Here, in the manner of saying *kaddish* for his first wife who passed away and she has only daughters, can they go to the synagogue and recite *kaddish*? And the answer is surely there is no place for this custom and all the more so in those countries where they do not know how to distinguish and they could make a mistake [and assume] that women could join the *minyan* of ten for *kedushah* and *barekhu*.... For a daughter should not recite *kaddish* in the synagogue for I have never heard of that in Poland, not at the synagogues that pray in the *Sefard* [Ḥasidic] liturgy nor at the synagogues that pray in the Ashkenazic liturgy. I have always been in association with *Ashkenazim* from the time I became a rabbi in 1916, [and] I never saw anything like this.... And even though he heard from someone entitled "Rabbi" who said that [she] could recite it in the synagogue, I do not want to know who this rabbi is. But now that all the latest [rabbinic] greats [Aḥaronim] agreed to forbid it, surely there is not in it any benefit for the soul of their mother. On the contrary, there is great evil to her soul and every recitation of *kaddish* is only with the intention to do good for the soul. And according to all the sources, only the son will do good for the soul of his father with the recitation of *kaddish* and *barekhu* and *maftir* but we have not

הנה בדרך אמירת קדש על אשתו הראשונה שמתה ואין לה כי אם בנות, האם יכולים ללכת לביהכ"נ [לבית הכנסת] לומר קדיש, תשובה ודאי אין שום מקום למנהג הזה וכ"ש [וכל שכן] במדינות אלו שאינם יודעים להבחין ויכולים לטעות כי נשים יש לצרף למנין עשרה לקדושה וברכו.... דאין לבת לומר קדיש בביהכ"נ [בבית הכנסת], ומעולם לא שמעתי במדינת פוילין לא אצל ספרדים ולא בביהכ"נ [בבית הכנסת] שמתפללין אשכנז, אשר הייתי תמיד בצוותא עם אשכנזים מעת היותי לרב משנת תרע"ז לא ראיתי כזאת.... והגם ששמע ממאן דהו אשר מכנהו בשם ראביי שאמר דיש לאמרה בביהכ"נ [בבית הכנסת], אין רצוני לדעת מי הוא הראביי הזה, אבל כעת ששמע שגדולי אחרונים כולם הסכימו לאסור, ודאי דאין בזה שום תועלת לנשמת אמם, ואדרבה יש בזה ריעותא גדולה לנשמתה, וכל אמירת קדיש הוא רק בכוונה לעשות טובה להנשמה ומכל המקורות ישנו רק דבן יעשה לטובת נשמת אביו באמירת קדיש וברכו ומפטיר אבל לא

found that also the daughter brings merit to the souls of her father and mother. Not only that, we have not found anywhere that there will be any merit for the soul with the recitation of *kaddish* [by the daughter]; on the contrary, it might, God forbid, provoke judgment for it destroys the words of *Ḥazal,* which are like coals of fire. Therefore, in my opinion, just as they receive reward in seeking, so will their reward be doubled in refraining, and her soul will be in the garden of Eden through the merit that they do not recite *kaddish* in the synagogue.

מצינו דגם בת מזכא לנשמת אביה ואמה וחוץ מזה שלא מצינו בשום מקום שיהי'[ה] שום זכות עבור הנשמה באמירת קדיש עוד נתעורר דינא ח"ו [חס ושלום] כי בזה מהרסים דברי חז"ל [חכמינו זכרונם לברכה] שהם כגחלי אש, ע"כ [על כן] לדעתי כשם שנוטלים שכר על הדרישה כך יהיה שכר כפול על הפרישה ונשמתה תהיה בג"ע [בגן עדן] בזכות שאינם אומרים קדיש בבהכ"נ [בבית הכנסת].

R. Zilberberg does not address R. Henkin specifically, but mentions an unspecified American rabbi's ruling, seemingly very similar to R. Henkin's, and disputes it. He states that the practice of women saying *kaddish* in the synagogue is something he has never seen in his rabbinic career and is not supported in the sources. R. Zilberberg worries that particularly in America, where people are less educated, they will mistakenly assume a woman could join the *minyan* for *kedushah* and *barekhu,* as well.[196] He maintains that women did not recite *kaddish* in any of the synagogues in Poland. He sees no merit for the soul of the girls' mother from her daughters reciting *kaddish,* as only a son can bring merit to the deceased through the recitation of *kaddish,* and he argues that the daughters' recitation would actually cause harm. In fact, he believes that by refraining from reciting *kaddish,* daughters bring twice as much merit to their mothers' souls.

196. It seems, from his language, that R. Zilberberg himself can possibly distinguish between these cases and understands that there is legal support for a woman to be able to recite *kaddish* even though it requires a *minyan* and despite the fact that he, himself, feels that it is only the role of the son.

R. Henkin's grandson, R. Yehuda Herzl Henkin, goes to great lengths[197] to defend his grandfather and respond to the critiques raised. He explains the reasoning behind his grandfather's legal ruling.

41. *Responsa Benei Banim* *Vol. 2, #7*

שו"ת בני בנים חלק ב סימן ז

R. Yehuda Henkin, United States and Israel (1945–)

The recitation of *kaddish* by a woman and the joining [with the *minyan*] from the women's section.

אמירת קדיש על ידי אשה וצרוף מעזרת נשים.

And they challenged him…and *She'erit Yosef* (Wahrman), Vol. 2, *kaddish* is only in a place with ten men, which is not the case in the women's section which the *meḥitsah* divides from the men and there is not a *minyan* there, and his honor requested to hear my opinion. And I did not speak with the *ga'on*, my teacher, my grandfather, about this.

והקשה עליו... ושארית יוסף (ווארמאן) חלק ב' שהלא אין קדיש אלא במקום עשרה גברים מה שאין כן בעזרת נשים שהמחיצה מבדלת בינה לבין הגברים אין שם מנין, וכבודו בקש לשמוע דעתי. ולא דברתי עם הגמו"ז [הגאון מורי וזקני] בזה.

But perhaps his honor thought that the *ga'on*, my teacher, my grandfather, permitted women to say *kaddish* in their own *minyan* without ten men, God forbid, and this is not so; rather in the majority of synagogues in the United States there is a joining of the

אך אולי כבודו חושב שהגמו"ז [הגאון מורי וזקני] התיר לנשים לאמר קדיש במנין שלהן בלי עשרה גברים חלילה, ואינו כן אלא שברוב בתי הכנסת שבארצות הברית יש צרוף

197. Besides the extensive responsum in *Benei Banim*, see R. Y.H. Henkin's exchange with R. Fink in: Reuven Fink, "The Recital of Kaddish by Women," *The Journal of Halacha and Contemporary Society* 31 (Spring 1996): 23–37; "Letters," *The Journal of Halacha and Contemporary Society* 32 (Fall 1996): 97–102 and 106–111; and his final rebuttal in Yehuda Henkin, "Women, Kaddish, and the Halachic Process," *Equality Lost*, 51–53. See also R. Henkin's post on the Avodah listserv, 11:60 (Sept. 1, 2003), http://www.aishdas.org/avodah/vol11/v11n060.shtml, and his article published in the Hebrew newspaper, *Hatzofeh*, on 23 *Iyyar* 5764, May 14, 2004.

minyan from the women's section to the men's section. And this is from a number of perspectives. First that the ceiling joins them...and therefore in a synagogue where the *meḥitsah* of the women's section does not reach the ceiling, one joins with the *minyan* from here and from there. And so it is in the majority of synagogues in the land of the *ga'on*, my teacher, my grandfather, as I wrote in *Benei Banim* [Vol. 1] #4, and so it was in the towns of Russia where the women sat up [high] in a balcony and they were not blocked; see there in section 2 and in the note. And the testimony [to this explanation is] that the *ga'on*, my teacher, my grandfather, wrote "that the woman should say *kaddish* in front of the women" and not in front of a *minyan* of women, and he wrote that she should recite at the time that the men are saying *kaddish* because she is dependent on their *minyan*. And the rest of the women and children in the women's section should answer after her "Amen" and "*Yehei shemeih rabbah*" and with this it is enough, as *Responsa Mishneh Sakhir* 11 stated, and even if there are not any women or children there, [she] can recite *kaddish* since the men answer "Amen" to the *kaddish* of the men and she is reciting with them word for word. And look in *Responsa Mishneh Sakhir* there, that it is possible that there is no objection [i.e., it is halakhically permissible] even if there is no answer of "Amen" at all; rather everyone says *kaddish*.... The outcome for us is that lawfully a woman can recite *kaddish* in the women's section where the

למנין מעזרת נשים לעזרת
גברים. והוא בכמה אופנים,
ראשית שהתקרה מצרפתם...
ולכן בבית כנסת שמחיצת
עזרת הנשים אינה מגיעה
לתקרה יש לצרף למנין מכאן
ומכאן וכן הם רוב בתי הכנסת
באתרא של הגמו"ז [הגאון מורי
וזקני] כמו שכתבתי בבני בנים
[חלק א'] סימן ד' וכן היו בערי
רוסיה כשהנשים ישבו למעלה
ביציע ולא היו מוסתרות
עיי"ש [עיין שם] בסימן ב'
בהגה. והעד שכתב הגמו"ז
[הגאון מורי וזקני] שהאשה
תאמר קדיש בפני נשים עכ"ל
[עד כאן לשונו] ולא בפני
מנין של נשים וכתב שתאמר
בשעה שהגברים אומרים קדיש
כי היא תלויה במנינם, ושאר
נשים וטף שבעזרת נשים יענו
אחריה אמן ויהא שמיה רבה
ובזה סגי כמו שכתב בשו"ת
משנת שכיר סימן י"א, ואפילו
אין שם נשים וטף יכולה
לאמר קדיש כיון שהגברים
עונים אמן לקדיש של הגברים
והיא אומרת אתם מלה במלה,
ועיין בשו"ת [שאלות ותשובות]
משנה שכיר שם שאפשר
שאין קפידא אפילו אין עניית
אמן כלל אלא כולם אומרים
קדיש.... היוצא לנו ששפיר
יכולה אשה לאמר קדיש
בעזרת הנשים כשאין המחיצה
מגיעה לתקרה... ואפשר

meḥitsah does not reach the ceiling…and it is possible that those who question the *ga'on*, my teacher, my grandfather, are not of his opinion, because in their places, since they are from Hungary, all the *meḥitsot* were up to the ceiling.	שהמשיגים על הגמו"ז [הגאון מורי וזקני] לאו אדעתייהו שכן במקומותיהם שהם מיוצאי הונגריה כל המחיצות היו עד התקרה.

The younger R. Y.H. Henkin states that he did not discuss with his grandfather the halakhic thought process by which R. Y.E. Henkin permitted a daughter to recite *kaddish* from the women's section; however, he offers a strong rationale for the decision based on the change in synagogue architecture.[198] The partitions in American synagogues with which R. Y.E. Henkin was familiar, unlike those in Europe, do not extend to the ceiling, and thus, the men's and women's sections are both part of one unified domain.[199] Consequently, a woman standing in the women's section is in the presence of the *minyan* in the men's section and so can recite *kaddish*. His grandson explains that surely, R. Y.E. Henkin did

198. Yehuda H. Henkin, "Women and Kaddish," *Equality Lost*, p. 43:

> The great majority of women's sections today are, for the purposes of a quorum, extensions of the men's section; i.e., nine men in the men's section and one man behind the *meḥitsah* in the women's section would constitute a *minyan*. There are two rationales for this: 1) In the absence of a floor-to-ceiling partition or separating wall which is rare today, the common roof unites the two into one room.… 2) the women's section is functionally subordinate (*beteilah nigreret*) to the men's section.… A woman saying *kaddish* behind the *meḥitsah* when there are ten men in the men's section, therefore, is indeed saying *kaddish* with a *minyan*. This explains, as well, the permission given by many authorities for a woman to recite *birkat hagomel* in the women's section, with the men in the men's section answering, even though *birkat hagomel* also requires the presence of a *minyan*.

199. R. Y.H. Henkin makes this argument as well as another one of *nigreret* to explain how women said *birkat hagomel* from even distinctly separate women's sections. *Nigreret* applies in cases where women follow the men's davening and not where they had their own prayer leader. Based on the legal argument of *nigreret*, a woman can say *kaddish* even when there is a floor-to-ceiling partition. For sources on both of these halakhic ideas (*nigreret* and/or one roof unites the women's section and the men's), see *Sefer Mitsvot Katan* commandment 282 and the notes of Rabbenu Perets note 5*; B.T. *Rosh Hash.* 27b, *Tosafot*, s.v. *ushma kol shofar*; *Responsa Harashba*, Vol. 1, #96; *Responsa Harashbash* 473; *Ḥiddushei Haramban* Tractate *Ber.* 45a and Tractate

not mean that the women in the women's section constitute a *minyan*; rather, the daughter reciting *kaddish* simultaneous with male mourners is relying on their male *minyan*. R. Y.H. Henkin adds an additional interesting point that was not explicitly stated by his grandfather. If the women and children answer the daughter's *kaddish* with "Amen" and "*Yehei shemeih rabbah*," it is sufficient and the men in the *minyan* do not need to hear or respond directly to her *kaddish*. Furthermore, even if there are no other women present to hear her, because the daughter is reciting *kaddish* word for word with the men, the responses to the men's recitation are sufficient to cover her *kaddish* even if it is inaudible in the men's section. R. Y.H. Henkin quotes both of these views in the name of R. Yissakhar Shelomo Teichtal[200] (Hungary, Czechoslovakia, 1885–1945), who maintained in *Mishneh Sakhir* 11 that one could recite mourner's *kaddish* even if no one responded to the recitation.[201]

Pesah. 85b; Rabbenu Yonah on B.T. *Eiruv*. 72b; *Or Zarua*, Vol. 2, #172, *Sh. Ar., O.H.* 55:19; *Magen Avraham* 55:14, *Responsa Avnei Nezer, O.H.* 34; *Mishnah Berurah* 55:2; and *Responsa Minhat Yitshak*, Vol. 4, #9.

200. R. Teichtal is the author of the famous work *Em Habanim Semehah*.

201. In a long responsum, R. Teichtal discusses the case of many mourners reciting *kaddish* together and the question of whether there has to be any specific number of people responding "Amen." He distinguishes between other forms of *kaddish*, which are obligatory and the leader is thus fulfilling the obligation of others, and the mourner's *kaddish*, which is not obligatory and does not fulfill an obligation. In the former case, one must have at least nine (plus the male reciter) answering; however, with mourner's *kaddish* he quotes a number of sources who find two responders to be sufficient. (R. Teichtal even suggests at the end of the responsum that they could possibly be minors.) After quoting the traditional explanation that it is the congregation's response that benefits the deceased, R. Teichtal offers his own unique view in which he, to a certain extent, reinterprets the meaning of mourner's *kaddish* and breaks from the traditional understanding that the son brings merit to his parents specifically because he causes the *minyan* to respond to his *kaddish*. R. Teichtal explains that, in his opinion, it is the unique *content* of the *kaddish* prayer that the child invokes that brings merit to the parent and so, specifically, now that it is the custom for many to say *kaddish* together, with the emphasis on the power of the communal prayer being called out in unison, it is the child's recitation that brings merit and not the community's response, which becomes inconsequential. He does admit at the end of his responsum that it would be best if each person remained in his place and the mourners did not come together as a group to recite in unison. This way, each would have individual people to respond to him so that

Once he has discussed the permissibility of the recitation of *kaddish* in the women's section, R. Y.H. Henkin continues with his argument[202] to defend his grandfather's ruling.

42. *Responsa Benei Banim* Vol. 2, #7

שו"ת בני בנים חלק ב סימן ז

R. Yehuda Henkin, United States and Israel (1945–)

ולעצם אמירת קדיש על ידי אשה אין להקשות משו"ת [משאלות ותשובות] שבות יעקב חלק ב' סימן צ"ג וכנסת יחזקאל סוף חלק יורה דעה שכתבו שאין לאשה קדיש בבית הכנסת כלל, כי הם כתבו לפי מנהגם שרק אבל אחד אמר קדיש בכל פעם שאז בודאי אין לאשה לאמר קדיש לבדה שיענו לה הגברים. ואפילו אין שם אבל מלבדה יש לאחד מן המתפללים לאמר קדיש כמו שהביא הרמ"א באורח החיים סימן קל"ב סעיף ב'. ומה שכתבו האחרונים שאשה תברך הגומל מעזרת הנשים קיל מאמירת קדיש כי ברכת הגומל היא באקראי מה שאין כן קדיש הוא לי"א [לאחד עשר] חודש, ועוד שהאשה חייבת בברכת הגומל ולכן התירו לה

And as for the recitation of *kaddish* by a woman, one should not challenge it based on the responsa of *Shevut Ya'akov* Vol. 2, #93 and *Kenesset Yeḥezkel* end of section *Yoreh De'ah*, who wrote that a woman does not say *kaddish* in the synagogue at all. For they wrote according to their custom that only one mourner recited *kaddish* each time for then, surely, a woman should not recite *kaddish* alone so that the men respond to her. And even if she is the only mourner, one of the people [men] praying should recite *kaddish* as the Rema stated in *Oraḥ Ḥayyim* 132:2. And that which the Aḥaronim wrote that a woman blessing *hagomel* from the women's section is more lenient than the recitation of *kaddish* because the blessing of *hagomel* is an occasional [event], which is not the case with *kaddish* which lasts eleven months and, also, a woman is obligated in the blessing of *hagomel*,[203] and so they

---

both understandings of *kaddish* would be fulfilled, something that cannot be done by a woman if there are no other women in the women's section and she is speaking quietly.

202. This text follows immediately after the previous one. It was just broken up for the ease of discussion and explanation.

203. Most of the texts in reference to women and *birkat hagomel* do not actually speak

permitted her to bless in the synagogue, which is not the case with *kaddish* which is obligatory only on sons....[204]	לברך בבית הכנסת מה שאין כן בקדיש שאינו חיוב אלא לבנים....
However, in the responsa of *Shevut Ya'akov*, there he permitted a minor girl to recite *kaddish* in a *minyan* in her home (see there) and even though the custom is not so, it appears that everything is according to the time and the place... but it is better for her to recite *kaddish* in the women's section together with the men as it is in private and is not comparable to a *minyan* in a home where there is a gathering and publicity as *Responsa Ḥavvot Ya'ir* wrote. And also *Responsa Ḥavvot Ya'ir* and *Kenesset Yeḥezkel* would admit to this [being permissible] according to our custom that many recite *kaddish* together and that is what the *ga'on*, my teacher, my grandfather, wrote "that it is possible there is no objection" [i.e., it is halakhically permissible].	ואולם בשו"ת שבות יעקב שם התיר לקטנה לאמר קדיש במנין בביתה עיי"ש [עיין שם] ואף שאין המנהג כן נראה שהכל לפי הזמן והמקום... אבל טוב יותר שתאמר קדיש בעזרת הנשים בהדי הגברים דהוי בהצנע ואינו דומה למנין בבית שיש שם אסיפה ופרסום כמו שכתב בשו"ת [בשאלות ותשובות] חוות יאיר. וגם שו"ת [בשאלות ותשובות] חוות יאיר וכנסת יחזקאל יודו לזה לפי מנהגנו שהרבה אומרים קדיש ביחד וזהו שכתב הגמו"ז [הגאון מורי וזקני] אפשר שאין קפידא עכ"ל [עד כאן לשונו].

about obligation. Many try to justify why women do not recite this blessing. See, for example, *Magen Avraham*, beginning of 219. See *Ḥayyei Adam* 65:6 *and Mishnah Berurah* 219:3, who encourage the practice, and *Ben Ish Ḥai Ekev* 5, who does state that women are obligated. For a more in-depth discussion, see "Giving Thanks: Women and *Birkat Hagomel*."

204. This statement is very difficult to understand as it has been well established that *kaddish* is not obligatory upon anyone, even sons. When asked in an e-mail about his use of the term *obligation*, R. Henkin responded, "The 'obligation' of men to say *kaddish* is in a manner of speaking, the way people ask if any male in shul has a '*ḥiyyuv*' to be a *sheliaḥ tsibbur* because of *avelut* or *yahrtseit*." (Private correspondence, February 15, 2006.) And so R. Henkin should be understood as saying that they permitted the woman to say *birkat hagomel* in synagogue as she is obligated in it, which is not the case with *kaddish* where she is not obligated or, rather, no one is obligated.

R. Y.H. Henkin suggests an interesting reading of the earlier rabbinic authorities to claim that even they would not disagree with his grandfather's ruling. He explains that *Shevut Ya'akov*'s and *Kenesset Yeḥezkel*'s objections to a daughter reciting *kaddish* in the synagogue are based on the custom that a single mourner recites *kaddish*. He then continues, agreeing with them, that in the synagogue[205] "surely a woman should not recite *kaddish* alone so that the men respond to her." R. Y.H. Henkin derives this notion from Rema, who after describing the hierarchy of mourners, states that in the absence of any (male) mourners, one of the other members of the congregation should recite *kaddish*. It seems that R. Y.H. Henkin understands the absence of the female mourner in the hierarchy as an indication that Rema did not intend a woman to recite *kaddish* alone in the synagogue.[206] R. Y.H. Henkin argues so strongly that a woman should not lead a prayer in the synagogue that he needs to explain why *birkat hagomel* does not disprove his point, as women do say that alone and aloud from the women's section. R. Y.H. Henkin states that now that *kaddish* is recited by many mourners in unison,

205. It is implied that in the synagogue, as opposed to the home, where *Shevut Ya'akov* permits a daughter to lead the men, there is some objective problem. However, R. Y.H. Henkin does not elaborate if it is an issue of her entering the male space or the worry that she might be confused with an eligible prayer leader, both of which were concerns of his grandfather. Most likely, it is the issue of being a prayer leader as R. Y.H. Henkin continues to explain why *birkat hagomel* is different. (His distinction is slightly difficult, as *kaddish* is not obligatory on sons. See n204 above.) It is unclear why, from his understanding, this problem of confusion does not also exist in the home where *Shevut Ya'akov* permitted a daughter to recite *kaddish* alone. In this author's view, it makes more sense to say that *Shevut Ya'akov* was concerned with a woman entering the men's domain, but felt comfortable with her leading the men as he permitted it at home, and therefore, nowadays, when the women's section is considered in the presence of the *minyan*, *Shevut Ya'akov* would likewise have no problem with her leading the men as a sole voice from her place on the other side of the *meḥitsah*.

206. Interestingly, in source #30 above, R. Grayevsky comes to a completely opposite conclusion. Basing himself on a similar law that a non-relative has the right to recite the *kaddish* in the synagogue hierarchy when there are no male relatives, he argues that a daughter, who is the deceased's offspring, would clearly be preferable to a non-relative and so she should have the right to recite *kaddish* as well.

Ḥavvot Ya'ir and *Kenesset Yeḥezkel*,[207] both of whom opposed daughters reciting *kaddish* in their day even in a separate *minyan*, would agree with the elder R. Y.E. Henkin's ruling that she should be permitted to say *kaddish* from the women's section. In fact, he states, it is preferable for her to recite *kaddish* in the women's section, where she is hidden and not heard, than to recite it in the mourner's home, which is more public and where she is more prominent.[208]

This desire both to show that his grandfather's *pesak* fits with all those who came before him and to defend him from anyone who tries to discredit his ruling is central to R. Y.H. Henkin's writings on the topic of women and *kaddish*.

43. *Y.H. Henkin,* "Women and Kaddish," *Equality Lost: Essays in Torah Commentary, Halacha, and Jewish Thought (Urim Publications, 1999), pp. 44–45*

R. Yehuda Henkin, United States and Israel (1945–)

This [the fact that only one person used to say *kaddish* for all], when combined with my observation that she can recite *kaddish* simultaneously with the male mourners in a quiet voice, and thus not be heard at all in the men's section, meets virtually all objections of the Aḥaronim:

1) The objection that the change in *minhag* would undermine established custom (*Responsa Ḥavvot Ya'ir*), or lead to confusion and to a woman acting as a *sheliaḥ*

207. As the *Kenesset Yeḥezkel* opposed a daughter saying *kaddish* in any circumstance, it is unclear why a change in custom of many reciting *kaddish* together should cause him to change his mind. Perhaps the fact that it is now the norm for many different relatives, such as grandsons through the daughter, to recite *kaddish* (which he originally opposed) would be a change that might be more likely to affect his view.

208. This terminology is the language used by *Ḥavvot Ya'ir* when decrying a daughter making a *minyan* to say *kaddish* in her home. Although, as explained above in source #19, it is not clear whether his opposition is directly linked to the daughter's recitation, which he defends halakhically, or, rather, to creating a separate *minyan*. If the latter is the case once everyone says *kaddish* in unison, *Ḥavvot Ya'ir* should agree even with a woman being the sole voice heard from the women's section.

tsibbur or being counted as part of a *minyan* (*Responsa Torah Lishmah*). The conspicuousness of a woman saying *kaddish* in such a fashion is virtually nil and the change in custom negligible – the men say *kaddish* exactly as before – as compared with her being the only person saying *kaddish* in the synagogue, even if she is behind the *meḥitsah* or *kal vaḥomer*, in a *minyan* in her home in full view of the men (the latter case is the one discussed by *Ḥavvot Ya'ir* and *Torah Lishmah*). Nor is a woman who remains in the women's section likely to be confused with a *sheliaḥ tsibbur* or counted in a *minyan*.

2) The objection that listening to her may violate the prohibition of *kol be'ishah* (*Matteih Efrayim, Elef Lammatteh*) and that her presence would be immodest and distract the men (*Aseih Lekha Rav* and others). When she recites *kaddish* simultaneously with men the principle "*trei kali lo mishtamei,*" two voices are not heard at once, applies, and if she is completely inaudible there is of course no *kol ishah* to start with. Nor is there immodesty or visual distraction when she remains behind the *meḥitzah*.

R. Y.H. Henkin demonstrates how, in his opinion, a woman reciting *kaddish* from the women's section dispels all the challenges raised to women's recitation of *kaddish* over the centuries. Central to his argument is the requirement that the woman must be saying *kaddish* along with a man[209] and, beyond that, in a quiet voice. In the best-case scenario, her voice is so quiet that it is rendered inaudible to the men or at least it will be drowned out by her male counterpart and become halakhically

209. Interestingly, R. Saul Lieberman held the same view. See Elijah J. Schochet and Solomon Spiro, *Saul Lieberman: The Man and His Work* (New York: JTS Press, 2005), 104n253:

> Alice Zlotnick (wife of Dov) asked Lieberman whether she was permitted, under Jewish law, to recite the *kaddish* in the synagogue after her father's death, in view of the fact that she had no brothers to say *kaddish*. Lieberman told her

inaudible, as in the halakhic principle that two voices cannot be heard at once. In a footnote to his responsum, R. Y.H. Henkin argues in a similar vein after quoting his grandfather's statements.

44. Responsa Benei Banim
Vol. 2, #7
*****(Note) on p. 26***
R. Yehuda Henkin, United States and Israel (1945–)

שו"ת בני בנים
חלק ב סימן ז
**** (הג"ה) עמוד כו**

And so in *Responsa Ḥavvot Ya'ir* and *Kenesset Yeḥezkel* they did not worry about the trill of her voice and all the more so according to our custom[210] that she says [*kaddish*] together with the men and [we hold] two voices [spoken together] are not clearly heard. And also, she does not need to raise her voice and [with] a modest woman it is possible that they [the men] will not sense her recitation at all. And it is not comparable to what the *Magen Avraham* (139:10) wrote because there, it is referring to one who recites *kaddish* or *barekhu* alone.

וכן בשו"ת [בשאלות ותשובות] חוות יאיר וכנסת יחזקאל לא חששו שתסלסל בקולה וכל שכן למנהגנו שאומרת בהדי גברים ותרי קולי לא משתמעי, וגם אינה צריכה להגביה קולה ואשה צנועה יכולה שלא ירגישו באמירתה כלל ואינו דומה למה שכתב המגן אברהם בסימן קל"ט סעיף קטן י' כי שם מיירי באומר קדיש וברכו לבדו.

In this instance, R. Y.H. Henkin states that the earliest sources discussing a daughter reciting *kaddish* were not concerned with hearing her voice. He, however, continues to focus on this issue and points out why and

that she was permitted to say *kaddish* if there was a male worshiper reciting it in the synagogue at the same time, so that the other worshipers would be responding to his *kaddish* (with "Amen" and other responses).

His view about a woman reciting *kaddish* might be affected by his overall view about *kaddish,* which can be seen from the statement in the book on which this footnote was made. On p. 61, it reads: "...his recitation of only one *kaddish* at each morning service during the year following Judith's death so as to permit the worshipers to respond 'Amen' to those with an obligation to recite the *kaddish*..."

210. Presumably, the custom he is referring to is that mourners recite *kaddish* in unison and not that there exists an established custom of women saying *kaddish* along with men, which would be a difficult claim to defend.

how there is no problem of *kol ishah*[211] in the case of her reciting *kaddish* from the women's section with a man. He points out that when she is reciting *kaddish* with a man, the legal principle of "two voices cannot be heard at once"[212] applies; consequently, there is no problem of *kol ishah*. R. Y.H. Henkin adds that the woman need not raise her voice at all and then, with a modest woman, the men would not even have the slightest indication that she was saying *kaddish* at all.[213]

This idea that the woman should not be heard and even that the *minyan* would not realize she was reciting *kaddish* is halakhically problematic from the essential nature of *kaddish* in general and mourner's *kaddish* in particular. As was shown above in Tractate *Soferim* 10:6 (source #1), the recitation of *kaddish* in general requires a *minyan*'s response, and cannot be said without a *minyan*. For this very reason, many of the earlier sources discussed the daughter entering into the men's section to recite *kaddish* in the *minyan*'s presence. Secondly, the key sources on mourner's *kaddish* understood it as the bringing of merit by the child to the deceased by

---

211. See source #47 and its discussion to follow for an analysis of R. Y.H. Henkin's personal view that *kol ishah* should not be a concern in a daughter's recitation of *kaddish*. See also R. Yitsḥak Yosef, R. Ovadiah Yosef's son, who thinks women should not recite *kaddish* at all in any situation but explains that this is solely because he is concerned with weakening customs and that there is no problem of *kol ishah* if she were to recite *kaddish* alone. See *Yalkut Yosef*, Vol. 7, 23:11, footnote end of 16. (He makes a similar argument to his father's logic in *Responsa Yeḥavveh Da'at*, Vol. 4, #15.)

    והנה מצד איסור קול באשה ערוה, אין לאסור בזה, מדאמרו בגמרא מגילה (כג.) הכל עולין למנין שבעה ואפילו קטן ואפילו אשה וכו', והרי אסור לקרוא בתורה בלי טעמים, ולא אסרו משום קול באשה ערוה, אלא משום כבוד הצבור, ועיין בזה בארוך בילקוט יוסף מועדים (עמוד רפח).

    See R. Ovadiah Yosef's more recent view in source #36 above.

212. Usually, this principle is applied in cases where the congregation needs to hear only one person's voice and so it is the reason for forbidding two people to recite or chant something at the same time. For example, with the laws of public Torah reading, see B.T. *Meg.* 21a–b, Rashi ad loc., s.v. *uvilvad shelo*; Rambam, *Hilk. Tefillah* 12:6 and 12; *Tur, O.Ḥ.* 141; *Sh. Ar., O.Ḥ.* 141:2, ad loc. *Magen Avraham* 3 and *Mishnah Berurah* 6; and *Sh. Ar., O.Ḥ.* 284:5. In the cases of *hallel* and reading the *megillah*, two voices are not a problem. See Rambam, *Hilk. Megillah* 2:7; *Sh. Ar., O.Ḥ.* 488:2, ad loc. *Taz* 2, *Magen Avraham* 2, and *Mishnah Berurah* 8; *Sh. Ar., O.Ḥ.* 690:2, ad loc. *Taz* 2, and *Magen Avraham* 4.

213. See the end of source #36 above, where R. Ovadiah Yosef's staff states that if the woman cannot be heard, there is no value to her *kaddish*.

causing the congregation to respond "*yehei shemeih rabbah*" in sanctification of God's name. For the congregation to be unable to hear the words of *kaddish* and respond, and all the more so, to not even know they are being recited, undermines the entire purpose of the act itself. R. Henkin, to some extent, acknowledges these problems by mentioning that the scenario he is suggesting is not compatible with the statements that *Magen Avraham* made on the ruling of the *Shulḥan Arukh*, which states as follows:

45. *Shulḥan Arukh*
Oraḥ Ḥayyim 139:6
Magen Avraham ad loc. #10
R. Yosef Caro, Spain and Israel (1488–1575)

שולחן ערוך
אורח חיים סימן קלט סעיף ו
מגן אברהם שם ס"ק י

One recites *barekhu* and the blessings [on the Torah] aloud. And the one who says them quietly makes a mistake.[214]

אומר ברכו והברכות בקול רם; והאומרם בלחש טועה.

[*Magen Avraham*:] **Quietly makes a mistake** – For one should only recite it with ten and the one who says them quietly does not benefit as it is [considered] a private recitation and so, too, for *kaddish* and *barekhu*.

[מגן אברהם:] **בלחש טוע'[ה]** – שאין לאומרו כ"א [כי אם] בעשר'[ה] והאומרם בלחש אינו מועיל דהוי יחיד וא"כ [ואם כן] ה"ה [ההוא הדין] לקדיש וברכו.

Shulḥan Arukh rules that one must say *barekhu* aloud and it is a mistake to recite it silently. *Magen Avraham* explains that saying it silently is tantamount to private prayer without a *minyan*; in his view, the same holds true for *kaddish*.[215] R. Y.H. Henkin suggests that a woman reciting *kaddish* silently is different than the case of *Magen Avraham*, since she is not saying *kaddish* alone. In his view, the *minyan*'s response to a

---

214. See also *Beit Yosef, O.Ḥ.* 139:6.

215. See also *Mishnah Berurah* 139:24:

> **טועה** - דלמי אומר ברכו כשאומר בלחש. ובלחש נקרא כל דלית עשרה דצייתי כדין דבר שבקדושה דאינו בפחות מעשרה. ועיין במ"א דה"ה בקדיש יש ליזהר שלא לאומרו בלחש מהאי טעמא.

man's *kaddish* said aloud is also a response to the woman's silent recitation of *kaddish*[216] and so it is not similar to private prayer, since the community is responding.

The behavior frowned upon by *Magen Avraham* of reciting *kaddish* quietly is also decried in responsa in reference to men's practice. A number of texts[217] discuss the problem of mourners reciting *kaddish* at different paces; often not every recitation of *kaddish* gets its own response in that case. It is interesting to note that R. Y.H. Henkin evokes *trei kalei* (the principle that two voices are not heard) as an advantage of a woman reciting *kaddish* with a man, as this principle is specifically raised as problematic by the opponents of the practice of reciting *kaddish* in unison,[218] because the individual voices cannot be distinguished and so no merit is brought to the parent by the specific child. These texts warn that the mourners should be careful to recite *kaddish* exactly at the same pace so that the community will respond to all, or, alternatively, each individual should make sure to have a group of at least nine others nearby who can hear and respond to the recitation and thus the purpose of *kaddish*, the bringing peace of spirit to the deceased, will be fulfilled. In one such text, R. Betsalel Stein directly addresses the case suggested by R. Y.H. Henkin, of a mourner reciting *kaddish* silently together with

---

216. This suggestion tries to deal with the halakhic challenge to his grandfather's *pesak* implied by *Magen Avraham*'s ruling. It would seem that his answer to the challenge must understand the core purpose of mourner's *kaddish* to be as explained in the ruling and thought process of R. Teichtal, which R. Y.H. Henkin cited above at the end of source #41. His view uniquely reconceptualizes the value of *kaddish* to be in reciting the content of the prayer and not in causing the response to it, which a quiet woman cannot do. See n201 above.

217. See *Responsa Mishpetei Uzziel*, Vol. 1, *O.Ḥ.* 2; *Responsa Halakhot Ketanot*, Vol. 2, #48; and *Pitḥei Teshuvah*, *Y.D.* 376:6.

218. See also *Responsa Tsits Eliezer*, Vol. 9, 16:4 and 5. He is greatly distressed by men reciting *kaddish* quietly in a group, as R. Y.H. Henkin is advocating for women, and he makes this case as part of the argument against reciting *kaddish* in unison. R. Waldenberg, in fact, feels that the principle of "two voices cannot be heard at once" should be applied as a reason to prohibit more than one person to recite *kaddish* at one time. In the middle of the responsum, R. Waldenberg also cites *Mishneh Sakhir*, on whom R. Y.H. Henkin relied above. See also n57 above.

others, although with regard to men, and finds this recitation to be halakhically problematic.

46. *Responsa Betsel Haḥokhmah* *Vol. 5, Oraḥ Ḥayyim, #135*

שו"ת בצל החכמה
חלק ה או"ח סימן קלה

R. Betsalel Stein, Hungary, Italy, and Australia (1911–1989)

The ruling of reciting *kaddish* and *barekhu* aloud.

דין אמירת קדיש וברכו בקול רם.

A) Apropos [of the words], I would say that the words of *Sefer Hamaḥkim* that I mentioned (previous entry #4[219]) [are] an open rebuke to many people who recite mourner's *kaddish* silently in a manner that even the people standing next to them do not hear the voice. And I already mentioned many times to those who recite *kaddish* like this, that it is appropriate to be meticulous to say *kaddish* with a loud voice that, in any case, the nine people closest to him will hear his voice so that with him [the mourner], together, it will be ten. That if this is not the case, then it is like he recites *kaddish* in his house alone and it does not help that ten people are present with him in the synagogue....

א. אגב אמינא כי מדברי ספר המחכים שהזכרתי (סימן הקודם אות ד') תוכחת מגולה להרבה בני אדם האומרים קדיש יתום בלחש באופן שאפי'[לו] האנשים העומדים על ידם סמוך להם אינם שומעין את הקול. וכבר הערותי הרבה פעמים לאומרי קדיש כאלה, שראוי לדקדק לומר קדיש בקול רם שעכ"פ [שעל כל פנים] תשעה בני אדם הקרובים אליו ביותר ישמעו קולו כך שיהיו אתה עמו ביחד עשרה. דאל"כ [דאם לא כן] הו"ל [הוה לה] כאומר קדיש בתוך ביתו ביחיד, ולא מהני מה שנמצאים עשרה בני אדם אתו בביהכנ"ס [בבית הכנסת]....

B) Apparently, this issue results from the fact that many times *kaddish* is recited by many people together and those who say it

ב. ומסתבר כי ענין זה נמשך ממה שהרבה פעמים אומרים קדיש אנשים רבים ביחד ואלה

219. R. Stein writes in his previous responsum (134:4):
וכן מצאתי מפורש בספר המחכים (בן דורו של הרשב"א והרא"ש) בדיני קרה"ת בשני וחמישי (עמוד ט"ו) שכתב, והקורא יאמר ברכו בהגבהת קול כדי להוציא אותם שלא שמעוהו ועוד שאין לאומרו אלא בעשרה ואם יאמרו בלחש הוי יחיד ולא הועיל עכ"ל.

silently themselves rely on that other people other than themselves recite *kaddish* aloud, and since those [other people] recite *kaddish* aloud in a manner that the congregation hears the recitation of *kaddish* from their mouths, then it is a proper *kaddish* with ten, and then there is no worry if he says it quietly without raising [his] voice. But, in my humble opinion, this is not [so] since, in the end, he is saying *kaddish* quietly and alone.... [220]

האומרי'[ם] בלחש סומכים עצמם על כי האנשים זולתם אומרים קדיש בקול רם, וכיון שאלה אומרים בקול רם באופן שהציבור שומע אמירת הקדיש מפיהם הר"ל [הוה לה] שפיר קדיש בעשרה, ושוב אין חשש אם הוא יאמרנו בלחש בלי הרמת קול. אבל לענ"ד [לעניות דעתי] זה אינו דסו"ס [דסוף סוף] הוא אומר הקדיש בלחש וביחיד....

What arises as *halakhah*: A) One who says *kaddish* or *barekhu* should be meticulous to say it aloud in a manner that, in any case, nine people excluding him will hear his recitation (A [above]). B) It appears that also when many are reciting *kaddish* together, each one of them should be careful to recite it aloud as appears above (B).

העולה להלכה: א. האומר קדיש או ברכו ידקדק לאומרו בקול באופן שעכ"פ [שעל כל פנים] תשעה אנשים זולתו ישמעו אמירתו (אות א'). ב. נראה דגם כאשר רבים אומרים קדיש ביחד, יזהר כל אחד מהם לאומרו בקול כהנ"ל [כהנמצא למעלה] (אות ב').

R. Stein acknowledges that those who recite *kaddish* quietly assume, as R. Y.H. Henkin suggests, that they can rely on those who are reciting *kaddish* aloud. R. Stein strongly disagrees with this practice and maintains that even when *kaddish* is recited in a group, each male mourner should be careful to recite it aloud so that at least nine other people can hear and respond, for as *Magen Avraham* explained (source #45), if they do not, it is as if he is just praying as an individual in his home without the presence of a *minyan*. It would seem that R. Stein would strongly

220. R. Stein goes on to suggest that the person who recites *kaddish* quietly is a *gazlan* (robber) who steals the *mitsvah* of responding from others.

disagree with the halakhic premise of R. Y.H. Henkin's ruling that it is acceptable, if not preferable, for women to recite *kaddish* quietly.[221]

This emphasis on women reciting *kaddish* quietly has even caused women to recite *kaddish* quietly in synagogues that permit them to say *kaddish* alone and aloud. In this situation, only the small group of women surrounding them can hear, which creates halakhic problems since the *minyan* cannot hear or answer at the right places and there is no male saying it along with her. In practice, this behavior ironically realizes the major fear of the opponents of the elder R. Y.E. Henkin's *pesak*, which was that ten women would function as a *minyan*.

Besides these possible halakhic problems with R. Henkin's position that women recite *kaddish* silently, there is also a sense that halakhic practice has moved backward,[222] for the earlier halakhic authorities who permitted a daughter to recite *kaddish*, as enumerated throughout this chapter, never stipulated that it be done silently or only in conjunction with a man. From a social and emotional perspective, much anguish results when women are instructed not to recite *kaddish* when there is

221. Clearly R. Y.H. Henkin is a Torah scholar and halakhic authority of stature in his own right and so can disagree with other responsa. However, the author finds it important to point out that not all authorities agree with his logic and that the silencing of women may be halakhically problematic. Also, R. Henkin himself makes a point of stating (*Equality Lost*, 49n31) that it is important to accurately present what is halakhically permitted and what is forbidden, all the more so in this case where a woman saying *kaddish* aloud and also alone is a permitted option backed by some authorities and the opposite practice of silence might even be forbidden by some. R. Henkin, at the end of *Benei Banim* 1:37, speaks out against one who mixes stringencies and customs with the core law. He states in the name of his grandfather:

    והגמו"ז זצלה"ה היה מתרעם על חיבורים כמו הקצור שלחן ערוך אשר כתבו דיני תורה ודיני התלמוד וחמרות הראשונים והאחרונים ומנהגים בלא לחלק, כי יוצא מהם חורבא בדור שלנו שאין הכל חסידים וכיון שרואים איסורי תורה ומנהגים בחדא מחתא ואין המנהגים נשמרים על ידם באים לזלזל בעיקרי הדין, וכל שכן להמציא איסורים חדשים והלואי שישמרו את המוטל עליהם.

In general, see also B.T. *Beits.* 2b, Rashi ad loc. s.v. *dehetera adifah leh* and *Shakh* "*pilpel behanhagat hora'ah be'isur veheiter,*" #9, end of 242 about forbidding that which is permitted.

222. Now, women who want to say *kaddish* alone and are upset when they are prohibited in situations where no man is there to say it with them are considered "feminist" in a derogatory sense and it has been forgotten by many that this stringency was not voiced in the sources of old.

no man available to recite it alongside them. Raise the subject of *kaddish* and women will tell stories of being hushed, or of men who were not mourners starting to shout over them, or of rabbis who would not permit them to recite *kaddish* without a male voice but would also not ensure that there would always be a man saying *kaddish* with them. At a time when women are already in pain over their personal loss and feel nervous and anxious about the great responsibility they hold toward their parent's soul, instead of being brought closer to the warmth and comfort of the Jewish community, they feel hurt and pushed away, exactly the opposite of what the elder R. Y.E. Henkin hoped to accomplish by allowing them to recite *kaddish* from the women's section of the synagogue.

The above analysis and discussion is based on R. Y.H. Henkin's written responsum and articles directly on the topic of *kaddish* to defend his grandfather's *pesak* from all possible challenges raised by earlier writings of the Aḥaronim. However, one might not be aware that R. Y.H. Henkin's personal view on a daughter's recitation of *kaddish* would not be concerned with the issues of *kol ishah* and hearing her voice. It is clear from his halakhic writings in reference to the topic of women's voice that R. Y.H. Henkin believes that both because of general habituation to hearing women's voices in modern times[223] and because there is no issue of *kol ishah* in synagogue ritual, such as with Torah and *megillah* reading,[224] one would not need to worry about this particular issue when a woman recites the *kaddish*. It seems that R. Y.H. Henkin, like his grandfather, is solely concerned with the worry that since the reciter is functioning like a prayer leader, if a woman were to "lead" the men, confusion could arise and one might think that a woman could fulfill the role of actual prayer leader in other situations. Since R. Y.H. Henkin feels her recitation does not involve immodest behavior, he rules that on an irregular basis, when no male says *kaddish*, she could recite it alone as women do with *birkat hagomel*. R. Henkin expresses this view in a footnote to his responsum on the question of a woman reciting the seven blessings at a wedding.

223. See *Equality Lost*, pp. 76–86.

224. See *Responsa Benei Banim*, Vol. 2, #10 and Vol. 4, #8. See also n211 above.

47. *Responsa Benei Banim*
Vol. 3, #27
**** (Note) on pp. 97–98***[225]

שו"ת בני בנים
חלק ג סימן כז
*** (הג"ה) עמוד צז-צח**

R. Yehuda Henkin, United States and Israel (1945–)

And that which he wrote[226] that in all of the generations they [women] did thus [recited *kaddish* in front of the men] does not contradict the words of the Aḥaronim, for in the responsum of *Ḥavvot Ya'ir*, it is explicit that he is dealing with the recitation of *kaddish* by the daughter in a fixed manner throughout the entire year of mourning. But in an occasional manner, it is possible that there is no objection [i.e., it is halakhically permissible], and from here, one can conclude that with a [female] mourner in the women's section, if she regularly recites *kaddish* with the [male] mourners as mentioned above, and one day it happened that there were no [male] mourners, she can recite *kaddish* by herself since it is only [an] occasional [event].

ומה שכתב שבכל הדורות היו עושות כן אינו נסתר מדברי האחרונים כי בשו"ת [בשאלות ותשובות] חות יאיר מפורש שמיירי באמירת קדיש על ידי הבת באופן קבוע לאורך שנת האבלות אבל באופן ארעי אפשר שאין קפידא, ומכאן יש לדון באבלה בעזרת הנשים אם היא רגילה לאמר קדיש ביחד עם האבלים כנ"ל [כמו שנזכר לעייל] ויום אחד אתרמי שלא היו אבלים, שיכולה לאמר קדיש לבדה כיון שאינו אלא באקראי.

---

225. At the beginning of the footnote, R. Henkin stresses that customs with regard to reciting *kaddish* have changed from one sole mourner saying it to a group reciting it in unison. He points out that people are not aware of this change and the halakhic ramifications of it:

ולפי זה נשתנה העינן. ורק הדורות לא שמו לב לשינוי.

He goes on to cite another example of this lack of understanding of change in custom in reference to welcoming mourners into the synagogue on Friday night.

226. R. Henkin is referring to R. Moshe Feinstein whom he had just quoted in the line before (see source #48 below). He makes the suggestion quoted in the source to reconcile R. Feinstein, who states that women in the past recited *kaddish* alone, with those Aḥaronim, such as *Ḥavvot Ya'ir*, who seem to oppose such a practice.

In R. Y.H. Henkin's view, a singular recitation of *kaddish* by a lone daughter will not lead anyone to misunderstand the general rule that women do not function as prayer leaders in the synagogue, especially if she recites *kaddish* in unison with a male on most days. In that temporary situation, when there are no male mourners present, it is perfectly permissible for her sole voice to be heard by the male *minyan*, and according to R. Y.H. Henkin it would seem that there would be no need for a male who was not a mourner to jump in and start reciting *kaddish* along with her or for anyone to try to prevent her from reciting *kaddish* on that specific occasion. R. Y.H. Henkin rules that in a temporary situation a daughter may recite *kaddish* alone and aloud from the women's section of the synagogue.

R. Y.E. Henkin, with the support of his grandson, drastically changed the reality for a daughter who desires to recite *kaddish* both positively, by reconceptualizing the synagogue architecture and structure and permitting her to recite *kaddish* from the women's section,[227] and somewhat negatively, by removing the possibility that she could consistently say it alone, as had been done in private homes and also in some synagogues[228] for many generations.

Rabbi Moshe Feinstein

R. Moshe Feinstein does not deal directly with the issue of women reciting *kaddish*. However, he does mention the topic indirectly in the following responsum on whether the presence of one or two women during the prayer service requires a *meḥitsah*.

---

227. R. Yisroel Taplin, in his book *Ta'arikh Yisra'el*, #19 n34 on pages 515–516, cites the views of the modern *ḥaredi* rabbinic authorities, R. Chaim Kanievsky and R. Chaim Pinchas Sheinberg, on a daughter reciting *kaddish* from the women's section.

    והנה שוב שאלתי את הגר"ח קניבסקי שליט"א אם הבת (גדולה או קטנה) מותרת לומר קדיש כשהיא אבילה או ביא"צ כשהיא עומדת בעזרת נשים כששאר אבלים אומרים קדיש או לא. והשיב וז"ל לא עכ"ל...והנה שאלתי את הגרח"פ שיינברג שליט"א בענין זה והשיב שיכולה לומר קדיש בעזרת נשים וכן זוכר שכן היו הנשים עושין עכת"ד.

228. As will be shown in the next source and n229 below, as well as what was already cited above in source #32.

48. ***Responsa Iggerot Moshe Oraḥ Ḥayyim Vol. 5, #12***

R. Moshe Feinstein, United States (1895–1986)

שו"ת אגרות משה
או"ח חלק ה סימן יב

B. Do you need a *meḥitsah* to block only a few women?

ב. אם צריך מחיצה לחצוץ רק בפני מעט נשים?

You asked if you need a *meḥitsah* to block only one or two women… for there is no obligation of *meḥitsah* to bar just a [small] number of women. And one needs to clarify, up until how many women is there no need for a *meḥitsah*. Such as in a house of mourning or in a house of study where they pray there on weekdays and *minḥah* on the Shabbat, where there is no *meḥitsah*, is it permissible to let a number of women enter and sit at the end of the room?

שאלת אם צריך מחיצה לחצוץ רק בפני אשה אחת או שתים.... שאין חיוב מחיצה להפסיק לפני כמה נשים בלבד. וצריך לבאר עד כמה נשים אין צריך מחיצה. כגון בבית אבל, או בבית מדרש שמתפללים שם בימי חול ובמנחה בשבת, שאין שם מחיצה, האם מותר להניח שכמה נשים יכנסו וישבו בסוף החדר.

And see, that in all of the generations, it was the practice that sometimes a poor woman would enter the house of study to collect *tsedakah* or a [female] mourner [would enter] to recite *kaddish,* and the practical law on this issue needs study and depends on many issues. Nevertheless, it appears that in a house of study where every Shabbat even one woman wants to come regularly for *minḥah,* one should not be lenient and pray without a *meḥitsah* and only in occasional situations can one permit it. And one can permit it in occasional situations only up to two women and not more.

והנה בכל הדורות נהגו שלפעמים היתה נכנסת אשה ענייה לבית המדרש לקבל צדקה, או אבלה לומר קדיש, וההלכה למעשה בעניין זה צריכה עיון ותלויה בהרבה עניינים. ומכל מקום נראה שבבית מדרש שבכל שבת תרצה אפילו אשה אחת לבוא למנחה בקביעות, שאין להקל להתפלל בלא מחיצה, ורק באקראי אפשר להתיר. ואפשר להתיר, באקראי, רק עד ב' נשים ולא יותר.

And there is a proof, as you mentioned, that according to the law, one can let one woman enter the house of study based on the law in the *Shulḥan Arukh O.Ḥ.* 282:3, that a woman goes up to be counted in the seven who are called [to read from the Torah on Shabbat].	והנה יש ראיה, כעין שהזכרת, שלדינא אפשר להניח לאשה אחת להכנס לבית המדרש, מן הדין בשולחן ערוך או"ח [אורח חיים] סי'[מן] רפ"ב סעיף ג' דאשה עולה למנין שבעה קרואים.

In his analysis of the issue, R. Feinstein lists a number of examples in which a woman might enter the men's section. He states quite simply that in the past[229] occasionally a female mourner would enter the synagogue

229. There are many anecdotal references to this phenomenon. See the following for a few.

Dr. Joel B. Wolowelsky, *Women, Jewish Law, and Modernity: New Opportunities in a Post-Feminist Age* (New Jersey: Ktav Publishing House, 1997), pp. 88–89:

> R. Pinchos Zelig Prag, *gabbai* of the Mir *minyan* in Brooklyn, New York, told me that one of the congregants, R. Moshe Maaruch, who was born and raised in Vilna and who studied at the Mirrer Yeshiva, recalled that when his cousin died, leaving an adult daughter and no sons, R. Ḥayyim Ozer Grodzinski allowed her to say *kaddish* daily in the synagogue; another recalled that the Ḥafetz Ḥayyim had made a similar ruling.
>
> Prof. Yaffa Eliach relates similar occurrences in her study of Eishenbok. Tsipora Hunter Kravitz, wife of R. Yosef Kravitz, recalled to Dr. Eliach that in 1935, when she was fourteen years old, her brothers were out of town when her father, R. Naftali Menaḥem Hunter, the *dayan* of the town, died. She said *kaddish* at the graveside and continued to say *kaddish* in both the town's new *bet midrash* and *shtibel* until her brother returned. She recalled that at the same time Gitel Gordon, then eighteen years old, said *kaddish* in the *shtibel*. Another townswoman recalled that when the girls said *kaddish*, they wore a beret and stood in the men's section in the first row to the right of the *amud*.

Dr. Joel B. Wolowelsky, *Hadarom* 57 (*Elul* 5748): 157–158:

> ומענין שהמשיך הכותב, שהרב שליט"א הוסיף שהוא זוכר שלפני החורבן באירופה שהוא היה בווילנה והתפלל בקלויז של הגאון, אשה היתה נכנסת אחורה לומר קדיש אחרי תפילת מעריב. ומקרה דומה הזכיר לי אחד מגבאי "מנין מיר" בברוקלין. (זה המנין המפורסס שהקימו יוצאי מיר באירופה שבאו משאנחי לארה"ב), שהעיד לפניו אחד ממתפללי המנין שהיה מוותיקי ישיבת מיר שנולד וגדל בווילנא, שכשבן - דודו נפטר ולא השאיר בנים פסק הגרח"ע גרודזנסקי זצ"ל לבתו המבוגרת לומר קדיש כל יום בביהכנ"ס בווילנא. וסיפר הרב הנ"ל שהיה רואה את הבת כל יום נחפזת לביהכנ"ס לומר קדיש בפסק הגרח"ע זצ"ל. והוסיף עוד אחד מחברי המנין שאביו למד אצל החפץ חיים זצ"ל שהוא גם פסק כהנ"ל.

or *beit midrash* to recite *kaddish*. R. Feinstein, without delving into the specifics, goes on to state that the *halakhah* is that a *meḥitsah* is required even for a small number of women, if they attend regularly. To R. Feinstein, the basic notion of a female mourner reciting *kaddish* in the presence of men is a normative and accepted fact that requires no explanation or discussion.[230] It is simply an example of an existing practice that he mentions to help determine the practical *halakhah* under discussion regarding if a

---

ורבה של בית וגן כתב לי שגם הוא שמע שלפני שנים נשים היו נכנסות לבתי הכנסת במאה שערים להגיד קדיש. והרבה זקנים זכרו מקרים דומים. וכך כנראה היה עמדתם ההלכתית של גאוני ליטא להתיר לנשים לומר קדיש יתום.

Herman Eliot Snyder, "The American Synagogue World of Yesterday, 1901–1925," *American Jewish Archives Journal* 42:1 (Spring–Summer 1990): 72, tells of a sixteen-year-old who entered the men's section to recite *kaddish*.

T. Parshel, Brooklyn, New York, *Hapardes*, Year 38, Booklet 7, #60 "The Recitation of *Kaddish* by the Daughter":

בירושלים ספרו לי על מקרה שבת קטנה אמרה קדיש. וכמדומה שנאמר לי שהיא עמדה בפתח או בפרוזדור בית התפילה. גם קראתי כי בימי הפרעות של כנופיות פטליורא כאשר בכפרים רבים באוקראינה הושמדו כמעט כל הגברים התאספו יחד בנות ישראל מיותמות לומר קדיש אחרי הוריהם.

Simḥah Raz, *Tsaddik Yesod Olam* (Jerusalem: Olam Hasefer Hatorani, 1996), p. 217:

האדריכל מאיר רובין, מי שתכנן את "היכל שלמה", ומי שלימים כיהן כסגן ראש עיריית ירושלים, שהיה אלמן, נפטר והותיר אחריו שתי בנות, שאחת מהן, נילי, הייתה אותה עת בת שתים עשרה. ר' אריה [לוין] ביקש להיות זה שיבשר להן את דבר מותו. וכך סיפרה נילי, כי "- הוא ביקשנו שנאמר 'קדיש' אחר אבינו, אף דפדף בסידור התפילה והראה לנו היכן מקומה של תפילה זו, ולימדנו כיצד יש לאומרה."

"*Yom Hashishi*" (newspaper) – 9 *Tammuz* 5755 (July 7, 1995):

ובמכתב למערכת עיתון מסויים כתב שלום זבולני מקיבוץ אושה בו הוא כותב בנושא של אמירת קדיש על ידי בת יחידה שהתיר הרב הספרדי הראשי בבאר-שבע לפני כמה שנים, במכתבו כותב כי הוא זוכר בילדותו בביאליסטוק בתחילת שנות השלושים הלך לעולמו ראש משפחה שהשאיר רק בת יחידה והיא אמרה קדיש כל השנה בתפילות מנחה וערבית בבית הכנסת וזאת לפי היתר הרבנים המקומים, לפי זכרונו, הרב דוד פאיאנס ז"ל וחתנו הרב שמואל מוהליבר ז"ל.

The author thanks R. Aryeh Frimer for bringing this excerpt to her attention.

230. See Amnon Shapira, *Amudim* 33:11 (#523), *Av* 5749, p. 352, who relates a conversation with R. Moshe Tendler, R. Feinstein's son-in-law:

וכך עמדת הרב מ.ט., פוסק מפורסם במונסי, ניו יורק (ופרופ' בישיבה אוניברסיטה):
אני: האם יכולות נשים לומר "קדיש"?
הרב: כן, שיגידו.
Let the women say *kaddish*: we are not afraid of the women.
אני: ואם הם אשכנזיות?
הרב: אז אפילו יש להן חיוב לומר קדיש!

meḥitsah is needed for just a few women.[231] The custom, as he knows it, is that women could recite *kaddish*[232] even in the men's section.

Rabbi Joseph B. Soloveitchik

R. Joseph B. Soloveitchik did not commonly write down his halakhic rulings and it is therefore difficult, at times, to state his halakhic opinions conclusively. However, his view on the issue of women reciting *kaddish* is clear, since a number of his prominent students and female congregants all relate strikingly similar understandings of his legal view on the topic.

Dr. Joel Wolowelsky recounts R. Soloveitchik's view on a female reciting *kaddish* in two different incidents.

49. *J. Wolowelsky,* Women, Jewish Law, and Modernity: New Opportunities in a Post-Feminist Age *(New Jersey: Ktav Publishing House, 1997), pp. 88–90*

R. Joseph B. Soloveitchik, United States (1903–1993)

In the early 1970s, when the issue came up in a chapter of Yavneh, the national association of religious Jewish college students, I asked one of the organization's leaders who was then learning with the Rav, R. Joseph B. Soloveitchik, to put the question to him. R. Ezra Bick[233] (now at Yeshivat Har Etzion) wrote back:

---

231. Yehuda Eisenberg writes in *Kaddish Yetomah–Teguvah Liteguvah, Tzohar* 9 (Winter 5762):

> כלפי מה אמורים דברי רמ"פ "וההלכה למעשה בעניין זה צריכה עיון ותלויה בהרבה עניינים"? כלפי המשפט הקודם לו, על אישה הנכנסת לומר קדיש, או כלפי הנושא כולו: לפני כמה נשים צריך לעשות מחיצה?... הנושא הוא מחיצה, ולא קדיש יתומה! בדקתי את הדבר עם הרב שבתאי רפופורט, שערך את כתבי רמ"פ, והוא אישר את הפירוש הזה. בנוסף לזה יש עדויות מאנשים שונים, שנוכחו באמירת קדיש על ידי נשים בבית הכנסת של ר' משה פיינשטיין.

232. See *Iggerot Moshe, Y.D.* Vol. 4, #61 where R. Feinstein mentions that there is no difference if it is a son or a daughter who hires another to recite *kaddish*, except that a daughter is, at times, less knowledgeable.

233. The author of this work contacted R. Bick via e-mail and (on July 9, 2006) the latter confirmed that, as far as he could remember, the story was accurate.

> I spoke with the Rav about the question you asked concerning a girl saying *kaddish*. He told me that he remembered being in Vilna at the "Ga'on's Kloiz" – which wasn't one of your modern Orthodox shuls – and a woman came into the back (there was no *ezrat nashim* [women's section]) and said *kaddish* after *ma'ariv*. I asked him whether it would make a difference if someone was saying *kaddish* along with her or not, and he replied that he would see no objections in either case – it's perfectly all right. Coincidently, checking around, I came across a number of people who remember such incidents from Europe, including my father (in my grandfather's *minyan* – he was the *rav* in the town). [R. Ḥayyim Yeḥiel Mikhl Bick was the rav in Medzhibush in Ukraine.] .... [234]

Rabbi Soloveitchik also insisted that a woman saying Kaddish had to remain in the women's section. When, in the early 1970s, I asked Rabbi Gerald J. Blidstein (then a faculty advisor to Yavneh and now at Ben-Gurion University) about the issue, he wrote to me:

> The *kaddish* matter is as follows. I [R. Gerald J. Blidstein] was asked about the question last year, and looking into it, could find no reason beyond "general policy" for forbidding it. I spoke to Aharon Lichtenstein [then Rosh Kollel at Yeshiva University and now Rosh Yeshivat Har Etzion], who had the same reaction and said he would ask the Rav [R. Joseph B. Soloveitchik, his father-in-law], which he did when I was on the other end of the phone. [R. Lichtenstein] put the question to him and then was directed to ask me whether the girl was stationed in the *ezrat nashim*. I, of course, answered in the affirmative and the Rav then said that of course she could say *kaddish*.[235]

234. This text also appears in Joel Wolowelsky, *Hadarom* 57 (*Elul* 1988), 157–158; Wolowelsky, "Modern Orthodoxy and Women's Self-Perception," *Tradition* 22:1 (Spring 1986): 80n9; and Wolowelsky, "Women and Kaddish," *Judaism* 44:3 (Summer 1995): 282–290.

235. This account was also published in Joel B. Wolowelsky, "Women and Kaddish,"

In both of these instances cited by Dr. Wolowelsky,[236] R. Soloveitchik offered a succinct, decisive ruling permitting a woman to recite *kaddish* from the women's section even if she is the only person doing so in the synagogue. The stories are recounted in the names of distinguished students of R. Soloveitchik and form a consistent and coherent picture.[237] Apparently, R. Soloveitchik ruled that the women's sections in the United States were built in such a manner as to be considered part of the same domain as the men's section,[238] and he did not share the concerns of those authorities who came before him.

Judaism 44:3 (Summer 1995): 282–290 and in R. Aaron Rakefet-Rothkoff, *The Rav: The World of Rabbi Joseph B. Soloveitchik*, Vol. 2 (New Jersey: Ktav Publishing House, 1999), 36.

236. See R. Neriyah Gutel's rebuttal of Wolowelsky's views in "*Kaddish Yetomah - Teguvah*," *Tzohar* 8 (Fall 5762): 21–37.

237. R. Shlomo Riskin, another student of R. Soloveitchik, recounts that he received a similar answer. In a post to the Women's Tefillah Network listserv (October 7, 2002, Digest #1099), he wrote:

> I certainly believe that a woman can recite *kaddish* if she is in mourning for a close relative from the *ezrat nashim* of a synagogue in which there is a *minyan* of ten men. She can even recite that *kaddish* if no one else other than she is reciting *kaddish*. I heard this view expressed by Rav Soloveitchik in response to a question I asked many years ago and this view has been published in the book *The Rav: The World of Rabbi Joseph B. Soloveitchik* by R. Aaron Rakefet-Rothkoff, Vol. 2 p. 36.

See also R. Saul Berman's statement in n243 below.

R. Hershel Schachter, in his book *Be'ikvei Hatson*, p. 24n5, also mentions R. Soloveitchik's view.

> וכן שמעתי בשם רבינו, ז"ל, שהי' סובר שמעיקר הדין הבת רשאה לומר קדיש, אלא שהדבר תלוי במנהג המקום.

In his *Hadarom* article Dr. Wolowelsky states:

> ועוד תלמידים מובהקים הזכירו את עמדתו הנ"ל של הרב שליט"א, וכן פשט המנהג בהרבה בתי כנסיות שמשמשים בהם חברי הסתדרות הרבנים.

238. This reality was certainly true of the women's section in the Maimonides School/Synagogue in Brookline, Massachusetts, at the time that R. Soloveitchik prayed there. It is likely that both R. Soloveitchik and R. Y.E. Henkin emphasized the need for her to be in the women's section because of the controversy in their day surrounding mixed seating and the removal of the *meḥitsah*.

R. Dr. Kenneth Chelst, in his self-published book, *Kaddish: The Unanswered Cry,*[239] also presents the ruling of R. Soloveitchik as well.[240]

---

239. R. Chelst wrote the book and titled it as such because he was concerned with the phenomenon that so many people in synagogue never even notice the person saying *kaddish* and do not respond appropriately.

240. Tamy Chelst, his wife, relates and R. Chelst confirms that, in 1984, R. Yitzhak Twersky arranged for her husband to see R. Soloveitchik at the Twerskys' home, where R. Soloveitchik was residing. R. Chelst showed his original text to R. Soloveitchik, who changed a few words. The endnote is exactly the text that R. Soloveitchik approved.

Tamy Chelst, in an e-mail of May 8, 2006 to Monique C. Katz, M.D., relates her story as follows:

> My dad, R. [Isaac] Simon, was a rebbe at Maimonides School in Brookline for 35 years. He treated male and female Talmud and Ḥumash students with equal respect. Even though he was from the Mirrer Yeshiva in Europe and then Shanghai, he valued boy and girl students similarly. Many a year, the school prize for *Limudei Kodesh* (Ḥumash, Gemara, etc.) would be given to a female. Indeed, I won the Talmud award at high school graduation. I felt that my father would be proud to have his daughter recite *kaddish,* no holds barred. I decided to recite *kaddish* without asking anyone. My dad's funeral was on Wednesday, and I recited *kaddish* in the home *minyan* with my husband and brother-in-law (they were not always there together) in all *minyanim* through Shabbat. On Shabbat, we went to the Maimonides School *minyan* where I continued to recite *kaddish* for *ma'ariv* on Friday night and then for *shaḥarit* and *minḥah* on Shabbat. Between *minḥah* and *ma'ariv,* the Rav always entertained congregants' halakhic questions. Rabbi Wohlgemuth, who was a teacher at Maimonides, asked the Rav about women reciting *kaddish.* The Rav said that it was fine and that this was often done in shuls in Europe. I believe he also said that after the Holocaust, women even said *kaddish* by themselves if they were the only person to recite *kaddish* in a shul. (He may have shared this experiential note with my husband at a later date, I'll get into this later.) My husband was in shul and heard this conversation as did many other people in shul. When the Rav came to be *menaḥem avel* in our home, I said that I had heard that he thought that I could say *kaddish* for my dad. He replied that I could, but that I should not take the responsibility lightly and that once I did this three times, it was like a "*neder*" and I would have to do it with regularity for the entire time period. There were several people in the *shivah* house at the time. One of them, Joyce Kosowsky, told me twenty years later that she heard the entire conversation and recited *kaddish* for her mother based on it. Several years later, my husband wrote a small pamphlet about the emotional aspects of his experience saying *kaddish* for his parents. He added a footnote stating the Rav's *pesak* to me. The

He relates[241] that R. Soloveitchik read the entire text of the book and specifically approved the statement of his view on a daughter's recitation of *kaddish*.

50. *K. Chelst,* Kaddish: The Unanswered Cry *(self-published, 1987), p. 23, endnote 29*

R. Joseph B. Soloveitchik, United States (1903–1993)

Rabbi Joseph B. Soloveitchik recently offered his opinion which can be summarized as follows: Although the Jewish women's role is not in the synagogue, a daughter could recite *kaddish* in honor of a deceased parent if there were no sons[242] to recite *kaddish*. She could recite *kaddish* even if she were the only one saying *kaddish* in the synagogue and the congregation could answer her *kaddish* but was not required to do so.[243] The Rav reminisced about a visit decades earlier to Vilna in which he saw a young woman

---

Rav was ailing at the time and his concentration wandered, but Yitzhak Twersky arranged for my husband to meet the Rav at home and show him the statement before publication. The Rav altered a few words but the *pesak* remains the same.

241. In private correspondence with this author (December 31, 2010), R. Chelst mentioned that if he had realized that there would be any debate about R. Soloveitchik's views on this matter (see Reuven Fink, "The Recital of Kaddish by Women," *The Journal of Halacha and Contemporary Society* 31 [Spring 1996]: 34 and n7, and "Letters," *The Journal of Halacha and Contemporary Society* 32 [Fall 1996]: 110), he would have explicitly stated in his book that R. Soloveitchik had reviewed its text.

242. R. Soloveitchik's statement concerning a woman saying *kaddish* in the case of no sons was made in direct reference to Tamy's particular situation of not having brothers.

243. It is hard to understand the end of this sentence halakhically. It would be difficult to understand R. Soloveitchik as truly saying that the congregation is not required to answer her, for *kaddish* requires a *minyan*'s response; without the *minyan* it may not be recited. It would make more sense for the sentence to read "a daughter could recite *kaddish* in honor of a deceased parent if there were no sons to recite *kaddish*, but was not required to do so. She could recite *kaddish* even if she were the only one saying *kaddish* in the synagogue and the congregation could answer her *kaddish*." The intention of R. Soloveitchik was to state that the daughter could recite *kaddish* but was not required to do so. The author thanks Joel Wolowelsky for suggesting this reading given the difficulty in the text. This explanation fits with the fact that R. Soloveitchik discussed with R. Chelst the seriousness of commitment that his wife would be

> recite kaddish after the evening services. His curiosity piqued, he checked around and discovered that this woman's actions were consistent with the prevailing custom in Vilna.

R. Soloveitchik's ruling is also recounted as his actual practice by Dr. Sara Reguer, describing a visit to Boston.

> ***51. S. Reguer, "Kaddish from the 'Wrong' Side of the Meḥitzah," On Being a Jewish Feminist, Susannah Heschel, ed. (New York: Schocken Books, 1983), pp. 180–181***
>
> R. Joseph B. Soloveitchik, United States (1903–1993)
>
> Then there was the time I visited Boston[244] and was praying in an Orthodox school attended by one of the most outstanding Jewish

---

imposing on herself if she chose to recite *kaddish*. However, R. Soloveitchik did not want him to include in writing a discussion of what constitutes a *neder* for a daughter reciting *kaddish*.

Dr. Amnon Shapira in "*Temurot Feministiyot Ba'ortodoksiyah Hamodernit,*" *Amudim* 33:11 (#523), *Av* 5749, p. 352 relates the following in the name of R. Saul Berman with regard to the community answering:

> כיון שמעיקר הדין נראה שאין כל לאיסור, עשויה מציאות חיינו לעודד דווקא הפן החיובי של אמירת "קדיש" ע"י הנשים. הרב ס.ב., רב של אחד מבתי הכנסת הגדולים בניו יורק, מראשי סטרן קולג' והסתדרות הרבנים בארה"ב: "יש תשובות הלכתיות מפורשות, ביניהן של הרב סולובייצ'יק, המתירות ואף מעודדות נשים לומר "קדיש". יתרה מזו. הרי אין שום בעיה לאשה הנמצאת בעזרת נשים לומר קדיש, כפי שהיא אומרת כיום עפ"י המקובל והמסורת, "קדושה" או "ברכו". הבעיה מתעוררת במקרה שבכל בית הכנסת אין איש האומר "קדיש", ורק אשה אחת למעלה, בעזרת הנשים, נשמעת אומרת "קדיש". האם צריכים החזן והקהל להמתין לה?"
>
> תשובת הרב - "כן, שימתינו!"

244. Rochelle L. Millen, in "The Female Voice of Kaddish," *Jewish Legal Writings by Women*, p. 179, recounts another story from the larger Boston community:

> When Rav Menachem Mendel Auerbach, a member of the *beit din* of Boston, died in 1952, his widow, Esther, said *kaddish* for her husband, although there were sons to do so. Mrs. Auerbach, scion of a rabbinical family from Kovno, recited *kaddish* in her home during the *shivah*, as well as for the remainder of the required thirty days in shul. She attended the services of the Bostoner Rebbe, then located in Dorchester, every day.

Tamy Chelst (in her e-mail of May 8, 2006 to Monique C. Katz, M.D.) corroborated this information:

scholars and rabbis of our day.[245] The sexton was nervous because I had already told him what I would be doing. He insisted on saying *kaddish* with me. But I saw a flurry of activity in the corner where the rabbi sat, and when it came time to say it, I said the *kaddish* alone and all answered, as they properly should have.

Similarly, Dr. Monique Katz recounts her experiences as R. Soloveitchik's congregant.[246]

52. M. Katz, Personal Correspondence, January 27, 2010

R. Joseph B. Soloveitchik, United States (1903–1993)

I am currently saying *kaddish* for my father who died this past July. I am doing this because 42 years ago [in 1963], when my mother died, I asked the Rav (Yosef B.) Soloveitchik, then the rabbi of Congregation Moriah in New York (he was the rabbi both in New York and Boston), whether I could say *kaddish*. Our family had a

---

> Recently, I visited Ada Jacobowitz (née Greenwald) from Boston. She told me that the women in her family said *kaddish* even at the Bostoner Rebbe's in Dorchester. She is relation to Rav [Shlomo Zalman] Auerbach of Jerusalem.

245. Dr. Reguer adds to the story:

> My mother died in August 1979. I was in Boston some time during that year – probably Pesaḥ of 1980.... I went to shul for *shaḥarit*, and did not tell the *shamash* my name, only that I was going to say *kaddish* aloud and alone, if no one else was obligated to say it. He went immediately to the Rav who saw me behind the *meḥitsah* – I am not sure if he recognized me then. I said it alone, and everyone answered me. After davening I went up to him to thank him for agreeing with my father. He said something to the effect of Briskers having the same view. By then he also knew that I too had brothers, and it made absolutely no difference. He then wished me *niḥumim*, for he knew my mother and was very concerned about how my father was holding up. No, my father did not publish anything on this, and the Rav was notorious for not publishing. Neither did his grandfather – that was the task of my grandfather, Simcha Zelig, the Brisker Dayan.

Conveyed in a personal e-mail to Monique C. Katz, M.D. (January 29, 2006). Published with permission of Dr. Reguer.

246. Text from a private e-mail (January 27, 2010). Permission was granted by Dr. Katz to the author to publish this correspondence.

close relationship with the Rav and when my mother died, he gave the eulogy and went with the men to the cemetery to perform the burial. As Moriah was a shul of Jews from Belgium, as is the custom even today, women were not permitted to go to the cemetery for the burial even of their own parents. Hence, I went home while my brother and father went with the Rav to the cemetery for the burial at which time they said the *kaddish*. When they returned from the burial, the Rav came up to our apartment to pay a *shivah* call to me. At that point I asked the Rav if I, too, could say *kaddish* for my mother. Without the slightest hesitation, he said that I certainly could say it, despite knowing my brother was perfectly capable of saying the *kaddish*.

In light of these clear testimonies covering a significant period of time and by different people all of whom had direct interactions with R. Soloveitchik, it is reasonable to conclude that R. Soloveitchik ruled that it was permissible and legitimate for a woman to recite *kaddish*, even if she had brothers who were reciting *kaddish* and even if she was the sole mourner reciting *kaddish* in the synagogue.

R. Joseph B. Soloveitchik's brother, R. Ahron Soloveichik,[247] at the end of a responsum on *kaddish* in general, addresses the issue of women reciting *kaddish*.

53. Od Yisra'el Yosef Beni Ḥai **#32**	**עוד ישראל יוסף בני חי סימן לב**
R. Ahron Soloveichik, Chicago (1917–2001)	
And look in *Teshuvot Ḥavvot Ya'ir* #242[248] who wrote that if the deceased did not have a son, only a daughter, and the daughter is married then the husband is required to say *kaddish*. And if the daughter is not	ועיין בתשובות חוות יאיר בתשובה רמ"ב שכתב שאם אין למת בן רק בת והבת נשואה אז הבעל צריך לומר קדיש. ואם הבת אינה נשואה אז מצד עיקר

247. The two families spell their last names slightly differently.

248. This text clearly states 242 even though the correct reference is 222. From his misquote of the content of *Ḥavvot Ya'ir*, it seems that he did not see the original.

married then from the essence of the law the daughter can recite *kaddish*; however, one should not do this as it will weaken the customs of Israel and since there is publicity, one should prevent it. And it appears that, nowadays, when a number of men and women of Israel are fighting for the equality of women vis-à-vis men on the issue of *aliyot* for women, therefore if the Orthodox rabbis prevent a woman from reciting *kaddish* in a place where it is possible that, as a result, the influence of Conservative and Reform rabbis will increase, then it is forbidden [for them] to prevent a daughter from reciting *kaddish*.	הדין הבת יכולה לומר קדיש אלא שלא תעשה כן שעל ידי זה יתחלשו מנהגי ישראל וכיון דאיכא פרסום יש למחות. ונראה עכשיו שכמה אנשים ונשים מישראל לוחמים בעד שיווי הנשים לעומת האנשים ביחס עם עליות בשביל הנשים א"כ [אם כן] אם הרבנים החרדים ימנעו אשה מלומר קדיש במקום שישנה אפשרות שע"י [שעל ידי זה] זה תתרבה ההשפעה של הרבנים השמרנים והריפורמים אז אסור למנוע בת מלומר קדיש.

After attributing to *Ḥavvot Ya'ir* a distinction that he does not make between a married and unmarried daughter, R. Soloveichik explains why the situation in modern times is diametrically opposite of that in the times of *Ḥavvot Ya'ir*. *Ḥavvot Ya'ir* believed that a daughter reciting *kaddish* would weaken the customs of Israel and therefore it should be prevented, whereas R. Soloveichik argues that, nowadays, stopping a daughter from reciting *kaddish* will weaken the stance of traditional Judaism. When Orthodox rabbis prohibit women from performing practices[249] when there is a halakhic

249. R. Daniel Sperber, quoted by Leila Speisman in *The Canadian Jewish News* on Nov. 25, 2004, uses this point of R. Soloveichik's in his own manner:

> The real issue, Rav Sperber said, is the true intention of those who want such innovations. "Is it *l'shem shomayom* [sic], for the sake of heaven [a spiritual need], or is it for political reasons, or to copy what others are doing?" This quandary is central to the question of whether women can say *kaddish* in the synagogue. R. Aaron Soloveitchik [sic] "realized that there was no halakhic reason to forbid it," R. Sperber said. R. Ovadia Yosheph [sic] said that those who have a genuine personal need to say *kaddish* should do so, as to forbid it would cause the mourner pain. Preventing mental anguish and maintaining a person's dignity is a basic concept in Jewish law, R. Sperber said. If a woman has a genuine spiritual need to say *kaddish*, forbidding her to do it would cause her mental anguish.

reason to allow them,[250] they run the danger of alienating women from Orthodox Judaism and strengthening the more liberal denominations. Unlike R. Wahrman and others,[251] who fear the innovations of reformers and so prohibit a daughter's recitation, R. Soloveichik ends his statement with extremely strong language: "It is therefore forbidden [for them] to prevent a daughter from reciting *kaddish*."

SUMMARY AND CONCLUSIONS

As described by *Or Zarua* (source #4) and *Responsa Maharil* (source #5), mourner's *kaddish* originally developed as a custom specifically for young minors to recite, since they could not function in the more preferable role of prayer leader. Even though they could not count in the *minyan* required for the recitation, they were permitted to say this additional,

---

250. Dr. Joel B. Wolowelsky, *Women, Jewish Law, and Modernity*, 93–94, eloquently states:

> The halakhic legitimacy of women to say *kaddish* is unassailable even if not universally accepted. No woman should feel constrained from pressing to say *kaddish* in her shul. If a rabbi feels that it is in the community's best interest to not allow an orphaned daughter to say *kaddish*, he should make it clear that his decision is based on public policy considerations rather than *halakhah*. He should be confident that in a healthy halakhic community people generally feel bound by their personal halakhic authority. Additionally, many daughters will pass up the opportunity to exercise an option that all agree is not obligatory, finding solace in a more passive role. But a woman who regularly attends shul will feel resentment when she eventually learns that a meaningful, legitimate option was withheld from her. The rabbi, in his role as counselor, has an obligation to bring all legitimate options to the attention of the mourner.

R. Maurice Lamm also voices similar concerns in *The Jewish Way in Death and Mourning (Revised and Expanded Edition)* (New York: Jonathan David Publishers, 2000 [revised and expanded]), 162:

> On the contrary, my worry is that if women in traditional synagogues are not given the opportunity to express themselves through *halakhot* in sensitive areas such as mourning, the consequences will be destructive. Here is a need to empower women religiously – not pander to political and cultural correctness – always staying within the framework of *halakhah*. There is a need to encourage women's participation in synagogue life; to allow women to express their innermost spiritual yearnings in a traditional mode; and to trust contemporary rabbinic leadership to be receptive to a woman's continuing religious needs. This was fundamentally R. Henkin's contention. It is fifty years later. Should we not finally hear his voice?

251. See source #39 and n194 above.

non-obligatory *kaddish*. At the time of its inception, *kaddish* was recited by only a single mourner so that the mourner could be the direct cause of the congregation blessing God's name in the parent's honor. Rema (source #8), the first code to mention the custom of mourner's *kaddish,* outlines a clear structure of prioritization for which type of mourner has the right to be the one to recite *kaddish*. Due to this defined hierarchical list, which did not include the daughter, and the rule that *kaddish* must be said in the presence of a *minyan,* which could not be done from the distinctly separate domain of the women's sections of old, the earliest sources discussing a daughter's recitation of *kaddish* all focus on her doing so in a private *minyan* in her home.

The three earliest sources regarding a daughter's recitation of *kaddish* (*Ḥavvot Ya'ir, Shevut Ya'akov,* and *Kenesset Yeḥezkel*) have different opinions on the matter. These became the three different models for how rabbinic authorities throughout the ages viewed and discussed a daughter's recitation of *kaddish*. The community of rabbis in Amsterdam cited by *Ḥavvot Ya'ir* (source #19), as well as *Shevut Ya'akov* (source #20), both unequivocally believe that a daughter may benefit her deceased father with the recitation of *kaddish* and so permit her to be the sole reciter of *kaddish* in the presence of a *minyan* in her home. *Ḥavvot Ya'ir* is the first to lay out a clear argument to prove that halakhically a daughter may recite *kaddish*. He states that she is clearly the deceased's offspring and that the story of R. Akiva was not speaking exclusively about sons. Women are obligated in the *mitsvah* to sanctify God's name and they may do so because there is a *minyan* of men present. However, despite justifying a daughter's recitation legally, *Ḥavvot Ya'ir* speaks out very strongly against this practice, saying that it must be prevented for it may weaken the customs of Israel. *Kenesset Yeḥezkel* (source #22) completely disagrees with the halakhic reasoning of the two responsa before him and outright denies that the daughter, as well as her son (the grandson from a daughter), has any right to recite *kaddish*. In the generations that follow these three different rulings, very few halakhic authorities follow in the footsteps of *Kenesset Yeḥezkel* to completely forbid a daughter to recite *kaddish* from the core of halakhic logic. Instead, the majority of responsa either follow *Shevut Ya'akov* and permit a daughter's recitation in the home or even go one step further and permit her recitation in the men's section of the synagogue or, as *Ḥavvot Ya'ir* did, defend its legality but either limit its application or prevent it due to social or public policy concerns.

For many generations after *Ḥavvot Ya'ir*'s first responsum on the topic of a daughter reciting mourner's *kaddish*, halakhic authorities referred back to both his halakhic analysis of the issue, which legally defended the daughter's right to recite *kaddish*, and to his concern that doing so would weaken the traditions of the rabbis and the Jewish people. Interestingly, in the modern period, responsa in both Israel and the United States do not focus on the worry of changing customs and two of them[252] even make the claim that *Ḥavvot Ya'ir* would permit a woman's recitation of *kaddish* in the women's section of the synagogue, a practice first suggested in the twentieth century. Possibly these authorities, when considering the application of R. Bacharach's social statement against change to the case of a daughter's recitation, implicitly acknowledged the many different customs concerning the recitation of *kaddish* that have changed and evolved over time. It would be difficult today to oppose a woman's recitation of *kaddish* based on the notion that customs of Israel should not be changed in any synagogue or community that permits mourning adult relatives of all kinds (and even paid non-relatives) to recite *kaddish* together, numerous times, every day of the week for only eleven months, all of which are innovations on the original practice. As shown above, so many customs have changed with regard to the recitation of mourner's *kaddish* that, in the larger picture, a daughter's desire to take an active role in ensuring her parents' welfare after death is just one of many innovations.

In the past sixty-five years or so,[253] since the responsum of

252. See sources #34 and 42.

253. The change in attitude in the modern day towards a daughter's desire to recite *kaddish* can be seen in the most famous Modern Orthodox manual on mourning and bereavement, R. Maurice Lamm's *The Jewish Way in Death and Mourning*. A comparison of the text from the original publication in 1969 to the revised and expanded edition from 2000 shows significant differences in his approach regarding a daughter's recitation of *kaddish*.

In the first edition R. Lamm writes: "The primary obligation to say *kaddish* falls upon the *son* of the deceased. It is he who is required to recite it – he and *not*

R. Uzziel (source #31), who states that only sons can physically replace their father in the *minyan* and so only they can halakhically recite *kaddish*, and *Mishnat Binyamin* (source #40), who had not heard of such a custom, none of the sources cited above deny the right, halakhic capacity, and spiritual efficacy of a daughter's recitation of *kaddish*. Some authorities did have concerns with issues of modesty and men's inappropriate thoughts and so limited the place or manner in which the daughter should recite *kaddish*. However, all affirmed her place as *ben* (offspring), capable of sanctifying God's holy name and eliciting a response from the community to benefit the soul of her departed parent.

An analysis of the halakhic discussion and debate in the rabbinic literature beginning with the Rishonim and proceeding to modern legal texts, in light of a serious examination of the customs of mourner's *kaddish* itself, produces a number of conclusions regarding a daughter's and,

---

his sister; he and not his relatives; he and not someone paid to substitute him...." (p. 164, emphasis added). In the newer edition this text has changed been to read in a more gender-inclusive way that does not actively exclude the daughter: "The primary obligation to say *kaddish* falls upon the *child* of the deceased. It is he who is required to recite it; he and not his relatives; he and not someone paid to substitute for him...." (p. 157, emphasis added). Whereas in the first edition he merely gives an explanation for why the sages did not require the daughter to recite *kaddish*, in the revised text R. Lamm presents an entire section entitled "Should Women Say *Kaddish*?" in which he cites halakhic sources through the ages supporting a daughter's right and legal eligibility to say *kaddish* for her parents.

Furthermore, in the first edition, R. Lamm acknowledges the possibility of a daughter reciting *kaddish* only if there are no sons, and says that she should only do so "quietly to herself" (p.167). In his revised text, R. Lamm states unequivocally: "Today, reciting the *kaddish* is open to all women who want to express their grief in this manner and speak to the Almighty on behalf of their beloved departed relatives.... She can stand and recite the full mourner's *kaddish* whenever she attends the synagogue – at every Sabbath, festival, or weekday service of the year, on *yahrtseit*, and at every *yizkor* service" (p.162). R. Lamm completely removes the requirement for daughters to recite *kaddish* quietly to themselves, although he does discuss reciting *kaddish* with reverence and modesty – values which, he points out, are relevant for both sons and daughters.

Finally, R. Lamm adds that, similar to a daughter for her parents, a wife may recite *kaddish* for her deceased husband.

by extension, another woman's (such as a wife's or sister's) recitation of mourner's *kaddish*. These conclusions are as follows:[254]

1. Mourner's *kaddish* must be recited in the presence of a *minyan* (ten males).
2. A daughter is considered offspring and so can successfully benefit a deceased parent's soul, especially when there are no sons, with the recitation of mourner's *kaddish*.
3. A woman is obligated to sanctify God's name and so, combined with #2 above, may halakhically recite mourner's *kaddish*.
4. As has been the tradition of those *posekim* of generations past who permit a daughter's recitation, modern *posekim* permit a daughter to recite mourner's *kaddish* in the presence of a male *minyan* at home.
5. Most modern *posekim* in the United States permit a daughter to recite mourner's *kaddish* in the women's section of the synagogue as well as in the home, and do not worry about changing customs.
6. As has been the tradition of those *posekim* of generations past who permit a daughter's recitation, many modern *posekim* permit a daughter to recite mourner's *kaddish* aloud and alone as the sole voice heard by a *minyan* of men in the home.
7. As has been the tradition of those *posekim* of generations past who permit a daughter's recitation within the men's section of the synagogue, some modern *posekim* permit a daughter to recite mourner's *kaddish* aloud and alone as the sole voice heard by

---

254. As R. Y.H. Henkin states in the Hebrew newspaper *Hatzofeh* on 23 *Iyyar* 5764, May 14, 2004, one cannot present a majority view. Each community will follow its own practice and different customs will exist.

הטענה המושמעת מדי פעם שרוב הפוסקים אוסרים אמירת קדיש על ידי אישה, אינה בדוקה וגם אינה רלוונטית. אין מנגנון לקבוע מי הם רוב הפוסקים היום, ומה היא דעתם, ואין תוקף לרוב מזדמן שלא במסגרת של מפגש ודיון פנים אל פנים. ולפע״ד היא מעידה על חוסר הבנה בתהליך ההלכתי... השלב החמישי יכיל את תגובות פוסקי היום ומחר לטיעונים הנ״ל, עד להכרעה או הסכמה סופית, או עד שהצבור יכריע בדרך של ״פוק חזי מאי עמא דבר״ וקביעת מנהג. ויתכן גם שקהילות שונות תאמצנה מנהגים שונים, ויש כבר סימנים לכך בשטח.

the male *minyan* in the synagogue, although they stipulate that she should now do so only from the women's section.

8. R. Yosef Eliyahu Henkin is the first to state that a daughter should recite mourner's *kaddish* in conjunction with a male in the synagogue.
9. R. Yehuda H. Henkin, his grandson, states that if a daughter wants to follow those Aḥaronim who are concerned about hearing a woman's singing voice under any circumstances, she should recite mourner's *kaddish* quietly from the women's section in conjunction with a male so that her voice cannot be distinguished by the men.
10. Reciting mourner's *kaddish* quietly may be halakhically problematic for two reasons: if the *minyan* cannot hear her, she may be reciting *kaddish* in the presence of only women or no male *minyan* and, second, if the *minyan* cannot hear and so does not respond to her recitation, it may undermine the entire benefit of *kaddish*. Therefore, some *posekim* state explicitly that she must recite *kaddish* aloud.
11. As in general, *halakhah*, unlike human behavior, does not hold the custom of *kaddish* in such high regard and it is not normative behavior for all daughters to recite *kaddish*, if a daughter feels uncomfortable with reciting *kaddish* and does not desire to do so then she should be encouraged to undertake a different *mitsvah* action for her deceased parent's merit, which will serve the same purpose of benefiting the parent's soul.
12. A number of authorities suggest that communal leaders and rabbis should be sensitive to women's feelings at this emotional time and look to bring them closer to the synagogue and ritual practice. Refusing them the option of reciting mourner's *kaddish* when they sincerely desire to do so may push them away from traditional Judaism.

Defending himself against opponents who wanted to preserve the practices of old, R. Oppenheim (source #14) brings the example of God's own behavior in the *sotah* ritual to endorse the new practice of reciting *kaddish* in unison. In this ritual, God was willing to even erase God's holy name for the sake of peace between people. So, too, for the sake of the peace and comfort of those mourners who would be denied the right to recite *kaddish* if the hierarchy system were still used, R. Oppenheim allows a radical new change in behavior and attitude by permitting all mourners to recite *kaddish* together. His message, modeled on God's actions, speaks to our modern-day situation when more and more women desire to recite *kaddish*.

This chapter was written with the hope that female mourners may find peace for themselves and their beloved parents with the recitation of mourner's *kaddish*. May they find comfort amidst communities and from leaders who are willing to acknowledge and support their desire and right to honor their parents in the model presented by Jewish tradition for generations. May God comfort the mourners of Zion and *Yerushalayim*.

Appendix A

R. MOSHE BLAIR

Dvinsk, Chicago, and Israel (1896–1967)

הרב משה לייב בלייער, שיקאגו
אמירת קדיש ע״י הבת[255]

מי שמת בלי בנים ויש לו בת אם היא מחייבת לאמר קדיש?

מצד השכל הישר אנו צריכים לאמר שהבת מחויבת לאמר קדיש כיון שחלים עליה כל דיני אבלות ואנו נוהגים שהקדיש הוא פרט של אבילות. א״כ מדוע לא חל עליה הדין של קדיש?

שנית - הטעמים שהיתומים אומרים קדיש הם: א) כי יש נחת רוח לנפש המת; ב) כשהבן מתפלל ומקדיש ברבים הוא פודה את אביו ואמו מן הגיהנום; ג) בשעה שהיתומים אומרים קדיש מרחמים עליו כי יצא ממנו זרע שמקדש שם שמים - ע׳ יו״ד ס׳ שע״ו הרמ״א ע׳ אליהו זוטא במנהגים חות יאיר ס׳ מ״ח. ילפי טעמים הנ״ל מדוע אין הבת מחוייבת בקדיש, היא בודאי מחוייבת לקדש שם שמים ולפדות את ההורים מן הגיהנום, וגם עליה לעשות נחת־רוח לנפש המת.

שלישית - בקדיש אין דברי אבלות והיא רק תפלה, ונשים חייבות בתפילה כמו אנשים - זה לשון המשנה. ופסק של הרמב״ם בהלכות תפילה - אף

255. Responsum published independently in Chicago circa 1955. Received from his granddaughter, Aviva Cayam.

ששחרית, מנחה ומעריב הן תפלות שהזמן גרמא מ"מ נשים חייבות כמו אנשים כי תפלה היא בקשת רחמים ע' או"ח פ' ק"ו מ' ק"א במשנה ברורה. אמת, המשנה והרמב"ם והא"ח מדברים אודות חיוב תפילה דאורייתא או דרבנן והקדיש אינו מתפילות הנ"ל. מ"מ כיון שנתקבל כבר בהרבה דורות המנהג לאמר תפילת קדיש לאבל מדוע תהיינה נשים פטורות? ובפרט במקום שאין בנים.

ועתה לדינא. נזכר בשם ר' אלחנן ב"ר מתתיה הובא בב"י וגם נזכר באוצר ישראל "קדיש" כרך ט' עמוד 115 ח"ל אם מת בלי בן או בת אז נהגו לשכור קדיש. אם כן אנו רואים מזה שגם על הבת חיוב הקדיש. ועוד אנו מוצאים שנזכר בחות יאיר שבאמשטרדאם נפטר אחד וצוה שילמדו עשרה אנשים בביתו תוך י"ב חודש ואחרי הלימוד תאמר הבת קדיש עליו, וחכמי העיר ופרנסיה לא מחו בדבר.

וע' בפתחי תשובה יו"ד שע"ו ס"ק ג שהוא ג"כ מבי[א] את החות יאיר בלשון אחרת ואומר שמדינא יש לה לאמר קדיש שגם בבת יש תועלת ונחת רוח לנפש ע"ש.

ד"ר די סולה פול בספרו על קדיש עמוד ק"ז מביא שנתנו רשות לבנות לאמר קדיש במקום שאין בנים.

ובכלל קשה לי על האחרונים ורבני זמננו. מנין להם שזה שאומרים הראשונים והאחרונים כמו הרמ"א ועוד שהבן אומר קדיש הוא בן דוקא ולא בת, כי בכל דיני תורה אנו אומרים שבמלה בן נכללת גם הבת - למשל "ולבני לוי נתתי את מעשר בני ישראל לנחלה." והרמב"ם בהלכות מעשר פ"א הל' א' "המעשר הזה ללוים זכרים ונקבות" ע"ש (ידוע לי המ"מ ולא קשה כלל. ע' בספרי פני משה מה שענה לי ע"ז הגאון ר' איצעלע מפאניוועז.) למשל אצל התענית של יום כפור רב נחמן אמר בן תשע בן עשר מחנכים אותו לשעות ע' ביומא דף פב. ושם בודאי כלל גם את הבת ע"ש בראש"י. וא"כ מדוע אנו פוסקים אצל קדיש יתום כזה שנאמר בהלכה בן הוא בן דוקא ע' בשדה חמ"ד מער' ב סק' וז"ל "בנים" כולל זכרים ונקבות וכו' דהא דאמרינן בנים ולא בנות היינו דוקא היכא דמיותר מלת בן לגמרי, אבל היכא דלא מייתר לא ממעטינן בנות דהן בכלל בנים ע"ש וגם זה לשון של הרב תוספות יום־טוב בנות נמי נכללות במלת בנים ע"ש.

במשמרת שלום אבלות ק' כתב שחתנו של המת הוא כמו בן לאמירת קדיש, אבל שאלתנו היא מה אם הבת אינה נשואה, ושנית מה אם לחתנו יש הורים ומנהגנו שאין אנו אומרים קדיש יתום במקום שיש הורים. ושלישית

הוא מדבר בדין קדימה או זכות במקום שיש הרבה קדישים, אבל הזכות הזאת היא באה מצד אשתו - שהיא הבת ועליה החיוב באמת.

רצוני פה להביא את החות יאיר בלשונו ולבארו, כי הוא מתנגד לאמירת קדיש לבת. הוא מביא את המעשה באמשטרדאם שהבאתי למעלה וז"ל "כי גם אשה מצוות על קדוש השם וכו' ואף כי ממעשה דר"ע שממנו מקור לאמירת קדיש ביתומים זכר היה (לא מובן לי שזכר דוקא-מפני שקרה בבן) מ"מ יש סברה דגם בבת יש תועלת ונחת רוח לנפש כי זרעו הוא". א"כ מזה אנו רואים שגם הוא מסכים שיש חובה של קדיש בבת. אבל בסוף הוא כתב וז"ל "מ"מ יש לחוש שע"י כך יחלשו כח המנהגים של בני ישראל שג"כ תורה הם ויהיה כל אחד בונה במה לעצמו עפ"י סברתו ומחזי מילי דרבנן כחוכא וטלולא ויבואו לזלזל בו" עכ"ל. דבריו האחרונים של החות יאיר צריכין באור. הוא מדבר שהאב צוה שילמדו עשרה אנשים תורה בביתו י"ב חודש ואח"כ תאמר הבת קדיש. זה הוא באמת בונה במה לעצמו ומבטל מנהג ישראל, כי גם בב"כ רק אנשים אומרים קדיש אחר הלמוד ולא נשים - אבל הוא אינו מדבר אודות הקדיש של הי"א חודש שהאשה אומרת בעזרת נשים או אפילו בעת שבעה בביתה כשמתפללים עשרה אנשים. על זה בודאי לא שייך לומר ומחזי מילא דרבנן כחוכא וטלולא. הנה כבר אנו רואים בזמננו בב"כ ארטודוקסיים שנשים עומדות אחרי עלינו וה"סיום", ואומרות קדיש ואין אנו מזלזלים באמירתן. אדרבה, אנו מביטים על זה בכבוד ולא ח"ו בזלזול. מדוע יעלה על דעת איזה רב לפסוק לשכר איש קל המוכן לפרעניות לאמר קדיש בעד בת במקום שאין בן! וטוב הדגיש הרב גרינוואלד בספרו "כל בו על אבלות" שכתב שם "נוהגים קלות ראש בזמננו, שוכרים איש עתי המוכן לפרעניות האומר קדיש אחרי תריסר יאהרצייטן ואחרי תריסר נפטרים וכו' ולא ידעו ולא יבינו כי הקדיש בשעה שיש בן ובכחו לאמר, ואינו אומר, אינה שוה אף פרוטה, אפילו אם אומרים אותו בירושלים או בחברון" עכ"ל. ובודאי הקלת ראש כזה בודאי שייך גם בבת, כיון שהיא חייבת מצד הדין, והיא יכלה לבוא לבה"כ לאמר א"כ לדעתי הקטנה על כל רבני זמננו לבאר לבת באבלות במקום שאין בן שעליה יש החיוב לבא בעזרת נשים ולאמר קדיש ולא לשכור קדיש.

ואין בדעתי להחמיר באבלות דבת. רק להעמיד על דיננו שהבת מחייבת לאמר קדיש. אדרבה, לדעתי זו היא קולה, ובאבלות אנו פוסקים כדבר המיקל - אף ביחיד נגד הרבים (ע' שדי חמד מער' ה' סק' קי"ת).

וגם אם לא תהיינה עשר נשים בעזרת נשים לענות אמן, ג"כ אינו מעכב - כי

לדינא כל הקדשים צריכין לאמר קדיש כל מלה ומלה ביחד א"כ האמן שאומרים האנשים חל גם על הקדיש שלה.

וזה שאנו אומרים שהמנהג מבטל הלכה, זה הוא רק שהוא תקנת הצבור ואין אנו מוצאים שאיזה צבור עשה תקנה שהבת במקום שאין בן לא תאמר קדיש (ע' מהרשד"ם ס' צו על א"ד).

חפצתי להדגיש פה לרבנו ארצנו שיצאו למחות נגד פסק הלכה כזה, כי בזמן הגאונים כשהתחיל המנהג לאמר קדיש יתום, יצאו הרבה גדולי ישראל בהתנגדות לזה כמו רב האי גאון ועוד. ומה אנו רואים עתה? שהקדיש נכלל בכלל אבלות וחשוב לה כמו מצוה דאורייתא. הקדיש הביא הרבה בני ישראל לבה"כ וקרב אותם ליהדות, וככה יקרה גם לבנות ישראל, אנו נקרב אותן ליהדות ולתורתנו הקדושה.

Appendix B

HENRIETTA SZOLD

United States and Israel (1860–1945)
Marvin Lowenthal, *Henrietta Szold: Life and Letters* (New York: Viking Press, 1942), 92–93

[To Haym Peretz]
New York, September 16, 1916
It is impossible for me to find words in which to tell you how deeply I was touched by your offer to act as "*kaddish*" for my dear mother. I cannot even thank you – it is something that goes beyond thanks. It is beautiful, what you have offered to do – I shall never forget it.

You will wonder, then, that I cannot accept your offer. Perhaps it would be best for me not to try to explain to you in writing, but to wait until I see you to tell you why it is so. I know well, and appreciate what you say about, the Jewish custom; and Jewish custom is very dear and sacred to me. And yet I cannot ask you to say *kaddish* after my mother. The *kaddish* means to me that the survivor publicly and markedly manifests his wish and intention to assume the relation to the Jewish community which his parent had, and that so the chain of tradition remains unbroken from generation to generation, each adding its own link. You can do that for the generations of your family, I must do that for the generations of my family.

I believe that the elimination of women from such duties was never intended by our law and custom – women were freed from positive duties when they could not perform them (because of family responsibilities) but not when they could. It was never intended that, if they could perform them, their performance of them should not be considered as valuable and valid as when one of the male sex performed them. And of the *kaddish* I feel sure this is particularly true.

My mother had eight daughters and no son; and yet never did I hear a word of regret pass the lips of either my mother or my father that one was not a son. When my father died, my mother would not permit others to take her daughters' place in saying the *kaddish,* and so I am sure I am acting in her spirit when I am moved to decline your offer. But beautiful your offer remains nevertheless, and, I repeat, I know full well that it is much more in consonance with the generally accepted Jewish tradition than is my family's conception. You understand me, don't you?

Giving Thanks: Women and *Birkat Hagomel*

Jennie Rosenfeld

INTRODUCTION[1]

The desire to give thanks to God upon being saved from danger is codified by the Talmud into a blessing known as *birkat hagomel,* the blessing of [God's] bestowing [kindness]. *Birkat hagomel* is generally recited publicly at the time of Torah reading,[2] with the entire community responding. Intuitively it makes sense that the requirement to give thanks to God should not be limited based on gender, and many of the earliest sources do not directly discuss women's recitation of the blessing. The explicit question of whether women are obligated to recite *birkat hagomel* only first emerges in the late fifteenth century in the context of whether a man may recite the blessing on his wife's behalf. An examination of the halakhic literature on women's obligation to recite *birkat hagomel* will address the following questions:

- What is the nature of the obligation to recite *birkat hagomel*?
- Who is required to recite *birkat hagomel*? Is a *yoledet* (postpartum woman) required to recite the blessing?
- How intrinsic to the requirement is the presence of a *minyan* (quorum of ten)? Can women be included in the *minyan* for *birkat hagomel*?
- If a person has not experienced a personal salvation, can they still recite *birkat hagomel* on behalf of someone else? Specifically, can a husband recite the blessing on behalf of his wife?

1. My heartfelt thanks to R. Dina Najman, who offered sage halakhic advice and several key sources throughout the writing process, going beyond the call of duty in her generosity to me. This piece was written in 2010 and appears here unaltered.
2. *Tosafot* to B.T. *Ber.* 54b, s.v. *ve'ema,* mentions the custom of the individual reciting *hagomel* after reading from the Torah. It seems likely that this custom developed due to the fact that one is ensured of having a *minyan* present at that time. See *Orḥot Ḥayyim, Hilkh. Sheni Vaḥamishi* 25 (also quoted in *Beit Yosef, O.Ḥ.* 219:3, s.v. *katuv be'orḥot ḥayyim; Sefer Haminhagim, Haggahot, Minhag Shel Shabbat;* and *Sh. Ar., O.Ḥ.* 219:3). *Sefer Pekudat Halviyyim* to B.T. *Ber.* 54b offers two different explanations for the custom to recite *birkat hagomel* at the Torah reading.

TANAKH

While the formal requirement to give thanks to God upon being saved from specific evils emerges from the Talmud, the roots of the general obligation to give thanks to God in certain circumstances can be traced to the Torah itself. The *korban todah* (thanksgiving offering), is described in Leviticus:[3]

1. Leviticus 22:29–30	**ויקרא כב:כט-ל**
And when you sacrifice a thanksgiving offering to God, you should offer it when you want to.[4] It may be eaten on that day, you may not leave over from it until morning; I am God.	וכי תזבחו זבח תודה, לי·הוה לרצנכם, תזבחו. ביום ההוא יאכל, לא תותירו ממנו עד בקר: אני, י·הוה.

A specific comparison between *birkat hagomel* and the *korban todah* emerges in medieval biblical commentaries,[5] as well as in commentaries to the Mishnah[6] and other halakhic works.[7] The Talmud itself,

---

3. See also Lev. 7:12–15.
4. The word לרצונכם can also be translated as "to please God." However, the translation in the text above would seem to indicate that the thanksgiving offering is not obligatory, since its very nature is as a spontaneous expression of thanks. This understanding could have ramifications as to how to view *birkat hagomel,* as well, depending on the extent to which the laws of *birkat hagomel* mirror those of the thanksgiving offering.
5. See Rashbam to Lev. 7:12, s.v. *im,* who makes explicit reference to the Talmudic discussion of *birkat hagomel* in his explanation of the *korban todah.* Rashbam sees the two as analogous. See also Rashi and Alshikh, ad loc., and *Ba'al Haturim* to Exod. 8:4, s.v. *vayizbeḥu.*
6. In his commentary to M. *Ned.* 1:4, s.v. *ha'omer,* R. Ovadiah Mibartenura writes that the *korban todah* (which one might think is optional) is like an obligatory sacrifice (such as an *olah* or *ḥattat*) because Rav says that four types of people *must* give praise.
7. See *Maḥzor Vitry, Hilkh. Pesaḥ* 53, pp. 254–310, s.v. *vehashalosh matsot* where he compares the *matsot* to *laḥamei todah.* See also the discussion of this matter by R. Aharon Lichtenstein in "*Birkat Ha-gomel* (II)" (http://vbm-torah.org/archive/halak66/26halak.htm) and the related discussion by R. Ya'ir Kahan in "*Birkat Ha-gomel*" (*Daf Kesher* 85:1, pp. 345–48; www.vbm-torah.org/archive/halak58/22gomel.doc).

however, bases some of the details of the obligation to recite *birkat hagomel* on Psalms 107, which discusses various situations in which one is called upon to praise God and give thanks.[8]

2. Psalms 107:1–32	**תהלים קז:א-לב**
"Give thanks to God for His kindness is everlasting" – [thus] will say those whom God redeemed...	הדו לי·הוה כי טוב כי לעולם חסדו יאמרו גאולי י·הוה...
Those who wandered in the wilderness of the desert and did not find the route to a city of habitation.... Let them praise God for His kindness and for the miracles which He does for people....	תעו במדבר בישימון דרך עיר מושב לא מצאו... יודו לי·הוה חסדו ונפלאותיו לבני אדם...
Those who sit in darkness in the shadow of death, who are tied up in chains and afflicted.... Let them praise God for His kindness and for the miracles which He does for people....	ישבי חשך וצלמות אסירי עני וברזל... יודו לי·הוה חסדו ונפלאותיו לבני אדם...
The foolish ones because of their transgression and those who suffer from their sins [through illness].... Let them praise God for His kindness and for the miracles which He does for people....	אולים מדרך פשעם ומעונתיהם יתענו... יודו לי·הוה חסדו ונפלאותיו לבני אדם...
Those who enter the sea in boats and who labor in the deep waters.... Let them praise God for His kindness and for the miracles which He does for people. And they should exalt Him in an assembly of people and in the seat of elders they shall praise Him.	יורדי הים באניות עשי מלאכה במים רבים... יודו לי·הוה חסדו ונפלאותיו לבני אדם וירממוהו בקהל עם ובמושב זקנים יהללוהו:

8. *Levush, O.Ḥ.* 219:1 states that it is King David who commands (*tsivvah*) the requirement to give thanks to God by reciting *hagomel.*

It is important to note with regard to both the thanksgiving offering mentioned in the Torah and those people who appear in Psalms 107 that no distinction is made on the basis of gender. It would seem that a simple reading of these texts assumes that women as well as men would call out to God in praise and thanks when encountering the kindness of their creator.

TALMUD

The formal requirement to recite *birkat hagomel* is first found in the Babylonian Talmud, at the beginning of the ninth chapter of Tractate *Berakhot* in the context of the *birkhot hare'iyyah* (blessings of seeing), which are recited upon seeing various miraculous or unusual things or the sites of personal or national miracles and special events.[9] *Birkhot hare'iyyah* are part of the broader category of blessings known as *birkhot hahoda'ah* (blessings of thanksgiving).[10] A number of different topics are raised in the Talmudic text, through the different historical layers of the discussion. In the earliest stratum of the text, Rav Yehudah in the name of Rav discusses who is obligated, what the text of the *berakhah* should be, and whether someone can say the *berakhah* on behalf of another. A later issue raised by Abbaye, and placed in the middle of the flow of the text, is whether a *minyan* is obligatory, and later, the issue of whether two additional rabbis are required (and whether they are included in or above and beyond the *minyan*) is raised.

3. Babylonian Talmud *Berakhot 54b*	**תלמוד בבלי מסכת ברכות נד:**
Rav Yehudah said in the name of Rav: Four [types of people] must give thanks: those who	אמר רב יהודה אמר רב: ארבעה צריכין להודות -

9. A few *posekim* actually understand this blessing to be voluntary rather than obligatory. See Ra'avad, *Torat Ha'adam,* Medicine, p. 49, and in his gloss on Rif to B.T. *Ber.* 44a, and the suggestion of *Magen Avraham* in source #17, below.
10. While the relationship between *birkhot hare'iyyah* and *birkhot hahoda'ah* is relevant to the broader discussion of *birkat hagomel,* such discussion is beyond the purview of this chapter.

travel at sea; those who walk in the deserts; and the one who was ill and became healed; and the one who was imprisoned in jail and came out....

יורדי הים, הולכי מדברות, ומי שהיה חולה ונתרפא, ומי שהיה חבוש בבית האסורים ויצא....

What blessing does he recite? Rav Yehudah said: Blessed is He who bestows good kindnesses.[11] Abbaye said: And he must give thanks in front of ten [people], as it says (Psalms 107:32), "And they should exalt Him in an assembly of people, etc."

מאי מברך? אמר רב יהודה: ברוך גומל חסדים טובים. אביי אמר: וצריך לאודויי קמי עשרה, דכתיב: (תהלים ק"ז) וירוממוהו בקהל עם וגו'.

Mar Zutra said: And two of them must be rabbis, as it says (Psalms 107:32), "And in the seat of elders they shall praise Him."

מר זוטרא אמר: ותרין מינייהו רבנן, שנאמר: (תהלים ק"ז) ובמושב זקנים יהללוהו.

R. Ashi challenged him: Then say that they must all be rabbis! But is it written in an "assembly of elders"? An "assembly of people" is written. Then say [that we require] ten regular people and [an additional] two rabbis. This remains a difficulty.

מתקיף לה רב אשי: ואימא כולהו רבנן! - מי כתיב בקהל זקנים? בקהל עם כתיב. - ואימא: בי עשרה שאר עמא, ותרי רבנן! - קשיא.

Rav Yehudah was ill and was healed. Rav Ḥana Bagdatta'ah [of Baghdad] and the rabbis came to visit him. They said to him: Blessed is the Merciful One who has given you to us and has

רב יהודה חלש ואתפח, על לגביה רב חנא בגדתאה ורבנן, אמרי ליה: בריך רחמנא דיהבך

11. Most manuscripts contain two textual variant in the form of the blessing: they substitute the word חייבים for חסדים and add an ending which personalizes the blessing. Their formula is: ברוך גומל לחייבים טובות שגמלנו כל טוב, "Blessed is the one who bestows good upon the guilty, who has bestowed upon us all good"; see Ms. Oxford Bodleian Library, cat. no. 366. The formula is very similar in Ms. Cambridge T-S F1 (1) 41 and Ms. Paris Bibliothéque Nationale, Héb. 671; Ms. Munich retains חסדים but adds the ending found in the other manuscripts. This formula is also used by many of the Rishonim.

not given you to the dust. He said to them: You have exempted me from [my obligation to] give thanks. But did not Abbaye say that one is required to give thanks in the presence of ten? They were a group of ten. But he [Rav Yehudah] did not give thanks. This is unnecessary, as he responded "Amen" after [their blessing].	ניהלן ולא יהבך לעפרא. אמר להו: פטרתון יתי מלאודויי. והא אמר אביי: בעי אודויי באפי עשרה! - דהוו בי עשרה. והא איהו לא קא מודה! - לא צריך, דעני בתרייהו אמן.

Rav defined four specific categories of people who are required to give thanks to God: one who has traveled the sea; one who has traversed the desert; one who was ill and has recovered; and one who was imprisoned and then freed. All of these were presumably life-threatening situations during that time. Rav Yehudah then codifies the wording of the blessing, which is recited as a means of giving thanks. The text also contains the requirement that *birkat hagomel* be recited communally; this requirement is first introduced by Abbaye, several generations after the original obligation appears. While Abbaye's position that a quorum of ten is required for the recitation of the blessing is undisputed in the Talmud, the further requirement of two rabbis or elders remains unclear – can the two rabbis be part of the *minyan*, or must they be in addition to it?[12] This question is raised by the Talmudic editors and left unanswered.[13]

12. The text does not explain why this blessing should specifically require two rabbis. R. Ya'ir Kahan in his article (see n6, above) suggests that this rule and the fact that subsequent *posekim* allow the blessing to be recited in front of women attest to the point that this quorum does not function in the manner that a normal prayer *minyan* does.

13. The Talmud uses the term קשיא (it is difficult), marking this question as unanswered (איבעיא דלא איפשיטא), which typically leads one to adopt the more stringent of two possible halakhic positions. Here, however, there is debate as to which position is actually the more stringent one and further debate about whether to rule stringently even though this blessing is rabbinic in nature. Some require twelve as the more stringent position (see, for example, Rosh to B.T. *Ber.* 9:3); others adopt the lenient position, requiring only a *minyan* which includes two rabbis (see, for example, Rif to B.T. *Ber.* 43a); others mention only the requirement of a *minyan*, without any mention of two rabbis (*Sefer Halakhot Gedolot* 1, *Hilkh. Berakhot*, p. 88); while still others argue that two rabbis are ideal but not essential (see, for example, *Sefer Mitsvot Gadol, Asin* 27, *Birkat Hahoda'ah*).

The Talmud recounts an actual story of Rav Yehudah himself, recovering from illness and fulfilling the obligatory recitation by answering "Amen"[14] to his colleagues' blessing.[15] Just as with the text in the Torah concerning the thanksgiving offering, the text of the Talmud which introduces the obligation of *birkat hagomel* does not distinguish between the genders. Clearly a woman who had experienced one of these life-threatening scenarios would be required to recognize God's hand in her salvation and thank God for her survival.

RISHONIM

One of the only Rishonim to mention women explicitly in connection to *birkat hagomel* is R. Eliezer of Worms (Roke'aḥ) in his commentary to the *siddur*. He writes on the Shabbat morning service:

4. ***Perushei Siddur Hatefillah Laroke'aḥ [9] lefikhakh anu ḥayyavim, p. 20***

פירושי סידור התפילה לרוקח [ט] לפיכך אנו חייבים, עמוד כ

R. Eliezer of Worms (Roke'aḥ), Germany (1165–1240)

Therefore we are obligated to give thanks to You for the great good by which You have benefited us. Thanks is appropriate to say in a place where much good was effected, such as, "Now I will thank God" (Gen. 29:35) who gave me four sons. When He gave me three, this was the appropriate number for each of the four matriarchs to bear; when He gave me an additional son, I will give thanks. Therefore, "Four [types of people] must give thanks" that He did good for them.

לפיכך אנחנו חייבין להודות לך על רוב טובה שהנאתנו. הודאה שייך לומר במקום שהשפיע רוב טובה. כמו: הפעם אודה את ה', שנתן לי ד' בנים, כשנתן לי ג' כך היה לד' אמהות לכל אחת להוליד, ונתן לי בן יותר אודה. על כן ארבעה צריכין להודות, שמטיב להם.

14. When an individual says "Amen" to a blessing it is as if he or she has personally recited the entire blessing.
15. The question of whether another person may recite the blessing on behalf of the individual who has been saved will be discussed below.

In what is perhaps the earliest association between *birkat hagomel* and childbirth, an event not mentioned in either Psalms or the Talmud as a time to thank God, Roke'aḥ links the foremother Leah's statement הפעם אודה את ה', "Now I will thank God," after the birth of Yehudah, with the Talmud's four categories of people who must give thanks in the form of *birkat hagomel*. Roke'aḥ speaks of *birkat hagomel* only as a response to the many good things which God has done for us, without any mention of sin and suffering.[16] Indeed, his paradigmatic example of that joyous calling out to thank and acknowledge God is a woman who, after a healthy and successful labor and childbirth, experiences the gift of a child. Clearly Roke'aḥ sees no distinction between men and women when it comes to the obligation to recite the *hagomel* blessing.

Although *Sefer Haḥinnukh* does not directly mention the codified blessing of *hagomel*, he writes in his description of the commandment for the *yoledet* to bring a sacrifice after childbirth, that she should give thanks to God.

5. *Sefer Haḥinnukh, Commandment #168* **ספר החינוך מצוה קסח**

"The Levite of Barcelona,"[17] Catalonia (thirteenth century)

...from the essence of the commandment, so that she should be roused by the action to give thanks to God, blessed is He, who saved her from the pangs of childbirth, which is a miraculous occurrence.	...משרשי המצוה, כדי שתתעורר מתוך הפעולה לתת הודאה לי·הוה ברוך הוא שהצילה מחבלי יולדה, שהוא דבר נס.

16. It is perhaps not accidental that the unilaterally positive way in which Roke'aḥ writes about *birkat hagomel* is mirrored in the *nusaḥ* (formula) that he cites for this blessing elsewhere: ברוך גומל חסדים טובים (*Sefer Haroke'aḥ, Hilkh. Berakhot* 343). This version of the blessing, which is found in the printed Talmud but not cited by any other halakhic source, focuses only on the positive good which God has bestowed, without the phrase לחייבים (to the guilty ones), or any mention of the iniquity which brought the person into hardship.
17. So states the introduction to the book. The author's identity is disputed by scholars. He is most likely from the school of Ramban, possibly a student of Rashba.

The experience of offering a sacrifice to God should connect the postpartum woman with the need to acknowledge God's hand in her salvation.

Apart from these two outside references, in the discussions of the Rishonim, which appear directly on the Talmudic passage discussing *birkat hagomel,* women are not singled out in any way, nor even mentioned. How should this silence be understood? One possible reading is that women's obligation is assumed by the Rishonim, though not explicitly stated. They simply felt that there was no need to address women specifically, for the general law applied to all.[18] This view, that women are naturally obligated in *birkat hagomel,* is the prevalent understanding in many of the sources to follow.[19] Alternately, one could possibly learn from this silence that women are not required to recite the blessing of thanksgiving.[20]

Before directly analyzing the texts which explicitly address women's participation in the ritual of *hagomel,* a review of several other Rishonim and the major codes will draw out a number of essential legal issues, following from the text of the Talmud. These issues will have direct and indirect ramifications for the question of women and *birkat hagomel,* such as whether the requirement for a *minyan* is essential to the recitation of the blessing and whether another person may

18. See n32, below, for those who read R. Caro's silence in this manner.
19. See, for example, below, sources #14, 16, 19, 21, 22, 23, 25, 26, and 29.
20. R. Yehuda Henkin in chapter 8 of his book, *Responsa on Contemporary Jewish Women's Issues* (Jersey City, N.J.: Ktav Publishing, 2003), "Women and Birkat haGomel," 53–60, argues that the Rishonim's silence with regard to women implies that they are exempt. He acknowledges that with regard to all other blessing they are also silent, yet in those cases women are obligated. However, he believes that the difficulty maneuvering the need for a *minyan* with *hagomel* requires a specific mention and discussion, and that the absence of such a discussion implies the Rishonim's belief in women's exemption. This is a difficult argument to support, as the very nature of the meaning of the word *patur,* "exempt," implies that someone would have originally been obligated and has specifically been exempted. The working assumption should be that all Jews are obligated in *mitsvot,* unless there exists an explicit statement exempting them. R. Henkin's belief that *hagomel* is voluntary for women leads him to conclude that they may recite it in the presence of only women. See below, sources #15 and 17, which also indicate that women are not obligated in *birkat hagomel.*

recite the blessing on behalf of the individual who actually experienced God's salvation.

CODES

Rambam discusses the laws of *birkat hagomel* in just one brief paragraph.

6. *Mishneh Torah*
Laws of Blessings 10:8

משנה תורה הלכות ברכות
פרק י הלכה ח

R. Moshe ben Maimon (Rambam), Spain and Egypt (1135–1204)

Four [types of people] must give thanks: one who was ill and became healed; a prisoner who has come out of prison; those who travel at sea, when they come up [onto land]; and travelers when they reach habitation. And they must give thanks in front of ten, two of whom are sages, as it says, "And they should exalt Him in an assembly of people and in the seat of elders they shall praise Him" [Psalms 107:32]. And how does he give thanks and how does he recite the blessing? He stands among them and recites, "Blessed are You, God, our Lord, Master of the Universe, who bestows good upon the guilty, [and] who has given me only good." And all those who hear [the blessing] respond, "[The one] who has bestowed good upon you, He should bestow [more good], *selah*."

ארבעה צריכין להודות, חולה שנתרפא, וחבוש שיצא מבית האסורים, ויורדי הים כשעלו, והולכי דרכים כשיגיעו לישוב, וצריכין להודות בפני עשרה ושנים מהם חכמים שנאמר וירוממוהו בקהל עם ובמושב זקנים יהללוהו, וכיצד מודה וכיצד מברך, עומד ביניהן ומברך, ברוך אתה יי׳ אלהינו מלך העולם הגומל לחייבים טובות שגמלני כל טוב, וכל השומעין אומרים שגמלך טוב הוא יגמלך סלה.

Rambam does not mention anything about women's obligation explicitly; however, it seems clear that he assumes women are included in this description of the four individuals who must thank God. For, if he wanted to exempt them he would have stated this clearly, as he does with numerous other *mitsvot.*[21] Nevertheless, for the purpose of the ensuing discussion of women's obligation in *birkat hagomel,* there are two significant points to note in Rambam. The first is that Rambam rules leniently on how many people must be included in the community of listeners (ten *including* the two Torah scholars, rather than ten *in addition to* the two sages), a point which the Talmud had left unresolved. While Rambam states that one must ("*tserikhin*") recite the blessing in front of a *minyan,* he does not clarify what happens when that is not possible: may one still recite the blessing in this less than optimal circumstance, or is it prohibited to do so? The second point to note is that the Talmudic story of Rav Yehudah and Rav Ḥana, which permits a person to fulfill obligation through someone else who recites *birkat hagomel* on their behalf, is entirely absent from Rambam.[22] Despite the fact that this story is quoted as *halakhah* by most Rishonim,[23] Rambam presumably feels that the declaration of thanks and gratitude to God can only truly be expressed by the individual who experienced salvation firsthand and not by another, who did not themselves live through it.

Rabbenu Yonah addresses the question of whether the presence of a *minyan* is essential (*me'akkev*) or only the ideal way (*lekhatḥillah*) of performing the *mitsvah* of reciting *birkat hagomel.*

7. *Talmidei Rabbenu Yonah on Rif Berakhot 43a, s.v. amar lehu*

תלמידי רבינו יונה על הרי"ף מסכת ברכות מג. ד"ה אמר להו

Students of R. Yonah ben Avraham of Gerona, Spain (d. 1263)

We learn from there [from the story of Rav Yehudah and the question and answer of the Talmud there] that if there are ten present and they recite this blessing and the

למדנו משם שאם יש שם עשרה וברכו ברכה זו וענה החולה אמן אין צריך לברך ברכה אחרת ואם אין שם י' צריך לברך.

21. See for example *Hilkh. Tsitsit* 3:9; *Hilkh. Talmud Torah* 1:1.

22. See Ḥafets Ḥayyim, *Be'ur Halakhah* 219, s.v. *ve'ein zeh,* who notes this fact.

23. See, for example: *Sefer Halakhot Gedolot* 1, *Hilkh. Berakhot,* p. 88; Rif to B.T. *Ber.* 43a; Ra'avan to B.T. *Ber.* 197; *Roke'aḥ, Hilkh. Berakhot* 343 (cont'd); *Torat Ha'adam, Sha'ar Hasof, Inyan Harefuah* 8; Rosh to B.T. *Ber.* 9:3.

sick person responds, "Amen," he does not need to recite another blessing. And if there are not ten [men] present, he must recite [*birkat hagomel* again in front of a *minyan*].

Rabbenu Yonah rules that the presence of a *minyan* is essential (*me'akkev*) and that one cannot fulfill one's obligation to recite *birkat hagomel* in its absence.[24] He learns this rule from the story of the rabbis' reciting the blessing on behalf of Rav Yehudah, who responds, "Amen." Unlike Rambam, it seems that Rabbenu Yonah believes that the recitation by another individual, who did not experience the actual event, still fulfills one's duty to give thanks.

However, a more moderate position regarding the need for a *minyan* can be found in the *Tur*'s codification of the law. *Tur*, like Rambam before him, presumably assumes women's obligation in *birkat hagomel*, as he does not explicitly mention them; however, he does weigh in on the surrounding issues.

8. *Tur*
Oraḥ Ḥayyim 219:3
R. Ya'akov ben Asher, Spain (ca. 1269–1343)

טור אורח חיים
סימן ריט סעיף ג

And if he recited [*birkat hagomel*] even with less than ten, he does not need to repeat the blessing again. For the language [of the Talmud], "And he must (*tsarikh*) give thanks in front of ten," means specifically as the ideal way [of performing the *mitsvah*].

ואם בירך אפילו בפחות מי' א"צ [אינו צריך] לחזור ולברך דלישנא וצריך לאודויי באנפי י' משמע דוקא לכתחלה.

24. Me'iri, *Beit Habeḥirah* to B.T. *Ber.* 54b, s.v. *arba'ah,* also writes that a *minyan* is needed and that the blessing may not be recited in its absence. Rabbenu Ḥananel is also quoted in agreement with this position (*Responsa Tashbets* 4:1 [*ḥut hameshullash*], *siman* 4, s.v. *teshuvah beni*).

Unlike Rabbenu Yonah, *Tur* learns from the language of the Talmud that a *minyan* is ideal (*lekhatḥillah*),[25] but not essential.[26] He then goes on to cite the Talmudic story of Rav Yehudah and Rav Ḥana Bagdatta'ah and explicitly permits one who has not experienced personal salvation to recite *birkat hagomel* on behalf of someone else.

9. *Tur*
***Oraḥ Ḥayyim* 219:4–5**
R. Ya'akov ben Asher, Spain (ca. 1269–1343)

טור אורח חיים
סימן ריט סעיף ד-ה

And if someone else blessed and recited, "Blessed are you God, our Lord, Master of the Universe, who has bestowed upon you all good," and he [the one obligated] responded, "Amen," he has fulfilled his obligation [as per the story of Rav Yehudah and Rav Ḥana] .... And it is not considered a blessing in vain, though they are not obligated to recite it, since they are giving praise and thanks to the Lord, as is the way of those who praise the Lord on the good that He has given them.

ואם בירך אחר ואמר בא"י אמ"ה [ברוך אתה י"י אלהינו מלך העולם] אשר גמלך כל טוב וענה אמן יצא.... ולא חשיב ברכה לבטלה כיון שהם לא נתחייבו בה שהם נתנו שבח והודאה למקום כדרך בני אדם שמשבחים למקום על הטובה שמזמין להם.

Tur extrapolates from the story of Rav Yehudah and Rav Ḥana that anyone, not just a student on behalf of one's teacher, can recite *birkat hagomel* on behalf of another, and he explains why he believes that

25. Commentators to *Tur* debate *Tur's* definition of the word *tsarikh*. See, for example, *Baḥ, O.Ḥ.* 219:2 and *Perishah, O.Ḥ.* 219:5, who defend *Tur* on this point, whereas *Beit Yosef, O.Ḥ.* 219:3 argues that "the language of *tsarikh* means that it is *me'akkev* [essential]." *Taz, O.Ḥ.* 219:1, agrees as well, pointing out that the original requirement stated in the Talmud also uses the word *tsarikh*. He argues that it would be ridiculous to say that the Talmud was only referring to a *lekhatḥillah* situation, as one who has not yet blessed has surely not fulfilled their obligation. See *Sh. Ar., O.Ḥ.* 219:3, who in the end gives more credence to *Tur*.

26. See also *Arukh*, quoted in *Shittah Mekubbetset* to B.T. *Ber.* 54b, s.v. *mar zutra*, and Ra'ah in *Sefer Pekudat Halviyyim* to B.T. *Ber.* 54b.

this practice is legally permitted. Quoting his father, Rosh, *Tur* raises the issue of whether this recitation is a *berakhah levattalah* (blessing in vain, which is forbidden because of the prohibition against taking God's name in vain) since the one reciting the blessing did not experience the salvation themselves, which could make the blessing a misuse of God's name. Rosh claims that there is no concern of *berakhah levattalah*, even when one who is not personally obligated recites *hagomel*, because they are simply giving praise and thanks to God for the divine act done for another, which is permitted to do voluntarily.

Tur does not place any limits on who is permitted to recite *birkat hagomel* on someone else's behalf. R. Yeshayah Ha'aḥaron gives specific examples of people who might choose to say this blessing for another:

10. *Piskei Riaz* | **פסקי ריא"ז**

***Berakhot* 9:1.4** | **ברכות פרק ט, א:ד**

R. Yeshayah ben Eliyah di Trani, Italy (d. ca. 1280)

It would seem to me that if a person wants to give thanks and to recite *birkat hagomel* for his loved one and for his relative for whom he feels pain, he is permitted to do so.

ונראה בעיניי שאם רצה אדם להודות ולברך הגומל על אוהבו ועל קרובו שהוא כואב עליו הרשות בידו.

Riaz states his position unequivocally, making no distinction between father, wife, or other relatives: any loved one can recite *hagomel*. Although he does not address this case explicitly, he is quoted by later halakhists as a source for those who would permit husbands to recite *birkat hagomel* on their wives' behalf.[27]

While both Riaz and *Tur* expand the category of who may recite *birkat hagomel* on behalf of another, R. Yosef Caro, in *Beit Yosef*, is the

27. *Piskei Riaz* here is quoted in *Shiltei Hagibborim* 6, on Rif to B.T. *Ber.* 43a; *Baḥ, O.Ḥ.* 219:3, and *Darkhei Moshe, O.Ḥ.* 219:1.

first to address the specific case of a husband reciting *birkat hagomel* on behalf of his wife.

11. *Beit Yosef, Oraḥ Ḥayyim* 219:4–5 s.v. *ve'im berekh*

בית יוסף אורח חיים סימן ריט אות ד-ה ד"ה ואם בירך

R. Yosef Caro, Spain and Israel (1488–1575)

And from that which our master [*Tur*] wrote: that it is not considered a blessing in vain, that which they recited, even though they were not obligated in it, since they gave praise and thanks to God on the good that He has given them. We can learn with regard to the practice of a few men that when their wives give birth, they [the husbands] stand up and recite *birkat hagomel* that it is not a blessing in vain. For just like Rav Ḥana Bagdatta'ah and the rabbis – even though they were not obligated in this blessing – recited it in order to give praise and thanks to God on the good that He gave them, that R. Yehudah was saved, so too one whose wife gave birth, even though he is not obligated in *birkat hagomel*, he can still recite it in order to give praise and thanks to God on the good that He gave him in saving his wife [from childbirth]. But I found that the Rashba (to B.T. *Ber.* 54b, s.v. *haro'eh*)[28]

וממ"ש [וממה שכתב] רבינו דלא חשיב ברכה לבטלה מה שבירכו הם אע"פ שלא נתחייבו בה שהם נתנו שבח והודאה למקום על הטובה שמזמין להם. יש ללמוד על מה שנוהגים קצת אנשים שכשיולדות נשותיהם עומדים ומברכים ברכת הגומל דלאו ברכה לבטלה היא דכשם דרב חנא בגדתאה ורבנן אע"פ [אף על פי] שלא היו חייבים בברכה זו היו מברכים אותה כדי לתת שבח והודאה למקום על הטובה שהזמין להם שנצול רב יהודה כך מי שילדה אשתו אע"פ [אף על פי] שאינו חייב בברכת הגומל יכול לברך אותה כדי לתת שבח והודאה למקום על הטובה שהזמין לו שניצולה אשתו. אבל מצאתי להרשב"א (נד. ד"ה הרואה) שכתב

28. See *Ḥiddushei Harashba* to B.T. *Ber.* 54a, s.v. *haro'eh*. Rashba here only discusses one's father and teacher and notes that the Babylonian Talmud answers a question here that the Jerusalem Talmud does not. While Riaz is clear about extrapolating from a father and teacher to all loved ones, and *Tur* is clear about extrapolating from a father and teacher to anyone, Rashba is not clear on this point and does not specifically address it. *Baḥ* (below, source #13) reads Rashba differently. See *Eliyah Rabbah* 219:11, who sides with *Beit Yosef*'s reading of Rashba and brings a list of other *posekim* who read Rashba in the same way as *Beit Yosef*.

wrote that even though it is asked in the Jerusalem Talmud (*Ber.* 9:1), what is the law with regard to [reciting a] blessing upon the miracle that happens to one's teacher, and they do not answer it, we can answer it from the story of Rav Ḥana which is found before us in the [Babylonian] Talmud (*Ber.* 54b). It seems that [Rashba] wants to say that Rav Ḥana Bagdatta'ah and the rabbis only blessed upon the healing of Rav Yehudah because he was their teacher. And thus wrote R. Mano'aḥ (*Sefer Hamenuḥah* 10:9).[29] And according to their words, we cannot learn from the story with regard to one who is not his teacher, even though he is as beloved to him as his own body [i.e., his wife], over which he should recite the blessing when he is healed. But nevertheless I found that R. Mano'aḥ wrote (ibid.), "But others do not need [to recite the blessing], and it makes sense that if they have some value in their [the other's] salvation that they would recite the blessing." And with regard to the law, since according to all opinions he is not obligated to recite the blessing, he should not recite the blessing, and if he does, we scold him, for perhaps it is a blessing in vain.

ואע"ג [אף על גב] דבעיא היא בירושלמי (ברכות פ"ט ה"א) מהו לברך אניסא דרביה ולא פשטוה איכא למיפשטה מהא דרב חנא דאיתא לקמן בגמרא (נד:) נראה שדעתו לומר דרב חנא בגדתאה ורבנן לא בריכו על רפואת רב יהודה אלא לפי שהיה רבם וכ"כ [וכך כתב] ה"ר מנוח (ספר המנוחה פ"י ה"ט) ולפי דבריהם אין ללמוד משם למי שאינו רבו אע"פ [אף על פי] שהוא חביב עליו כגופו שיברך על רפואתו. ומ"מ [ומכל מקום] מצאתי לה"ר מנוח שכתב (שם) אבל אחרים אין צריכים ומסתברא דאי אית להו תועלת בהצלתם שמברכין ע"כ [עד כאן] ולענין הלכה כיון דלדברי הכל אינו חייב לברך לא יברך ואם בירך גוערין בו דדילמא ברכה לבטלה היא.

R. Caro reports a custom of "a few men" who recite *birkat hagomel* on their wives' behalf after childbirth. He opens by defending this practice of the husband, and explains that based on the simple reading of the Talmudic story it should not be considered a blessing in vain. R. Caro ulti-

29. The reference in the printed versions is *Sefer Hamenuḥah, Hilkh. Berakhot* 10:8.

mately concludes the opposite, however, basing his opinion on Rashba,[30] who reads the Talmudic story as allowing only students to bless for their teachers. R. Caro infers that husbands should not adopt this practice and those who do so should be admonished out of concern for *berakhah levattalah*.[31] The discussion only focuses on the husbands' actions, and R. Caro does not explicitly address the question of women's fundamental obligation in *birkat hagomel*. However, it is clear from the husbands' behavior that they assume that postpartum women are required to recite *hagomel*.[32] Many authorities understand from R. Caro's analysis and his willingness to discuss the husbands' practice that he agrees that women are obligated; for, if he felt that a postpartum woman did not need to recite *hagomel* then he would have said so.[33] In his view, according to

---

30. Though he quotes R. Mano'aḥ in this context, as well, it is clear from the second quotation that *Beit Yosef* realizes that R. Mano'aḥ meant only that others *are not obligated* to recite the blessing on someone else's behalf. But, if they experience relief and joy at another's redemption, they most certainly may recite *birkat hagomel*. Therefore, by the end, R. Caro's argument rests solely on Rashba.
31. R. Ḥayyim Abulafia, *Sefer Nishmat Ḥayyim, O.Ḥ.* #2, comments about an episode in the community, where it was customary for the husband to recite *birkat hagomel* on behalf of his wife who had given birth. Once a "wise" person visited and scolded them for this practice, claiming that it was a blessing in vain. However, when they asked R. Ḥayyim Abulafia for his opinion, he claimed that the visitor did not act appropriately, for though that is the ruling of *Beit Yosef*, there are many important Aḥaronim who rule that a husband can recite *birkat hagomel* on behalf of his wife. The community could rely on those Aḥaronim in their practice. R. Yitsḥak Abulafia (published in Aleppo 1871) quotes *Nishmat Ḥayyim* in this regard.
32. R. Caro does not discuss why the husband would assume this task in place of his wife. This question will be discussed in subsequent sources.
33. See, for example, *Responsa Tsits Eliezer* 19:53, who argues that R. Caro certainly felt that women were obligated to recite *birkat hagomel*, and if the woman recited it herself that would certainly be fine, according to his opinion. R. Caro's only question was whether the husband can step in and fulfill the obligation on his wife's behalf. R. Waldenberg writes:

    ונמצאנו למדים שכל דיונו ופקפוקו של הב״י [הבית יוסף] שם הוא מפני שלבעל הא לא נתרחש שם נס בלידת אשתו, ומזה איפוא שאבל הא ליולדת בעצמה היה פשוט ליה להב״י [להבית יוסף] שליכא בזה ברכה בטלה אם תברך, דאל״כ [דאם לא כן] אין כל מקום ללימוד הזכות שרוצה הב״י [הבית יוסף] שם ללמד על הבעלים המברכים כמובן.

    See also *Yosef Et Eḥav* 2:1 (below, source #22), who also thinks that R. Caro obligates women in *hagomel*. See n19 above for R. Henkin's view that the Rishonim's silence indicates that women are not obligated in *hagomel*.

this reading, the husband does not have the obligation to give thanks to God for his wife's salvation. Only the woman herself, who experienced the life-threatening travails of childbirth, can fully bless God and fulfill the obligation incumbent upon her to thank her creator for her survival.

Interestingly R. Yosef Caro himself rules differently with regard to the husband's behavior in his *Shulḥan Arukh*.

12. *Shulḥan Arukh, Oraḥ Ḥayyim 219:4–5*

R. Yosef Caro, Spain and Israel (1488–1575)

שולחן ערוך אורח חיים סימן ריט סעיף ד–ה

4) If someone else recited the blessing and said, "Blessed are You God, our Lord, Master of the Universe, who has bestowed upon you all good," and he [the one obligated] responded, "Amen," he has fulfilled his obligation. And similarly, if he said [in Aramaic], "Blessed are You God, King of the universe, who has given you [back] to us," and he responded, "Amen," he has fulfilled his obligation.[34]

ד) אם בירך אחר ואמר: בא״י אמ״ה [ברוך אתה י״י אלהינו מלך העולם] אשר גמלך כל טוב, וענה אמן, יצא. וכן אם אמר: בריך רחמנא מלכא דעלמא דיהבך לן, וענה אמן, יצא.

5) If someone recited *birkat hagomel* for himself and intended for his friend to fulfill the obligation [too], and his friend heard

ה) אם בירך אחד הגומל לעצמו, ונתכוין להוציא את חבירו, ושמע חבירו וכוון

34. Rema adds a note as to why the blessing would not be in vain:

ואין זה ברכה לבטלה מן מברך, אף על פי שלא נתחייב בברכה זו, הואיל ואינו מברך רק דרך שבח והודאה על טובת חבירו ששמח בה.

Rema rules according to *Tur* with the addition of the phrase ושמח בה ("and he was glad of it") and adds that this is not to be considered a blessing in vain, since he is simply praising God for the good bestowed upon his friend. *Taz, O.Ḥ.* 219:3, takes this addition extremely seriously and rules that someone else may recite *birkat hagomel* only when he is truly glad that his friend has been saved. But, if one does not feel joy in his heart and is only reciting the blessing to preserve peace, then he should recite it without *shem umalkhut* so that it will not be a blessing in vain. *Seder Birkhot Hanehenin Untilat Yadayim* 13:4 concurs with *Taz* regarding the requirement that the third party genuinely feel the joy of the person who was saved.

and intended to fulfill the obligation, he has fulfilled his obligation, even without responding, "Amen."	לצאת, יצא אפילו בלא עניית אמן.

Here R. Yosef Caro permits a third party to recite *birkat hagomel* on someone else's behalf and makes no caveat as to who this third party must be. There is no mention in *Shulḥan Arukh* – as there was in *Beit Yosef* – that it must be his rabbi, and so presumably there would be no issue with a husband reciting *hagomel* on his wife's behalf, although she must be present to respond, "Amen." There is a clear discrepancy between what R. Caro writes in his commentary to the *Tur* (*Beit Yosef*) and what he writes later in his own halakhic code, *Shulḥan Arukh*. Has R. Caro retracted his earlier position as expressed in *Beit Yosef*? Or does he assume that those learning *Shulḥan Arukh* will already know from *Beit Yosef* that only a student may recite on behalf of his teacher? This question is debated by many later authorities.[35] Although it was clear from his statements in *Beit Yosef* that the *yoledet* is obligated in *hagomel*, in the *Shulḥan Arukh*, R. Caro does not single out women in any way. Their obligation is simply assumed similar to the norm for all Jews.

AḤARONIM

Whatever R. Caro's motivation may have been for not including his caveat regarding a husband reciting *birkat hagomel* for his wife in *Shulḥan Arukh*, the custom continues to be discussed in later halakhic texts. R. Yo'el Sirkis engages with the same Rashba as R. Caro but comes to a different conclusion:

35. It is abundantly clear to *Magen Avraham, O.Ḥ.* 219:4 that R. Caro retracted his earlier comments in *Beit Yosef*. *Eshel Avraham, O.Ḥ.* 219:4, agrees, as does, to a lesser extent, *Mor Uktsiah* 1:219. Others, such as *Kaf Hahayyim, O.Ḥ.* 219:33, disagree. *Responsa Tsits Eliezer* 19:53 also reads R. Caro differently and makes a general statement about the relationship between *Beit Yosef* and *Shulḥan Arukh*: one can never assume a retraction of what is written in *Beit Yosef* simply because it was omitted or not reiterated in *Shulḥan Arukh*; only when R. Caro does so explicitly. Thus, the caveat in *Beit Yosef* that a husband should not say *birkat hagomel* for his wife would still apply even though it is not reiterated in *Shulḥan Arukh*. Many of the sources below agree and believe that R. Caro did not change his mind and still maintains the position he held in *Beit Yosef*.

13. *Baḥ (Bayit Ḥadash)*
Oraḥ Ḥayyim 219:3
R. Yo'el Sirkis, Poland (1560–1640)

ב"ח (בית חדש)
אורח חיים סימן ריט סעיף ג

And there is no greater value to a man than his wife's salvation, for she is as his own body, and similarly the salvation of his children and loved ones.... And even though *Beit Yosef* wrote in the name of Rashba that the fact that Rav Ḥana Bagdatta'ah and the rabbis recited the blessing on the healing of Rav Yehudah was [only] because he was their rabbi, meaning that if he was not their rabbi he should not recite the blessing, as if he has no value in their salvation. But his loved one or his relative – how much more so his father or his wife and his children – he should recite the blessing as he would for his teacher. Thus, it seems to me that this is *halakhah lema'aseh* (the practical law), and not as *Beit Yosef* [ruled]...for even according to Rashba he [the husband] should recite the blessing.

ואין תועלת לאדם יותר מהצלת אשתו שהיא כגופו והוא הדין הצלת בניו ואוהביו.... ואף על פי שבית יוסף כתב על שם הרשב"א דהא דבריך רב חנא בגדתאה ורבנן על רפואת רב יהודא היינו לפי שהיה רבם משמע דאם אינו רבו לא יברך היינו באין לו תועלת בהצלתו אבל אוהבו וקרובו כל שכן אביו או אשתו ובניו יש לו לברך כמו על רבו כך נראה לי להלכה למעשה ודלא כבית יוסף... דאף להרשב"א יש לו לברך.

Baḥ directly takes issue with R. Caro's conclusion, based on his own reading of Rashba. In disputing *Beit Yosef*, both with regard to his practical conclusion and with regard to his reading of Rashba, *Baḥ* quotes Riaz,[36] discussed earlier. Surely a loved one or relative should be able to rejoice and recite *hagomel* on behalf of a family member just as is done for a teacher. And who is more important to a man than his own wife, who is considered to be an extension of his own body and flesh? In *Baḥ*'s view, a husband can certainly make the thanksgiving blessing

36. *Baḥ* assumes that Rashba would agree with Riaz, and therefore reads Rashba maximally, whereas *Beit Yosef* does not quote Riaz and reads Rashba minimally.

on behalf of his wife, who, *Baḥ* assumes, like those who came before him, is required to recite *hagomel.*

R. Avraham Schor continues this discussion, but with a significant variation and innovation to the husband's behavior.

14. *Torat Ḥayyim* / תורת חיים
Sanhedrin 94a / מסכת סנהדרין צד.

R. Avraham Ḥayyim ben Naftali Tsevi Hirsch Schor, Belz, Galicia (d. 1632)

And for this reason[37] this custom also seems [correct]: that one whose wife has given birth, when she gets up after giving birth and goes to the synagogue, then her husband reads from the Torah. And there are places where the deputy [such as the *gabbai*] is required to call him [up to the Torah], for the woman must give thanks for her miracle – that she gave birth safely – and the custom of giving thanks at the time of the Torah reading is in order to publicize the matter. And also when he says, "Blessed is the Lord who is blessed" etc. [the phrase recited when receiving an *aliyah* to the Torah], that too is like giving thanks, for blessing and thanks are one and the same.... And because a woman does not read from the Torah, therefore her husband thanks in her place. And therefore the husband must intend thusly when he recites, "Blessed is the Lord who is blessed," that he is blessing and giving thanks to God for his wife. For with regard to blessings of thanksgiving, if someone recites the blessing on behalf of his friend, he [the friend] has fulfilled his obligation. And all the more so with a husband and wife, who

ומהאי טעמא נמי נראה מה שנוהגין מי שילדה לו אשתו כשעומדת אחר לידתה והולכת לבית הכנסת אז בעלה קורא בתורה וביש מקומות מחוייב הסגן לקרותו לפי שהאשה צריכה להודות על נסה מה שילדה בשלום והמנהג להודות בשעה שקורא בתורה לפרסומי מלתא וגם כשאומר ברכו את ה' המבורך וכו' ה"ל [הוה ליה] נמי כהודאה דברכה והודאה כי חדא נינהו.... ולפי שאין אשה קוראה בתורה לכך בעלה מודה תחתיה ולפי זה צריך הבעל להתכוין לכך כשאומר ברכו את ה' המבורך שנותן ברכה והודאה לה' בשביל אשתו דברכת הודאה אם בירך אחר בשביל חברו יצא וכ"ש [וכל שכן] בבעל

37. In the previous paragraph he writes about the importance of using the word "*Barukh*" (Blessed) in giving thanks for being saved.

are as one body. And certainly when the wife responds "Amen" to her husband's blessing, then the wife is exempt from giving [further] thanks.[38]	ואשה דכחד גופא דמו וכ"ש [וכל שכן] כשהאשה אומרת אמן על ברכתו דפטורה האשה מלאודויי.

R. Schor is the first to state explicitly that a woman is obligated to thank God by reciting *birkat hagomel.* Yet, he suggests that her husband fulfil that obligation for her at the traditional time of public Torah reading. He describes the custom that a man read from the Torah and receive an *aliyah* on the same Shabbat on which his wife returns to synagogue after giving birth. R. Schor explains that since women do not read from the Torah, the husband must function in her place. Rather than reciting the *hagomel* blessing, R. Schor states that the husband must have the intention to fulfil his wife's obligation to thank God when he recites the normative blessings on the Torah and that the wife should answer "Amen," thereby fulfilling her obligation of thanks through his blessing. R. Schor's suggestion is completely novel. It avoids the potential pitfall of *berakhah levattalah* which concerned *Beit Yosef,* since the husband's recitation of the blessing for the *aliyah* cannot be construed as being in vain, but preserves the husband's ability to fulfil the *mitsvah* on his

38. R. Schor is also quoted *lehalakhah* in *Eliyah Rabbah* 219:5. Although *Eliyah Rabbah* 219:12 quotes *Kenesset Hagedolah* but suggests that it is actually preferable for a husband to recite *birkat hagomel* on his wife's behalf, rather than her reciting *birkat hagomel* herself, since a woman is mainly punished for the sins of her husband. While he maintains the general obligation for a woman to say *birkat hagomel,* he creatively argues that this obligation is best fulfilled through her husband rather than through her own recitation of the blessing. He also invokes the concept of *ishto kegufo* (his wife is like his own body) as a rationale for why a husband is permitted to recite *birkat hagomel* on his wife's behalf even though, in general, friends and relatives should not do so. *Mor Uktsiah* 1:219, s.v. *ul'inyan halakhah,* uses the concept of *ishto kegufo* to make a different point. See *Responsa Divrei Yetsiv, E.H.* #35, who reads this passage of *Eliyah Rabbah* as saying that *birkat hagomel* should not be recited for a woman at all (either by her husband or for herself). See also *Mishnah Berurah* 219:17, who supplies the proper formula to use when reciting *birkat hagomel* for one's wife but concludes in 219:18 that it is better not to do so, following *Beit Yosef.*

wife's behalf. However, by giving thanks through receiving an *aliyah*, the actual recitation of *birkat hagomel* is bypassed.[39]

Similarly to R. Schor, R. Ya'akov Hagiz feels that internal factors linked to *birkat hagomel* make it impractical for women to recite. He likewise suggests an alternate way of expressing thanks which does not involve reciting *birkat hagomel* for either the woman or her husband.

15. *Responsa Halakhot Ketanot* Vol. 2, #161 — **שו"ת הלכות קטנות חלק ב סימן קסא**

R. Ya'akov Hagiz, Morocco, Turkey, Italy, Jerusalem (1620–1674)

It is a question whether a woman should recite *birkat hagomel*. The answer, according to one who says that a *minyan* and two rabbis are essential: it is possible that a woman is not obligated [to bless in this manner] since "all the honor of the daughter of a king is internal [private]."[40] And it is possible that she should recite the *sheheḥeyanu* blessing... for if on the purchase of a new utensil one says it, on the renewal and acquiring of one's body [i.e., one's life being saved] would it not all the more so [be warranted to bless]? ... But if there are not ten present, who exempts him from blessing his creator by reciting *sheheḥeyanu*?

שאלה אם אשה תברך הגומל. תשובה למ"ד [למאן דאמר] דעשרה ותרי רבנן מעכב אפשר דאשה לא מיחייבא דכל כבודה ב"מ [בת מלך] פנימה. ואפשר דתברך שהחיינו... דאם על קניית כלי חדש אומרו (כמבואר באו"ח סי' רכ"ג) על חדוש וקנין גופא לכ"ש [לא כל שכן].... אבל אם אין שם עשרה מי פטרו מלשבח את יוצרו בברכת שהחיינו.

39. See also *Responsa Tsits Eliezer* 17:9 and *Responsa Yeḥavveh Da'at* 4:15. R. Yosef refutes this position and explains that *barekhu* cannot substitute for *birkat hagomel*, since *birkat hagomel* requires *shem umalkhut*, and *barekhu* does not contain *malkhut*. Therefore, a husband's recitation of *barekhu* – while it is not a blessing in vain – cannot exempt his wife from her obligation to recite *birkat hagomel*. *Responsa Hitorerut Teshuvah* 1:59, endorses *Torat Ḥayyim* and argues that the formula for *birkat hagomel* is not authoritative. Everyone knows that the wife's childbirth is the reason behind the husband's *aliyah*, and therefore she can fulfill her obligation in this manner.

40. Psalms 45:14.

R. Hagiz suggests that women may be exempt from reciting *hagomel*, a blessing in which it was assumed, up until this point, that they were obligated. He bases this view on the grounds of modesty,[41] for according to the opinion that *hagomel* may only be recited in the presence of a *minyan*, this setting may be improper for women.[42] Twice he uses the language of "it is possible," which acknowledges that the opposite is possible as well, and thus women may in fact be obligated. His wording also implies that according to those authorities who do not view the *minyan* as an essential requirement for reciting the blessing, modesty would not be an issue and women would be required to thank God through *hagomel*. However, within the criteria that he establishes, R. Hagiz raises the unprecedented suggestion that women must recite the *sheheḥeyanu* blessing, which can be recited even alone, without a quorum, for how could they be completely exempt from praising God for their salvation?[43]

---

41. R. Hagiz also rejects the option of a husband reciting *birkat hagomel* on his wife's behalf.

42. He does not explain what exactly is immodest about her recitation in front of a *minyan*. Possibly he assumes she would need to physically enter the men's section of the synagogue to bless in the presence of the prayer quorum. Presumably, a woman would need to do this in a synagogue which did not have an actual women's section or where the women's section was a distinct and separate domain, and thus not halakhically considered to be in the presence of the *minyan*. (See, for example, *Arukh Hashulḥan, O.Ḥ.* 55:20.) This assumption is the basis for concern among a number of authorities who discuss women's reciting mourner's *kaddish* in the men's section, in order to do so in the presence of a *minyan*. See, for example, *Teshuvah Me'ahavah*, Vol. 2, *O.Ḥ.* 229:10. This seems to be a possible reading of this situation as well. Much later, *Torat Ḥakham* 17 explicitly cites this idea:

    > גם נשים חייבות לברך ברכת הגומל דמאי שנא נשים מאנשים לענין ברכה זו? ואמאי לא יתחייבו וא"כ [ואם כן] אף שאנין יכולות לברך ברכה זו בפני עשרה אנשים דדרך פריצותא הוא ליכנס האשה לבין האנשים לבית הכנסת לברך שם ברכת הגומל... וכיון שאין לה להכנס לברך ברכה זו לפני עשרה אנשים הו"ל [הוה ליה] כמו דיעבד... אבל להך מ"ד [מאן דאמר] דס"ל [דסבירא ליה] שאם בירך בפחות מעשרה אפילו בדיעבד לא יצא הא ודאי שנשים לא יברכו ברכה זו כלל שאם תברך בתוך ביתה או בעזרת נשים אינה יצאה ידי חובה בזה כיון דלא הויא הברכה בפני עשרה.

    See below, source #30 and n94, for R. Yosef's response to *Torat Ḥakham*.

43. The legal link between *hagomel* and *sheheḥeyanu* appears in the writings of R. Hagiz with regard to men, as well. See *Halakhot Ketanot*, Vol. 1, #122, and Vol. 2, #1. In fact, the last line of the text quoted above is stated in the masculine even though the responsum is dealing only with the case of a woman. This could be either because

The suggestion that women actually recite *birkat hagomel* themselves to fulfil their own obligation, rather than via their husbands, first emerges in the seventeenth century. The most significant source in this regard is *Kenesset Hagedolah*,[44] who takes issue with the idea that modesty should prevent women from reciting *hagomel*.[45]

16. *Kenesset Hagedolah*
Oraḥ Ḥayyim #219
s.v. amar hame'asef

כנסת הגדולה או"ח
סימן ריט
ד"ה אמר המאסף

R. Ḥayyim ben Israel Benveniste, Turkey (1603–1673)

The collator said: I am astonished at the popular custom that women do not recite *birkat hagomel*. And it would appear to me that this is an erroneous custom, for since [*birkat hagomel*] is a blessing of thanksgiving, who exempted women from this blessing?! And if it is because one is obligated to give thanks before ten [men] two of whom are rabbis, and it is not proper for women to stand amongst men for "all the honor of the daughter of a king is internal," this claim is not satisfactory in order to exempt her from a blessing in

אמר המאסף תמה אני על מנהג העולם שנהגו שאין הנשים מברכות ברכת הגומל, ויראה לי דמנהג בטעות הוא דכיון דברכת הודאה היא זו מי פטר לנשים מברכה זו. ואי משום שצריך לאודויי באנפי עשרה ותרי מינייהו רבנן ואין כבודה של אישה לעמוד בפני האנשים דכל כבודה בת מלך פנימה, אין טענה זו היא מספקת לפטרה מברכה שנתחייבה בה. ועוד שהרי אפשר לאישה לעמוד

R. Hagiz is not precise with his Hebrew grammar or because the formulation of the rule that one must recite *sheheḥeyanu* when one does not have a *minyan* is also applicable to men.

44. *Kenesset Hagedolah* is quoted repeatedly; see R. Ḥayyim David Azulai (Ḥida) in *Birkhei Yosef, O.Ḥ.* 219:2, who quotes *Kenesset Hagedolah* and is later quoted by many in regard to this ruling.

45. It is possible that *Kenesset Hagedolah* was actually referring to *Halakhot Ketanot* (above, source #15) in discussing those who make the argument from "all the honor of the daughter of a king." While *Kenesset Hagedolah* was first printed in 1658 and *Halakhot Ketanot* was published in 1704, and while *Halakhot Ketanot* actually makes reference to *Kenesset Hagedolah* at the very end of the text above, which was not quoted in the body of the paper, given the overlap in time and place, it is quite likely that the two knew each other personally or at least knew of each other's rulings.

which she is obligated. And furthermore, it is possible for a woman to stand in the women's synagogue and recite *birkat hagomel* and for the men to hear it in their synagogue. And additionally, it only states that one must give thanks in front of ten *lekhatḥillah* (ideally), but *bediavad* (after the fact) one has fulfilled their obligation even in the absence of ten, as per the opinion of our rabbi *Tur* even though this is not the opinion of Rav Yonah or our rabbi, *Beit Yosef, z"l.*

בבית הכנסת של נשים ולברך ברכת הגומל וישמעו האנשים בבית הכנסת שלהם. ועוד דלא נאמר שצריך לאודויי באנפי עשרה אלא לכתחלה אבל בדיעבד אפילו שלא באנפי עשרה יצא, וכמו שהוא דעת רבינו בעל הטורים, אף על פי שאין כן דעת הרב יונה ורבינו בית יוסף ז"ל [זכרונו לברכה].

And for a woman who is unable to recite the blessing in front of men *lekhatḥillah,* she should recite the blessing without the presence of ten [men]. And therefore it seems fitting that a woman should recite *birkat hagomel* in front of ten [people], or at least in front of one man or [several] women, and if she recites the blessing between herself and herself [i.e., alone], she has fulfilled her obligation. And I believe that I heard from some Ashkenazic scholars that in Ashkenaz a woman recites *birkat hagomel* like a man, and this is correct practice.

ובאשה שאינה יכולה לברך בפני האנשים לכתחלה תברך שלא בפני עשרה, ולכן נראה שראוי שתברך האשה ברכת הגומל באנפי עשרה ולפחות בפני איש אחד או נשים, ואם בירכה בינה לבין עצמה יצאת. וכמדומה לי ששמעתי מקצת חכמי אשכנזים שבאשכנז האשה מברכת הגומל כמו האיש וכן נכון לעשות.

Kenesset Hagedolah comes out very strongly against the practice, which existed in his day, of women not reciting *birkat hagomel.* He does not explain whether he is referring to the practice of the husband reciting the blessing for her,[46] in which case she is not saying it herself, or whether

46. The option of a husband reciting *birkat hagomel* on his wife's behalf is not even raised by *Kenesset Hagedolah.* Perhaps the reason for this omission is that he has seen *Beit Yosef* (since he quotes him on another point), and he accepts *Beit Yosef*'s concern of *berakhah levattalah.*

there is an assumption that women have absolutely no part in this ritual, which seems to be the implication of his words. He argues that *birkat hagomel* is obligatory for both men and women, and he rejects the claim that it is immodest for women to recite this blessing in front of a *minyan* of men. Further, he argues that if modesty is a concern, a woman can stand in the women's section of the synagogue and recite *birkat hagomel,* while the men respond from the men's section.[47] Though the thrust of *Kenesset Hagedolah*'s argument seems to be encouraging women to recite *birkat hagomel* in front of a *minyan,* as men do – he ends by stating that this behavior is the correct practice – he eventually steps back from arguing for this position alone and also allows for cases where a woman cannot recite *birkat hagomel* in front of a male *minyan* (though he does not say why this would be the case). In such a *bediavad* (non-ideal) situation, a woman should still aim to publicize God's wonderful actions and recite *birkat hagomel* in front of a group of women,[48] or one man.[49] However, even if she recites the blessing alone, he concedes she will have fulfilled her obligation. He concludes by citing the custom in Ashkenaz, where women recite *birkat hagomel* just as men do,[50] and he endorses this practice as the ideal.

While some later Sephardic authorities criticize *Kenesset Hagedolah* for stepping back from his ideal position and ruling against R. Caro's view that a *minyan* is required,[51] he does nonetheless preserve the implication of the ruling in the *Beit Yosef* that women must recite *hagomel* themselves. *Kenesset Hagedolah* is the first to explicitly argue that a woman should always recite *birkat hagomel* for herself and not resort

47. This suggestion seems to assume that the women's section and the men's section are part of one united domain.
48. R. David Auerbach, in his book *Halikhot Beitah* 13:7 n13, suggests that this passage (and possibly also the view of the *yesh omerim* in *Shulḥan Arukh, O.Ḥ.* 219:3) is intended to refer to reciting *hagomel* in front of ten women. He cites his uncle R. Shlomo Zalman Auerbach and *Arukh Hashulḥan* (below, source #25) as disagreeing with that possibility.
49. See *Magen Avraham* (below, source #17) and *Mishnah Berurah* (below, source #24).
50. *Kenesset Hagedolah* does not cite a source for this Ashkanazic custom and, interestingly, many of the sources to follow actually attest to the opposite custom that women refrain from reciting *hagomel.*
51. See, for example, *Berekh Et Avraham* 88b and R. Yosef (below, source #30).

to having a man reciting it on her behalf. *Kenesset Hagedolah* is quoted repeatedly by later sources. Any halakhist who tries to make a claim for exempting women must first refute the incisive arguments made by *Kenesset Hagedolah*. One of the first to respond is R. Avraham Gombiner.

17. Magen Avraham
#219, Introduction

מגן אברהם
סימן ריט פתיחה

R. Avraham Halevi Gombiner, Poland and Lithuania (1637–1683)

Kenesset Hagedolah wondered why women do not recite this blessing [*birkat hagomel*], and [he argues that] if it is because one needs ten, then *bediavad* it is enough without ten, and therefore, she should bless in front of one man or in front of women. And it is possible that their custom is because they believe that these blessings are optional [but not obligatory].

בכ"ה תמה למה אין הנשים מברכות ברכה זו ואי משום דבעי י' הא דבדיעבד סגי בלא י' ולכן תברך בפני איש א' או בפני נשים עכ"ל [עד כאן לשונו] ואפשר שמנהגן מפני שס"ל [שסבירא ליה] שברכות אלו רשות.

Magen Avraham suggests that the reason women do not recite *hagomel* is not for reasons of modesty, as *Kenesset Hagedolah* thought, but rather that the women's custom is based on a different halakhic premise. He posits that it is possible that women believe that *birkhot hare'iyyah* in general, which include *birkat hagomel*, are optional (*reshut*) rather than mandatory (*ḥovah*) and, as such, they choose not to recite them. This idea exists in general rabbinic thought, not specifically linked to women, particularly with regard to life-threatening situations other than the four cited explicitly in the Talmud.[52] Certainly labor and childbirth are not

52. See for example Me'iri to B.T. *Ber.* 54b, who lays out this argument, although he ends by saying that even if it is optional, one surely ought to recite the blessing of thanks:

> יש מי שאומר שאין הדברים הללו אמורים אלא בהולכי מדברות שתעו ויורדי הים שעמד עליהם נחשול שבים וחולה שיש בו סכנה שבאלו יש בהם נס והרי הן כעין היוצא מבית האסורים אבל אם לא אירע להם כן אין צריך לברך וכן הולכי דרכים שלא במדברות אין צריכין לברך ואף על פי שפשוטי המקראות מוכיחים כך אין אני מודה בכך אלא כל שעלה למטה וירד מברך כבר אמרו עליה למטה הרי הוא כמי שעלה לגרדום וכן כל

listed there, nor do they appear in *Shulḥan Arukh*. However, the idea that the women themselves have gone through a real halakhic analysis to determine their practice seems a bit farfetched. It seems more reasonable to assume that *Magen Avraham* is looking for a legal support to justify their behavior.[53] More problematic for *Magen Avraham*'s understanding is that Ra'avad, whose position is most famously identified with these blessings' being non-obligatory, still believes an expression of thanks is required, which seems lacking in these women's practice according to *Magen Avraham*. As *Peri Megadim* wonders in his famous commentary on *Magen Avraham*:

18. *Peri Megadim*
Oraḥ Ḥayyim, Eshel Avraham #219

פרי מגדים אורח חיים
אשל אברהם סימן ריט

R. Yosef ben R. Meir Te'omim, Poland (1727–1792)

Nevertheless, we learn that one who is unsure whether he blessed *hagomel* or not should go back and repeat the blessing without *shem umalkhut* [God's name and kingdom, the fixed liturgical structure], as the blessings are not essential – just the thanksgiving is needed. And

ומכל מקום למדנו מי שספק לו אם בירך הגומל או לאו דחוזר ומברך בלא שם ומלכות, דברכות אין מעכבות רק הודאה בעינן. ומה שכתב נשים דסבירא

הולכי דרכים במשמע בתלמוד המערב אמרו בפ׳ תפלת השחר כל הדרך בחזקת סכנה וכל החולי בחזקת סכנה והוא הדין לכל הליכת ים ולא עוד אלא שנראה לי שלא נאמרו אלו בפרט אלא שאע״פ [שאף על פין] שלא אירע להם סכנה צריכין להודות הואיל והדבר מצוי להסתכן אבל כל שאירע לו סכנה הן סכנת נפשות וניצל ממנה בכל דבר צריך להודות ויש בזה חולקים מתורת חובה הא מתורת רשות ודאי מברך.

See also *Responsa Betsel Haḥokhmah* 1:37, who mentions this view in the *posekim*. Some assume this view that *hagomel* is optional to be *Magen Avhraham*'s position in general, not just for women. See, for example, *Responsa Minḥat Yitsḥak*, who tries to clarify what he means by voluntary. See *Responsa Har Tsevi, O.Ḥ.* 1:118, who discusses *Magen Avraham*'s suggestion and offers an alternative idea for the women's logic based on the fact that *hagomel* is not recited at night and therefore might be considered a time-caused *mitsvah*.

53 Returning to the analogy between *birkat hagomel* and the *korban todah*, it makes sense that *birkat hagomel* could be optional. One could ask (and there are those who do) why men accepted this blessing and not women; however, *Magen Avraham* was only trying to defend the custom of women. See also R. Akiva Eiger's response, *Haggahot* 219:7.

that which he [*Magen Avraham*] wrote, that women think it is optional, I do not know who says optional, for even the Ra'avad[54] only said that one does not need *shem umalkhut*, but surely one needs to thank [God].	ליה רשות, איני יודע מאן אומרים רשות, דאף הראב"ד לא אמר אלא שאין צריך שם ומלכות אבל וודאי צריך להודות.

Peri Megadim challenges *Magen Avraham*'s logic and claims that he has misinterpreted the original intent of Ra'avad, the minority position, which believes these blessings to be optional in general (not just for women). The traditional liturgical structure of a blessing is not required, as it would be if these blessing were obligatory; however, the need to thank God surely still exists.[55] *Peri Megadim* does not understand how, even according to *Magen Avraham*'s suggestion, these women would not be required to utter some acknowledgment of the good God has bestowed upon them.

Interestingly a few *simanim* later, in 219:4, R. Gombiner rules "that anyone who is happy [at the salvation of another] may recite *birkat hagomel*, and certainly over his wife who has given birth he may do so." Here *Magen Avraham* seems to revert back to the normative tradition that came before him, which considers *hagomel* something that a woman must recite and which can be performed by her husband.[56]

R. Ya'akov Emden also believes that women can say the blessing themselves and presents a radical suggestion.[57]

54. *Hassagot Hara'avad* to B.T. *Ber.* 44a (in the commentary of Rabbenu Yonah).
55. See also a similar idea in Me'iri's comment, above n51.
56. See a similar example where *Magen Avraham* tries to justify legally the practice of women of not praying the *amidah* daily, which seems to be halakhically problematic. He presents an innovative, non-normative idea in *O.Ḥ.* 106:2 and then reverts back to the accepted rabbinic tradition that women are obligated in rabbinic prayer in *O.Ḥ.* 299:10.
57. R. Emden writes elsewhere (*Mor Uktsiah* 1:219) about a husband's recitation of *birkat hagomel* on behalf of his wife. See also *Mor Uktsiah*, *O.Ḥ.* 55, where he discusses the possibility of women counting in a *minyan* and reading from the Torah.

19. *Birat Migdal Oz*	**בירת מגדל עוז**
(Siddur Haya'avets, Vol. 3)	**(סדור היעב"ץ חלק ג)**
Shoket 2 Lanekevah #10	**שוקת ב׳ לנקבה אות י**

R. Ya'akov Emden (Ya'avets), Germany (1697/1698–1776)

And it seems that when they pray and read [from the Torah] with precisely ten men, in the home of the woman who has given birth, when her husband is not present, we should establish the matter according to the law, that a woman may receive an *aliyah* and read from the Torah in these circumstances.	ונראה דכשמתפללין וקורין עשרה בצמצום. בבית היולדת ואין בעלה כאן. יש להעמיד הדבר על הדין. שאשה עולה וקוראה בתורה כהאי גוונא.
Even though the sages said (B.T. *Meg.* 23a) [she] should not read in public because of honor, they only said this in [reference to] a large congregation and that it should not be done regularly. But in these circumstances, which are uncommon and in order to help her, we can say that they [the rabbis] did not make this decree. In any event, they explicitly said that a woman can be counted in the quorum of the seven people [who are called to, and read from, the Torah on Shabbat]. And if not now [in this circumstance] then when [would this ruling be applicable]? These statements, where were they said? And certainly nothing they [the sages] said can fall to the ground and not have a place. And in this manner it is like a case of *bediavad*. Thus is my inclination [to rule], if my colleagues will agree with me.	אף על גם שאמרו חכמים (מגילה כג.) לא תקרא בצבור מפני הכבוד. לא אמרו. אלא בקהל רב. ושלא לעשות תדיר. אבל בהאי גוונא דהויא מילתא דלא שכיחא. ומשום תקנתא דידה. איכא למימר לא גזרו. על כל פנים הרי בפירוש אמרו שעולה למנין שבעה. ואם לא עכשיו אימתי. אלה הדברים איפוה הם אמורים. ובודאי לא יפול שום דבר מדבריהם ארצה. שלא יהא לו מקום. ובאופן זה כדעבד דמי. כך דעתי נוטה אם יסכימו עמי חברי.

Ya'avets goes in a new direction here. None who raised the possibility of women reciting *birkat hagomel* in front of a *minyan* have suggested that she also receive an *aliyah* or read from the Torah. However, R. Emden points out that perhaps women's obligation in *birkat hagomel* is the very reason why the Talmud allows for the legal possibility (however infrequent) of women reading from the Torah. Certainly, he argues, the statements of the rabbis must have applicability in practice. He states that the circumstances under which a woman would be called to the Torah are *bediavad*, and he limits the phenomenon to a *minyan* in the privacy of the woman's home, which in his view would not violate the principle of communal honor, *kevod hatsibbur*, as it is not in a large congregation and occurs infrequently. Interestingly, the scenario he describes is one in which the woman's husband is not present (although he does not explain why this might be the case – perhaps he is traveling). This statement seems to imply that if her husband had been present then surely he would have been called to the Torah in her place as is described in many previous sources. This fact reinforces the understanding that the husband is fulfilling an obligation that is truly incumbent upon his wife, and not something that he voluntarily does; for, when he is unavailable, Ya'avets follows the idea through to its logical end and requires the woman to receive the *aliyah* herself. Later *posekim* do not engage with R. Emden's suggestion that a woman receive an *aliyah* and recite *hagomel*.[58]

Other Ashkenazic *posekim* are not bothered at all by the logistical problems created by having women recite *hagomel*. Rather, they simply state it as the norm in their law codes.

20. *Ḥayyei Adam*
חיי אדם

Kelal 65, Perat 6
כלל סה פרט ו

R. Avraham Danzig, Danzig and Vilna (1748–1820)

And also women, it is appropriate that they bless in front of ten.	וגם נשים ראויות לברך בפני עשרה.

58. It was even censored in certain editions of Ya'avets, which could be why it did not receive any response.

R. Avaraham Danzig rules simply that women should recite *birkat hagomel* in front of a *minyan*.[59] With one word, he dismisses any issues of impropriety or immodesty. He states that this behavior is appropriate.

At the same time in Eastern Europe, R. Shne'ur Zalman of Liadi concurs with *Kenesset Hagedolah*'s original suggestion and rules accordingly that women are obligated to recite *hagomel*.

21. *Seder Birkhot Hanehenin Untilat Yadayim 13:3*

סדר ברכת הנהנין ונטילת ידים פרק יג אות ג

R. Shne'ur Zalman of Liadi, Belarus (1745–1812)

But women and slaves are obligated in this blessing [*birkat hagomel*]. Therefore, any woman who has given birth, when she is healed, should recite [*birkat hagomel*] in the women's section with ten men listening from inside [the main sanctuary].

אבל נשים ועבדים חייבים בברכה זו, לכן כל אשה יולדת כשתקום מחליה תברך בבהכ"נ [בבית הכנסת] של נשים וישמעו עשרה אנשים מבפנים.

He also sees no problem of immodesty, for women can recite the blessing from the women's section, and assumes that the postpartum mother falls into the category of those who are required to give thanks.

In the nineteenth century, a series of Sephardic rabbis ruled in favor of women's reciting *birkat hagomel*. The nineteenth-century, Turkish R. Yosef Palaji presents both the theoretical underpinnings of this obligation as well as an actual case in which he applied this ruling as practical law (*halakhah lema'aseh*).

---

59. While this passage from *Ḥayyei Adam*, which is a normative and significant work, seems important, it is not cited by most of the later sources. The one later halakhist who refers to it (*Responsa Vayitsbor Yosef* #41) only quotes it in the context of the question and proceeds to refute this position in his response.

22. *Yosef Et Eḥav*
2:1
R. Yosef Palaji, Izmir (1815–1896)

יוסף את אחיו
מערכת ב׳ אות א׳

Why should a man who is healed recite *birkat hagomel* and not a woman, as I have seen is our custom, the custom of Izmir, may God protect the city, that women do not recite *birkat hagomel.* Do not they both [men and women] have a heavenly soul?!... And in the laws of saving a life, there is no difference between man and woman, they are both equal....[60] And the law is the same when a woman has suffered a mortal illness and has received heavenly mercy and been healed, that she is obligated to recite *birkat hagomel* and to thank God, just like a man who recites *birkat hagomel* when he is saved.

ולמה האיש שנתרפא מברך ברכת הגומל ולא האישה שכן ראיתי מנהגינו מנהג איזמיר יע״א [יגן עליה אלהים] שאין הנשים מברכות ברכת הגומל. והלא נפש אחד להם מן השמים.... ובדין זה של פקוח נפש לא יש הפרש בין איש לאשה שניהם שוים כאחד.... והוא הדין נמי כשהאשה אירע לה חולי של סכנה וירחמו עליה מן השמים ונתרפאה היא חייבת לברך ברכת הגומל ולהודות לה׳ כמו האיש שמברך ברכת הגומל להצלתו.

And so I did on *Pesaḥ Sheni* in the year 1895 where there was a sick woman, the illustrious woman Diana Vera, may she be blessed among women of the tent, with a life-threatening illness, and praised be God that she recovered and returned to health.... I told her that according to what I learned in the rulings of our master in *Shulḥan Arukh*... she must bless. You, my dear woman, should stand to recite *birkat hagomel,* and one man entered with me, a neighbor and relative... and the woman answered and said *birkat hagomel*...and we answered, "Amen," and

וכן עשיתי מעשה בפסח ב׳ שנת כתמר יפרח לפ״ג שהיתה חולנית המעטירה נ״ב מ׳ דיינא וירא מב״ת בחולי סכנה ושלי״ת שנתרפאה ובאתה בגדר הבריאות.... אמרתי לה לפי מה שלמדתי בדין מרן בש״ע [בשלחן ערוך]... צרכה שתברך אנת אנתתי תעמוד לברך ברכת הגומל ונכנס עמדי איש א׳ שכן וקרוב... וענתה ואמרה האשה ברכת... וענינו אמן

60. In the section skipped, he discusses how seriously *halakhah* views the experience of childbirth.

said to her, "Who has bestowed good upon you, He should bestow[61] all good to you forever, *selah*. Amen."	ואמרנו לה אשר גמלך כל טוב הוא תגמלך כל טוב נצח סלה אמן.

Interestingly, also in R. Palaji's community, in Izmir, the women did not recite *hagomel* and he argues strongly against that practice. He sees no difference between women and men with regard to this obligation, for, just as one may equally save a woman or a man when their life is in danger from illness on Shabbat, so too women and men are equally required to recite *birkat hagomel* upon being saved. This logic is not just theoretical for R. Palaji. He actively works to educate women about their obligation to thank God. He describes how he instructed a woman in his community to recite *hagomel* after her life-threatening illness and responded to her blessing, although he did not require her to recite it in the presence of a *minyan*. In the continuation of the text, not quoted above, R. Palaji writes with joy about how he then found the opinion of *Kenesset Hagedolah* and was glad to have made a decision which concurred with it. R. Palaji makes a strong and clear statement for women's obligation to recite *birkat hagomel* being on par with men's obligation.[62]

Another contemporary Sephardic authority, *Ben Ish Ḥai,* is also concerned with instructing women on how to recite *hagomel* properly, in order to fulfill their obligation.

61. The Hebrew refers to God in the feminine form as תגמלך ("*she* should bestow").
62. See *Responsa Yeḥavveh Da'at* (below, source #30); and *Responsa Vayitsbor Yosef* #41 (who reads the story as having happened to R. Palaji's wife), though R. Schwarz eventually rejects his position. R. Schwarz writes that perhaps the reason women do not say *birkat hagomel* is because it must be said within three days, at which time women are still in *niddah* from the childbirth and therefore cannot recite blessings. See also *Responsa Vaya'an Avraham* 17, who brings the same argument. However, this does not explain why women do not recite *birkat hagomel* upon leaving the other dangers mentioned in the Gemara, which do not relate to their *niddah* status. See Devorah Zlochower, "May Women Touch a Torah Scroll?" (in forthcoming volume in this series), https://www.jofa.org/Education/Ritual_Opportunities/May_Women_Touch_A_Torah_Scroll, who explains why a woman's *niddah* status does not bar her from reciting blessings. See n91, below.

23. Ben Ish Ḥai ***First Year, Parashat Ekev #5*** R. Yosef Ḥayyim of Baghdad, Iraq (1834–1909)	**בן איש חי** **שנה א פרשת עקב אות ה**
Women are obligated in *birkat hagomel*, and they should recite the blessing with a *minyan* in order to recite it with *shem umalkhut*. And if it is difficult for her to recite the blessing with a *minyan* due to embarrassment, she should recite the blessing without *shem umalkhut*. And if she does not know [how to recite *birkat hagomel*], her husband or another should teach her, since it is a short blessing.	הנשים חייבין בברכת הגומל ויברכו בעשרה כדי לברך בשם ומלכות. ואם קשה לה לברך בעשרה מחמת הבושה תברך בלא שם ומלכות. ואם אינה יודעת ילמדו אותה בעלה או אחר כי ברכה קצרה היא.

He rules that women should ideally recite *birkat hagomel* in front of a *minyan*, so that they can recite the blessing with *shem umalkhut*[63] and thereby fulfill their obligation in the optimal manner; like the *Shulḥan Arukh*, he holds that a *minyan* is essential.[64] In his mind, there is nothing immodest in that behavior. However, *Ben Ish Ḥai* acknowledges that this requirement may place the woman in an awkward situation and she may be embarrassed in front of the men.[65] In such a case, he suggests that she recite the blessing by herself but without the usual liturgical structure of God's name, thus circumventing the prohibition of taking God's name in vain (*berakhah levattalah*) due to the fact that there is no *minyan*.[66] This view bears some similarities to the opinion of *Peri Mega-*

63. *Responsa Penei Yitsḥak* 1:69 also writes that if a woman who has given birth is unable to recite *birkat hagomel* with a *minyan*, she should recite it without *shem umalkhut*.
64. See *Ben Ish Ḥai*'s statements in *Ot* #2.
65. Interestingly, this way of articulating the problem – she will feel embarrassed, as opposed to saying that it is immodest – takes the woman's perspective and feelings into account.
66. See also the Sephardic *posek Kaf Haḥayyim, O.Ḥ.* 219:3, who rules similarly. He writes that women should recite *birkat hagomel* in front of a *minyan*, going so far as to say that if they cannot do so, the blessing should be recited without *shem umalkhut*, due to the concern of reciting a blessing in vain. If one is concerned with issues of modesty, *Kaf Haḥayyim* does offer the solution of a woman reciting the blessing

dim (source #18). For, despite the fact that she will not be fulfilling the obligation of reciting *hagomel,* per se, she is still required to articulate her thanks to God. *Ben Ish Ḥai* also realizes that some women may not know the blessing, so he encourages her husband or others to teach her the relatively straightforward formula.

MODERN CODES

Throughout the ages there has been a clear tension in the rabbinic sources with regard to women's recitation of *birkat hagomel.* On the one hand, the rabbis frequently attempt to understand and justify the fact that women appear regularly to have refrained from reciting *hagomel.* On the other hand, most *posekim* believe, based on logic and a reading of earlier sources, that women should be required to recite *birkat hagomel* just as men are. This tension is expressed in the modern codes, as well, with slightly different emphasis and outcomes.

As opposed to trying to change ritual practice through education, as was suggested by R. Yosef Palaji (source #22) and *Ben Ish Ḥai* (source #23), *Mishnah Berurah* seems at first glance to accept the women's behavior as a foregone conclusion.

24. *Mishnah Berurah* #219 — **משנה ברורה סימן ריט**

R. Israel Meir (Hakohen) Kagan, Poland (1839–1933)

3) And also women, it is the custom of the world that they do not recite this blessing, and the Aharonim wrote that the reason is because the way this blessing is [to be recited] is before ten, as stated before, and it is not appropriate for a woman. And there are those who wrote that nevertheless it is correct for her to bless in front of ten [men], or at least in front of women and one man.	ג) וגם נשים מנהג העולם שאין מברכין ברכה זו וכתבו האחרונים הטעם משום דסדר ברכה זו הוא בפני עשרה וכדלקמיה ולא אורח ארעא לאשה. ויש שכתבו דמ"מ [דמכל מקום] נכון הוא שתברך בפני עשרה עכ"פ [על כל פנים] בפני נשים ואיש אחד:

from the women's section, but in 219:33 he does not allow for the option of a husband reciting *birkat hagomel* on his wife's behalf, explaining that R. Caro's ruling in *Beit Yosef* is authoritative.

17) **For the good of his friend** – and all the more so for his wife, who is like his own body, he is permitted to bless. And from this a few men have the custom that when their wives give birth and return to good health, they [the husbands] stand up and bless *birkat hagomel.* And when she responds "Amen" to his blessing, she fulfills her obligation. And the version of the blessing he should say is, "who bestows good upon the guilty, [and] who has given you only good." And if he recites the blessing not in her presence, he should say, "who has given my wife only good."	יז) **על טובת חבירו** - וכ"ש [וכל שכן] על אשתו שהיא כגופו דרשאי לברך ומזה נוהגים קצת אנשים שכשיולדות נשותיהם וחוזרות לבורין עומדים ומברכים ברכת הגומל וכשהיא תענה אמן על ברכתו יוצאת בזה ונוסח הברכה יאמר הגומל לחייבים טובות שגמלך כל טוב. ואם בירך שלא בפניה יאמר שגמל לאשתי כל טוב.

Mishnah Berurah opens his discussion on women by making a sweeping statement that it is the custom of all women throughout the world not to recite *hagomel*. He explains that the Aḥaronim have justified this practice by saying that it is inappropriate for women to bless in front of the required *minyan* of men.[67] He does acknowledge that there are authorities who believe it would be acceptable and correct for women to recite the blessing in front of ten men, or at least in public in front of a group of other women and one man.[68] Later in his commentary, *Mishnah Berurah* also describes the husbands' custom of reciting *hagomel* for their wives. This practice clearly stems from the belief that the women's experience of labor and childbirth requires a statement of thanksgiving. This is reflected in *Mishnah Berurah*'s own language when

67. See also *Responsa Kol Mevasser*, Vol. 2, #44, s.v. *ve'od yesh lomar*, who cites this reasoning, despite the fact that *birkat hagomel* is required by the Talmud, as support against a *bat mitsvah* celebration.

68. This language makes it seem like the group must be composed of both women and one man, whereas in *Kenesset Hagedolah* (above, source #16), the originator of the idea, and subsequent authorities who quote him like *Magen Avraham* (above, source #17), the suggestion was either a group of women *or* one man. Later authorities such as R. Feinstein (below, source #26) understand him to be saying that women can make up part of the *minyan*.

he states, "and when she responds 'Amen' to his blessing, she fulfills her obligation." Although he obviously accepts and refrains from criticizing women's practice not to recite the blessing, *Mishnah Berurah* does leave open the possibility that women could or are possibly even required to recite *birkat hagomel.*

R. Epstein takes the opposite approach.[69] Although he also tries to offer an explanation for the custom of women not saying *birkat hagomel,* his tone is more critical, and he clearly rules that women are required to recite this blessing.

25. *Arukh Hashulḥan* *Oraḥ Ḥayyim 219:6*

ערוך השלחן אורח חיים סימן ריט סעיף ו

R. Yeḥiel Mikhl Epstein, Lithuania (1829–1908)

And it was customary for women not to recite the blessing, and there is no reason for this. And it is only because the custom is to recite the blessing at the time of the Torah reading, and therefore they [men] imagine that women are not obligated in this blessing. And it is therefore correct that they should bless.[70] And perhaps because

ונשים נהגו שלא לברך ואין בזה שום טעם ורק מפני שהמנהג הוא לברך בעת קריאת התורה לכן מדמים שאין הנשים חייבות בברכה זו, ולכן נכון שיברכו. ואולי מפני דכתיב בקהל עם ונשים לא מקרו קהל ולברך בפני

69. See *Benei Banim,* Vol. 2, #8 (and Vol. 1, #22). R. Yehuda Henkin quotes his grandfather R. Yosef Eliyahu Henkin:

גדול כח הערוך השלחן בהלכה יותר מהמשנה ברורה ושבמקום שחולקים יש לפסוק כערוך השלחן.

He explains that R. Epstein published his work after *Mishnah Berurah* and in many places cites it or refers to it. Accordingly, *Arukh Hashulḥan* also functions as a response to *Mishnah Berurah,* representing the traditions of Lithuania and White Russia, as opposed to those of Poland. R. Henkin explains his grandfather's statement as follows:

שהערוך השלחן והמשנה ברורה חולקים בשוה בסברת עצמם או בפרוש דעת אחרים שבזה בודאי הערוך השלחן חריף יותר.

70. It is very possible that R. Epstein means they should recite it in front of a *minyan.* However, this is not completely clear, especially given the fact that earlier, when discussing the general laws for men of *hagomel,* he quotes *Tur,* who says that a *minyan* is not necessary for this blessing. It would seem that recitation in front of a *minyan* would be the ideal situation; however, the absence of a *minyan* should not deter a

it says, "In an assembly of people" (Psalms 107:32), and women are not called an assembly [*kahal*], and to bless in front of men is not appropriate, for that reason they [women] refrained from it.	אנשים אינו מדרך ארץ ולכן נמנעו מזה.

As a synagogue rabbi, R. Epstein is frustrated that it is not the prevailing custom for women to recite *hagomel.* He offers two different possible reasons, one from the perspective of the men and one from the perspective of the women, for how this negative practice could have developed. He suggests that the fact that it is customary for men to recite *hagomel* during the public Torah reading in synagogue may have led men to imagine that women are not obligated in *hagomel.* Alternatively, perhaps since one must recite the blessing in front of a *minyan* of ten men, and not in the presence of women, the women themselves felt uncomfortable and refrained from doing so. Whatever the reason for the evolution of this practice, R. Epstein does not consider these sufficient justification, and he states clearly that there is no legitimate legal explanation for women to refrain from thanking God. Clearly, women are obligated to recite *birkat hagomel.*[71]

American *posek* R. Moshe Feinstein's ruling relates to both R. Epstein and *Mishnah Berurah* (it was also the last responsum that he wrote himself before his death).

---

woman from reciting *hagomel* and fulfilling her obligation. This policy is in marked distinction from the Sephardic *posekim* above, most of whom stress the importance of a *minyan* for *birkat hagomel,* following the ruling of R. Yosef Caro.

71. R. Epstein reiterates this ruling later on in *Arukh Hashulḥan, O.Ḥ.* 219:6, stating "that a woman who is obligated in *birkat hagomel,*" her husband may recite *birkat hagomel* on her behalf; however, he comments that the custom was not to do so, presumably encouraging her to recite the blessing herself.

26. *Responsa Iggerot Moshe Oraḥ Ḥayyim, Vol. 5, #14*

שו"ת אגרות משה אורח חיים חלק ה סימן יד

R. Moshe Feinstein, United States (1895–1986)

There is essentially no rhyme or reason to distinguish between a man and a woman with regard to the obligation of blessings of thanksgiving.... And since a man is obligated to recite the blessing, certainly a woman is also obligated to recite the blessing. However, there are matters where the sages were stringent in the manner of practice, that [they required] the one who is obligated to recite the blessing [to do so] specifically in front of ten, and on the day of the Torah reading, and at the time that they call him to the Torah [for an *aliyah*]. And only if it is impossible for him to be called to the Torah may he bless on the *bimah* immediately after the reading of the Torah. And this is even though this [blessing] is not connected to the blessing on the Torah. For example, this is the custom with *birkat hagomel*.... And this [behavior] is not relevant for a woman in our times, as we do not call a woman to the Torah [for an *aliyah*].[72]

הנה בעצם אין מקום ואין טעם לחלק בחיוב ברכות ההודאה בין איש לאשה.... וכיון שאיש מחוייב לברך, וודאי שגם אשה מחוייבת לברך. אך איכא דברים שהחמירו חכמים באופן העשייה, שיברך החייב לברך דווקא בעשרה, וביום הקריאה, ובשעה שקראוהו לתורה ורק אם אי אפשר לו שיקראוהו לתורה, מברך על הבימה תיכף אחר הקריאה בתורה. והוא אף שלא שייך זה לברכת התורה. כהמנהג בברכת הגומל... שזה לא שייך באשה בזמנינו, שאין קורין אשה לתורה.

[Editor's note:] Until here is the holy writing of our teacher [R. Moshe Feinstein], may his holy memory be a blessing. This was the last responsum written in his hand,

עד כאן כתי"ק [כתב יד קדוש] של מרן זצוק"ל [זכר צדיק וקדוש לברכה]. זו היתה התשובה האחרונה שכתב

72. It is interesting to speculate what R. Feinstein might have said today about those places in which women do receive *aliyot*, and whether in those communities she would be required to receive an *aliyah* to fulfill her obligation to recite *birkat hagomel*.

and he tried to write it three times, until he put it aside due to difficulty with his vision. The writing of these lines lasted a number of hours. Orally he added that it is not as *Mishnah Berurah* (219:3) brought, that the woman should recite the blessing in front of ten, who are comprised of women and one man. Rather there is no significance to a *minyan* of women, and it is enough if she recites the blessing in front of one person, man or woman. And ideally, if she is married, she should recite the blessing in front of her husband.[73]	בעצם כתב ידו, וניסה לכתבה שלש פעמים, עד שהניח מחמת קושי הראייה. כתיבת שורות אלה נמשכה כמה שעות. על־פה הוסיף שלא כדהביא במשנה ברורה ס"ק ג' שתברך בפני עשרה, עכ"פ [על כל פנים] בפני נשים, ואיש אחד. אלא שאין עניין במניין של נשים, ודייה אם תברך בפני אדם אחד, איש או אשה, ולכתחילה, אם היא נשואה, תברך בפני בעלה.

R. Feinstein makes a distinction here between the pure halakhic obligation and the practical way in which the obligation can be fulfilled. While, like R. Epstein, he rules emphatically that women are obligated in *birkat hagomel* just as men are, since there is no logical reason to distinguish between the genders, he nonetheless explains that women cannot practically fulfill the *mitsvah*. The sages were stringent about certain aspects of the recitation of *hagomel*, most significantly the link between the blessing and the Torah reading. Thus, even a man who did not receive an *aliyah* would come up to the *bimah* after the Torah reading to recite the thanksgiving blessing. R. Feinstein explains that since women in his day are not called to the Torah, their recitation becomes difficult. What is noteworthy here is that, for R. Feinstein, the practical hindrance is not one of immorality, promiscuity, or even modesty, as others have claimed. Rather, the connection made between *birkat hagomel* and the Torah reading, coupled with the fact that women do not receive *aliyot* to the Torah, is at the root of the problem. It seems to be a purely tech-

73. This notion of saying the blessing specifically in front of her husband is a new idea, not mentioned in earlier sources. However, it fits naturally with the overall concern that there is something inappropriate or uncomfortable with a woman standing before other men. Or, possibly, since R. Feinstein does not mention the issue of immodesty, he simply suggests her husband as the most available audience, who is most likely to enable her to recite the blessing.

nical issue. At this point the written responsum ends. Orally, as pointed out by R. Shabtai Rappaport in his editor's note,[74] R. Feinstein seeks to answer the question of how women are actually supposed to fulfill their obligation to recite *birkat hagomel.* He concludes that women should recite the blessing in front of one other person; if she is married, the person should ideally be her husband.[75] He rejects *Mishnah Berurah*'s suggestion that the *minyan* can be composed of women. Unfortunately, due to his poor health it is clear that R. Feinstein did not fully flesh out the issue, and he leaves a number of matters unaddressed.[76]

In Israel, in the *ḥaredi* world, the concern regarding modesty continues to be the primary issue. In the same responsum where R. Halberstam, Rebbe of Sanz, discusses whether it is appropriate to build a women's section in a synagogue,[77] he also address the issue of women's reciting *birkat hagomel.*

---

74. The responsum above is included in the eighth volume of *Iggerot Moshe,* which was published after R. Feinstein's death and edited by his grandson-in-law R. Shabtai Rappaport.

75. R. Feinstein does not explain the requirement for a listener, but perhaps one can understand it as his desire to preserve the public nature of the thanksgiving, without violating other halakhic imperatives. It would seem as though R. Feinstein does not believe than a *minyan* is essential for *birkat hagomel.* He seems to separate the essential obligation of reciting *birkat hagomel* from the practical aspects of *minyan* and Torah reading that were added later. Though, as shown above, *minyan* is mentioned in the Talmud, while Torah reading is added hundreds of years later by the Tosafists. See n11, above.

76. R. Feinstein does not address the question of whether a woman can recite the blessing in the synagogue during the Torah reading from the women's section, rather than from the *bimah.* He also does not indicate whether it would be better for her to recite the blessing in front of a male *minyan* at a time other than the Torah reading, rather than in front of just one person, or whether, once the link to the Torah reading has been severed, the issue of *minyan* is no longer relevant. He also does not discuss the issue of a husband's reciting the blessing on behalf of his wife.

77. He mentions that many synagogues did not have a women's section and that, if they did, there was only a hole in the floor through which to hear. The women surely should not see the men, and young, unmarried girls should not come to synagogue at all, for fear of inappropriate thoughts.

27. *Responsa Divrei Yetsiv Even Ha'ezer #35*[78]

שו"ת דברי יציב חלק אה"ע סימן לה

R. Yekutiel Yehudah Halberstam, Kiryat Sanz (1905–1994)

[It is written] in the notebook on *birkhot hanehenin* by the Rav *Ba'al Hatanya,* chapter 13, paragraph 3, that every postpartum woman when she arises strong should bless in the woman's section of the synagogue and ten men will hear her inside [the sanctuary]. But in our places our custom is not thus, and one could say that they were concerned about the licentiousness of hearing the voice of a woman…and in general they recite the blessing in a voice that is slightly pleasant. And also, if they [women] should err in the language of the blessing and the men correct them, it would be like a case where a man answers a woman [which is inappropriate]. Seek and you will find.

ובקונטרס על ברכות הנהנין להרב בעל התניא בפרק י"ג אות ג', דכל אשה יולדת כשתקום מחליה תברך בבית הכנסת של נשים וישמעו עשרה אנשים מבפנים עכ"ל [עד כאן לשונו]. אבל במקומותינו לא נהגו כן, וי"ל [ויש לומר] שחששו משום פריצותא של שמיעת קול אשה... ובדרך כלל מברכים בקול נעימה קצת. וגם אם יטעו בנוסח הברכה והאנשים יתקנו אותם, הוי כהך דעני גברי ודו"ק [ודייק ותמצא קל].

And furthermore, we can say that women do not get anything through their own merit, but only through the merit of their husbands. And in several matters we find that they are punished for the sins of their husbands,

ויש לומר עוד דנשים אין להם בזכות עצמן אלא בזכות בעליהן, ובכמה דברים מצינו שנענשים בעון הבעל, וכגון בעון נדרים [שבת ל"ב ע"ב]

78. It is worth noting the context in which R. Halberstam's discussion of women's recitation of *birkat hagomel* is codified. *Shulḥan Arukh* discusses *birkat hagomel* along with the other *birkhot hare'iyyah* in *O.Ḥ.*, where daily matters such as prayer and blessings are discussed, and almost all later commentaries and halakhists also discuss *birkat hagomel* in this context. Though R. Halberstam has a lengthy, general discussion of *birkat hagomel* in *O.Ḥ.* #86, those who compiled his responsa after his death included the question of women's recitation of *hagomel* in *E.H.*, in the context of הלכות הרחקה מעריות (the laws of distancing oneself from forbidden sexual relations).

such as the sin of vows (B.T. *Shab.* 32b), and elsewhere. And for this reason, when they recite, "who bestows good upon the guilty," it is a sort of disparagement of their husbands, and you should understand this. And I was very happy to find it written in *Eliyah Rabbah* 219:12 that the reason for the custom is as with a minor, since the main punishment for a woman is for her husband's sin.	ועוד, ולזה כשמברכות הגומל לחייבים טובות הוי כעין זלזול בבעליהן והבן. ומאוד שמחתי שמצאתי בא"ר סי' רי"ט ס"ק י"ב שכתב, דטעם המנהג כמו בקטן דעיקר עונש אשה בחטא בעלה.

R. Halberstam notes that, although there exists an older Ḥasidic tradition for women to recite *hagomel* from the women's section, in his community, they do not do so. R. Halberstam raises two main points as rationales for excusing women from *birkat hagomel.* The first relates to concerns of modesty and the prohibition against *kol ishah* (hearing a woman's voice, usually singing voice), which he claims would apply here.[79] This concern about hearing women's voices had not been raised in the earlier sources; neither those which allow women to recite *hagomel* in front of men nor those which justify women's custom to refrain from blessing find any issue with a women's speaking voice. The modesty concerns which were raised focused solely on the issue of women's appearing before men. R. Halberstam supports his argument by noting that women's recitation of blessings tends to sound slightly pleasant, even if it is not exactly singing, and that if she were to make a mistake the men would respond directly to her to correct it.[80] This reason does not explain why women would not be able to recite the blessing in front of other women, to themselves, or in front of their husbands. His second suggestion for why women should not recite *hagomel* is that women are

79. R. Halberstam is not alone in invoking the concept of immorality and promiscuity in this context. *Torat Ḥakham* (*siman* 17, page 28c–29c) invokes the concern of sexual immorality with perhaps even more vehemence. He is strongly rejected by R. Ovadiah Yosef (source #30, below).

80. This concern is an odd one as presumably even when she recites the blessing correctly the men listening would respond with the traditional rejoinder said by the congregation to *birkat hagomel.*

neither punished nor rewarded through their own merit, but through the merit or demerit of their husbands. It is, therefore, demeaning for a woman to recite *birkat hagomel,* as it implies some fault ("guilt") in her husband. This argument would preclude women from ever reciting *hagomel,* an idea also unprecedented in prior sources. Even those like *Magen Avraham,* who suggested that women might be exempt from reciting *birkat hagomel,* believed that is was an option available to women if they so chose.[81]

R. Halberstam's contemporary, R. Shlomo Zalman Auerbach also cites immodesty as the primary concern in women's recitation of *birkat hagomel* but allows women to recite *hagomel* in certain circumstances:

28. *Responsa Minḥat Shelomo Tinyana (2–3), 60:10*

שו"ת מנחת שלמה תנינא (ב-ג) סימן ס אות י

R. Shlomo Zalman Auerbach, Jerusalem (1910–1995)

However, the reason that it is not customary for women [to recite *birkat hagomel*] is, as everyone knows, for reasons of modesty, for "the honor of the daughter of a king is internal." And only with a woman who has given birth, since it is common for the relatives to gather in the house, and she is obligated in sacrifices (even though this is not a *korban todah*), in Jerusalem many [women] have the custom to recite this blessing. And there are those who just come to the synagogue to hear *barekhu,*[82] which is not the case with one who miscarries. For even though [one who miscarries] is

אמנם הטעם שנשים אינן נוהגות בכך הוא כידוע מפני הצניעות שכבודה בת מלך פנימה, ורק ביולדת הואיל וכרגיל הקרובים מתאספים בבית וגם חייבת בקרבנות (אע"ג [אף על גב] שאין זה קרבן תודה), רבים נוהגים בירושלם בברכה זו, ויש שרק באות לביהכנ"ס [לבית הכנסת] לשמוע "ברכו", משא"כ [מה שאינו כן] במפלת אע"ג [אף על גב] שחייבת בקרבן אבל כיון דליכא כלל אסיפת קרובים לכן

81. Even *Eliyah Rabbah,* who R. Halberstam joyfully exclaims agrees with him, mentions that the husband would recite *hagomel* for his wife, not that he would find it degrading.

82. This clause is not found in *Minḥat Shelomo* II, 4:31, in which the text is almost identical to the text of the above responsum. However, R. Auerbach offers this suggestion in the personal note quoted at the end and cited below.

<table>
<tr>
<td>obligated to bring a sacrifice, since there is no gathering of relatives, therefore, they do not bless [birkat hagomel]. However, I think that according to everyone bringing the korban todah after childbirth is only a mitsvah but not an obligation, and even birkat hagomel (as explained in Magen Avraham at the beginning of section 219) is considered only optional.... But what should be done for his wife who was ill [unconnected with childbirth] or traveled at sea? According to this, surely he [the husband] can correctly bless [for her].</td>
<td dir="rtl">אינן מברכות. אמנם חושבני דלכו"ע [דלכולי עלמא] הבאת קרבן תודה ליולדת זו רק מצוה אבל לא חיוב, ואף גם ברכת הגומל מבואר במ"א ריש סי' רי"ט דנחשב רק רשות.... אבל מה נעשה באשתו שחלתה או היתה מיורדי הים, דלפי"ז [דלפי זה] הרי יכול שפיר לברך.</td>
</tr>
</table>

Though R. Auerbach mentions the concern of modesty, he notes with approbation the custom of women in Jerusalem to recite *birkat hagomel* in the presence of a *minyan* at a family gathering or party after childbirth.[83] He is the first authority to mention a custom in which women actively recite *hagomel* as opposed to refraining from doing so. R. Auerbach differentiates between a woman's reciting *birkat hagomel* in front of a *minyan* in the synagogue and in front of a *minyan* in her home. By bringing the *minyan* to the woman's house, she can simultaneously remain in the private realm ("All the honor of the daughter of a king is internal") while reciting *birkat hagomel* in front of a *minyan*. The weight R. Auerbach gives to the obligation of women to bring a thanksgiving sacrifice is also noteworthy, although he distinguishes the blessing from the sacrifice; as is the connection he establishes between situations in which women are obligated to bring a sacrifice and situations in which they would desire to recite *birkat hagomel*. He explains that a woman does not recite *hagomel* after a miscarriage, even though she would bring a

83. It is interesting to compare R. Auerbach to others. See, for example, the contemporary *Shorshei Minhag Ashkenaz* (4 vols.; Benei Berak: Machon Moreshes Ashkenaz, 1995–2004) where R. Binyomin Solomon Hamburger cites a number of other practices with regard to the *yoledet*, all in order to avoid allowing her to recite *birkat hagomel*.

sacrifice, because, although she might want to bless, she does not have a structure in which to do so, as there is no celebratory gathering of relatives. After placing significant emphasis on the requirement to recite the blessing in the presence of a *minyan*, R. Auerbach ends by suggesting, following *Magen Avraham*, that *hagomel* is not actually an obligatory ritual. This statement may refer only to the recitation of *hagomel* after childbirth and not to the four situations mentioned in the Talmud; for he mentions that in those situations a husband should recite *hagomel* for his wife and thus avoid any problem of immodesty. Likewise, in another responsum R. Auerbach discusses women's recitation of *birkat hagomel* after recovering from an illness and states that the blessing is essentially obligatory.

29. *Responsa Minḥat Shelomo* Vol. 2, 4:31

שו"ת מנחת שלמה חלק ב סימן ד אות לא

R. Shlomo Zalman Auerbach, Jerusalem (1910–1995)

In regard to your question [whether a woman should recite *birkat hagomel* after an operation], although for reasons of modesty it is the custom that women do not recite the blessing except after childbirth, since they are also obligated in sacrifices, there are those who bless in front of ten [men], and there are those who only come to synagogue to hear *barekhu*. Nevertheless, since in any case there will be a *minyan* by you [at your home], God willing, for Shavuot, it is appropriate that she should bless, since from the essence of the law they [women] are obligated in it [*birkat hagomel*].

בנוגע לשאלתך [אם תברך אשה ברכת הגומל לאחר ניתוח] אף שמטעמי צניעות נהגו שנשים אינן מברכות פרט לאחר לידה הואיל וגם חייבות בקרבנות לכן יש שמברכות בפני עשרה ויש שרק באות לביהכ"נ [לבית הכנסת] לשמוע "ברכו" מ"מ [מכל מקום] הואיל ובלא"ה [בלאו הכי] יהיה בעהי"ת [בעזרת השם יתברך] מנין אצלך בחג העצרת מן הראוי שכן תברך הואיל ומעיקר הדין חייבים הן בכך.

R. Auerbach explains that some women do recite *hagomel* in front of men, while others, who are concerned with issues of modesty, simply listen to the recitation of *barekhu*. In this specific case, where the questioner will be having a *minyan* in his house anyway, R. Auerbach recommends that the wife recite the blessing at that time. Because she is legally obligated to say *hagomel* after an operation, this situation is comparable to the recitation of the blessing in front of a *minyan* at home after childbirth, which is not immodest as it is recited in the home.

The most thorough discussion of women's obligation to recite *birkat hagomel* can be found in the writings of former Sephardic chief rabbi of Israel R. Ovadiah Yosef, who addresses this topic in a number of places.[84]

30. *Responsa Yeḥavveh Da'at* 4:15 R. Ovadiah Yosef, Israel (1920–2013)	**שו"ת יחווה דעת** **חלק ד סימן טו**
And therefore it is correct to practice in accordance with the ruling of *Kenesset Hagedolah*, that a woman should recite the blessing in the women's section when there are ten men in the synagogue and they are reading from the Torah…. And similarly if they are making a party in their house for the birth of a son or daughter, and there are ten men present, the woman should enter and recite *birkat hagomel* in front of them, and for this she will be blessed…. And I saw in the book *Torat Ḥakham* (28c) by the *ga'on* R. Yosef Yedid Halevi,	ולכן הנכון שיש לנהוג כדברי הכנסת הגדולה שהאשה תברך בעזרת נשים כשיש עשרה אנשים בבית הכנסת וקוראים בתורה.... וכן אם עושים מסיבה בבית להולדת הבן או הבת, ויש שם עשרה אנשים, יש לאשה להיכנס ולברך בפניהם ברכת הגומל ותבוא עליה ברכה.... וראיתי להגאון רבי יוסף ידיד הלוי בספר תורת חכם (דף כ"ח ע"ג) שהאריך בזה, וכתב,

84. See *Responsa Yabbia Omer*, Vol. 8, *O.Ḥ.* #15:15, s.v. *besiman*, and #22:10, s.v. *be'ot*. In those responsa, as well as in the one quoted here, R. Yosef comes out strongly against the practice of women reciting *birkat hagomel* in front of a group of women and one man, since there are those (Rabbenu Yonah and Me'iri, and later *Sh. Ar.*) who rule that the presence of a *minyan* for *birkat hagomel* is essential. Therefore, no man or woman should recite *birkat hagomel* without a *minyan*. See R. Yosef's online responsa for a concise discussion of his views on women's obligation in *hagomel*: http://halachayomit.co.il/DisplayRead.asp?readID=472&txtSearch=%D7%91%D7%A8%D7%9B%D7%AA%20%D7%94%D7%92%D7%95%D7%9E%D7%9C.

who wrote on this matter at length, saying that a woman should not enter amongst the men to recite *birkat hagomel,* because of [concern for] sexual immorality and thoughts of sin. See there.[85] But I say that the evil inclination is not present for such a short time as this....[86] And especially in our times when the women are in the habit of going into the marketplace [public realm] among men....

שאין לאשה להיכנס בין האנשים לברך הגומל, משום פריצות, והרהורי עבירה. ע"ש [עיין שם]. ואני אומר שאין יצר הרע מצוי לשעה קלה כזאת.... ובפרט בזמן הזה שהנשים רגילות לצאת לשוק בין האנשים....

That which they said the singing voice of a woman is licentiousness, nevertheless in a place where there is fear of the *Shekhinah,* one does not worry about such [things]....

שזה שאמרו קול זמר של אשה ערוה, מכל מקום במקום דאיכא אימתא דשכינה, אין לחוש לכך....

And at first glance how did they permit to call up a woman to read from the Torah with the cantillation?[87] Is it not [a violation of the prohibition of] a woman's singing voice?... And one must say that they permitted a woman to read [from the Torah] in public when there are not seven [men] who are expert in reading, as in a place where the *Shekhinah* resides the rabbis did not worry about inappropriate sexual thoughts. And from this we may say that also in our case since the woman enters exclusively for the recitation of *birkat hagomel* and in the place where there are ten [a *minyan*], the *Shekhinah* resides [there] (B.T. *Sanh.* 39a).

ולכאורה איך התירו להעלות אשה לקרות בתורה בטעמי המקרא, והרי זה כקול זמר באשה.... ובע"כ [ובעל כרחך] לומר שהתירו לאשה לקרות בצבור כשאין שבעה בקיאים לקרות, משום שבמקום השראת שכינה לא חששו חכמים להרהור. ומעתה יש לומר שגם בנ"ד [בנידון דידן] הואיל והאשה נכנסת אך ורק לברכת הגומל ובמקום בי עשרה שכינתא שריא, (סנהדרין ל"ט ע"א), לפיכך אין לחוש לברכת הגומל באופן

85. See R. Yosef Yedid Halevi, *Torat Ḥakham* 17 (28c–29c) quoted in n41, above.
86. Proof of this idea is in the permission given for a *ḥatan* to place a ring on the finger of his *kallah* when she is menstruating.
87. See B.T. *Meg.* 23a.

Therefore, we should not be worried about sexual immorality when *birkat hagomel* is recited in this manner....[88] With regard to the issue of *kol ishah*, women's voice... in the case of *birkat hagomel* surely according to all opinions it is permissible, as is made clear in the commentary of the Rashba (to B.T. *Ber.* 24a). See there. And this is not the place to go on at length.	כזה משום פריצות.... לענין קול זמר של אשה... לענין ברכת הגומל, בודאי שלכל הדעות מותר. וכמו שנתבאר בחידושי הרשב"א (ברכות כ"ד ע"א). ע"ש [עיין שם]. ואכמ"ל [ואין כאן מקום להאריך].

Beyond ruling positively that women should recite *birkat hagomel* in the synagogue in front of a *minyan* at the time of Torah reading,[89] as was suggested by *Kenesset Hagedolah* (above, source #16), or else in front of a *minyan* in the woman's home,[90] if they are making a party to celebrate the birth of the child,[91] R. Yosef also comprehensively refutes those who

88. R. Yosef brings several proofs to this point: see B.T. *Nid.* 13a and B.T. *Meg.* 23a. See also *Responsa Yabbia Omer*, Vol. 8, *O.Ḥ.* #23:15, s.v. *be'erekh*, where he states the same response more concisely. R. Yosef takes pains to prove that there is nothing untoward about women reciting this blessing in front of a *minyan* of men and that the claim that this represents a lack of modesty (or even a type of immorality) is erroneous and not normative in contemporary culture. In this context, he quotes *Levush Haḥur, Minhagim* #36, who writes that nowadays men and women are so used to each other's presence that the concern of thoughts of sin is basically moot.

89. In R. Yosef's online responsum, cited above, n84, he states their obligation more emphatically:

   נשים, אף הן חייבות בברכת הגומל, שהרי דבר פשוט הוא שאין שום חילוק ביו אנשים לנשים, שהכל חייבים להודות לה' על הטוב אשר גמלם.

   He references the following authorities, who concur: Ḥida in *Birkhei Yosef*, R. Yitsḥak Abulafia in *Responsa Penei Yitsḥak*, and R. Yosef Ḥayyim of Baghdad in *Ben Ish Ḥai*.

90. Putting these two suggestions on par with each other makes sense, because there is more significance to reciting *birkat hagomel* in front of a *minyan* than there is in reciting it at the time of Torah reading. See n1, above.

91. Interestingly, he mentions the birth of either a son or a daughter, and in R. Yosef's online responsum, cited above, he specifically suggests the women recite the blessing at a *brit milah* or *simḥat bat:*

   ורשאית לברך בביתה כאשר יש שם עשרה אנשים, או אם נולד לה בן, תוכל לברך בזמן סעודת ברית המילה, וכן אם נולדה לה בת ועשו לכבודה "זבד הבת" וכדומה, תברך שם, ויענו כל הקהל לברכתה. (ואין לאשה למנוע עצמה מלברך ומלהתפלל ומלקיים את המצוות שלא בזמן טהרתה.)

challenged such a ruling on the grounds that there is something immodest or inappropriate about a woman's blessing before men.[92] R. Yosef makes a two-tiered argument to make his point. First, he argues that in modern times, when it is common for men and women to intermingle in the public domain,[93] a short encounter with a woman should not arouse a man's evil inclination. All the more so, he continues, when she is reciting *hagomel* in the synagogue or elsewhere in the presence of a *minyan*, the seriousness of the religious space and moment and the fear and awe in the surrounding divine presence would surely protect against any improper thoughts. R. Yosef also explains that for this same reason one does not need to worry about hearing the woman's voice. He learns from the fact that the rabbis permit a woman to receive an *aliyah* to the Torah in certain circumstances and to read with the traditional cantillation that there must not be any problem with hearing her voice, singing or otherwise, during a religious ritual. R. Yosef makes it very clear in his

92. R. Yosef also refutes those (such as R. Avraham Palaji, *Responsa Vayitsbor Yosef*, and *Sefer Torat Ḥayyim*) who claim that since the woman has not yet gone to the *mikveh* she cannot recite blessings. He states that this argument is invalid since words of Torah are not susceptible to impurity and, therefore, women may pray and recite blessings when in *niddah*. See n61, above.

93. The argument that attitudes toward modesty have changed in our time, used to support women's recitation of *hagomel*, is also stated by another prominent Israeli rabbi, R. Dov Lior, in an online responsum found at http://www.yeshiva.org.il/ask/67367, based on a telephone response.

שאלה:

בסימן ריט׳ באו״ח המשנ״ב סק״ג: טוען שנשים לא יברכו ברכת הגומל. מצד שני בסק״יז הוא פוסק שבעל יכול לברך לאשתו היולדת ולהוציאה ידי חובה. מצד שלישי רוה״פ שראיתי כן מחייבים את האשה לברך. מה דעת הרב בעניין? כיצד להדריך את הציבור בדין זה?

תשובה של הרה״ג דוב ליאור:

פעם היה בעיה של צניעות, וכיום זה די מקובל שנשים מברכות בבית הכנסת או שבעלה מזמין הביתה עשרה גברים ותברך לפניהם. פעם זה לא היה מקובל ולכן היה לזה בעיה צניעותית אבל כיום זה לא שייך. וכמובן שאישה חייבת להודות לה׳, אם היא יולדת וכדו׳, שניצלה מסכנה.

Also on that site, see other responsa on this topic by R. Lior and R. Ya'akov Ariel, all of which support the position that the woman herself must recite *birkat hagomel* in front of a *minyan*.

refutation that any concerns related to promiscuity and sexual immorality do not apply to women's recitation of *birkat hagomel.*[94]

CONCLUSIONS

From the very nature of what *birkat hagomel* represents – a public acknowledgment and expression of thanksgiving to God upon being saved from a life-threatening experience – logic dictates that any Jew, irrespective of gender, should thank and praise their creator in this manner. As such, the Talmud itself and the Rishonim appear to hold that there is no difference between men's and women's obligations to recite *birkat hagomel.* A large majority of the Aḥaronim who discuss this issue explicitly also rule that women are obligated to recite *hagomel,* despite the fact that there seems to have been an erroneous practice for women to refrain from reciting this blessing. In their discussions, a number of issues and halakhic considerations arise:

- How intrinsic to the obligation of *birkat hagomel* is the presence of a *minyan*?
- If a *minyan* is essential, how much weight should be given to the concerns of modesty which were raised by earlier *posekim*?
- Is a husband permitted to recite *birkat hagomel* for his wife, or does this create the problem of a *berakhah levattalah*?

94. Interestingly, from the language used by R. Yosef in his citation of Yedid Halevi concerning promiscuity, it is clear that Yedid Halevi is addressing an extreme situation where the woman reciting *hagomel* actually enters into the men's section of the synagogue to be in the presence of the *minyan.* Presumably a woman would need to do this in a synagogue which did not have an actual women's section or where the women's section was a distinct and separate domain, and thus not considered halakhically to be in the presence of the *minyan.* (See for example *Arukh Hashulḥan, O.Ḥ.* 55:20.) In his response supporting women's recitation of *hagomel* in front of men, R. Yosef uses the same language of "the woman enters," thus seemingly sanctioning not just her recitation from the women's section but also the possibility that she could enter into the all-male domain. From this context, it seems he would even permit her to enter into the men's section; however, in his online responsum concerning a woman's reciting *kaddish,* R. Yosef only permits a male *minyan* gathering in the women's section or at home to respond to a woman's recitation of *kaddish.* See n41, above.

Based on the different methods used by the rabbinic authorities to answer the above questions, the following conclusions can be drawn:

- Both women and men are equally obligated in the recitation of *birkat hagomel* upon experiencing a salvation; minimally, one of the four salvations listed in the Talmud, and maximally, any salvation.
- There are many significant *posekim* who rule that the optimal way for a woman to fulfill her obligation is for her to recite *birkat hagomel* in front of a *minyan*.
- In the case of a woman who is unable to be in the presence of a *minyan*, there are some significant *posekim* who rule that she should recite *birkat hagomel* in front of either other women or her husband, or even possibly alone.[95]
- There are some *posekim* who would allow for the husband's recitation of *birkat hagomel* on behalf of his wife, if need be, without the concern of *berakhah levattalah*.

Whichever route is most comfortable for a woman and for her community to fulfill the obligation to recite *birkat hagomel*, it is important not to lose sight of the point of *birkat hagomel*: to offer public thanksgiving to God in lieu of the *korban todah*. In communities which welcome women's recitation of *birkat hagomel* in front of a *minyan*, women should do so prominently, either during or after the Torah reading, or publicly at the *kiddush*, *brit milah*, or *simḥat bat* celebration. For those communities for which modesty is still a concern, alternate ways for women to fulfill this *mitsvah* should be presented, so that it is not forgotten or sidestepped. Women can be encouraged to recite *birkat hagomel* in front of a group of other women, or at a family gathering, ideally with a *minyan* present.

Furthermore, the gratitude and the desire to give thanks which *birkat hagomel* (and the thanksgiving offering) express are a part of human nature. Upon being cured from an illness, surviving a serious car accident, or giving birth to a baby, there is a desire to express abundant

95. It seems from the sources that it would be better to have another hear the expression of thanks than to recite the blessing alone.

gratitude to God. In the absence of awareness of *birkat hagomel* or the ability to recite it comfortably, people have turned and will continue to turn to other, non-ritualistic modes of giving thanks. But given that Jewish texts and tradition contain the formula for expressing such gratitude, it behooves Jewish communities to make *birkat hagomel* a central part of the thanksgiving ritual for men and women alike.

Appendix

SHOULD *BIRKAT HAGOMEL* BE RECITED AFTER CHILDBIRTH?

The issue of childbirth presents a unique question, which also relates directly to women's obligation to recite *birkat hagomel*. While much of the discussion of women and *birkat hagomel* focuses either on women saying it for themselves or on a husband saying it for his wife after childbirth,[96] there is another aspect to the discussion which avoids the question entirely by saying that *birkat hagomel* is either irrelevant or inappropriate to the situation of childbirth.

R. Tsevi Pesaḥ Frank addresses this question of childbirth in the context of a discussion of whether someone who survived a stroke which paralyzed half of his face should recite *birkat hagomel*.

96. Interestingly there are those who discuss *birkat hagomel* as an "obligation" upon the baby rather than the mother. *Sefer Maharil (Minhagim), Hilkh. Milah* 6 mentions that the phrase *Hodu lashem ki tov* ("give thanks to God for He is good") is used in the circumcision liturgy as if to recite *birkat hagomel* on behalf of the newborn baby, who in leaving the confines of his mother's womb, is as one who was freed from imprisonment. This idea is also found several hundred years later in *Eliyah Rabbah* 114:1. Other sources mention the even more radical custom of the father bringing the baby to the synagogue at age one or two and reciting *birkat hagomel* on its behalf; see, for example, *Sefer Nishmat Ḥayyim, O.Ḥ.* #2.

31. Responsa Har Tsevi Oraḥ Ḥayyim 1:113

שו״ת הר צבי אורח חיים א סימן קיג

R. Tsevi Pesaḥ Frank, Lithuania and Jerusalem (1873–1960)

And with regard to what they said in their reasoning that specifically one who is confined to his bed from illness and experienced suffering, that only then is it relevant to recite [*birkat hagomel*]. But if by a miracle, [the suffering] has not yet reached him, there is no reason to recite the blessing. And they said this because the principle is that there is no suffering without [prior] sin, and therefore it is appropriate to recite "who bestows good upon the guilty," which is not the case in these circumstances where he is saved before even experiencing suffering, for this is not "upon the guilty." According to this reasoning we can question the *ga'on* R. Ya'avets who questioned the practice, outside of Israel, of not reciting *birkat hagomel* on behalf of a woman who has given birth. But according to the aforementioned reason, it works well, for it is not relevant in this case [childbirth] to recite "who has bestowed [good] upon the guilty," for it [childbirth] is not specifically for the wicked.

ולענין שאמרו בטעמא דדוקא מושכב חולה והיו לו יסורין אז שייך לברך, אבל בנס שלא הגיע עדיין אליו כלל אין לברך, ואמרו משום דהכלל הוא דאין יסורים בלי חטא ולכן שייך לברך הגומל לחייבים טובות, משא״כ [מה שאין כן] בכה״ג [בכהאי גוונא] שניצול בטרם שבא לכלל יסורין, אין זה לחייבים, הנה לסברא זאת יש לתמוה מדברי הגריעב״ץ שתמה על הא דאין מברכין בחו״ל [בחוץ לארץ] על יולדות, ולפי הטעם הנ״ל [הנזכר לעיל] אתי שפיר, דלא שייך בכה״ג [בכהאי גוונא] הגומל לחייבים, דאין זה לרשעים דוקא.

R. Frank has a lengthy discussion of exactly what type of salvation necessitates the recitation of *birkat hagomel*. He makes a difficult theological claim that one need only recite *birkat hagomel* when one first experiences suffering, since suffering comes as a result of sin, and it is then fitting to recite, "who bestows good upon the guilty." R. Frank suggests that the understanding of the necessary link between sin, illness, suffering, and *birkat hagomel* could explain the practice of those who do not recite *birkat hagomel* on behalf of a woman who has given birth. According to this logic, it is not an appropriate blessing, as childbirth is not suffering experienced by the wicked but rather a natural phenomenon.[97] Along these lines, R. Shimon Sofer questions whether a woman who has given birth needs to recite *birkat hagomel,* since it is a danger which everyone faces and overcomes (*Responsa Hitorerut Teshuvah* 1:59).[98]

The most salient source in this regard is the response of R. Dr. Marcus Horovitz, whose innovative logic is repeatedly engaged by later halakhists. He explains at the beginning of his responsum the custom in Frankfurt, which he verified with the elderly righteous women of the community and found in the book *Noheg Ketson Yosef,* a compendium of laws and customs in Frankfurt. R. Horovitz discusses the custom that neither the woman who has given birth nor her husband recite *birkat hagomel* and then explains his own deduction of the reasoning behind this custom.

32. *Responsa Matteih Levi*
Vol. 2
Oraḥ Ḥayyim #8

שו"ת מטה לוי
חלק ב
אורח חיים סימן ח

R. Dr. Mordekhai (Marcus) Halevi Horovitz, Frankfurt (d. 1910)

And I will not hide from my friend (who should live and be well), what seems in my humble opinion to be at the heart of the matter. For we must investigate that which our rabbis of blessed memory established in the formula of the blessing "who has bestowed good upon the guilty".... And the intention of the

ולא אכסה מידידי נ"י [נרו יאיר] מה שנראה לענ"ד [לעניות דעתי] בעיקר הדבר, דהנה יש לחקור שיסדו רבותינו ז"ל [זכרונם לברכה] בנוסח הברכה הגומל לחייבים טובות.... ולא נפלאת בעינינו ולא רחוקה כוונת הברכה שבודאי מרב

97. R. Frank does not explain his thought process completely. R. Auerbach (below, source #33) understands him to mean that since suffering in childbirth is part of nature and not just suffering which affects those who have sinned, therefore, a woman who has given birth does not need to recite *birkat hagomel.* This is similar to *Matteih Levi*'s argument in the following source. See also *Tsits Eliezer* 17:9.

98. In this context, it is interesting to note that R. Sofer fathered fifteen children. However, he then concludes based on *Kenesset Hagedolah* and *Beit Yosef* that she is obligated to recite the blessing.

blessing is not wondrous or far away, for certainly because of our many sins and iniquities we come to danger and God, Blessed be He, saves us with His mercy. But this is specifically when we come to danger for a [specific] reason, which is not the case if we are obligated to perform a *mitsvah* which cannot be performed without danger. [In such a case], God, Blessed be He, is the one who commands and He is the one who protects, and it is not relevant to bless, "who bestows [good] upon the guilty," and they did not decree in such a case blessing and thanks that God, Blessed be He, has saved us. Quite the opposite, one who blesses on something like this is lacking in faith (Heaven forbid), that he does not trust in God to save him in the performance of His holy commandments. And if so, with regard to a woman who has given birth, there exists a *mah nafshakh* ["what is your desire to say"] argument: if birth is possible without danger, then why should she recite the blessing? And if it is impossible without danger, behold we were not created for nothingness, and we were created to settle [the world through procreation], and God sanctified us through His commandments [so, here too why should she recite the blessing?]. And perhaps it is for this reason that *Beit Yosef* himself did not mention in his *Shulḥan Arukh* the blessing of *birkat hagomel* at all [regarding childbirth] – not for the woman and not for the husband.

עונותינו ופשעינו אנו באים בסכנה והש״י [והשם יתברך] ברחמיו הצילנו. אבל זה דוקא אם באנו בסכנה ע״י [על ידי] שום סיבה, משא״כ [מה שאין כן] אם אנחנו מצווים לעשות מצוה שאי אפשר לקיימה בלי סכנה הרי הש״י [והשם יתברך] הוא המצוה והוא השומר ולא שייך לברך הגומל לחייבים, ולא תקנו בזה ברכה והודאה שהצילנו הש״י [והשם יתברך], ואדרבה מי שמברך בכגון זו הוא ממחוסרי אמונה ח״ו [חס ושלום] שלא יבטח בד׳ שיצילהו בקיום דברי מצותיו הקדושים. ואם כן ביולדת ממ״נ [ממה נפשך] אם הלידה אפשר בלי סכנה אמאי תברך, ואם אי אפשר בלי סכנה הרי לא לתוהו בראנו ולשבת יצרנו וקדשנו במצותיו, ואולי מטעם זה לא הזכיר הב״י [הבית יוסף] עצמו בש״ע [בשלחן ערוך] שלו כלל ברכת הגומל לא לאשה ולא לבעל.

Matteih Levi posits that one should not recite *birkat hagomel* when the performance of a *mitsvah* puts one into danger, rather than one's own transgressions. For God has commanded us to perform *mitsvot*, and God will, therefore, protect us in their performance.[99] Therefore, however one looks at it, a woman who has given birth should not recite *birkat hagomel*: if she is not in danger in giving birth, then there is no reason to recite it; and if she *is* in danger, then she also should not recite it, since God should protect her in her performance of the *mitsvah* of having children. This *mah nafshakh* argument of *Matteih Levi* is engaged with by later halakhists.[100]

33. *Responsa Minḥat Shelomo Tinyana (2–3), 60:10*

שו"ת מנחת שלמה תנינא (ב-ג) סימן ס אות י

R. Shlomo Zalman Auerbach, Jerusalem (1910–1995)

I do not understand [*Har Tsevi*'s and *Matteih Levi*'s argument]. For even those who are at sea for the purpose of a *mitsvah*, such as one who travels in a boat in the heart of the ocean from overseas to the	ולא הבינותי, הרי גם יורדי הים לצורך מצוה כגון הבא באניה בלב ים מחו"ל [מחוץ לארץ] לא"י [לארץ ישראל] דקעביד מצוה או סיכן עצמו

99. A similar argument is made by *Berekh Et Avraham* 88a–b, though he does not bring the example of childbirth. R. Avraham Perisco writes that one need not recite *birkat hagomel* for a danger into which he willingly enters:
בצרה הבאה לאדם בעל כרחו ושלא מדעתו ונעשה לו נס... אבל בדבר שהוא במאמר השם לעשותו... אף שהקב"ה יעשה לו נס אינו מברך כיצחק.

100. *Responsa Tsits Eliezer* 19:53 and 17:9 refutes *Matteih Levi* on several counts. First, he refutes both sides of the *mah nafshakh* argument. On the one hand, R. Waldenberg claims that it is impossible for childbirth to be free from danger. For that very reason, there exists a whole set of laws relating to *mitsvot* which can be violated on behalf of a woman in childbirth (e.g., the prohibitions of Shabbat and Yom Kippur). On the other hand, despite the fact that procreation is a *mitsvah*, nevertheless childbirth is a time of danger as is seen from the Talmud, which discusses the three sins for which women are punished during childbirth (B.T. *Shab.* 31b). Thus, he has effectively nullified both sides of *Matteih Levi*'s argument. He also adds that *Matteih Levi*'s proof from R. Caro's omission is invalid, since he did discuss the issue in *Beit Yosef*. R. Waldenberg concludes by quoting *Torat Ḥayyim*, *Mishnah Berurah*, and *Shalmat Ḥayyim*, who either state plainly or clearly presume that a woman who has given birth is obligated to recite *birkat hagomel*.

land of Israel, who is performing a *mitsvah*, or one who endangers himself to save others from an army, he also recites the blessing and says "upon the guilty." And if so, why should a woman who has given birth not say [*birkat hagomel*]?... And it also seems that with a woman who has given birth, it is possible that the language of "the guilty" is indeed relevant since it [the pain] is because of the verse, "With pain you will give birth" (Gen. 3:16), which is a punishment for a sin.	להציל אחרים מן הגייס ג"כ [גם כן] מברך ואומר לחייבים, וא"כ [ואם כן] למה לא תגיד יולדת.... וגם נראה דביולדת אפשר דשפיר שייך לשון חייבים, כיון שהוא משום קרא דבעצב תלדי בנים שהוא עונש על חטא.

R. Shlomo Zalman Auerbach refutes the arguments of both *Har Tsevi* and *Matteih Levi* and makes two points in his explanation. The first is that even people who encounter danger in the context of performing a *mitsvah,* such as those who travel the sea in order to make *aliyah* to the land of Israel, must still recite *birkat hagomel.* Therefore, a woman who has given birth should be no different. His second point is that the pain of childbirth is not just part of nature, but rather it is a direct result of Eve's actions and God's punishment. Therefore, a woman who has given birth is just as "guilty" as the person who becomes ill as punishment for their sins. And thus, a woman who has given birth should certainly be obligated to recite *birkat hagomel.*

This last claim raises a challenge for the modern women who desire to perform *mitsvot* in a meaningful fashion: should they or should they not recite *birkat hagomel* after childbirth? On the one hand, R. Auerbach is arguing against the custom of women's refraining from reciting *hagomel* after childbirth and rules that they should recite the blessing. This view certainly sits well with the modern woman who desires to give thanksgiving to God for the good done to her. On the other hand, his reasoning for this requirement is one which is disturbing to most modern sensibilities. Many women strongly embrace the notion that childbirth is a wonderful and unique biological phenomenon, a belief that fits better with R. Frank's view that childbirth is a natural event and therefore the concept of sin is entirely inapplicable. Accordingly, this conceptualization and understanding of childbirth supports the custom of postpartum women not to recite *hagomel* after childbirth.

Part of the Miracle: Women and *Megillah*

Sara Tillinger Wolkenfeld

INTRODUCTION*

On Purim, Jewish communities gather together to engage in *pirsumei nissa* – public recognition of the miracles that God has performed on behalf of the Jewish people – by reading *Megillat Ester*, which tells the story of the miraculous salvation of the Jews of Persia from the wicked Haman. From a verse in the book of Esther itself, the Talmud in Tractate *Megillah* derives a *mitsvah derabbanan* (rabbinic commandment) to read the *megillah* each year, on both the evening and the morning of the holiday.[1] This obligation may be fulfilled either by reading the *megillah* oneself or by hearing it read by another.[2] To properly fulfill this *mitsvah*, ideally the *megillah* should be read out loud in the presence of a *minyan* (prayer quorum) of ten.[3]

This chapter explores the nature of a woman's obligation in *megillah* reading. There are many different views on this topic in the halakhic discourse, and to this day a variety of opinions exists of how women may participate in the reading of *Megillat Ester*.[4] The following ques-

* The author acknowledges the contributions of Devorah Zlochower to a portion of the research for this chapter and to Raḥel Berkovits for a portion of the research, writing, and editing of this chapter.

1. See Esth. 9:28: והימים האלה נזכרים ונעשים בכל דור ודור. In B.T. *Meg.* 2b, the Talmud interprets this statement as follows:

   אשכחן עשייה זכירה מנלן? אמר קרא והימים האלה נזכרים ונעשים איתקש זכירה לעשייה.

   For the obligation to read in the evening and morning, see B.T. *Meg.* 4a.
2. See Rambam, *Hilkh. Megillah* 1:2; and *Sh. Ar., O.Ḥ.* 689:2.
3. See B.T. *Meg.* 5a. Although the text may be read by an individual, a public reading is preferable. For a full discussion of this issue, see the section "Women as Part of a Quorum."
4. Much has been written on this topic in recent years. See R. Alfred S. Cohen, "Women and the Reading of the Megilla," *Journal of Halacha and Contemporary Society* 30 (1995): 25–41; Joel Wolowelsky, "Women's Megillah Readings," *Women, Jewish Law and Modernity* (1997): 94–98; R. Zevulun Zaks, "*Keriat Hamegillah Al Yedei Nashim*," *Tehumin* 18 (1998): 357–60; R. Ariel Picard, "*Keriat Hamegillah Al Yedei Nashim Lifnei Nashim*," *Tehumin* 18 (1998): 361–70; R. Avraham Weiss, "Women and the Reading of the Megillah," *The Torah U-Madda Journal* 8 (1998): 295–317; R. Aaron Cohen, "Women Reading Megillah for Men: A Rejoinder," *The Torah U-Madda Journal* 9 (2000): 248–63; R. Yehuda Henkin, *Equality Lost: Essays in Torah Commentary, Halacha, and Jewish Thought* (Jerusalem: Urim Publications, 1999); R. Aryeh Frimer, "Women's *Megilla* Reading," in *Traditions and Celebrations for the Bat Mitzvah* (ed. Ora Wiskind Elper; Jerusalem: Urim Publications, 2003),

tions are explored through an examination of Tannaitic and Amoraic views preserved in the Talmud, followed by Geonic, medieval, modern, and contemporary decisors:

- What is the nature of a woman's obligation in *megillah* reading?
- May a woman read the *megillah* for men?
- May a woman read the *megillah* for other women?
- Do ten women constitute a quorum for the public reading of the *megillah*? May they count as part of a quorum with men?
- What blessings does a woman recite when she reads the *megillah*?

MISHNAH AND BABYLONIAN TALMUD

The Mishnah in Tractate *Megillah* addresses the issue of who is fit to read *Megillat Ester*:

1. ***Mishnah Megillah 2:4***	**משנה מסכת מגילה ב:ד**
All are eligible to read the *megillah,* except for one who is deaf,[5] mentally incompetent, or a minor. R. Yehudah declares the minor eligible.	הכל כשרין לקרות את המגילה חוץ מחרש שוטה וקטן. רבי יהודה מכשיר בקטן.

281–304, accessed July 29, 2015, http://www.daat.ac.il/daat/english/tfila/frimer2.htm; R. Dr. Benjamin Lau, "*Keriat Megillah Lenashim – Al Yedei Nashim,*" accessed July 29, 2015, http://ramban.org.il/קריאת-מגילה-לנשים-על-ידי-נשים/; Yair Ettinger, "Top Sephardi Rabbi Rules Women May Chant Scroll of Esther for Men," *Haaretz Online,* March 2, 2009, accessed July 29, 2015, http://www.haaretz.com/print-edition/news/top-sephardi-rabbi-rules-women-may-chant-scroll-of-esther-for-men-1.271212; R. Daniel Landes, "The Reading of the Megilla on Purim Night," accessed July 29, 2015, http://elmad.pardes.org/holidays/the-reading-of-the-megilla-on-purim-night/; David Brofsky, *Hilkhot Mo'adim: Understanding the Laws of the Festivals* (Jerusalem: Maggid Books, 2013).

5. Usually, the definition of *ḥeresh* is one who is both deaf and unable to speak. The Gemara (B.T. *Meg.* 19b) assumes that the Mishnah here is discussing one who cannot hear but can speak and could physically read the *megillah* aloud.

The Mishnah states that all are fit to read the *megillah* with the exception of three categories of people: the deaf, the mentally incompetent, and minors. R. Yehudah disagrees regarding minors. These three groups are often linked together and are entirely exempt from the performance of *mitsvot*.[6] Presumably, this *mishnah* follows the general principle that only one who is obligated in a *mitsvah* may discharge the obligation of another. The assertion that these categories of people are not fit to read implies that they are not obligated in this *mitsvah*.[7] Women are not mentioned in this *mishnah*, which indicates that they are part of the "all" who are eligible to read the *megillah* for others because they share equally in the obligation.[8]

The *gemara* that follows this *mishnah* does not discuss the issue of a woman's reading of the *megillah* but instead focuses on the disagreement concerning minors. However, earlier in Tractate *Megillah*, the Gemara states:

6. The assumption underlying the linking of these groups is that all of them lack *da'at* – the intelligence, awareness, and understanding to be held responsible for the yoke of *mitsvot*. (In the time of *Ḥazal*, because the deaf-mute could not communicate clearly, it was thought that he was also intellectually disabled. Today this assumption is known to be incorrect in the vast majority of cases of deafness.) See, for example, *Mekhilta Derabbi Yishma'el, Ki Tissa, Masekhta Deshabbata, Parashah* 1; Rambam, *Perush Hamishnah* to M. *Menaḥ.* 9:8; R. Ovadiah of Bartenura to M. *Git.* 2:5; and Rashi to B.T. *Ḥag.* 2a, s.v. *ḥuts*.
7. See M. *Rosh Hash.* 3:8: כל שאינו מחוייב בדבר אינו מוציא את הרבים ידי חובתן. Since this is a rabbinic *mitsvah*, R. Yehudah's assertion that a minor may discharge the obligation of others may be predicated on an opinion that minors do in fact have a rabbinic obligation to hear the *megillah* because they must be educated to observe *mitsvot* properly (due to the *mitsvah* of educating children). Therefore, his statement that minors may read *megillah* on behalf of others conforms to the same general principle that one must be obligated in an act in order to discharge another's obligation. See *Tosafot*, s.v. *R. Yehudah makhshir*.
8. Two major commentators on the Mishnah, Rambam and R. Ovadiah of Bartenura, both understand the Mishnah to include women among those who are fit to read the *megillah*. See Rambam, *Perush Hamishnah* to M. *Meg.* 2:4; and R. Ovadiah of Bartenura to M. *Meg.* 2:4. Similarly, B.T. *Arakh.* 2b–3a (source #3, below) clearly understands the Mishnah in this way.

2. ***Babylonian Talmud Megillah 4a***	**תלמוד בבלי מסכת מגילה ד.**
R. Yehoshua b. Levi said: Women are obligated in the reading of the *megillah,* for they too were part of the same miracle.	ואמר רבי יהושע בן לוי: נשים חייבות במקרא מגילה שאף הן היו באותו הנס.

According to R. Yehoshua b. Levi, women are obligated to read *megillah* despite the fact that it is one of the time-caused *mitsvot* from which women often are exempt.[9] His rationale is that since women also experienced the miracle of being saved from Haman's evil decree,[10] they, too, are obligated in the ritual act that commemorates and publicizes this miracle.[11]

R. Yehoshua b. Levi's position on a woman's obligation in *megillah* reading is also cited elsewhere in the Babylonian Talmud. In Tractate

9. See M. *Kid.* 1:7: וכל מצות עשה שהזמן גרמה אנשים חיבין ונשים פטורות. A full discussion of this principle is beyond the scope of this chapter; however, the reader should be aware that this "rule" is not a useful guide for predicting a woman's obligation in *mitsvot.* In fact, there are almost as many exceptions to the rule as commandments that constitute the rule itself. See R. Saul Berman, "The Status of Women in Halakhic Judaism," in *Jewish Woman: New Perspectives* (ed. Elizabeth Koltun; New York: Schocken Books, 1976), 118. See n11.
10. Commentators debate the meaning of R. Yehoshua b. Levi's explanation. *Tosafot* and Rashi explain *af hen* to mean that women, like men, were *beneficiaries* of the miracle (see Rashi to B.T. *Meg.* 4a, s.v *she'af hen hayu be'oto hanes,* and *Tosafot* ad loc.). Rashbam, on the other hand, argues that this phrase means that a woman was the *primary agent* of salvation. Either way, the implication is that women's involvement in the miracle is sufficient to obligate them in this *mitsvah.*
11. This positon is one of three similar statements attributed to R. Yehoshua b. Levi in the Babylonian Talmud. He also obligates women in the commemorative *mitsvot* of lighting Ḥanukkah candles (B.T. *Shab.* 23) and drinking four cups of wine at the Seder (B.T. *Pesaḥ.* 108a–b) based on this principle. There is much discussion about the implications of these statements. *Tosafot* to B.T. *Pesaḥ.* 108b reminds us that we would normally assume that women would be exempt because all three are positive, time-caused *mitsvot.* R. Yehoshua b. Levi then presents either a rationale or a source for a woman's obligation, which overrides the general exemption. Rashi and R. Tam, on the other hand, assume that exemption from time-caused *mitsvot* is limited to biblical commandments, whereas positive, time-caused, rabbinic *mitsvot* are equally

Arakhin it is linked to M. *Megillah* 2:4 (source #1, above) and the question of who is eligible to read the *megillah* on behalf of others:

3. *Babylonian Talmud* *Arakhin 2b–3a*	**תלמוד בבלי מסכת ערכין ב:-ג.**
All are obligated in the reading of the *megillah*; all are eligible to read the *megillah*. To include whom? To include women, in accordance with R. Yehoshua b. Levi. For R. Yehoshua b. Levi said: Women are obligated in the reading of the *megillah*, for they too were part of the same miracle.	הכל חייבין במקרא מגילה, הכל כשרין לקרות את המגילה. לאיתויי מאי? לאתויי נשים וכדר' יהושע בן לוי. דאמר ר' יהושע בן לוי: נשים חייבות במקרא מגילה שאף הן היו באותו הנס.

The Gemara links and explains two Tannaitic statements, both of which use the term *hakol* (everyone, all). The first statement is from a *baraita* (a Tannaitic source not included in the Mishnah) that asserts that all are obligated in the reading of the *megillah*.[12] The second is from the *mishnah* cited above, "All are eligible to read the *megillah*." The Gemara assumes that in both cases the word *hakol* suggests the inclusion of a category of individuals who might otherwise be excluded. Based on the statement of R. Yehoshua b. Levi, the Gemara concludes that the word *hakol* comes to include women, meaning that women are both obligated in the reading of the *megillah* and are fit agents to read it for others. By including women in the category of "all" who are obligated in *megillah* reading, the text equates the obligation of women and men.

The straightforward implication of M. *Megillah* 2:4 is that women, like men, are eligible to read the *megillah* on behalf of others. This understanding of the Mishnah is confirmed by the Gemara in Tractate *Arakhin*,

obligatory on men and women. According to this reading, *megillah* is simply an illustration of this principle. See Rashi to B.T. *Ber.* 20b, s.v. *hakhi garsinan*; *Tosafot* ad loc., s.v. *bitfillah peshita*; and R. Tam, *Sefer Hayashar*, Responsa 70:4.

12. This same statement is found at the beginning of the Tosefta passage cited below (source #5). Unlike there, the Gemara here clearly intends *hakol* to include women.

which explicitly states that women are obligated in the reading of the *megillah* and are therefore fit agents to read for others. R. Yehoshua b. Levi provides an explanation for this obligation: women were also part of the miracle of Purim.

JERUSALEM TALMUD

The Jerusalem Talmud also records a version of the statement of R. Yehoshua b. Levi, although with slight variations:

4. ***Jerusalem Talmud Megillah 2:4, 73b***	**תלמוד ירושלמי מסכת מגילה ב:ד (דף עג טור ב)**
Bar Kappara said: It is necessary to read it [the *megillah*] before women and minors, for they too were in doubt. R. Yehoshua b. Levi did so; he gathered his children and the members of his household and read it before them.	בר קפרא אמר צריך לקרותה לפני נשים ולפני קטנים שאף אותם היו בספק. ר' יהושע בן לוי עבד כן מכנש בנוי ובני בייתיה וקרי לה קומיהון.

Bar Kappara asserts that the *megillah* must be read for women and minors because they too were in danger of being destroyed by Haman's plot. His rationale sounds very similar to that of R. Yehoshua b. Levi as cited in the Babylonian Talmud.[13] The Jerusalem Talmud then cites a case that supports this statement: R. Yehoshua b. Levi behaved accordingly and read the *megillah* for all the members of his household.

Unlike the Babylonian Talmud, which clearly addresses the question of reading *megillah* and articulates a woman's obligation, Bar Kappara's statement is ambiguous. He says that the *megillah* must be read *for* women but does not raise the possibility of women reading for themselves (or for others). The story of R. Yehoshua b. Levi emphasizes this passivity: the women of his household have the *megillah* read to them.

13. In this source, it is clear that women are included in the *mitsvah* because they were in danger of being destroyed, not because a woman was the agent of divine salvation, as Rashbam argues. See Rashi and *Tosafot* to B.T. *Meg.* 4a; and n10, above.

It is possible that the account in the Jerusalem Talmud simply reflected the reality that women at that time did not know how to read. In this case, the fact that R. Yehoshua b. Levi read the *megillah* to them was simply an indication of his opinion that women are actually obligated in the reading of the *megillah*, as he articulated in the Babylonian Talmud. However, some commentators read these statements in the Jerusalem Talmud as prescriptive, indicating that there is a different type of obligation for women.[14] While it is clear from this source that women are obligated to hear the *megillah*, perhaps they are not included in the obligation to read the *megillah*. The correct *peshat* (straightforward reading) of the Jerusalem Talmud is ambiguous. However, given his statement in the Babylonian Talmud, it makes sense to understand R. Yehoshua b. Levi's actions in light of his opinion that women are obligated in the reading of *megillah*.

TOSEFTA

The Tosefta, a Tannaitic text roughly contemporary with the Mishnah, often contains opinions not codified in the Mishnah. The Tosefta in Tractate *Megillah* presents a view that is radically different from that of the Mishnah:

5. *Tosefta* *Megillah 2:7* *(Lieberman edition)*	**תוספתא מסכת מגילה ב:ז (מהדורת ליברמן)**
All are obligated in the reading of the *megillah*: priests, Levites, and Israelites; converts and freed slaves; *ḥalalim*,[15]	הכל חייבין בקריאת מגלה: כהנים לוים וישראל, גרים ועבדים משוחררין, חללים

14. This possibility is discussed at length in the section on Geonic sources, "Ge'onim."
15. A *ḥalal* (pl. *ḥalalim*) is the son of a *kohen* (priest) who is barred from Temple service because his father married a woman whom he was forbidden to marry (e.g., a divorcee, a woman who has had sex with a non-Jew, or a woman who is the offspring of a prohibited priestly marriage).

netinim,[16] and *mamzerim;*[17] men who were castrated, men born castrated, men with crushed testicles or cut penises; all are obligated and discharge the obligation of the many. *Tumtum*[18] and *androginos*[19] are obligated but do not discharge the obligation of the many. *Androginos* discharges the obligation of its kind and does not discharge the obligation of those who are not of its kind. *Tumtum* does not discharge the obligation either of its kind or of those not of its kind. Women, slaves, and minors are exempt and do not discharge the obligation of the many.	נתינים וממזרים, סריס אדם סריס חמה, פצוע דכא וכרות שפכה, כולן חייבין ומוציאין את הרבים ידי חובתן. טומטום ואנדרוגינוס חייבין ואין מוציאין את הרבים ידי חובתן. אנדרגינוס מוציא את מינו ואינו מוציא את שאינו מינו. טומטום אינו מוציא לא את מינו ולא את שאינו מינו. נשים ועבדים וקטנים פטורין ואין מוציאין את הרבים ידי חובתן.

According to the Tosefta, "all" refers only to men, even those who might otherwise seem to have a lesser status. The first section of this passage lists all the different categories of males who are obligated and who may therefore read on behalf of all others who are obligated.[20] Women, as well as slaves and minors, are not obligated and cannot therefore discharge

16. A *natin* (pl. *netinim*) is a descendant of the Gibeonites, who converted in the times of Joshua to avoid Israelite conquest (Josh. 9:3–27). They are not permitted to marry Jews.
17. A *mamzer* (pl. *mamzerim*) is the child of a forbidden sexual relationship (e.g., adultery or incest).
18. A *tumtum* is an individual, either male or female, whose sexual organs are covered and whose sex is therefore unknown.
19. An *androginos* is an intersex individual, with both male and female sexual characteristics. There are two classical understandings of the category of *androginos,* either *safek zakhar safek nekevah* (possibly male, possibly female) or *biryah bifnei atsmah* (a being, i.e., category, unto itself). See *Beit Yosef, O.Ḥ.* 689.
20. R. Saul Lieberman, *Tosefta Kifshutah* to T. *Meg.* 2:7, notes that this detailed listing appears in T. *Ber.* 5:14–17, in reference to *birkat hamazon*; in T. *Rosh Hash.* 2:5, in reference to *shofar*; and in T. *Menaḥ.* 10:13 and 10:18, in reference to *semikhah* and *tenufah.* In all these cases, the Tosefta states that men are obligated and women, slaves, and minors are exempt.

the obligations of others. The Tosefta also deals with the obligations of people who are not readily categorized as male or female. This becomes a particular concern once men and women have different obligations. Because a *tumtum* might be male, the *tumtum* is obligated to read *megillah*. However, because the *tumtum* might be female, the *tumtum* cannot discharge the obligations of others, even another *tumtum*, for the listener might actually be a male. An *androginos*, on the other hand, is obligated to read *megillah* because s/he is definitely partly male. However, because s/he is not fully male, s/he may discharge the obligation only of another, similarly half-male *androginos*.

The Tosefta directly contradicts the Mishnah quote above, which implies that women may read *megillah* on behalf of others, and the two Talmudic passages, which explicitly state that women are obligated in *megillah* reading. The Gemara, which often quotes relevant Tannaitic material not preserved in the Mishnah, does not mention this source at all as a challenge to the Mishnah or to the position of R. Yehoshua b. Levi. In fact, the Gemara in *Arakhin* (source #3, above) quotes a *baraita* with the exact same opening line, "All are obligated in the reading of the *megillah*," and goes on to state explicitly that women are included in that obligation, in direct opposition to the Tosefta.[21]

What are the implications of this contradiction? Normally, when the Tosefta is not quoted in the Talmud, it may not be considered in the halakhic process at all. One can argue that it should be ignored if it contradicts the mainstream texts.[22] Indeed, many of the later sources discussed below explicitly reject the position of the Tosefta as being

---

21. There is no way to know whether the Gemara was aware of the Tannaitic reading of the word "all" that appears in the Tosefta and chose to directly reject and challenge it, or whether it was unaware of this contradictory Tannaitic position.

22. R. Amram Ga'on wrote the following in response to a question about how the Tosefta is weighed in the halakhic decision-making process: "Any *baraita* that is not contradicted by the Talmud of our rabbis the Amora'im, the accepted law is according to it.... Any *baraita* that is contradicted by the Talmud, the accepted law is not according to it.... Therefore, there is no absolute [status] to the Tosefta, *Sifra* and *Sifrei*." See Louis Ginzberg, *Geonica* (2 vols.; New York: Jewish Theological Seminary of America, 1909), as quoted in Meir Sendor, "The Rule for the Admissibility of Kabbalah in Halakhah," in *Be'erot Yitzhak: Studies in Memory of Isadore Twersky* (ed. Jay M. Harris; Cambridge, Mass.: Harvard University Press, 2005), 274.

outside of the conventional halakhic tradition.[23] However, other commentators and halakhic decisors do attempt to reconcile the Tosefta with the Mishnah and Gemara.[24]

GE'ONIM

During the Geonic period, two new ideas are introduced into the discussion of a woman's obligation in *megillah* and become part of the normative halakhic discussion from that point forward.

Unlike other works of its time *Sefer Halakhot Gedolot,* an influential Geonic work of disputed authorship, privileges the Tosefta in its explanation of a woman's obligation in the reading of the *megillah*:[25]

23. See, for example: Rashi to B.T. *Arakh.* 3a (source #8, below); *Sefer Or Zarua,* Vol. 2, *Hilkh. Megillah* #368 (source #9, below); Rambam, *Hilkh. Megillah Vaḥanukkah* 1:1 (source #10, below); *Sefer Hamanhig, Hilkh. Megillah,* p. 249; *Sefer Shibbolei Haleket, Purim* 198; *Ḥiddushei Harashba* to B.T. *Meg.* 4a; Me'iri to B.T. Meg. 4a (source #13, below); *Avraham Min Hahar* to B.T. *Meg.* 4a (source #14, below); *Ḥiddushei Haran* to B.T. *Meg.* 4a; *Ḥiddushei Haritva* to B.T. *Meg.* 4a (source #16, below); *Sefer Kol Bo* #45 (source #17, below); *Orḥot Ḥayyim, Hilkh. Megillah Ufurim* 2; *Sefer Hame'orot* to B.T. *Meg.* 4a, 19b; *Sefer Hamikhtam* to B.T. *Meg.* 4a; Riaz to B.T. *Meg.* 4a (in *Shiltei Hagibborim*); and *Nimmukei Yosef* to B.T. *Meg.* 4a (source #55, below).
24. See, for example: R. Ḥananel to B.T. *Meg.* 4a; *Tosafot* to B.T. *Meg.* 4a (source #18, below); *Tosefot Harosh* to B.T. *Meg.* 4a and Rosh to *Meg.* 1:4 (source #19, below); *Tosafot* to B.T. *Arakh.* 3a; *Sefer Ha'ittur, Aseret Hadibberot, Hilkh. Megillah* 113b; *Sefer Ra'avyah,* Vol. 2, *Megillah* #569 (source #63, below); *Sefer Haroke'aḥ, Hilkh. Purim* #236; *Sefer Mitsvot Gadol, Aseih Derabbanan* 4; R. Yeruḥam, *Toledot Adam Veḥavah* 10:3.
25. Other Geonic sources, such as *Seder Rav Amram Ga'on* and *She'iltot Derav Aḥai Ga'on, Parashat Vayak'hel* 67, quote R. Yehoshua b. Levi without comment: ואמר רבי יהושע בן לוי נשים חייבות במקרא מגילה שאף הן היו באותו הנס. *Halakhot Ketsuvot Derav Yehudai Ga'on, Hilkh. Purim,* mentions an exemption for the deaf, the mentally incompetent, and minors but, like the Mishnah in *Megillah,* does not single out women.

6. *Sefer Halakhot Gedolot*
Laws of Megillah
Vol. 1, pp. 405–6
(Hildesheimer edition)

Authorship in dispute, Babylonia (ninth century)

ספר הלכות גדולות
הלכות מגלה
חלק א, עמ' 405-6
(מהדורת הילדסהיימר)

All are obligated in the reading of the *megillah*: priests, Levites, and Israelites; converts and freed slaves; *ḥalalim, netinim, mamzerim*; men who were castrated and men born castrated; men with crushed testicles or cut penises; all are obligated and discharge the obligation of the many. *Tumtum* and *androginos* are obligated but do not discharge the obligation of the many. *Androginos* discharges the obligation of its kind and does not discharge the obligation of those who are not of its kind. *Tumtum* does not discharge the obligation either of its kind or of those not of its kind. One who is half slave and half free does not discharge the obligation either of his kind or of those not of his kind. Women, slaves, and minors are exempt from the reading of the *megillah* [and do not discharge the obligation of the many], but they are obligated in listening. Why? For everyone was in danger [lit., doubt] of being destroyed, killed, and eradicated, and since everyone was in danger everyone is obligated in hearing. R. Yehoshua b. Levi would gather all the people of his household and read *Megillat Ester* before them. R. Yonah, father of R. Muna, would intentionally read it before the women of his house, for everyone was

הכל חייבין בקרית מגלה: כהנים לויים וישראלים, גרים ועבדים משוחררים, חללים נתינים ממזרים, סריס אדם וסריס חמה, פצוע דכא וכרות שפכה, כולן חייבין ומוציאין את הרבים ידי חובתן. טומטום ואנדרוגינוס חייבין ואין מוציאין את הרבים ידי חובתן. אנדרוגינוס מוציא את מינו ואינו מוציא את שאינו מינו. טומטום אינו מוציא לא את מינו ולא את שאינו מינו. מי שחציו עבד וחציו בן חורין אינו מוציא לא את מינו ולא את שאינו מינו. נשים ועבדים וקטנים פטורים מקרית המגילה [ואין מוציאין רבים ידי חובתן] אלא שחייבין במשמע. למה? שהכל היו בספק להשמיד ולהרוג ולאבד והואיל והכל היו בספק הכל חייבין במשמע. ר' יהושע בן לוי היה מכנש אל כל אנשי ביתו וקורא לפניהם מגילת אסתר ור' יונה אביו של ר' מונא היה מתכוין לקרות אותה בפני הנשים שבביתו שהכל היו בספק והכל היו במשמע אחד הנשים ואחד

in doubt and everyone is included in the hearing, women, slaves, and minors.[26]	העבדים ואחד הקטנים.

The author of *Sefer Halakhot Gedolot* (known as Ba'al Halakhot Gedolot or Behag) begins by citing the Tosefta, but with a significant change. Following the statement that women, slaves, and minors are exempt from the reading of the *megillah*, *Halakhot Gedolot* adds that women nonetheless have an obligation to hear the *megillah* read. In this understanding of the Tosefta, the word "exempt" does not imply a full exemption, but rather a different type of obligation. Why are women, slaves, and minors obligated in hearing the *megillah*? Behag paraphrases Bar Kappara's explanation in the Jerusalem Talmud that they, too, were endangered by the decree of Haman. He cites the story of R. Yehoshua b. Levi's reading for the members of his household in support of the idea that women are obligated to hear, but not to read, *Megillat Ester*.[27]

Behag's reading reconciles the Tosefta's exemption of women with R. Yehoshua b. Levi's assertion that women are included in the *mitsvah*

26. The nature of the exact source material for *Halakhot Gedolot* and the precise intention of the author of the work are beyond the scope of this article. The author thanks Prof. Robert Brody for his assistance in thinking through these issues. Further study is warranted to understand Behag's position in its historical context and in greater depth. This chapter focuses on how his words have been interpreted by later halakhic thinkers.

27. Whereas in the printed version of the Babylonian Talmud, R. Yehoshua b. Levi simply states that women are obligated in the reading of *megillah*, the Hildesheimer edition of Behag notes (p. 403) that he quotes a different version of the text:

ואמר ר' יהושע בן לוי נשים חייבות לשמוע מקרא מגלה שאף הן היו באותו הנס.

In this version of R. Yehoshua b. Levi's statement, he clearly says that women are obligated only to hear, rather than to read *Megillat Ester*. If this version informs Behag's position, then a different type of obligation for women is inherent in the text of the Talmud. *Arukh Hashulḥan, O.Ḥ.* 689:5, uses the Hebrew *garas* when discussing this source from *Halakhot Gedolot*. This indicates his view that the version of the Gemara in front of Behag stated explicitly that R. Yehoshua b. Levi thinks that women are obligated to hear, but not to read, *Megillat Ester*. However, this is not the version of the Talmudic text that is preserved in printed editions or in the manuscripts. The version in *Halakhot Gedolot* also fails to appear in other early commentaries. All of the manuscripts of B.T *Meg.* (MS Göttingen Cod., MS Hebr. 3, Or. 13; MS London Harley 5508; MS Munich 95; and MS Vatican Ebr. 134) read that women are obligated in the reading of *megillah*, just as it appears in the printed version. This is also the

of *megillah* because they were part of the miracle.[28] Women were saved along with men, and therefore women are obligated to hear the *megillah* read. However, Behag does not contend with either the Mishnah in Tractate *Megillah* or with the Gemara in *Arakhin,* both of which indicate that a woman may be the one to read and perform this *mitsvah* on behalf of others because she, too, is obligated to read the *megillah.* Later sources struggle to explain this contradiction.[29]

Most notably, Behag is the first to introduce the idea that hearing the *megillah* read is a separate *mitsvah.* The Talmudic material presents only two categories: one is either obligated to read *megillah* or one is exempt from this obligation. The Mishnah in *Megillah* and the Gemara in *Arakhin* teach that women are obligated to read, while the Tosefta states that they are exempt. Behag's distinction between an obligation to read the *megillah* and an obligation to hear the *megillah* creates a middle ground between the Mishnah and the Tosefta and a means of resolving the tension between these sources. This innovation is a radical departure from the straightforward implications of the Mishnah and Gemara, yet Behag's position influences all subsequent halakhic discussion on this matter.

Another Geonic position of note is preserved in *Teshuvot Hage'onim,* which separates the question of the level of a man's and a

---

case for the manuscripts of B.T. *Arakh.* (MS Munich 95; MS London Add. 25,717; MS Vatican Ebr. 119; and MS Vatican Ebr. 120–21). Interestingly, R. Ḥananel, in his commentary to B.T. *Meg.* 4a, also quotes R. Yehoshua b. Levi's position as follows: וא"ר יהושע נשים חייבות לשמוע מקרא מגילה שאף הן היו באותו הנס כלומר שגם הן היו בכלל להשמיד להרוג ולאבד.

28. It remains unclear what motivates Behag to try to reconcile the Tosefta with the mainstream texts. Did his assumptions about a woman's status, based on the social mores of his day, fit better with the idea that women would not be required to read, leading him to prioritize the Tosefta? Did he have a different version of the Talmud text as discussed in n27, above? This suggestion, however, does not explain how he read the Mishnah or Gemara in *Arakhin.*

29. See, for example, *Tosafot* to B.T. *Arakh.* 3a, s.v. *la'atuyei nashim*; *Ḥiddushei Harashba* to B.T. *Meg.* 4a; *Tosefot Harosh* to B.T. *Meg.* 4a and Rosh to *Meg.* 1:4 (source #19, below); R. Yeruḥam, *Toledot Adam Veḥavah* 10:3, where the statement is read to mean that women are fit to read for other women. See also *Sefer Ra'avyah*, Vol. 2, *Megillah* #562, where it states that the *hakol kesherin* means, "all [men] who are fit."

woman's obligation from the question of who may discharge the obligation of another. Unlike the Tosefta and Behag, this responsum does indicate that a woman is obligated in the reading of the *megillah*; however, it also challenges the ruling of the Mishnah and Gemara that a woman is eligible to read, though from a different perspective than Behag:

7. *Teshuvot Hage'onim, Sha'arei Teshuvah #345*

תשובות הגאונים שערי תשובה סימן שמה

Anthology, Babylonia (seventh–eleventh centuries)

A woman should not recite Grace after Meals in order to discharge the obligation of others, even though she is obligated. In a situation in which her husband does not know how to bless, this is comparable to a pressing matter [as the only choice is for her to bless], and a curse shall come upon him [when she blesses for him]. A woman is obligated in the reading of the *megillah*, but she should not discharge the obligation of the many; so too with Grace after Meals.

אשה לא תברך ברכת המזון להוציא אחרים ידי חובתן אע״פי שהיא מחוייבת ובמקום שאין בעלה יודע כמקום הדחק דמי ותבוא עליו מארה. אשה מחוייבת במקרא מגילה אבל לא תוציא את הרבים כך בברכת המזון.

Unlike the Gemara in *Arakhin*, which linked a woman's obligation directly to her eligibility to perform *mitsvot* for others, the responsum in *Teshuvot Hage'onim* takes the opposite approach. Technically speaking, women are obligated in reading *Megillat Ester*, just as they are obligated in Grace after Meals. However, a man who is forced to have a woman discharge this obligation on his behalf is worthy of being cursed. This source does not suggest that there is any difference in the level of obligation between the man and the woman – they are both equally obligated. Rather, it introduces an external, social problem with a woman's reading *megillah* for men. The responsum articulates a strong policy statement against a woman performing a *mitsvah* on behalf of a man because it assumes that the only scenario in which this might occur is when a man is uneducated and cannot perform the act himself. A number of later authorities expand upon this type of concern, and this issue will be addressed in detail in Rishonim #2 of the following section.

RISHONIM

The early medieval authorities work to resolve the question of a woman's eligibility to read *Megillat Ester* on behalf of men through careful readings and elucidations of the Talmudic material and the positions of the Ge'onim. Sources from the era of the Rishonim fall into three categories:

- Rishonim who prioritize a straightforward reading of the Babylonian Talmud and therefore rule with the Gemara in *Arakhin* that women are eligible to read the *megillah* for men because they are equally obligated in this *mitsvah*.
- Rishonim who are similarly convinced that a woman is equally obligated in the reading of the *megillah* but nonetheless rule that a woman should not read on behalf of men for other reasons.
- Rishonim who give precedence to the position in the Tosefta exempting women from reading *megillah*. They reconcile this with the Talmud by accepting Behag's ruling that women are obligated to hear but not to read *Megillat Ester* and, therefore, may not read for men, who have a different obligation, but may read for other women.

Below is a selection of the main sources that represent arguments of each of these three groups.

Rishonim #1: Women Are Obligated to Read and May Read for Men

The *peshat* of the Talmudic texts indicates that women are, in fact, obligated just like men in the reading of the *megillah*. Many Rishonim maintain that this ruling of the Mishnah and Gemara should be upheld. Some of these authorities explicitly address their willingness to discount the Tosefta because it stands outside the halakhic discourse; others mention the Tosefta or Behag as legitimate sources for halakhic decision-making but nonetheless rule in accordance with the Talmud; yet others do not address the issue at all and rely only on the mainstream texts in their analysis.

One early example of this third approach is Rashi's commentary on B.T. *Arakhin*. Commenting on the statement that the word "all" includes women, Rashi explains the simple meaning of the text:

8. ***Rashi*** ***Arakhin 3a*** R. Shelomo ben Yitsḥak, France (1040–1105)	**רש"י** **מסכת ערכין ג.**
To include women – who are obligated in reading the *megillah* and are eligible to read it and discharge the obligation of men.	**לאתויי נשים** - שחייבות במקרא מגילה וכשרות לקרותה ולהוציא זכרים ידי חובתם.

According to Rashi, the words "to include women" mean that women are both obligated in *megillah* and fit to read for others. Rashi follows the general principle that one who is obligated may discharge another's obligation in a given *mitsvah*. He therefore concludes that women may read *megillah* on behalf of men.[30]

Or Zarua, a slightly later Ashkenazic authority, considers Behag's position and the implications of his reading but ultimately rejects his approach in favor of Rashi's.

9. ***Sefer Or Zarua, Vol. 2*** ***Laws of Megillah #368*** R. Yitsḥak ben Moshe, Vienna (ca. 1180–1250)	**ספר אור זרוע חלק ב** **הלכות מגילה סימן שסח**
Behag ruled that women are only obligated in hearing, but with regard to reading they may not discharge the obligation of men… and he brought proof from that which is	וה"ג פסקו שהנשים אינן חייבות אלא בשמיעה אבל בקריאתה לא תוציא הזכרים י"ח... והביאו ראיה דתניא

30. Similarly, *Sefer Hamikhtam*, a thirteenth-century French work, says as follows in a comment to B.T. *Meg.* 4a:

נשים חייבות במקרא מגילה פירוש אם יודעת לקרות מוציאה אפילו אנשים.

taught in the Tosefta.... And according to the Tosefta, the Gemara in *Arakhin* which says that women are eligible to read the *megillah* must be explained to mean that they can discharge the obligation of other women but not of men. For one would have thought that that they may not even discharge the obligation of women, since they cannot do so for men – and so this comes to teach us [that they may].

בתוספתא.... ולפי התוספתא יש לפרש ההיא דערכין דנשים כשירות לקרות את המגילה להוציא נשים אחרות אבל לא להוציא הזכרים דסד״א שלא יוציאו גם נשים כיון דאין מוציאין אנשים קמ״ל.

But I find this difficult because why would I have mistakenly assumed that since women cannot discharge the obligation for men, they perforce cannot discharge the obligation for women either? This is the case in other instances: with regard to *zimmun*, women create a *zimmun* [to recite Grace after Meals] for themselves, but do not create a *zimmun* with men. And why does [the Gemara] not use this *tosefta* to challenge R. Yehoshua b. Levi, for it [the *tosefta*] teaches that a woman is exempt? It should have responded by distinguishing between reading and hearing, as does Behag.

וקשיא לי דמאי סד״א הוא זה שהייתי טועה לומר דכיון דנשים אינן מוציאות את האנשים ע״כ לא יוציאו גם נשים כמו כן אחרות? הרי זימון שנשים מזמנות לעצמן ואינן מזמנות עם אנשים. ואמאי לא פריך מההיא דתוספתא לריב״ל דקתני שהאשה פטורה והוה ליה למפרך ולחלק בין קריאה לשמיעה כמו שמחלק בה״ג.

And it seems to me that since the teaching of the Tosefta is not mentioned in our Talmud, we do not rely on it. And it seems to me that Rashi's explanation is correct that "to include women" means that they are obligated in the reading of *megillah* and are fit to discharge the obligation of men. And now it makes sense, for one might have thought that the statement of R. Yehoshua b. Levi means that a woman may discharge the

ונראה בעיני דהואיל דברייתא דתוספתא לא הוזכרה בתלמוד שלנו לא סומכין עלה ונראה בעיני עיקר כדפי׳ רבי׳ שלמה לאתויי נשים שחייבות במקרא מגילה וכשירות להוציא אנשים והשתא אתי שפיר דסד״א הא דריב״ל היינו שהאשה מוציאה אחרת אבל לא את הזכרים קמ״ל שהנשים חייבות

obligation on behalf of another woman but not on behalf of men. Therefore it comes to teach us that women are obligated and may discharge the obligation on behalf of men, for all are obligated for the same reason – because of the miracle, and women too were included in that miracle....

ומוציאות את הזכרים דכולהו חד טעמא נינהו בעבור הנס והרי גם הנשים היו בכלל הנס....

And on the matter of *megillah*, it seems to me that the law that should be practiced is that a woman is obligated in the reading of the *megillah* and may discharge the obligation of men.

ולענין מגילה כך נ"ב הלכה למעשה שהאשה חייבת במ"מ ומוציאה את הזכרי' י"ח.

Or Zarua presents two logical arguments for adhering to the *peshat* of the Talmudic text, and then he ultimately rejects the Tosefta because it is not mentioned in the Talmud. He presents the position of Behag and acknowledges that Rishonim who accept Behag's ruling may reconcile the statement in *Arakhin* – that women are fit to read – with the Tosefta by asserting that the Gemara means that they may read only for other women.[31] However, *Or Zarua* contends that it is farfetched to claim that the Talmud would have made a point of including women in this obligation for the sole purpose of teaching that they may read only for other women! In cases where women are obligated but may not discharge men's obligation, it is obvious that they may nonetheless discharge the obligation of other women. The invitation to recite *birkat hamazon* (Grace after Meals) as a group is one such case; according to *Or Zarua*, women may not lead the blessing on behalf of men but can clearly do so on behalf of other women.[32] Given this context, *Or Zarua*

31. This idea is also presented in *Tosafot* to B.T. *Meg.* 4a, s.v. *nashim ḥayyavot bemikra megillah* (source #18, below); and *Tosefot Harosh* to B.T. *Meg.* 4a and Rosh to *Meg.* 1:4 (source #19, below).

32. A discussion of whether a woman may lead the *zimmun* on behalf of men is beyond the scope of this chapter. See Ritva, *Hilkh. Berakhot* 7:2; *Responsa of Maharam Merotenburg*, Vol. 4, #227; and *Tur, O.Ḥ.* 199 for views that differ from the one presented here by Or Zarua.

argues that the Talmud's statement that women are fit to read must surely be a broader instruction that they may discharge the obligation of men as well. Furthermore, if there is a distinction between the requirement to read *megillah* and the requirement to hear it read, as Behag claims, the Talmud should have provided that information by challenging R. Yehoshua b. Levi's original statement that women are obligated, which the Talmud does not do.

Or Zarua concludes: the Gemara in *Arakhin* quotes a *baraita* but not this *tosefta*. Therefore, one should not rely on the Tosefta because it is the Talmud, and not external material, that is binding in *halakhah*. The Babylonian Talmud is clear: women and men are equally obligated because both were included in the miracle of Purim. They share the same obligation to read the *megillah*. Thus *Or Zarua* rules as law to be acted upon – that women may read *megillah* for men.

The early Sephardic tradition also follows the *peshat* reading of the Talmudic text. R. Yitsḥak Alfasi, in his halakhic distillation of the Talmud, simply records the statement of R. Yehoshua b. Levi that women are obligated in the reading of *megillah* because they, too, were included in the miracle.[33] Similarly, Rambam includes women on the list of those who are obligated to read *megillah*:

10. ***Mishneh Torah***	**משנה תורה**
Laws of Megillah and Ḥanukkah	**הלכות מגילה וחנוכה**
1:1–2	**פרק א הלכה א–ב**
R. Moshe ben Maimon, Spain and Egypt (1135–1204)	
1) The reading of the *megillah* at the proper time is a positive, rabbinic *mitsvah*... and all are obligated to read it – men, women, converts, and freed slaves; and minors must be educated to read it.	א) קריאת המגילה בזמנה מצות עשה מדברי סופרים... והכל חייבים בקריאתה אנשים ונשים וגרים ועבדים משוחררים, ומחנכין את הקטנים לקרותה.
2) Both one who reads and one who hears it read fulfills the obligation, and this is if one	ב) אחד הקורא ואחד השומע מן הקורא יצא ידי חובתו

33. *Hilkhot Harif, Meg.* 2b.

hears it from one who is obligated to read it. Therefore, if the reader was a minor or mentally incompetent, the hearer has not fulfilled the obligation.	והוא שישמע ממי שהוא חייב בקריאתה, לפיכך אם היה הקורא קטן או שוטה השומע ממנו לא יצא.

According to Rambam, women are obligated in the rabbinic *mitsvah* of reading *Megillat Ester* just as men are. Interestingly, his language echoes that of the *baraita* in *Arakhin* that "all" includes women,[34] whereas the rest of the list, which mentions converts and freed slaves, parallels the words of the Tosefta. In 1:2, Rambam explains that it is possible to fulfill this obligation by hearing *megillah* from a qualified, obligated reader; those who are not eligible to read include minors and the mentally incompetent. Since women and men share the same obligation, Rambam rules that women may read *megillah* on behalf of men.

Maggid Mishneh, a commentary on *Mishneh Torah*, explains Rambam's position:

11. ***Maggid Mishneh*** ***Laws of Megillah and Ḥanukkah*** ***1:2*** R. Vidal of Tolosa, Spain (fourteenth century)	**מגיד משנה** **הלכות מגילה וחנוכה** **פרק א הלכה ב**
"Both one who reads," etc. Mishnah: … "All are eligible to read the *megillah* except for one who is deaf, one who is mentally incompetent, and a minor. R. Yehudah declared the minor eligible." The law is in accordance with the unattributed section of the *mishnah*. But a woman, it appears from the words of our teacher, may discharge the obligation of others, and this is correct.[35]	אחד הקורא וכו'. משנה.... הכל כשרים לקרות את המגילה חוץ מחש"ו ור' יהודה מכשיר בקטן והלכה כסתם משנה. אבל אשה נראה מדברי רבינו שהיא מוציאה את אחרים וכן עיקר.

34. See Rambam, *Perush Hamishnah* to M. *Meg.* 2:4, where he states: הכל ואפילו אשה.

35. *Haggahot Maimoniyyot* to Rambam, *Hilkh. Megillah Vaḥanukkah* 1:1, also reads

Maggid Mishneh links Rambam's ruling to the original texts, and he explains that the Mishnah in Tractate *Megillah* states that all are fit to read the *megillah*, with only three specific exceptions. He states that the general principle is that the law is in accordance with the unattributed first section of the *mishnah*.[36] Therefore, women may read for others, according to "our teacher," Rambam. *Maggid Mishneh* adds that this position is, in fact, the correct practice. Women may read *megillah* on behalf of men.

Nimmukei Yosef, another Sephardic authority, presents a similar ruling and is the first to explicitly address the blessing a woman would recite.

12. ***Nimmukei Yosef***
Megillah 4a
R. Yosef ibn Ḥabib, Spain (fourteenth–fifteenth centuries)

נימוקי יוסף
מסכת מגילה ד.

So too, women recite the blessing "on the reading of the *megillah*," and discharge the obligation of men. For anyone who is obligated in a matter may discharge the obligation of others.

וכן נמי נשים מברכות על מקרא מגילה ומוציאות האנשים שכל המחויב בדבר מוציא אחרים ידי חובתן.

Because women are obligated to read the *megillah*, *Nimmukei Yosef* asserts that it follows legally that they bless and read *Megillat Ester* on behalf of men, based on the Mishnaic principle that anyone who is obligated in a ritual may discharge the obligation of others.[37]

This approach, to apply the general rule of agency to a woman's obligation, is found among Provençal authorities as well:

Rambam this way, as does *Or Same'aḥ* ad loc. *Shiltei Gibborim* #2 (2b in the pages of the Rif) also suggests this reading of Rambam. See also *Avraham Min Hahar* to B.T. *Meg.* 19b (source #14, below). Similarly, *Bayit Ḥadash, O.Ḥ.* 689, records this as the positon of Rambam, and R. Caro's addition of the *yesh omerim* (there are those who say) after he quotes Rambam verbatim also attests to this reading.

36. See B.T. *Shab.* 112b, 147b, 148b, and 156b; B.T. *Beits.* 2a–b; and B.T. *Menaḥ.* 52b.

37. M. *Rosh Hash.* 3:8. See n7.

13. ***Beit Habeḥirah***
Megillah 4a
R. Menaḥem ben Shelomo Me'iri, France (1249–1315)

בית הבחירה
מסכת מגילה ד.

Women are obligated in the reading of the *megillah*; they too were included in the miracle, for the decree was upon them as well.... Since women are obligated, they too may discharge the obligation of the many. [The rabbis] have stated a general principle: anyone who is obligated in a matter [may discharge the obligations of the many]. And so too at the beginning of Tractate *Arakhin* they said: "All are eligible to read the *megillah*...to include women." Nevertheless, Behag ruled that women are obligated but may only discharge the obligation of women....[38] And the correct reading is that one should not reject the edited Talmud that we have in our hands because of a *baraita* or because of the words of the Jerusalem Talmud, and how much more so not because of *sevara* (logical reasoning)! Rather, come let us rely on the well-known rule that anyone

נשים חייבות במקרא מגלה אף הם היו בכלל הנס שהרי אף עליהם נגזרה גזרה.... מאחר שהנשים חייבות אף הן מוציאות את הרבים ידי חובתן. כלל גדול אמרו כל המחוייב בדבר [מוציא את הרבים ידי חובתן] וכן בראש מסכת ערכין אמרו הכל כשרין לקרות את המגלה... לאתויי נשים. ומ"מ בהלכות גדולות פסקו שהנשים חייבות אבל אינן מוציאות אלא נשים.... ועיקר הדברים שלא לדחות תלמוד ערוך שבידינו מברייתא או מדברי תלמוד המערב וכל שכן מסברא אלא בואו ונסמוך על הכלל הידוע כל המחוייב בדבר מוציא את הרבים ידי חובתן.

38. In the omitted passage, Me'iri points out a difficulty in the text of the Tosefta, which is the basis of Behag's position. Having stated that women are exempt from the obligation to read *megillah*, it is redundant for the Tosefta to add that they cannot read on behalf of others. If they are exempt, they are obviously ineligible to read! Me'iri concludes that there must be a scribal error in the Tosefta, and he emends the text to say that women are obligated but nonetheless may not read on behalf of others:

> ופירשו זו של ערכין לאתויי נשים להוציא את מינן. ואף מה שאמרו בברייתא נשים ועבדים וקטנים פטורים ואין מוציאין את הרבים ידי חובתן נראה להם ששיבוש נפל בברייתא על ידי סופרים שאם הם פטורין מה הוצרך לומר שאין מוציאין אלא כך הוא הענין חייבין ואין מוציאין והוא שאמרו שם טומטום ואנדרוגינוס חייבין ואין מוציאין אנדרוגינוס מוציא את מינו טומטום לא מינו ולא שאינו מינו.

who is obligated in a matter may discharge the obligation of the many.

Me'iri focuses on the Mishnaic rule that anyone who is obligated in a *mitsvah* may fulfill that *mitsvah* on behalf of another. He explains that because women are obligated to read *megillah,* they may discharge the obligation of others. He then cites as support the Gemara in *Arakhin* that makes it clear that women are included among those who are fit to read the *megillah* for others. Me'iri mentions the position of Behag, whose ruling, when reconciled with the text in *Arakhin,*[39] would lead to the conclusion that women may read only for other women. Me'iri ultimately rejects Behag's position and rules that it is preferable to act in accordance with the received text of the Babylonian Talmud and not based on the Tosefta or the Jerusalem Talmud. He maintains the principle that one who is obligated may discharge another's obligation and thus rules that women may read *megillah* for men.[40]

In summary, this first group of Rishonim gives precedence to the authority of the Mishnah and Gemara over the Tosefta and rejects or does not discuss Behag's approach. Women are obligated in *megillah* because they, too, were a part of the miraculous salvation from Haman's decree; as a result, they may also discharge the obligation of men.

Rishonim #2: Women Are Obligated to Read but Should Not Read for Men

Among the Rishonim who agree that women are fully obligated in the reading of *megillah,* there are those who nonetheless express concerns about women's reading *megillah* on behalf of men. A number follow in the footsteps of the responsum from *Teshuvot Hage'onim* (source #7, above), which raises social concerns regarding a woman performing *mitsvot* on behalf of men, in connection with *birkat hamazon.*

39. Although Me'iri cites this view as the actual ruling of Behag, Behag himself did not address this issue. Rather, later Rishonim are the ones who attribute this view to Behag when trying to reconcile his position with the text of the Gemara. See the following section.

40. See also Me'iri to B.T. *Ber.* 47b.

Commenting on Rambam's ruling that anyone who is obligated in *megillah* reading may discharge another's obligation, R. Avraham ben Yitsḥak explains:

14. *Avraham Min Hahar*
Megillah 19b

אברהם מן ההר
מסכת מגילה יט:

R. Avraham ben Yitsḥak, Montpellier, Provence (d. 1315)

If he hears [*megillah*] from a woman, he has fulfilled his obligation, for a woman is [obligated] like a man. This is clearly stated in the beginning of *Arakhin*: "All are obligated in *megillah*...'all' to include women, in accordance with R. Yehoshua [b. Levi]," etc. However, ideally she certainly should not discharge the obligation of others, as it says in [chapter] *mi shemeto*: "Let a curse come upon a man whose wife and sons bless [Grace after Meals] on his behalf."[41] And it says in chapter *omed veyoshev*: "All may go up as part of the count of seven [*aliyot*], even a woman or a minor. However, the sages declared that a woman should not read in the congregation because of the honor of the congregation."[42]

ואם שומע מאשה יצא, דהא אשה כאיש. והכי איתא בהדיא בריש ערכין הכל חייבין [במקרא מגילה]... הכל לאתויי נשים וכדר' יהושע וכו'. מיהו ודאי לכתחלה לא תוציא אחרים, כדאמרינן במי שמתו תבוא מאירה לאדם שאשתו ובנין מברכין לו. ואמרינן פרק עומד ויושב הכל עולין למנין שבעה אפילו אשה או קטן אבל אמרו חכמים אשה לא תקרא בצבור מפני כבוד הצבור.

41. B.T. *Ber.* 20b.

42. B.T. *Meg.* 23a. The question of whether *kevod hatsibbur* (the honor of the congregation) is an objective, unchanging standard, or whether a community has the right to determine for itself which behaviors are and are not honorable, is beyond the scope of this chapter. See *Responsa Maharam Merotenburg*, Vol. 4, #8; *Beit Yosef, O.Ḥ.* 53:6; and *Responsa Benei Banim* 2:11, who think that a community has the right to waive its honor depending on the situation and social norms. See also *Bayit Ḥadash, O.Ḥ.* 53:2, who thinks the honor in question is actually God's and that humans have no right to change the standards.

Based on the Gemara in *Arakhin,* R. Avraham ben Yitsḥak rules that a woman is legally fit to read *megillah* on behalf of a man and that if he hears her read, he has filled his obligation. He does not cite Behag, and he clearly states that men's and women's obligations in this *mitsvah* are identical. However, he expresses the concern that it is inappropriate or in some way undignified for a woman to read *Megillat Ester* on behalf of men, and he cites two other cases where this objection is raised. Although women are obligated in *birkat hamazon,*[43] the Gemara proclaims, "let a curse come upon" any man whose wife or sons recite it on his behalf, for this would imply that he is incapable of reciting the blessing himself.[44] Similarly, although the *baraita* explains that women may receive one of the seven *aliyot* to the Torah on Shabbat, the rabbis state that women should not read from the Torah publicly, as it is in some way dishonorable to the community. In both of these cases, despite a woman being legally eligible to perform the ritual under discussion, the Gemara states that she should not do so because it reflects negatively on men.[45]

These concerns do not change the fact that women and men are equally obligated in *megillah,* nor do they invalidate a woman's legal eligibility to read it on behalf of men. However, R. Avraham ben Yitsḥak argues that these social concerns regarding men's dignity are relevant to *megillah* reading, as well. Thus, he argues, *a priori* a woman should not read for men.[46] If a woman does so, the man would nevertheless have fulfilled his obligation.

Tosafot also link a woman reading *megillah* to a woman leading *birkat hamazon* and to the idea that a man should be cursed for allowing

43. It is not clear if this obligation is biblical or rabbinic in nature. See M. *Ber.* 3:3; J.T. *Ber.* 25b; B.T. *Berakhot* 20b; J.T. *Suk.* 54d; and B.T. *Ber.* 49a. A majority of Rishonim actually think that women are obligated in *birkat hamazon* from the Torah. See, for example, Ritva, *Hilkh. Berakhot* 7:2; Ra'avad, *Teshuvot Ufsakim* 12; *Milḥamot Hashem* to B.T. *Ber.* 12a (in Rif); *Ḥiddushei Harashba* to B.T. *Ber.* 20b; *Ḥiddushei Haritva* to B.T. *Suk.* 38a; and *Perush Harashbats* to B.T. *Ber.* 20b. However, both Rambam, *Hilkh. Berakhot* 5:1, and *Sh. Ar., O.Ḥ.* 186:1, rule that women are obligated, but they are unsure whether this obligation is biblical or rabbinic.

44. See *Teshuvot Hage'onim,* source #7, above.

45. Why this would be the case is beyond the scope of this chapter.

46. *Arukh Hashulḥan, O.Ḥ.* 689:5, basing himself on *Magen Avraham* 689:5 (source #29,

his wife to bless for him. However, they approach the matter from the opposite direction. In trying to understand why a man may lead a woman in *birkat hamazon* but not the reverse, *Tosafot* bring the case of *megillah* as a support for their explanation:

15. ***Tosafot***
Sukkah 38a
s.v. be'emet ameru ben mevarekh le'aviv
French and German Talmudists (twelfth–fourteenth centuries)[47]

תוספות מסכת סוכה לח.
ד"ה באמת אמרו בן מברך לאביו

They [women] do not discharge the obligation [of men] even though a man discharges theirs. A man is different, for he is considered more important, or also because in public it is beneath their [men's] dignity,[48] for [with regard to] *megillah*,

אין מוציאות אף על פי שהאיש מוציאן שאני איש דחשיב טפי א"נ משום דרבים זילא בהו מילתא, דהרי מגילה דנשים חייבות בה ופירש בה"ג דאין נשים מוציאות את הרבים ידי

below), points out that this concern over the honor of the community would still preclude one woman from reading *megillah* for one man based on the legal concept of *lo pelug* – a rule should have no exceptions that contradict it:
והטעם משום כבוד ציבור וכמ"ש בסעיף א' ולכן אפילו ליחיד אינה מוציאה דלא פלוג.

47. The Tosafists were not one person but rather an entire school of thought that lasted about two hundred years in both France and Germany. The earliest Tosafists were Rashi's grandsons, and the name of the commentary indicates that it was originally considered an "addition" (*tosefet*) to Rashi's commentary on the Babylonian Talmud. As such, not all pieces of commentary that appear in the printed Talmud are from the same commentator and thus may at times present different or somewhat conflicting views.

48. The term *zila milleta*, when referring to a woman's practice, is often translated as "contemptible" or "disgraceful," intimating that there is something severely objectionable about the act itself. However, a careful examination of the usage of this phrase in the Talmud reveals that it is always used in reference to diminishing or insulting someone's honor or dignity. It means that the matter is beneath him or her. See, for example, B.T. *B. Bat.* 110a: ולא תמא גברא רבא אנא וזילא בי מילתא. See also B.T. *Git.* 80b, where the phrase is used with its opposite שביחא להו מילתא (the matter is honorable to him). On two occasions, the Gemara explicitly distinguishes between how the act would be perceived by others if it were performed in public, where it would be considered beneath one's dignity, instead of in private, where it would not. See, for example, B.T. *Menaḥ.* 67b and B.T. *Git.* 38a. This translation of *zila milleta* also is supported by Yitzhak Frank, *Practical Talmud Dictionary*, s.v. *zil.*

חובתן במגילה.

in which women are obligated, Behag explained that women may not discharge the obligation of the many in *megillah.*

Tosafot think that women are obligated in the *mitsvah* of reading *Megillat Ester,*[49] even according to Behag.[50] However, *megillah* reading is a very public affair, and it would be degrading to men for women to perform this *mitsvah* on their behalf, just as it would be degrading to men for women to recite *birkat hamazon* in a mixed group.[51] Presumably this affront to men's honor is based on the lower social status of women within the community at large in those times because no purely legal

See his example there and Marcus Jastrow, *A Dictionary of the Targumim, the Talmud Bavli and Yerushalmi, and the Midrashic Literature,* s.v. *zul.* See B.T. *Ketub.* 54a, 70b; B.T. *Kid.* 32a; B.T. *B. Kam.* 84a; B.T. *B. Mets.* 72b, 76a; B.T. *Shevu.* 30b; and B.T. *Avod. Zar.* 18a, 53b.

49. This perspective seems slightly different from that presented in *Tosafot* to B.T. *Arakh.* 3a; and to B.T. *Meg.* 4a (source #18, below). It is important to note that our *Tosafot,* in the printed volumes of the Talmud, consist of comments composed by different Tosafists in different locations and times.

50. There appear to be two different understandings of Behag's position that existed among Rishonim. One, as appears in the text of *Sefer Halakhot Gedolot* (source #6, above) is that women are obligated only to hear the *megillah.* As a result, men and women have different levels of obligation, and thus women are unable to read for men. This position is discussed in greater detail in the next section. The other reading, expressed by *Tosafot* here, seems to understand Behag differently. According to this reading, similar to the tradition found in *Teshuvot Hage'onim* (source #7, above), women are in fact obligated in the reading of *megillah* but should not read on behalf of men. See also *Tur, O.Ḥ.* 689; and *Bayit Ḥadash, O.Ḥ.* 271. These different understandings of Behag's position might account for the disagreement between *Baḥ* and *Taz, O.Ḥ.* 271:2.

51. A similar idea is expressed by Maharil (R. Ya'akov ben Moshe Moellin of Mainz, 1365–1427), who says that although women are obligated in *megillah,* it is preferable to publicize the miracle by having men read:

    אמר מהר״י סג״ל שרבינו שמחה כתב שנשים חייבות לקרא הלל בליל פסח שאף הן היו באותו הנס. ולפי זה אפשר שנשים אומרות הודו ועונים אחריהן. ואמרתי לפניו והא חייבות במגילה משום דהיו באותו הנס מ״מ פסק המרדכי שאין מוציאות אנשים. והשיב לי שאני מגילה דצריכה לקרוא ברבים ולפרסומי ניסא **ויותר יפה באנשים.**

issue with a woman reading *megillah* for men exists as their levels of obligation are equal.[52]

Ritva similarly argues that women are obligated to read the *megillah* but should not do so for men, citing the affront to men's dignity and the community's honor:

16. *Ḥiddushei Haritva*
Megillah 4a
R. Yom Tov ben Avraham Ashvili, Spain (1250–1320)

חידושי הריטב"א
מסכת מגילה ד.

It seems that since women are obligated in the reading of *megillah*, the law is that they may discharge the obligation of others, as it is taught (below, 19b), "All are eligible to read the *megillah*," and the language of "eligible" implies to read for others. The Gemara in *Arakhin* says (3a), "All to include women," and similarly the Mishnah includes them.... That which is taught in the Tosefta (2:4), "Women and slaves and minors are exempt from the reading of the *megillah*" – this is a mistake, and there is no sense in it, for they too were included in the same miracle, and yet this exempts them entirely.... Since we follow the opinion of R. Yehoshua b. Levi that they are obligated, they may also discharge

ונראין דברים שכיון שחייבות במקרא מגילה ה"ה שמוציאות לאחרים, וכדתנן (לק' י"ט ב') הכל כשרים לקרות את המגילה, ולישנא דכשרים משמע לקרוא לאחרים, ואמרינן בערכין (ג' א') הכל לאתויי נשים ודומיא דמתני' מרבי להו.... והא דתני תוספתא (פ"ב ה"ד) נשים ועבדים וקטנים פטורים ממקרא מגילה, ההיא משבשתא היא ולית בה טעמא שאף הן היו באותו הנס דהא פטר להו לגמרי.... וכיון דקי"ל כר' יהושע בן לוי דחייבות, אף מוציאות, אלא שאין זה כבוד לציבור והן בכלל מארה.

52. R. Henkin, *Responsa Benei Banim* 2:10, argues that according to this logic a woman could read for a small group of men. He disagrees with *Magen Avraham*'s argument of *lo pelug* (source #29, below).

והנה מלשון התוספות במסכת סוכה דרבים זילא בהו מילתא עכ"ל והביאו ראיה ממקרא מגילה משמע ששפיר אשה קוראת להוציא גברים בודדים, וכן משמע ממה שהריטב"א דימה קריאת המגילה לכבוד צבור ואלמא לא גזרו אלא שלא תקרא במגילה להוציא צבור גברים דומיא דקריאת התורה... ובמגן אברהם בסימן תרפ"ט סעיף קטן ה' כתב... שאפילו לזכר יחיד אינה מוציאה דלא פלוג עכ"ל... ומיהו קשה לי בדברי המגן אברהם והלא הוי מענין לענין שאין אומרים בו לא פלוג.

> [the obligation of others]. However, this is not [in accordance with] the honor of the congregation, and it falls into the category of [those who are to be] cursed.

Women are obligated in the reading of *megillah,* asserts Ritva, and their obligation allows them to read *megillah* on behalf of others, including men. He quotes the Tosefta but dismisses it as a mistake.[53] Clearly, women must be obligated because they too were included in the miracle! However, although a woman's reading would legally fulfill men's obligation, it would be beneath the honor of the congregation were a woman to perform this function.[54] In the end, she should not do so as it would reflect badly upon her male listeners – indeed, they should be cursed.

Kol Bo records a different concern about women's reading *megillah* for a mixed audience:[55]

---

53. See also *Ḥiddushei Harashba* to B.T. *Meg.* 4a that arrives at the same conclusion regarding the Tosefta but nevertheless concludes that women are only obligated to hear the *megillah* and, therefore, cannot read for men. See *Arukh Hashulḥan, O.Ḥ.* 689:1, who echoes Ritva's understanding of the Tosefta.

54. Interestingly, *Bayit Ḥadash, O.Ḥ.* 689:2, explains that the concern over *kevod hatsibbur* exists regarding Torah reading but is negated with regard to *megillah* reading by the reasoning of *af hen.*

    ואף על פי שהקילו במגילה יותר מבתורה לענין אשה שמוציאה לאיש במגילה מה שאין כן בתורה שאני התם דכיון דאפילו בקריאת התורה היתה אשה עולה למנין אלא שאמרו חכמים אשה לא תקרא בתורה מפני כבוד הצבור כדתניא התם (ע"א) הילכך במגילה לא חשו לכך מאחר שאף הן היו באותו הנס.

    See *Responsa Benei Banim* 2:10, where R. Henkin makes it clear that *kevod hatsibbur* is a separate concern from *kol be'ishah ervah* (the voice of a woman is sexual incitement). Both explanations stem from the opinion that women, though obligated, may not read for men. However, *kevod hatsibbur* is about that which is demeaning to the honor of the congregation, whereas *kol ishah* is a concern about provoking sexual thoughts in men.

55. See also *Orḥot Ḥayyim, Hilkh. Megillah Ufurim* 2.

17. ***Sefer Kol Bo #45*** **ספר כלבו סימן מה**

Authorship in dispute, France and Spain (thirteenth–fourteenth centuries)

Reading the *megillah* at its proper time is a positive, rabbinic *mitsvah*, and all are obligated to read it: men, women, converts, and freed slaves; and minors must be educated to read it.... Since women are obligated, for they too were part of the same miracle, it may be said that they may discharge even the obligation of men.... And the author of *Aseret Hadibberot* wrote that women should not fulfill the obligation of men through their reading, and the reason is because a woman's voice is sexual incitement.[56]

קריאת מגילה בזמנה מצות עשה מדברי סופרים והכל חייבין בקריאתה אנשים ונשים וגרים ועבדים משוחררין ומחנכין הקטנים לִקרותה.... נשים כיון שהן חייבות שאף הן היו באותו הנס י"ל שמוציאות אף האנשים.... והבעל עשרת הדברות כתב שאין נשים מוציאות אנשים בקריאתם והטעם משום דקול באשה ערוה.

Like Ritva (source #16) and R. Avraham ben Yitsḥak (source #14), *Kol Bo* rules that women and men have exactly the same obligation in *megillah*. However, *Kol Bo* records an opinion from *Aseret Hadibberot*, by R. Yitsḥak ben Abba Mari (Ba'al Ha'ittur, a Provençal authority in the twelfth century), that women should not read on behalf of men because of the problem of *kol ishah*, the potential for sexual incitement inherent in a woman's singing voice. *Kol Bo* is the only Rishon to raise this issue

56. The idea that it is problematic for a man to hear a woman singing stems from B.T. *Ber.* 24a. See *Sh. Ar., O.Ḥ.* 75:3, as well as the comment of Rema there; and *E.H.* 21:2. However, there is considerable debate as to the exact circumstances in which this restriction applies. A full discussion of the parameters of the restriction of *kol ishah* is beyond the scope of this chapter. For more information, see R. Howard Jachter, "The Parameters of Kol Isha," accessed August 18, 2015, http://koltorah.org/ravj/The%20Parameters%20of%20Kol%20Isha.htm; R. Howard Jachter and R. Saul Berman, "Kol 'Isha," in *Rabbi Joseph H. Lookstein Memorial Volume* (ed. Leo Landman; New York: Ktav Publishing, 1980); R. Yehuda Henkin, "*Kol Ishah* Reviewed," in *Equality Lost*, 66–76.

of women's voice,[57] and interestingly, the idea does not appear in extant editions of *Sefer Ha'ittur, Aseret Hadibberot*.[58]

In summary, these Rishonim agree that men and women share the same obligation with regard to reading *Megillat Ester*. Technically, one who is obligated in a *mitsvah* may fulfill that obligation on behalf of another. Therefore, after the fact, a man would have fulfilled his obligation if a woman were to read for him. However, these Rishonim feel that other social considerations make it unacceptable or undignified for a woman to read on behalf of a man and thus rule that she should not do so.

57. R. Henkin, *Responsa Benei Banim* 2:10, rejects the idea that *kol ishah* is a valid reason to prevent women from discharging the obligation of men. He bases his ruling on the statements of the rest of the Rishonim, and he softens *Kol Bo*'s intentions:

    ובכל הראשונים לא נזכר חילוק בין קריאת נשים בטעמים לבין קריאה בלי טעמים ובודאי אין מחלוקת ביניהם במציאות האם סתם נשים קוראות המגילה בטעמים או לא, ולכן ממה נפשך, אם סתם אשה קוראת המגילה בטעמים אם כן לדעת רש״י ודעמיה שהתירו לצאת על ידה אין בנגון הטעמים משום קול באשה ערוה ולדעת בה״ג ודעמיה שאסרו לאשה לקרוא לגברים על כל פנים לא משום קול באשה ערוה נגעו בה ונמצא שדעת הכלבו לפי פרוש שו״ת עצי חיים היא יחידאה ואינה הלכה, ואם סתם אשה קוראת בלי נגון הטעמים וכמו שמסתבר אזי אין כאן נגון כלל ומהיכי תיתי דהוי קול ערוה ממש ומאי שנא מקידוש. אלא מוכרח כמו שכתבתי שגם לדעת ספר הכלבו וארחות חיים אינו אלא מעין קול אשה וחשש בעלמא ורק במגילה חששו טפי.

58. See *Sefer Ha'ittur, Aseret Hadibberot, Hilkh. Megillah* 110a; and 113c–d. See also *Hilkh. Ḥanukkah* 116a (ed. Vilna; 46a–b in ed. Zemberg 1860). R. Henkin, *Responsa Benei Banim* 2:10, also confirms that this quote does not exist in contemporary editions of this work. It is only quoted by *Kol Bo* and *Orḥot Ḥayyim*, two works which may share an author. The issue of *kol ishah* is also raised by *Sefer Ha'eshkol* (in the 1863 edition), which is likely a forgery created by R. Benjamin Hirsch Auerbach. *Sefer Hame'orot*, a twelfth-century work, also quotes *Sefer Ha'ittur*; however, he merely quotes his comment that women should not read for men and then goes on to suggest in his own words, **ואפשר לומר טעם לספרא זה**, that the reason is *peritsut* (promiscuity), as in the case of *birkat hamazon*. He suggests that a woman's voice would be a form of *peritsut*, which explains why women may not bless for men. However, he then backtracks and states that *peritsut* only applies to slaves but not to free men. Thus, women would be eligible to read *megillah* for men, although one should still worry about the opinion of Behag.

Rishonim #3: Women Are Obligated Only to Hear and So May Read Only for Other Women

A third group of Rishonim prioritizes the Tosefta over the plain meaning of the Mishnah and attempts to harmonize the Tosefta with the material in the Babylonian Talmud by adopting the position of Behag. Like Behag, these authorities rule that women have an obligation to hear, but not to read, *Megillat Ester*. Therefore, these sources must reinterpret the Gemara in *Arakhin* and conclude that while women may not read the *megillah* on behalf of men, they may read it for other women.[59]

Although the Gemara implies that women are obligated to read *megillah* and may do so on behalf of men, *Tosafot* question this understanding in light of the Tosefta. As a result, they also must explain the statement of R. Yehoshua b. Levi (that women are obligated in the reading of the *megillah*) in light of this new understanding.

18. *Tosafot* *Megillah 4a* *s.v. nashim ḥayyavot bemikra megillah* French and German Talmudists (twelfth–fourteenth centuries)	**תוספות מסכת מגילה ד. ד"ה נשים חייבות במקרא מגילה**
Women are obligated in the reading of the megillah – From here we learn that women fulfill the obligation of others, since it does not say "to hear the reading of the *megillah*." We also learn this from *Arakhin* (2b) where it says, "All are eligible to read the *megillah*," and deduces, all are eligible, "to include whom?" and it learns, "to include women," meaning even to fulfill the obligation of men. And this is difficult, since in the Tosefta it teaches explicitly that a *tumtum* does not discharge the obligation either of its kind or of those not	**נשים חייבות במקרא מגילה** – מכאן משמע שהנשים מוציאות את אחרים ידי חובתן מדלא קאמר לשמוע מקרא מגילה והכי נמי משמע בערכין (דף ב: ושם) דקאמר הכל כשרים לקרא את המגילה ומסיק הכל כשרים לאתויי מאי ומשני לאתויי נשים, משמע להוציא אפילו אנשים. וקשה דהא בתוספתא תני בהדיא דטומטום אין מוציא לא את מינו ולא שאין מינו ואנדרוגינוס מוציא

59. Some of the sources state clearly that this interpretation is one way of understanding Behag, whereas others imply that Behag himself rules this way.

of its kind, and an *androginos* discharges the obligation of its kind and does not discharge the obligation of those who are not of its kind. It is obvious that a woman is not preferable to an *androginos*.[60] Thus ruled *Halakhot Gedolot*, that a woman discharges the obligation of her kind but not of men. It may be explained that one might have thought that their [women's] reading would not even be effective to fulfill the obligation of other women; therefore [this Gemara] taught us that they are obligated, since all are obligated in the hearing [of *megillah*] – slaves, women, and minors.	את מינו ואין מוציא את שאין מינו, ופשיטא דלא עדיפא אשה מאנדרוגינוס. וכן פסקו ההלכות גדולות דאשה מוציאה מינה אבל לא אנשים, ויש לומר דסלקא דעתך דלא יועיל קריאתן אפילו להוציא הנשים קא משמע לן דחייבין, דהכל חייבין בשמיעה עבדים נשים וקטנים.

Tosafot open by carefully analyzing the wording of the Gemara in *Megillah* in light of Behag's ruling. The text explicitly states that women are obligated to read *megillah*; nowhere in the Gemara does it say that they are obligated only to hear it. This understanding is supported by the Gemara in *Arakhin*, which teaches that women may read *megillah* for men. However, *Tosafot* cite the Tosefta as a challenge to this understanding. Since the Tosefta does not permit the *androginos* to read for other men, it is inconceivable to *Tosafot* that a woman would be eligible to do so, when one who is at least partially male cannot.[61] They attribute to Behag the view that women, like *androginos*, may only read for their own kind, that is, for other women. *Tosafot* then explain that this is in fact the view of the Gemara in *Arakhin*, as well. One might have mistakenly thought that women may not read the *megillah* at all – not even for other women.[62] The Gemara's statement about a woman's obligation teaches us that

60. See *Korban Netanel* 1:4 on Rosh to B.T. *Meg.* 4a, note 50. See n71 for the view of *Peri Ḥadash* that women are preferable to *androginos*.
61. It seems from this text that the Tosafists did not have the last line of the *tosefta*, which explicitly exempts women, in their version of the text. As a result, they only deduce this ruling from the statements about *tumtum* and *androginos*.
62. See *Ḥiddushei Harashba* to B.T. *Meg.* 4a, s.v. *R. Yehoshua b. Levi*, who goes so far as

women may in fact read for other women because all women have the same type of obligation, namely, to listen to the reading of the *megillah*. Therefore, *Tosafot* conclude that to rule in accordance with Behag,[63] one must interpret the Gemara's statement in *Arakhin* – "all are obligated in the reading of the *megillah*" – to mean that women may discharge the obligation of other women, not that they may read for men.[64]

Rosh also rules that women may read only for other women. Like *Tosafot*, he argues that the Gemara must inform us that women are obligated in *megillah* reading, lest one think that they may not read even for other women. Rosh first acknowledges that the Gemara indicates that women and men share the same obligation in the reading of the *megillah*. In principle, therefore, women should be eligible to read on behalf of men. However, Behag rules that women may not do so, and Rosh must explain how to read the Gemara in light of this more restrictive position.

19. ***Rosh*** **רא"ש**

Megillah 1:4 **מסכת מגילה פרק א סימן ד.**

R. Asher ben Yeḥiel, Germany and Spain (1250–1327)

"R. Yehoshua b. Levi said: Women are obligated in the reading of the *megillah*, for they too were part of the same miracle." ...[65] But Ba'al Hahalakhot [Behag] ruled that women are only

אמר ריב"ל נשים חייבות במקרא מגילה שאף הן היו באותו הנס.... ובעל ההלכות פסק שהנשים אינן חייבות אלא בשמיעה אבל קריאתה אינה מוציאה אנשים

to say that there is a mistake in the language of the Tosefta. For, if women were completely exempt, they would not be able to read at all! Rather, they are obligated, and that obligation allows them to read for other women. See above, n53.

63. *Arukh Hashulḥan, O.Ḥ.* 689:6 does not think that *Tosafot* rule in accordance with Behag. In his opinion, *Tosafot* just cite his opposing view. *Arukh Hashulḥan* thinks that *Tosafot* accept the opinion first cited, namely, that one learns from the language of the text that women may read for men.

64. See also *Tosafot* to B.T. *Arakh.* 3a, s.v. *la'atuyei nashim* that comes to the same conclusions.

65. In the omitted section, Rosh quotes Rashi's view that women can fulfill men's obligation based on the Gemara in *Arakhin*. *Beit Yosef, O.Ḥ.* 689:2 states:

והרא"ש כתב בריש מגילה (סי' ד) דברי רש"י ודברי הלכות גדולות ולא הכריע ומכל מקום דבריו נוטים כדעת בעל הלכות גדולות.

ידי חובתן שחייבין בקריאה עד שישמעו מפי אנשים המחוייבין בקריאה כמותן ואין שמיעתן מנשים חשובה כאלו הן עצמן קורין והביא ראיה מן התוספתא (פרק ב) דקתני הכל חייבין בקריאת מגילה וכו׳.... נשים ועבדים וקטנים פטורין ממקרא מגילה ואין מוציאין רבים ידי חובתן עכ״ל התוספתא והוסיף בהלכות גדולות אלא שחייבות בשמיעה....

obligated in hearing [the *megillah*], but her [a woman's] reading does not discharge the obligation of men, who are obligated in reading [and do not fulfill their obligation] until they hear it read from the mouth of men, who are obligated in reading like they are. Their hearing it from a woman is not as significant as if they [men] themselves read it. And he brings proof from the Tosefta (chapter 2), which teaches: "All are obligated in the reading of the *megillah*, etc.... Women, slaves, and minors are exempt from the reading of the *megillah* and do not discharge the obligation of the many." This is the end of the Tosefta. And he added in *Halakhot Gedolot*:[66] "But they are obligated in hearing."...

וצריך לתרץ לפי ה״ג ותוספתא הא דאמר בערכין הכל כשרין לקרות לאתויי נשים לא שיוציאו אנשים בקריאתן אלא דוקא נשים דלא תימא אף נשים אינן יוצאות אלא בקריאה חשובה של אנשים קא משמע לן שהאשה מוציאה חבירתה.

One must explain, according to [the view of] Behag and the Tosefta, that which is said in *Arakhin*: "All are eligible to read – to include women." This does not mean that they may discharge the obligation of men by their reading, but [that they may discharge the obligation] specifically of women. [This is necessary] lest one should say that women, too, do not fulfill their obligation other than through the significant reading of men. This [Gemara] comes to teach that a woman may discharge the obligation of her [female] friend.

66. It is clear that Rosh, like *Tosafot*, views this comment as an addition by Behag, not a part of Behag's version of the Tosefta.

Rosh explains Behag's position that women are obligated only to hear the *megillah* read, and, therefore, their reading is not sufficient to fulfill a man's obligation. For Behag to avoid contradicting the Gemara, Rosh interprets the text in *Arakhin* to mean specifically that women are permitted to read for other women. His language is even sharper than that of *Tosafot*: one might have thought that only a man's reading is significant, that is, that only one who is obligated to read, and not one who is obligated merely to hear, may read for others. In that case, one would mistakenly conclude that women can fulfill their obligation only by hearing the *megillah* read by men. Therefore, the Gemara explains that everyone, even women, are eligible to read and may fulfill the *mitsvah* for others, but only for those who share the same level of obligation. Thus, according to *Tosafot* and Rosh,[67] the Gemara teaches that although women may not read for men, they nonetheless may read for other women. This explanation is echoed by a number of other Rishonim.[68]

Ran, the fourteenth-century Spanish Talmudist, is another early authority who rules that women should read *megillah* only on behalf of other women. However, unlike *Tosafot* and Rosh, he clearly views Behag's position as a stringency that runs counter to the simple reading of the Gemara.

20. *Ran on Rif Megillah 2b (in Rif)*

ר"ן על הרי"ף מסכת מגילה ב: (בדפי הרי"ף)

R. Nissim ben Re'uven of Gerona, Spain (1320–1380)

Women are obligated in the reading of *megillah*, for they too were part of the same miracle. The correct explanation is that they too were in danger, and this is how it appears in the Jerusalem Talmud.... And there are those who say that since they are obligated,	נשים חייבות במקרא מגילה שאף הן היו באותו הנס. ועיקר הפי' דאף הן היו בסכנה והכי איתא בירושלמי.... ואיכא מ"ד דכיון שהן חייבות מוציאות את הזכרים ידי חובתן שכל

67. See n65 and n73.

68. See, for example, *Ḥiddushei Harashba* to B.T. *Meg.* 4a; *Sefer Ha'ittur Aseret Hadibberot, Hilkh. Megillah* 113b (who says that women are obligated only to hear the *megillah*); Mordekhai *Megillah* 4, *remez* 779; Ra'avyah Vol. 2 *Megillah* 569; and *Or Zarua*, Vol. 2, *Hilkh. Megillah* 368 (source #9, above, who discusses and rejects this logic).

they may discharge the obligation of men, for anyone who is obligated may discharge the obligation of the many. This also seems to be the case in the first *sugya* in *Arakhin* (3a), where it says: "All are obligated to read the *megillah*. To include whom? To include women." And this teaches that their [women's] rule is the same as anyone else who is obligated – [women are eligible] to fulfill the obligation of the many. Thus is the view of Rashi *z"l* ad loc., but in the name of *Halakhot Gedolot* they wrote that they [women] are obligated to hear the *megillah* but are not obligated to read it, and therefore they may not fulfill the obligation of the many. He brings proof from that which is taught in the Tosefta of the *Mekhilta*: "All are obligated in the reading of the *megillah*, etc., women and slaves and minors are exempt from the reading of the *megillah*." And he explains that they are exempt from reading but are obligated in hearing, as the Jerusalem Talmud reads: "R. Yehoshua b. Levi gathered his children and the members of his household and read it before them." And this [view that women are only obligated to hear] is not apparent, but it is appropriate to worry about his position and be stringent.

המחויב בדבר מוציא את הרבים ידי חובתן וה"נ משמע בשמעתא קמייתא דערכין (ג.) דאמרינן הכל חייבין לקרות את המגילה לאיתויי מאי לאיתויי נשים ומשמע שדינם כשאר החייבין להוציא רבים ידי חובתן וכן דעת רש"י ז"ל שם אבל בשם ה"ג כתבו שהן חייבות לשמוע את המגילה אבל אין חייבות בקריאתה ולפיכך אין מוציאות הרבים ידי חובתן והביא ראיה מדתניא בתוספתא דמכילתא הכל חייבין בקריאת מגילה וכו' נשים ועבדים וקטנים פטורין ממקרא מגילה ופירש בו שהן פטורות מהמקרא אבל חייבות בשמיעה וכדגרסי' בירושל' ריב"ל מכניף בניו ובני ביתו וקרי ליה קמיהון. ואין זה מחוור אלא שראוי לחוש לדבריו להחמיר.

Like *Tosafot* (source #18) and Rosh (source #19), Ran notes that the Gemara clearly states that women, like men, are obligated in the reading of the *megillah* because they, too, were in danger of annihilation. Therefore, Ran explains, following Rashi, women may discharge the obligation of men. He also quotes the opposing ruling of Behag and the Tosefta on which it is based. Ran concludes that one should be stringent in this regard and follow the ruling of Behag despite the fact that his reading is "not apparent" because women are clearly obligated to read the *megillah* according to the Gemara.[69] Out of concern for the view of Behag that women may not really have the same obligation as men, women should only read for other women.[70]

This third group of Rishonim represents the most limiting and restrictive view of a woman's obligation and participation in the *mitsvah* of *megillah* reading. Unlike the first two groups of Rishonim, these authorities prioritize the Tosefta over the normative texts of the Mishnah and Gemara and rule that women and men have different types of obligations with regard to *megillah* reading. Based on the opinion of Behag, these Rishonim conclude that the obligation to which R. Yehoshua b. Levi refers is an obligation to hear, but not to read, *Megillat Ester,* and that women may not read for men. However, these Rishonim must grapple with the Gemara's statement in *Arakhin,* which definitively states that women are eligible to read *megillah.* They interpret this text to mean that women are eligible to read *megillah* only for other women. It is clear from these medieval sources that the practice of women's reading for other women is not a progressive reading of the Gemara, but rather the most conservative possible interpretation of the Talmudic text in light of the Tosefta.

TUR AND *SHULḤAN ARUKH*

The two great law codes of the late medieval period, R. Ya'akov ben R. Asher's *Tur* and R. Yosef Caro's *Shulḥan Arukh,* each codify rulings about the question of a woman reading *megillah* for men. Both codes, however, contain ambiguity in the way they present their respective positions.

---

69. See source #54, below, on the question of a woman counting toward a *minyan,* where it is clear that Ran thinks that women can legally discharge the obligation of men.

70. *Sefer Hame'orot* to B.T. *Meg.* 19a uses very similar language:

ואפשר לומר דדוקא בעבדים ונשים אמרינן בזימון דחיישינן לפריצותא וכדאמרינן בעלמא דעבדים פרוצים הם, אבל באנשי אחריני לא אמרינן הכי, והילכך אפילו במגלה מוציאות את האנשים. ומכל מקום ראוי לחוש לכתחלה לדברי הרב בעל ההלכות שאוסר מכח התוספתא והירושלמי.

It is clear that the position of *Sefer Hame'orot* is that if a woman did read for men, they would have fulfilled their obligation. Logically, this would also be the view of Ran.

21. ***Tur***
Oraḥ Ḥayyim #689
R. Ya'akov ben R. Asher, Spain (1269–1343)

טור
אורח חיים סימן תרפט

All are obligated in the reading of the *megillah*: priests, Levites, and Israelites; slaves, a defiled priest, *mamzer, natin, tumtum,* and *androginos.* We also educate the minor in it, and women are also obligated in reading it. Rashi explained that they [women] discharge the obligation of men, and Behag wrote that even though they are obligated in the reading of the *megillah,* they do not discharge the obligation of men.[71]

הכל חייבין בקריאת מגילה כהנים לוים וישראלים עבדים חלל ממזר נתין טומטום ואנדרוגינוס ומחנכין נמי הקטן בה ונשים נמי חייבות בקריאתה ופירש"י שמוציאות לאנשים ידי חובתן ובה"ג כ' אע"ג שחייבות במקרא מגילה אינן מוציאות לאנשים.

Tur echoes the language of the Tosefta in his list of all those who are obligated in *megillah* reading; however, he does include women tacked on at the end of the list. He cites two interpretations of this ruling: that of Rashi, who states that women may read the *megillah* on behalf of men, and that of Behag, who argues that women may not discharge a man's

71. *Tur* goes on to say: ואנדרוגינוס מוציא מינו ולא שאינו מינו וטומטום ומי שחציו עבד וחציו בן חורין אפי' מינו אינו מוציא. *Beit Yosef* ad loc., note 3, explains that even according to Rashi, who holds that women may read for men, it still makes sense that a *tumtum* (a person of indeterminate sex) may not read even for another *tumtum.* It is important to know the sex of the person reading and the sex of the person listening, and thus it is better to know that the reader is definitely female:

> וטעמא משום דטפי עדיף כשהמוציא הוא ודאי אשה והשומע זכר מכשהמוציא הוא טומטום אפילו אם השומע נקבה ואפילו אם השומע טומטום דסלקא דעתך אמינא כיון דתרווייהו חד מינא נינהו נפקו אהדדי ידי חובתן קא משמע לן דלא משום דבעינן שהמוציא את אחרים ידי חובתן יהא ניכר אם הוא זכר או אם הוא נקבה.

The same logic would presumably apply in the case of an *androginos*; one might also argue that it is a dishonor to the community. See *Peri Ḥadash* 689:3, who explains:

> והנה דין האנדרוגינוס איכא למימר דאפילו לדעת רש"י ודעמיה ז"ל שס"ל דנשים מוצאות את הרבים י"ח מודה הכא דאינו מוציא אלא מינו דאנדרוגינוס גרע מאשה.

See *Sh. Ar., O.Ḥ.* 689:3, who rules similarly regarding *tumtum* and *androginos* despite the fact that women are obligated to read.

obligation. Interestingly, *Tur* does not explain his understanding of the reasoning behind Behag's ruling; presumably it is a social concern like those stated in the second section of Rishonim above.[72] *Tur* does not rule conclusively between the two perspectives.[73]

Shulḥan Arukh, the authoritative sixteenth-century law code, also presents two different positions regarding a woman's reading of the *megillah*.

22. *Shulḥan Arukh* *Oraḥ Ḥayyim #689* R. Yosef Caro, Spain and Israel (1488–1575)	**שולחן ערוך אורח חיים סימן תרפט**
1) All are obligated in reading it: men, women, converts, and freed slaves, and we educate minors to read it.	א) הכל חייבים בקריאתה אנשים ונשים וגרים ועבדים משוחררים ומחנכים את הקטנים לקרותה.
2) Both one who reads and one who hears from the reader fulfills the obligation, and this is if one hears it from one who is obligated to read it. Therefore, if the reader was a deaf-mute, a minor, or intellectually disabled, the listener has not fulfilled their obligation. There are those who say that women do not discharge the obligation of men.[74]	ב) אחד הקורא ואחד השומע מן הקורא יצא ידי חובתו והוא שישמע ממי שהוא חייב בקריאתה. לפיכך אם היה הקורא חרש או קטן או שוטה, השומע ממנו לא יצא. וי"א שהנשים אינם מוציאות את האנשים.

72. *Tur* does not mention the idea that women are obligated to hear the *megillah*, but not to read it. Thus, he presumably understands Behag's ruling in light of the idea that it is inappropriate or undignified for women to read *megillah* on behalf of men. See the discussion of *Arukh Hashulḥan* (source #23, below), who suggests this interpretation of *Tur*'s halakhic ruling.

73. *Beit Yosef*, commenting on *Tur*, brings positions on both sides. He quotes Rosh, *Tur*'s father, who cites both Rashi and Behag. *Beit Yosef* explains that Rosh does not rule conclusively between them. However, he feels that Rosh leans more toward Behag's position. See Rosh's position in source #19, above.

74. Rema comments here:

וי"א אם האשה קוראה לעצמה מברכת: לשמוע מגילה, שאינה חייבת בקריאה.

This statement is discussed in greater detail, below (see source #66).

6) It is a good custom to bring boys and girls to hear the reading of the *megillah*.[75]	ו) מנהג טוב להביא קטנים וקטנות לשמוע מקרא מגילה.

The first two *se'ifim* (paragraphs) of *Shulḥan Arukh* are exact quotes from Rambam's *Mishneh Torah* (source #10 above). The first paragraph, a list of those who are obligated in the reading of *megillah*, includes women. The second is an explanation of how one may fulfill this obligation: anyone who is obligated may either read or hear the reading from another who is obligated. Again quoting Rambam, *Shulḥan Arukh* lists examples of those whose reading would be insufficient to discharge a listener's obligation. Women are not included in this list because they are indeed obligated, just as men are, and a woman reading would therefore suffice to discharge a man's obligation[76] according to this initial ruling of *Shulḥan Arukh*.[77]

In the final clause of the second *se'if*, *Shulḥan Arukh* records a contrary opinion under the heading *yesh omerim*: "There are those who say that women do not discharge the obligation of men." No explanation or reasoning is recorded for this opinion, and R. Caro does not explicitly state which position, the initial statement or the *yesh omerim*, represents his ruling for practical *halakhah*.[78] These two elements leave

75. The idea to bring both young boys and girls to hear the *megillah* is also expressed by *Tur*:

    וכ"כ בה"ג ירוש' ריב"ל הוה מכניש בני ביתיה וקרי קמיהון מכאן נוהגין במקצת מקומות להביא קטנים וקטנות לשמוע מקרא מגילה.

    It is also codified by *Arukh Hashulḥan, O.Ḥ.* 689:3, who stresses that young children, both male and female, should be educated to behave appropriately during the reading. See *Mishnah Berurah* 689 (source #35, below), who also raises the issue of decorum when bringing children to the synagogue.

76. See also R. Yosef Caro's statement in *Beit Yosef, O.Ḥ.* 689:2, where he mentions that *Maggid Mishneh* thinks that Rambam rules like Rashi, that women may read *megillah* on behalf of men.

77. *Kaf Haḥayyim, O.Ḥ.* 689:13, suggests that the *yesh omerim* might be concerned with a man's hearing a woman's voice, whereas the view of the initial ruling is not concerned: וכ"ז לדעת י"א אבל לדיעה הראשונה אין חושבין זה הקול ערוה כיון שאינו של שיר.

78. In general, there is a clear rule for how to determine the *pesak* of *Sh. Ar.* when he first brings one ruling *setam* and then follows it with a different ruling under the heading *yesh omerim*: the *halakhah* is according to the initial ruling. This rule is stated by *Shakh, Y.D.* 242 (*Pilpul Behanhagat Hora'ot Be'issur Veheter*), end of #5:

room for much discussion and speculation. Perhaps the *yesh omerim* reflects the views of Behag and of those Rishonim in the third group discussed above that women, unlike men, are obligated only to hear but not to read *Megillat Ester*.[79] However, given that in the first *se'if* R. Caro cites without comment Rambam's position that both women and men are obligated in the reading of *megillah*, it seems unlikely that he would record an opposing view that excludes women from the obligation to read the *megillah* without explicitly mentioning this tension. If it was

---

> זה שתמצא בכמה מקומות בדברי המחבר והרב או שאר אחרונים שמביאים בתחילה סברא אחת בסתם ואחר כך יש מי שמתיר או יש מי שאוסר או יש מתירין או יש אוסרים או יש מי שחולק או יש חולקים הוא מפני שנראה להם עיקר כהסברא שכתבו בסתם והסברא האחרת היא טפלה בעיניהם.

It also appears in *Peri Megadim, O.Ḥ., kelallim* 11 and 34: הלכה כדיעה ראשונה בסתם ...כבר כתבנו [לעיל אות יא, טו] הלכה כדיעה א' בסתם, ויש אומרים הלכה כסתם. This rule is applied by numerous *posekim* in their rulings on many topics in *halakhah*. A simple search in the Bar Ilan Responsa Project for סתם וי"א הלכה כסתם brings up hundreds of sources. R. Ovadiah Yosef applies this rule over forty-five times in his responsa, including in reference to this specific topic of women and *megillah* reading. See *Responsa Yeḥavveh Da'at* 3:53:

> וכן פסק מרן השלחן ערוך /א"ח/ (סימן תרפ"ט סעיף א') בסתם, אלא שסיים אחר כך: ויש אומרים שהנשים אין מוציאות את האנשים. וידוע הכלל שסתם ויש הלכה כסתם. וכן כתב מרן החיד"א בברכי יוסף (סימן רע"א סק"א).

Mishpatim Yesharim 1:53 cites this rule, as well, but expresses some hesitation: if R. Caro wanted to rule according to the initial ruling, why would he bring the *yesh omerim* at all? In his view, these cases are ones in which R. Caro was unsure about how to rule.

> כלל מורגל בפי הכל שכל מקום שמביא בש"ע סברות הרבה פוס' כי"א בתרא אם היה דרך י"א וי"א. ואם הביא האחד בסתם הלכה כסתם ולדעתי נראה שכלל זה משתבר ונופל מכמה מקומות בש"ע כאשר אבאר אלא שעיקר הוא שדעת הרב ז"ל דהוי ספיקא דדינא והמוציא מחבירו עליו הראיה והסיבה שכתב הסברא הא' סתם וכתב עליה וי"א הוא לסיבה שיעתיק הרב דברי הרמב"ם ככתבם וכלשונם ושוב כותב עליו וי"א ולפעמים מעתיק לשון הטור וכותב וי"א וכוונתו להודיענו שיש חולקים בזה והוה ספק כי אין בידו להכריע. ותדע שאם כוונתו היתה שלא לחוש כלל לסברת י"א והלא מעטים הם הדינים שהם מוסכמים ורובא דרובא יש בהם מחלוקת ולמה אינו מביא סברותיהם אלא ודאי כמ"ש עיקר. ואמת ויציב שהרב בשלחנו בא לסלק המחלוקות וכל מקום שאין בידו להכריע מפאת הצדדים שהם שקולים כותב שניהם או בדרך סתם וי"א או בדרך י"א וי"א כששניהם מחודשים לא נזכרו בדברי הרמב"ם או הטור ולעולם אינו מזכיר ראשונה בסתם אלא שהיא מהרמב"ם או מהטור שהמה העמודים שעליהם נבנה הש"ע או אם הפוסק שממנו העתיק הדין כתב ראשונה בסתם ושניה בשם י"א מעתיק הרב כן.

79. The third group of Rishonim is discussed above, pp. 240–246.

his intention to record this understanding of Behag's position, then he should state not only that those authorities rule that women may not read for men but also that they do not think that women are obligated to read the *megillah* in the first place.[80] It makes more sense to say that this second opinion cited by R. Caro reflects the views of the second group of Rishonim,[81] who rule that although women are obligated in the reading of *megillah,* they may not read on behalf of men because it is beneath the dignity of the congregation or for some other social reason.[82] *Shulḥan Arukh* does not explicitly endorse one position over the other, although the natural structure of the language suggests that his own view is in accordance with the first opinion, cited without attribution (*setam*) and elaborated, after which he records the differing opinion of other authorities. This ambiguity generates a great deal of controversy in subsequent halakhic works. The many commentators on *Shulḥan Arukh* and other later *posekim* are divided as to which of the two positions *Shulḥan Arukh* gives precedence.[83]

Interestingly, in the final *se'if* of this chapter, *Shulḥan Arukh*

80. Rema ad loc. does so specifically. When citing those authorities who think that women should recite a different blessing, he explicitly states that they think women are not obligated to read *megillah.* See n74 and source #66.

81. Or, of Behag, according to *Tur.* For discussion of this second group of Rishonim, see above, pp. 231–239.

82. See *Magen Avraham* ad loc., #5, *Arukh Hashulḥan, O.Ḥ.* 689:1, and R. Halevi's view in n179, who all read the *yesh omerim* in *Sh. Ar.* in this way. *Arukh Hashulḥan* states:

    וכ"כ בש"ע בשם י"א והטעם מפני שאין זה כבוד הציבור כמו בס"ת אין אשה קוראה בציבור מפני כבוד הציבור.

83. R. Ovadiah Yosef, *Responsa Yeḥavveh Da'at* 3:51 and 4:34, says that in cases such as these the ruling is in accordance with the first position cited (see n78, above). *Responsa Tsits Eliezer* 22:38 holds like R. Yosef:

    ולפי"ז הא מצינו גם למרן המחבר בשו"ע דפוסק בזה ג"כ כהרמב"ם כי בסימן תרפ"ט סעי' ב' פוסק בסתמא כלשונו של הרמב"ם בהלכה ב' שם דאם היה הקורא חרש או קטן או שוטה השומע ממנו לא יצא, אשר מזה מדייק המגיד משנה שם דמשמע דאבל אשה נראה מדברי רבינו שהיא מוציאה את אחרים ושכן עיקר. ורק מוסיף וכותב די"א שהנשים אינן מוציאות את האנשים. וידוע כללי הב"י דכשכותב סתמא וי"א ס"ל לעיקר כסתמא. וא"כ הא יש הוכחה ג"כ מהשו"ע דס"ל גם זאת לעיקר דנשים חייבות גם לרבות בשמיעת פרשת זכור.

    Eshel Avraham 689:4, *Eliyah Rabbah* 689:2, and *Levush* 689 all disagree and hold that the *halakhah* is in accordance with the *yesh omerim. Kaf Haḥayyim, O.Ḥ.* 689:14, agrees, but because of the lack of clarity in *Sh. Ar.,* he holds that a man who heard

records the "commendable custom" of taking both young boys and young girls to hear the reading of the *megillah*. This supports R. Caro's point in the first *se'if*: both men and women are obligated in this *mitsvah*, and, therefore, all children should become accustomed to hearing *Megillat Ester* as part of their religious education.[84]

It seems that neither *Tur* nor *Shulḥan Arukh* codifies the view of Behag that women are obligated only to hear the *megillah*. For they both initially rule that women are obligated in the reading of *megillah*. They explain that, as a consequence, women would be eligible to read for men. However, both codes subsequently introduce the alternate view that women should not read for men, thus leaving some uncertainity about their final ruling.

AḤARONIM

Following the publication of *Tur* and *Shulḥan Arukh*, the Aḥaronim struggled to make sense of the ambiguity contained in those two major codes and to understand them in light of the positions of the Rishonim.

Halakhic discourse about women and *Megillat Ester* during this time period (ca. 1400–1900) largely centers on whether or not women must hear the *megillah* read by a man or whether they may hear it read by other women. The straightforward reading of the Talmud, which indicates that women may discharge the obligation of men, is rarely discussed.

The Aḥaronim may be divided into three groups:

---

the *megillah* read by a woman should hear it again from a man but without the blessings. Although, see source #39, below, where he states that if it is the man's only option, he may rely on R. Caro's initial ruling and have a woman read for him: וא"כ כיון דאיכא פלוגתא בזה אם שמע מן האשה צריך לחזור ולקרות כדי לצאת אליבא דכ"ע אבל לא יברך משום דק"ל ספק ברכות להקל.

84. In the first *se'if*, he specifically says that *ketanim*, which could mean all children but probably means young boys, should be educated to read. This could be understood to mean that boys, but not girls, need this training. Or, it could just reflect the reality that it was men who usually read *megillah* and so boys were taught to do so (or that only boys were educated to read at all!). It is also possible that *Sh. Ar.* simply quotes Rambam directly, and this language has no further significance.

- A small number of Aḥaronim rule that women may read *megillah* on behalf of men. This position is supported by the first opinion presented in *Shulḥan Arukh*. It reflects a straightforward reading of the Gemara and is well documented among Rishonim in the first group discussed above.
- Some Aḥaronim follow the position of Behag and the third group of Rishonim who believe that women have a different obligation from men and therefore rule that women may not read *megillah* on behalf of men. A number of them actually reinterpret the exact distinction between men's and women's obligations to explain why women cannot read for men. However, they do support the idea of women reading on behalf of other women.
- Others claim that it is preferable for women to hear *megillah* read by a man, except perhaps if she has no alternative. This new idea, explored in detail below, seems to result from a misreading of certain texts and is without precedent anywhere in the Gemara, Rishonim, or codes.

Aḥaronim #1: Women May Read *Megillah* for Men

R. Yeḥiel Mikhl Epstein, in his influential halakhic compilation *Arukh Hashulḥan*, thoroughly analyzes the issues raised by earlier sources.[85] He spends a significant amount of time in his introductory paragraphs discussing and trying to understand the Tosefta and Behag's ruling[86] before ultimately arguing that this position is untenable. He concludes

---

85. R. Epstein thinks that women are obligated in the reading of the *megillah* and, therefore, finds that the wording of the Tosefta must be mistaken. He suggests that it should read that women are obligated but cannot read for men because of the honor of the community. According to R. Epstein, this is the understanding presented in *Tur* and the *yesh omerim* in *Sh. Ar.* Because women are obligated, he holds that one should ensure that girls of *bat mitsvah* age hear the *megillah* and also references a custom when young children – both boys and girls – are brought to synagogue to hear the reading. See n72, n75, and n82, above.

86. R. Epstein weighs two possible understandings of Behag. In the first, women are obligated to read, but it is dishonorable to the congregation for them to do so. In this case, due to the legal concept of *lo pelug*, even one woman may not read for one man (as stated by *Magen Avraham* 689:5, source #29, below). Alternatively, women are only obligated to hear *megillah* but not to read it. He is uncertain why Behag

that women have the same obligation as men and may therefore read *Megillat Ester* on their behalf.[87]

23. *Arukh Hashulḥan Oraḥ Ḥayyim 689:6*

ערוך השולחן אורח חיים סימן תרפט סעיף ו

R. Yeḥiel Mikhl Epstein, Lithuania (1829–1908)

Tur and *Shulḥan Arukh* wrote in *se'if* 3: "*Androginos* discharges the obligation of its kind but not of those who are not of its kind. *Tumtum* and half-slaves do not discharge even the obligation of their own kind." The reason is that every *androginos* is the same, which is not the case with *tumtum*, for one can be male and another female.... This law is in the Tosefta at the beginning of *Megillah*, and it seems that this is only according to the position of Behag that women may not discharge the obligation of men. For if this were not the case, why could an *androginos* not discharge the obligation of those not of its kind, and why could one *tumtum* not discharge the obligation of another *tumtum*?... But in fact, this is a very forced position. It seems more [correct] according to Rashi and *Tosafot*, who do not include all of these rules. The law is not like the Tosefta, according to our Talmud. A clear proof for this is the fact that Rambam does not

כתבו הטור והש"ע סעיף ג' אנדרוגינוס מוציא מינו ולא שאינו מינו טומטום ומי שחציו עבד אפילו מינו אינו מוציא עכ"ל והטעם משום דאנדרוגינוס כולם שוים משא"כ טומטום יכול להיות זה זכר וזו נקבה.... ודין זה הוא בתוספתא ריש מגילה ונראה דזה אינו אלא לשיטת בה"ג דהנשים אינן מוציאות לאנשים דאל"כ למה אנדרוגינוס אינו מוציא שאינו מינו וטומטום למה אינו מוציא טומטום אחר.... אבל באמת כמה מהדוחק הוא זה ונראה יותר דלרש"י ותוס' ליכא כל הני דינים ולית הלכתא כהתוספתא לפי ש"ס דילן [ב"ח] וראיה ברורה לדבר זה שהרמב"ם לא הזכיר כלל מדינים אלו ע"ש משום דס"ל כרש"י ותוס' דנשים שוות לאנשים א"כ גם

might suggest such a possibility and suggests that perhaps an obligation derived from the principle of *af hen* might not be as forceful as a man's obligation. This idea is expressed by later Aḥaronim. See sources #26–28, below.

87. He quotes the ruling of Rambam that one who is obligated may read for another; and before going on to analyze the ruling of Behag, he states:

ולכאורה אשה כיון שחייבת מוציאה גם אנשים בקריאתה.

mention these laws [about *tumtum* and *androginos*] at all, see there, because he rules like Rashi and *Tosafot* that women are equal to men. If so, *tumtum* and *androginos* may also discharge the obligation of those who are definitely male, and so too half-slaves whose situation is like a woman's. [So it appears in my humble opinion.]

טומטום ואנדרוגינוס מוציאין את הזכרים הוודאין וכן חציו עבד דדינו כאשה [כנלע"ד].

Arukh Hashulḥan cites *Tur* and *Shulḥan Arukh*, who both rule that an *androginos* can read only for its own kind and that a *tumtum* cannot read for anyone, even another *tumtum*. According to *Arukh Hashulḥan*, this ruling reflects the language of the Tosefta and is in accordance with Behag's interpretation. If women are not obligated to read as men are, then someone who is partially female (*androginos*) or who actually might be female (*tumtum*) would not be permitted to read for men either.[88]

However, *Arukh Hashulḥan* concludes that the entire argument of Behag and the Tosefta is forced and runs counter to the Talmud. Rather, he says, it makes more sense to follow Rashi and *Tosafot* who do not discuss these cases as exceptions.[89] R. Epstein strengthens his argument by pointing out that Rambam does not cite the laws of *tumtum* and *androginos* because he also thinks that men and women have equal obligations. Therefore, concludes *Arukh Hashulḥan*, it is in fact the case that women may legally read *megillah* on behalf of men as can *tumtum* and *androginos*.[90] In rejecting the Tosefta, R. Epstein also dismisses both of the rationales that he proposed in earlier paragraphs

88. See n71, above, for R. Caro's explanation of how this ruling nonetheless accords with Rashi's view and is not solely the view of Behag.
89. The position of *Tosafot* (source #18, above) seems to be in accordance with that of Behag. Interestingly, *Arukh Hashulḥan* groups *Tosafot* and Rashi together. It seems that R. Epstein reads *Tosafot* as ruling in accordance with Rashi; that is, women may read for men. In his understanding, *Tosafot* simply quotes the position of Behag but does not actually adopt his view.
90. R. Yehuda Henkin, who is quoted at length in sources #44–46 and 60, below, has ruled that in the event of differing opinions, one should follow the position of *Arukh Hashulḥan* over that of *Mishnah Berurah* (*Responsa Benei Banim* 2:8).

to explain its reasoning. In fact, women and men do not have different obligations, and *kevod hatsibbur* does not preclude women from reading *Megillat Ester* for men.

In the early twentieth century, R. Ḥanokh Eigis formulated a very different approach to the question of women's reading *megillah* on behalf of men. R. Eigis explores the position of Behag through an examination of the essence of the *mitsvah* of *megillah* reading and develops an intricate and completely innovative approach. Ultimately, though he claims to adhere to the conceptual framework of Behag, his practical conclusions regarding women's ritual participation differs greatly from a straightforward reading of Behag or any previous source.

24. ***Marḥeshet Vol. 1, #22*** **מרחשת חלק א סימן כב**

R. Ḥanokh Henekh Eigis, Vilna (1864–1941)

1) It is the opinion of Behag that women are not obligated in reading the *megillah*, but only in hearing the *megillah*, and therefore they cannot discharge the obligation of men, and they recite the blessing "on hearing the *megillah*."[91] Many have already examined this to understand his reasoning. It seems to me that it is based on what is written in Tractate *Megillah* (18a), "one who reads [*megillah*] by heart has not fulfilled [the obligation]." The reasoning is explained by means of a *gezerah shavah* (analogy; lit., equal decree):[92] it says here, "*remembered* and enacted" (Esth. 9:28), and it says there, "write this [what Amalek did] as a *remembrance* in the book" (Exod. 17:14); just as there it should be in a book, so here [in the case of *megillah* reading]	א) דעת הבה"ג הוא שנשים אינן חייבות במקרא מגילה רק בשמיעת המגילה וע"כ אינן מוציאות אנשים ומברכות על משמע מגילה, וכבר חקרו רבים להבין טעמו, והנראה לי בזה עפ"י מה דאיתא במגילה (יח.) קראה ע"פ לא יצא ומפרש טעמא משום גז"ש כתיב כאן נזכרים ונעשים וכתיב התם כתוב זאת זכרון בספר מה להלן בספר אף כאן בספר.... משום

91. The question of which blessings women should say is discussed in detail below in "Women and Blessings."

92. A *gezerah shavah* is a hermeneutical tool in which two similar words or phrases are compared for the purpose of drawing a conclusion about one case from information that is already known about the other.

it should be in a book [i.e., the reader must read from the *megillah* rather than by heart]… because we learn from similar things, since the reading of *megillah*, aside from publicizing the miracle, also contains the aspect of remembering the eradication of Amalek….

דילפינן מדבר הדומה משום דקריאת המגילה מלבד פרסום הנס יש בה ג"כ משום זכירת מחיית עמלק....

Indeed, we learn from this that the reading of *megillah* contains two *mitsvot*, one related to the publicizing of the miracle, and the other related to the commandment to remember [that which was done by Amalek], which the Men of the Great Assembly established, [namely] to remember it on this day through the reading of the *megillah* because of an event that happened….

והרי אנו למדין מזה שקריאת המגילה יש בה שתי מצוות, חדא משום פרסום הנס ועוד משום מצוות זכירה שתקנו אכה"ג לזכור ביום זה ע"י הקריאה של המגילה משום מעשה שהיה....

2) With regard to the *mitsvah* of remembering the eradication of Amalek, the [*Sefer*] *Haḥinnukh* wrote at the end of *Parashat* [*Ki*] *Tetsei* that women are not commanded regarding this because they are not eligible for war (lit., daughters of war), and are not commanded regarding the *mitsvah* of eradicating Amalek. Therefore, they are also not included in the *mitsvah* of remembering…. If this is the case, according to what I wrote, [namely] that the reading of the *megillah* has within it also this aspect of the *mitsvah* of remembering [Amalek], if so, it follows that even though women are obligated in the reading of *megillah*, this is only because of [the aspect of] publicizing the miracle because they too were part of the same miracle. However, the *mitsvah* of remembering does not apply to them. If so, this clearly explains Behag's position that women are obligated only to hear the *megillah*, since the essence of their

ב) והנה בדין מצות זכירת מח"ע כתב החינוך סו"פ תצא שהנשים לא נצטוו ע"ז משום שאינן בנות מלחמה ואינן מצוות על מצות מחיית עמלק ע"כ אינן ג"כ במצות זכירה.... א"כ לפ"מ שכתבתי שקריאת המגילה יש בה ג"כ משום מצות זכירה א"כ בנשים אף שמחוייבות במקרא מגילה היינו רק משום פרסום הנס משום שגם הן היו באותו הנס, אבל מצות זכירה אין בהם, א"כ מתבאר בזה היטב דעת הבה"ג שאין נשים מחייבות רק בשמיעת המגילה והיינו כיון דעיקר חיובן הוא משים פרסום

obligation is publicizing the miracle. If so, it is sufficient for them simply to hear because this constitutes publicizing. This is not the case for men, since beside the *mitsvah* of publicizing the miracle they are also obligated in the *mitsvah* of remembering, and this is the obligation to read. It then follows that women may not discharge the obligation of men, according to his opinion, since they are not [included] in the *mitsvah* of remembering. If so, they are not obligated in this matter and cannot discharge the obligation of men, who are also obligated in the *mitsvah* of remembering.

הנס א"כ די להם בשמיעה לבד שזה הוי פרסום, משא"כ האנשים מלבד מצות פרסום הנס חייבים ג"כ במצות זכירה, וזהו חיוב קריאה, וממילא ניחא מה שאין נשים מוציאות אנשים לפי דעתו כיון דבמצות זכירה ליתנהו א"כ הוו אינן מחוייבות בדבר ואינן יכולות להוציא אנשים שמחוייבין ג"כ במצות זכירה.

R. Eigis explains, based on the Talmud, that the obligation to read *Megillat Ester* from a scroll rather than reciting it by heart stems from a homiletical interpretation of the word *zikkaron* (remembrance). The events of the Purim story are to be "remembered and enacted," just as the story of Amalek's attack on the children of Israel is meant to be written "as a remembrance in the book." Thus, it is learned that in both instances, the remembering of a story is intrinsically linked to a written account.

Based on this connection, R. Eigis argues that the obligation to read the *megillah* on Purim consists of two components. One is the obligation to publicize the miracle of Purim, and the other is the obligation to remember the actions of Amalek, the ancestors of the wicked Haman. Reading *Megillat Ester* simultaneously accomplishes both of these *mitsvot*. Women are fully obligated in *pirsumei nissa* (publicizing the miracle) because they, too, were included in the miracle. However, based on the analysis of the obligation to remember Amalek in *Sefer Haḥinnukh*, R. Eigis concludes that women are not obligated in the *mitsvah* of remembering the eradication of Amalek.[93] Men, on the other

93. A full discussion of the question of a woman's obligation in remembering Amalek is beyond the scope of this chapter, as indeed is the larger question of how this obligation is derived and interpreted for men as well as for women. It is sufficient to note here that there is considerable debate as to whether women are obligated.

hand, are obligated in both. This theory, proposes R. Eigis, perfectly explains the position of Behag regarding women and *megillah* reading.[94] Women are obligated to hear the *megillah* because hearing the story read aloud fulfills the aspect of the *mitsvah* that is relevant to them: publicizing the miracle. Men, on the other hand, must also satisfy the aspect of remembering Amalek, which is directly linked to reading the *megillah* from a scroll. Therefore, men are obligated to read, not merely to hear the reading of *Megillat Ester*. Since women are not obligated in this regard, they cannot fulfill the obligation on a man's behalf.

R. Eigis then takes this reasoning a step further.

Sefer Haḥinnukh clearly holds that they are not (see *Sefer Haḥinnukh* #603), and a number of Aḥaronim adopt this position. Nonetheless, the majority of *posekim* disagree and think that women are obligated to remember Amalek. For examples and further discussion, see *Responsa Binyan Tsiyyon Haḥadashot* #8; *Responsa Yeḥavveh Da'at* 1:84; *Responsa Yabbia Omer*, Vol. 8, *O.Ḥ.* #54; *Responsa Tsits Eliezer* 22:38; and a summary of the issue in *Halikhot Beitah* 9:5 and n8, as well as in R. Tsevi Pesaḥ Frank's *Mikra'ei Kodesh* on Purim, chapter 5.

94. In *se'if* 8, R. Eigis explains that the position of Rambam (and, by extension, other authorities), who thinks that women may, in fact, read *megillah* on behalf of men, follows the same rubric.

> נחזור לענינינו דלפי דעת החינוך שהנשים אינן מחויבות במצות זכירה של מחיית עמלק, משום שאינן בנות מלחמה ולא נצטוו במצות מחיית עמלק א״ש דעת הבה״ג שאין הנשים מוציאות אנשים במקרא מגילה׳.... אולם דעת הרמב״ם ז״ל בפ״א מה׳ מגילה ה״ב שנשים מוציאות אנשים במקרא מגילה וכמו שכ׳ הה״מ שם, ולפמש״כ הרמב״ם ז״ל לטעמיה אזיל, שבפיה״מ סוטה פ׳ משוח מלחמה כתב וז״ל: אין מחלקת ביניהם שמלחמת שבעה עממין ומלחמת עמלק חובה יעו״ש, הרי מפורש דעתו ז״ל שגם מלחמת עמלק היא בכלל מלחמת חובה שע״ז שנו במשנתנו שם שכלה יוצאה מחופתה, ולטעמיה אזיל שאינו מונה מצות יא״י למצ״ע וע״כ ס״ל דהטעם שלמלחמת חובה הכל יוצאין הוא משום מצות מלחמה ולא מטעם כבוש א״י, ולדידיה גם הנשים נצטוו במלחמת חובה וגם מלחמת עמלק בכלל, וכיון שס״ל שהנשים נצטוו במחיית עמלק נצטוו ג״כ בזכירה של מח״ע, וע״כ ס״ל שנהשים מוציאות אנשים במקרא מגילה משום שחיוב הנשים והאנשים שוה בזה, היוצא מדברינו שמה שנסתפקו האחרונים אם נשים חייבות בקריאת פ׳ זכור תלוי במחלוקת הרמב״ם והבה״ג.

R. Eigis points out that Rambam thinks women are obligated in the *mitsvah* of eradicating Amalek and also in the *mitsvah* of remembering Amalek. It therefore stands to reason that he rules that women and men are equally obligated in the the reading of the *megillah*, as they are fully obligated in both components of this *mitsvah* – publicizing the miracle and remembering Amalek. See n83, where R. Yosef also links women's obligation to read to remembering Amalek.

25. *Marheshet Vol. 1, #22*

מרחשת חלק א סימן כב

R. Ḥanokh Henekh Eigis, Vilna (1864–1941)

3) One can also add to the reasoning of *Ḥinnukh*, who wrote that women are not included in the *mitsvah* of remembering and eradicating because they are not eligible for war, based on what Rashi wrote in *Megillah* (3a), s.v. *emesh*: that the time for war is not at night, after dark.... Since the obligation to wage war is only during the day, this is a positive, time-caused *mitsvah*, from which women are exempt, and therefore they are also not included in the *mitsvah* of remembering, since they are not fit for war, as it is a positive, time-caused *mitsvah*.

ג) ויש עוד להוסיף על טעם החינוך שכתב שנשים אינן במצוות זכירה ומחייה מפני שאינן בנות מלחמה, לפמש״כ רש״י ז״ל במגילה (ג.) ד״ה אמש שאין זמן מלחמה בלילה משתחשך.... וכיון שאין חיוב מלחמה אלא ביום הר״ז מצו״ע שהז״ג שנשים פטורות מהן וע״כ אינן ג״כ במצוות זכירה משום שאינן בנות מלחמה משום דהיי מצ״ע שהז״ג.

4) According to my opinion about Behag's reasoning, and according to what we have written, that night is not a time for war, and according to the words of the *Ḥinnukh* that the *mitsvah* of remembering is dependent on the *mitsvah* of war – according to [all] this: because night is not a time of war, the *mitsvah* of remembering also does not [apply] at night. Therefore, [though] the reading of *megillah*, which is commanded during the day and at night – as R. Yehoshua b. Levi said (B.T. *Meg.* 4a): "A person must read the *megillah* at night and repeat it during the day" – nonetheless there is a difference between the daytime obligation and the nighttime obligation. For during the day, the *mitsvah* is also for the sake of

ד) ולפ״ד בטעם הבה״ג ולפ״מ שכתבנו שאין זמן מלחמה בלילה ולפי דברי החינוך דמצות זכירה תלי׳ במצות מלחמה, לפ״ז בלילה שאינו זמן מלחמה מצות זכירה ג״כ אינה בלילה, מעתה גם קריאת המגילה שמצותה ביום ובלילה כמו שאמר ריב״ל (ד.) חייב אדם לקרוא את המגילה בלילה ולשנותה ביום, מ״מ יש בזה הבדל בין חיוב היום ובין חיוב הלילה, דביום מצותה ג״כ משום זכירת מחיית עמלק, אבל בלילה אין מצות קריאתה אלא משום פרסום הנס אבל לא משום מצוות זכירה, ולפ״ז

remembering the eradication of Amalek, but at night the *mitsvah* is only for the sake of publicizing the miracle, but not because of the *mitsvah* of remembering. According to this, the nighttime obligation is the same for men and for women, since for both of them the *mitsvah* is only for the sake of publicizing the miracle. Therefore, at night, even according to Behag, women may discharge the obligation of men, for in this [case] their obligations are the same.[95]	בלילה חיוב קריאת האנשים והנשים שוה, דבשניהם אין מצותה אלא משום פרסום הנס. מעתה בלילה גם לדעת בה"ג נשים מוציאות אנשים שבזה חיובן שוה.

R. Eigis builds on the view in *Sefer Haḥinnukh* that women are not required to fight the war against Amalek by citing Rashi's idea that war is only fought during the daytime. Linking these two ideas together, R. Eigis conceptualizes the war against Amalek as a positive, time-caused *mitsvah*, in which women are not obligated. Since the obligation to eradicate Amalek does not apply at night, it must be that the obligation to remember the eradication of Amalek also does not apply at night. Based on this distinction, R. Eigis argues that there is a difference between the two acts of reading *Megillat Ester* mandated by the Talmud. The nighttime reading is simply an act of *pirsumei nissa*, whereas the daytime reading also fulfills the *mitsvah* of remembering the obligation to eradicate Amalek. R. Eigis suggests that since women, like men, are obligated in *pirsumei nissa*, they are fully obligated to read the *megillah* at night. He concludes that even according to Behag women may in fact fulfill the obligation of reading *megillah* on behalf of men during the nighttime reading because they share an equal obligation. However, they may not read for men during the day, as their obligation is unequal.[96] In R. Eigis'

95. R. Eigis then suggests that this understanding, that women may read for men at night, can explain the Gemara in *Arakhim* and the Mishnah in *Megillah* and is surely the view of Behag.
96. In *se'if* 9, R. Eigis brings another idea to buttress this reading of Behag. He explains that the Talmud considers the daytime reading of the *megillah* on Purim as a

analysis, the only potential issue with women's reading *megillah* for men is the possibility that their obligations might be unequal. In a case where the obligation is equal, he does not raise the issue of *kevod hatsibbur* as a potential problem. Thus, in his view, women are permitted to read *megillah* for men at night, even according to Behag.

This explanation of Behag's position, while fascinating, is certainly not an intuitive understanding of the language of Behag or of the Tosefta. R. Eigis seems to think that Behag would allow women to read for men at night, but there is absolutely no indication of this in the text of *Halakhot Gedolot*, nor is the idea of a distinction between the daytime and nighttime readings mentioned in any earlier source. In addition, while this carefully constructed theory may be convincing for those who follow the halakhic positions cited in *Marḥeshet*, there is significant disagreement on a number of the issues he references, such as whether or not reading *Megillat Ester* constitutes a fulfillment of the commandment to remember Amalek and whether or not women are obligated in this commandment.[97]

---

replacement for the recitation of *hallel*. Since women are not obligated in *hallel*, they are not fully obligated in the daytime reading. At night, when there is no obligation to recite *hallel*, men and women are on equal footing, and both are equally obligated to publicize the miracle of Purim.

עוד אפשר לי לומר בטעם הבה״ג שאין נשים מוציאות אנשים לפ״מ דאיתא בגמ׳ (יד) דעת רנב״י דמשו״ה אין אומרין הלל בפורים משום שקרייתה היינו הלילא, הרי שבמצות קריאת המגילה נכללת ג״כ מצות קריאת ההלל, ובהלל נשים פטורות, וע״כ אין נשים מוציאות אנשים המחיובין בקריאת הלל שיוצאין ע״י קריאת המגילה, ולפ״ז אפי׳ לדעת הבה״ג אין זה אלא בקריאת היום, אבל בקריאת המגילה בלילה שאז אין חיוב קריאת הלל שחיוב הלל אינו אלא ביום כדילפינן במגילה שם וקריאת המגילה בלילה אינה אלא משום פרסומא ניסא, בזה נשים מוציאות אנשים שחיובן אז שוה.

A full treatment of a woman's obligation in the recitation of *hallel* is beyond the scope of this chapter. For basic sources on *hallel* as a time-caused obligation from which women are exempt, see M. *Suk.* 3:10 and the corresponding *gemara* in B.T. *Suk.* 38a; *Magen Avraham* 422:5; and *Be'ur Halakhah* ad loc., s.v. *hallel*. The question of whether *hallel* on Passover, Ḥanukkah, and Rosh Ḥodesh is different than that on Sukkot and, therefore, women would be obligated, is debated within rabbinic literature.

97. Halakhic sources discuss whether only the reading of *Parashat Zakhor* (Deut. 25:17–19) fulfills this obligation. The general consensus is that *Zakhor* is the preferred, and possibly the only, way to fullfill the *mitsvah* of remembering Amalek. *Magen Avraham* 685:1 justifies the practice of those who do not hear *Parashat Zakhor* with

Aḥaronim #2: Women May Not Read *Megillah* on Behalf of Men Due to Differing Levels of Obligation

A number of Aḥaronim explore the idea that women are indeed obligated to read *megillah* and yet may not do so on behalf of men. Unlike the second group of Rishonim, discussed above, these scholars do not base their conclusions on the extralegal issue of *kevod hatsibbur* but rather on a halakhic explanation that a woman's obligation in *megillah* is somehow different from a man's and is derived from a different source. As a result, women may not legally discharge a man's obligation. Although these Aḥaronim do not necessarily advocate the idea that women may read on behalf of other women, they seem to leave open that possibility.

One such opinion is found in R. Ya'ir Ḥayyim Bacharach's *Responsa Ḥavvot Ya'ir*. In a long responsum dealing with the rabbinic nature of the obligation of *megillah*, he touches on this issue and argues that women and men have different types of obligations with regard to *megillah* reading because their obligations stem from different sources.

26. *Responsa Ḥavvot Ya'ir #10* **שו"ת חוות יאיר סימן י**

R. Ya'ir Ḥayyim Bacharach, Germany (1639–1702)

Why is it necessary for R. Yehoshua b. Levi to say that women are obligated in *megillah* because they too were part of the same miracle? Let him say it is because they are included in *lo tasur* ("do not turn aside," Deut. 17:11) and this is a negative commandment, and women are included in all negative commandments....

ל"ל לריב"ל לומר דנשים חייבין במגילה מטעם שאף הם היו באותו הנס לימא משום שהוא בכלל לא תסור וה"ל ל"ת ונשים חייבות בכל ל"ת....

a *minyan* by explaining that one may fulfill the obligation by going to synagogue on Purim and hearing on that day the Torah reading (Exod. 17:8–16), which tells the story of Amalek. Then, immediately following, one would hear the *megillah*. However, *Mishnah Berurah* ad loc. disagrees. Although some argue that the obligation may be fulfilled just by hearing about Amalek at a point during the year or at some point in one's life, they do not endorse the idea that one may choose the *megillah* reading as the opportunity to fulfill the *mitsvah* of remembering Amalek. See also above, n93.

The words of *Tosafot* in [chapter] *Arvei Pesaḥim* [B.T. *Pesaḥ.*] 108b [are as follows]: "They too were part of the same miracle. And if not for this reason they would not be obligated, since women are exempt from positive, time-caused *mitsvot.* Even though the four cups are [a] rabbinic [commandment], they established it like a Torah [commandment]." If so, it should also apply to *megillah* and Ḥanukkah candles, which require the reason of "they too were part, etc."... for if this is not the case, I would think that they are positive, time-caused *mitsvot,* because they were instituted like a Torah commandment, and so he [R. Yehoshua b. Levi] comes to teach us [that this is not the case].

דברי תוס׳ בפ׳ ערבי פסחים דף ק״ח ע״ב וז״ל שאף הן היו באותה הנס ואי לאו האי טעמא לא היו חייבי׳ משום דנשים פטורות ממ״ע שהזמן גרמא אע״ג דארבע כוסות דרבנן כעין דאורייתא תיקנו עכ״ל וא״כ ה״נ מגילה ונ״ח דצריכין הטעם שאף הן וכו׳... דאל״כ ה״א שהם מ״ע שזמן גרמא דכעין דאורייתא תיקון וק״ל.

And this also allows me to understand why women may not discharge the obligation of men in *megillah* as [they can] with *kiddush*.... For since they are obligated for the general reason that they too were part of the same miracle and men are obligated because of *lo tasur* [because it was established] like a Torah commandment, if so it is for this reason that they cannot discharge the obligation of men.

ובזה מיושב לי נמי למה במגילה אין הנשים מוציאי׳ האנשים כמו קידוש היום.... דכיון דהם חייבי׳ מטעם בעלמא שאף הן היו באותו נס ואנשים מחויבים מל״ת כעין דאורייתא א״כ להכי אין מוציאי׳ האנשים.

Ḥavvot Ya'ir begins with a question: Why does R. Yehoshua b. Levi need the justification that "they, too, were included in the same miracle" in order to obligate women? All rabbinic commandments are considered to fall within the biblical injunction against deviating from the instructions of later religious authorities. This biblical *mitsvah,* referred to as *lo tasur* (do not turn aside), is a negative commandment, and women, like men, are obligated in all negative commandments. Therefore, women should be obligated in *megillah* without any additional justification.[98]

Expanding on a comment in *Tosafot* concerning a woman's obligation in the four cups of wine at the Passover Seder, *Ḥavvot Ya'ir* responds that when rabbinic obligations are instituted, the rabbis generally model the structure and magnitude of the obligation on other Torah-level commandments (*ke'en de'oraita*).[99] In this case, then, the exemption of women from positive, time-caused *mitsvot* should apply, and they should be exempt.[100] It is only due to R. Yehoshua b. Levi's invocation of the principle of *af hen* that women are obligated. *Ḥavvot Ya'ir* suggests that this thought process could explain why women may not read *megillah* for men. A man's obligation is *ke'en de'oraita,* whereas a woman is obligated only rabbinically because women also were included in the miracle. Thus, the obligations of a woman and a man are not sufficiently similar to allow a woman to discharge the obligation of a man in reading *megillah.*

Ḥavvot Ya'ir does not discuss the possibility of a woman

98. See M. *Kid.* 1:7. The idea that women automatically should be obligated in all rabbinic commandments by the very force of the commandments being rabbinic, which *Ḥavvot Ya'ir* ultimately rejects, is seemingly upheld by Rashi. See Rashi to B.T. *Ber.* 20b, s.v. *veḥayyavim bitfillah,* regarding a woman's obligation in prayer. Rashi feels so strongly that prayer is rabbinic and that a woman's general exemption from time-caused commandments does not apply that he is willing to change the text of the Gemara to reflect this idea. R. Tam also supports this idea in *Sefer Hayashar* 70:4, where he states in reference to a woman's obligation in *leḥem mishneh*:

ועוד דמ'[צות] עשה דרבנן שוה בכל.

99. The concept appears in the Gemara a number of times (not specifically in connection to women) as: כל דתקון רבנן כעין דאורייתא תקון. See, for example, B.T. *Pesaḥ.* 30b, 39b, and 116b.

100. *Tosafot* posited that the drinking of four cups of wine at the Seder was rabbinically instituted in the spirit of the general biblical commandments to observe the Passover holiday. *Ḥavvot Ya'ir* applies this same logic to the rabbinic *mitsvah* of reading the *megillah.* The difficulty with this reasoning is that there is no biblical commandment or rubric to which this new *mitsvah* is added. The entire holiday of Purim is a rabbinic decree. B.T. *Git.* 65a states:

כי אמרינן כל דתקון רבנן כעין דאורייתא תקון - במילתא דאית לה עיקר מה"ת,
אבל מילתא דלית לה עיקר מן התורה - לא.

reading *megillah* on behalf of other women, though presumably he would permit it, as all women share the same level of obligation.[101] Rather, he focuses on explaining that women may not read for men because their obligation is qualitatively different from that of men, disqualifying them as fit agents to read on behalf of men.[102]

R. Aryeh Leib Gunzberg, author of *Turei Even*, also argues that a man's obligation in *megillah* is derived from a semi-divine source, while a woman's obligation is added by rabbinic enactment. He opens by discussing the difficulties of Behag's position:

27. *Turei Even* **טורי אבן**
Megillah 4a **מסכת מגילה ד.**

R. Aryeh Leib ben Asher Gunzberg, Lithuania and France (ca. 1695–1785)

Nonetheless, I find this difficult, because the idea itself requires a reason: what is the reason they cannot discharge the obligation of men? For since they too were part of the same miracle, they are entirely similar to men [with regard to this obligation].... Also, the distinction between women's obligation to hear and to	ומ"מ ק"ל דהא גופי' טעמא בעי מ"ט אינ' מוציאה אנשים דהא כיון דאף הם היו באותו הנס דמו לגמרי לאנשים.... וגם מה שמחלקין בין חיוב שמיעה לחיוב קריאה גבי נשים לא נתברר חילוק זה. ובאמת דברי בה"ג אינו נראה להרבה

101. *Arukh Hashulḥan, O.Ḥ.* 689:5, proposes a similar reading of Behag: that *af hen* is not a strong enough level of obligation for a woman to be able to fulfill the *mitsvah* on behalf of men. He clearly states that in his view Behag would rule that women may read *megillah* for other women:

ונ"ל דבה"ג ס"ל דא"א לומר דמטעם שאף הן היו באותו הנס יהיה חיוב גמור כאיש דא"כ למה לן על חיוב מצה לנשים הקישא דבל תאכל חמץ בפסחים [מ"ג:] לימא מטעם דאף הן היו באותו הנס [תוס' מגילה ד'. ד"ה שאף] אלא וודאי דמטעם זה אינו חיוב גמור כאיש לקריאה אלא די בשמיעה וגם בחנוכה י"ל כן דאין חיובן בהדלקה אלא בראיית נר חנוכה אא"כ יש לה בעל דמדלקת בשביל הבעל ולכן אין מוציאות בקריאתן את האנשים ומיהו נשים מוציאות כיון דחיובן שוה.

102. *Ḥavvot Ya'ir* never mentions Behag by name and also never links a woman's obligation with the specific act of reading or hearing; he simply discusses a woman's obligation in *megillah*. It, therefore, seems likely that *Ḥavvot Ya'ir* thinks that women are obligated to read *megillah* but that they may not do so for men. His explanation deals with this seemingly difficult legal position.

read – this is not clear. And, in fact, Behag's opinion does not seem correct to many commentators, who think that women may even discharge the obligation of men, as a straightforward reading of Tractate *Arakhin* suggests. However, according to this, the Tosefta is quite difficult.	מפרשים וסברי שהנשים מוציאות י"ח אפי' אנשים וכפשטא דשמעתא דמס' ערכין. ומיהו לפ"ז הא תוספתא ודאי קשיא.
It seems to me that women are certainly obligated in reading *megillah*, as are men, because they too were part of the same miracle, for there is no reason to distinguish between reading and hearing. Nonetheless, they may not discharge the obligation of men, as the Tosefta says. It seems to me that this is because the reasoning that they too were part of the same miracle is certainly not effective in obligating women at the level of a Torah commandment....[103] Since this is the case, one can say that since everyone agrees that [the book of] Esther was given with *ruaḥ hakodesh* (the Divine Spirit)[104]... as such surely it was said as if [it were part] of the Torah, since one God said them [the Torah and the book of Esther], from the mouth of the Master of All Things, Blessed	ול"נ דודאי נשים חייבות בקריאה כאנשים מה"ט שאף הן היו באותו הנס דאין טעם לחלק בין קריאה לשמיעה ואפ"ה אין מוציאות אנשים כדברי התוספתא, וטעמא דמילתא נ"ל משום דודאי ה"ט שאף הן היו באותו הנס מה"ת לא מהני לחייב נשים.... וכיון שכן י"ל כיון דאסתר נאמרה לכ"ע ברוח הקודש... הא ודאי כעין של תורה נאמרה כיון דאל אחד אמרן מפי אדון כל המעשי' ב"ה לאנשים נאמרה חיובה ולא לנשים אלא מדרבנן תיקנו והוסיפו לחייב נשים נמי....

103. He cites *Tosafot* as the source of this idea without providing a source reference. According to *Turei Even*, *Tosafot* asks: Why does the Gemara learn a woman's obligation in *matsah* from the Torah; why not just say that they, too, were part of the same miracle? In the printed version of the Talmud there is no *Tosafot* that states this idea in reference to *matsah*. *Tosafot* to B.T. *Pesaḥ*. 108b, s.v. *hayu be'oto*, does explain that the reason women are not included in the *mitsvah* of *sukkah* is because it is biblical, and *af hen* does not apply to biblical commandments.

104. See B.T. *Meg.* 7a. The Talmud debates the status of the five *megillot* as compared to the rest of the Bible. Various prooftexts are offered, and the conclusion is that *Megillat Ester* has the status of being given through divine inspiration.

be He, the obligation was communicated to men and not to women, but on a rabbinic level they decreed this and added it to obligate women as well....

Similarly, since the essence of the obligation for women to read *megillah* does not derive from *ruaḥ hakodesh* but rather from the addition of the sages, therefore it is only for stringency [to make sure women fulfill the obligation] and not for leniency to discharge the obligation of men, for [men's obligation] is essentially an obligation of *ruaḥ hakodesh*. They [women] are not obligated in the matter and cannot discharge the obligation of men who are fundamentally obligated through *ruaḥ hakodesh*....

וה"נ דכוותי' וכיון דעיקר חיוב מקרא מגילה לנשים ברוח הקודש ליתא אלא מהוספת חכמים ע"כ אינו אלא לחומרא ולא להקל להוציא את האנשים י"ח דהא מעיקר חיוב של רוח הקודש. אינן מחוייבות בדבר וא"א להו להוציא את אנשים המחוייבים מעיקר רוח הקודש....

It must be for this reason that our Mishnah mentioned above (B.T. *Meg.* 19b) that all are fit to read the *megillah*. Where it says [in the Gemara] that this comes to include women, it means [that women are eligible] to discharge the obligation of [other] women, who are like them, but not [the obligation] of men....

ומהשתא בע"כ מתניתין דלקמן (יט:) דהכל כשירים לקרות המגילה דאמרינן לאתויי נשים אתיא דהיינו להוציא נשים דכוותייהו ולא אנשים....

And it is worth considering whether or not this reason – that they too were part of the same miracle – works to obligate men rabbinically, as well, apart from their fundamental obligation through *ruaḥ hakodesh*.... The practical implication [of this question] is [in a case] where the only one who knows how to read the *megillah* is a woman and there is a man there who does

ויש לעיין אי מהני ה"ט שאף הן היו באותו הנס לחייב נמי לאנשים מדרבנן מלבד עיקר חיובן של רוח הקודש או לא.... ונ"מ אם אין כאן אלא אשה היודעת לקרות את המגילה ויש כאן איש שאין יודע לקרות המגילה ולא לענות אחרי' מה שהיא אומרת כגון שהוא אלם

not know how to read *megillah* and cannot repeat what she says after her, for instance if he were mute. Is he nonetheless obligated to hear *megillah* from her? For if one says that apart from the *ruaḥ hakodesh* obligation, the rabbinic obligation is also binding on them [men], as on a woman, then he is obligated to hear [*megillah*] from her, in order to fulfill at least his rabbinic obligation, even though he would not fullfill his fundamental *ruaḥ hakodesh* obligation through this hearing. But if you say that the rabbinic obligation does not devolve upon him, then he does not need to hear [*megillah*] from her, since he cannot fulfill his fundamental *ruaḥ hakodesh* obligation through this hearing. And it makes sense to me that he is obligated to hear from her, for the rabbinic obligation does devolve upon him, as on a woman.	אם חייב מ"מ לשמוע ממנה מקרא מגיל' דאי אמרת מלבד חיוב של רוח הקודש חל נמי עליהם מדרבנן כמו אשה חייב לשמוע ממנה כדי לצאת מיהא מחיוב דרבנן אע"ג שאין יוצא ע"י שמיעה זו מעיקר חיוב של רוח הקודש ואי אמרת דאינו חל עליו חיוב דרבנן א"צ לשמוע מינה כיון שא"א לו לצאת ע"י שמיעה זו מעיקר חיוב של רוח הקודש. ומסתבר לי דחייב לשמוע ממנה דחל עליו חיובא דדבריהם כמו לאשה.

Turei Even begins by summarizing the position of Behag that women may not read on behalf of men because men are obligated to read *megillah* whereas women are obligated only to hear it read. He then questions these assertions in light of the Talmudic statement that women are obligated in *megillah* reading. Why would the logic that "they, too, were part of the same miracle" not obligate women and men equally? And why would there be a distinction between the obligation to read *megillah* and the obligation to hear *megillah*? Nothing in the Talmudic material indicates that there should be any difference between the respective obligations of men and women, and for this reason, notes *Turei Even*, many authorities in fact rule that women may read on behalf of men. For these reasons *Turei Even* rejects Behag's ruling, arguing that one cannot distinguish between hearing and reading. He states that women are indeed obligated to read the *megillah*. However, he is still concerned with understanding what basis the Tosefta could have for the opposing view that women cannot fulfill the obligation of men.

To explain the problem posed by the Tosefta, *Turei Even* makes a different type of distinction between a man's and a woman's obligation: the obligation to read itself is the same, but the source of the obligation is different. The Talmud tells us that *Megillat Ester*, and by extension the obligation to read it, was divinely inspired. *Turei Even* suggests that a man's obligation derives from this divine revelation, and only later did the rabbis add the obligation for women to read *megillah*, based on the principle of *af hen*.[105] This rabbinic reasoning is not sufficient to allow women to read on behalf of men since it does not carry the same significance as a man's divine obligation.[106] However, women may read *megillah* on behalf of other women because they have an equal level of obligation.

The interesting question for *Turei Even* is whether a man has an additional obligation that derives from the principle of *af hen*, separate from his *ruaḥ hakodesh* obligation. If so, then a man who cannot read for himself should listen to the reading of a woman if she is the only person who can read on his behalf. He would thereby fulfill his rabbinic obligation to read *megillah*, though not his *ruaḥ hakodesh* obligation. However, if a man's only obligation derives from *ruaḥ hakodesh*, and he has no rabbinic obligation, then hearing a woman read would in no way fulfill his obligation. *Turei Even* indicates that he thinks that a man does have a rabbinic obligation in addition to his *ruaḥ hakodesh* obligation. Thus, in such a situation, a man should listen to a woman's reading of *megillah* and thereby fulfill at least the rabbinic aspect of his obligation.[107]

---

105. *Turei Even* does not explain how he knows this fact or why it might be that women were excluded from the original *ruaḥ hakodesh* obligation. Considering that Esther 9:29, the commentaries ad loc., and B.T. *Meg.* 19a all seem to consider Queen Esther herself as the author of the scroll and, therefore, the one to receive the divine inspiration, this premise is difficult to understand. *Or Same'aḥ* (source #28, below) thinks that women do have a part in the *ruaḥ hakodesh* obligation.

106. Later in his discussion of this *mitsvah*, *Turei Even* explains that a *ruaḥ hakodesh* obligation has a status that is somewhere in between a rabbinic *mitsvah* and a Torah-level *mitsvah*:

> וי״ל דודאי דבר שחיובו ברוח הקודש ל״ד לשל תורה לגמרי ולא לשל דבריהם אלא היא מילתא מציע׳ בין של תורה לשל סופרים.

107. *Turei Even* adds that a woman's eligibility to read *megillah* on behalf of a man in certain situations and to discharge this one aspect of a man's obligation provides a better explanation as to why the Gemara in *Arakhin* states that women are fit to

No objection is raised to such a reading; the dignity of the man seems not to be an issue. Like *Ḥavvot Ya'ir, Turei Even* is simply interested in unpacking the nature of a man's and a woman's obligation. The only reason that a woman cannot discharge the obligation of a man is, in his view, because their levels of obligation differ.[108]

R. Meir Simḥah of Dvinsk, author of *Or Same'aḥ,* also tries to explain the position of Behag. Commenting on Rambam's statement that all, including women, are obligated to read the *megillah,* he proposes, unlike *Turei Even,* that both a man's and a woman's obligation is based on *ruaḥ hakodesh.* Instead, he applies the ruling of the *Sefer Haḥinnukh,* which was cited by R. Eigis (source #24, above), to explain how the obligation of a man differs fundamentally from that of a woman:

---

read the *megillah. Tosafot* read this *gemara* as proving that women may discharge the obligation of other women, but *Turei Even* points out that this should be obvious! Rather, he argues, the Gemara is teaching that if there is no other option, a woman can read on behalf of a man and thereby help him to fulfill his rabbinic obligation in the reading of *megillah.* According to him, there is no reason to avoid this practice out of fear that it may lead to a more widespread practice of women reading for men.

ובהכי ניחא לי האי דהכל כשרים לקרות המגילה דאתא לאתויי נשים דלדברי התוס׳ שפי׳ דאתא לאתויי דאשה מוציאה אשה י״ח דסד״א שלא יועיל קריאתה אפי׳ להוציא נשים ק״ל מהיכי תיתי לומר כן כיון דכל הנשים שוות בחיובן בין למאי דפי׳ תוס׳ דחייבין בשמיעה ולא בקריאה בין למאי דפי׳ דחייבין מדבריהם ולא מעיקר חיובא של רוח הקודש. ולפי מה שפי׳ אתי שפיר דאתא לאתויי נשים שמוציאו׳ אנשים מחיוב׳ דדבריהם שיש על אנשים כמו על הנשים וכה״ג דפי׳ וקמ״ל דלא גזרינן דאשה לא תוציא איש דילמא אתי למיסרך להוציאם י״ח במקום שיש איש שיודע לקרות ולהוציאם י״ח עיקר קריאה של רוח הקודש קמ״ל דלא גזרינן הא אטו הא.

108. Yet another variation on this theme is proposed by R. Ḥayyim David Azulai, in *Birkhei Yosef, O.Ḥ.* 689:1. He explains that saying that women are *ḥayyavot* (obligated) implies only that women are personally obligated, whereas *kasher* (fit, eligible) means that they may read for others. He uses this distinction to show that the principle of *af hen* means only that women may read for other women because they are personally obligated; however, they are not fit to read for men.

28. ***Or Same'aḥ***
Laws of Megillah and Ḥanukkah
Chapter 1
R. Meir Simḥah of Dvinsk, Lithuania (1843–1926)

אור שמח
הלכות מגילה וחנוכה
פרק א

All are obligated in its reading: men and women etc. Behold, Behag rules that women may discharge the obligation of their kind but not of those who are not of their kind…and many have struggled to understand his reasoning. It appears to be simple. [With regard to the aspect of] remembering the miracle, we are obligated to read the *megillah,* but we can read it by heart and not [necessarily] from a written text….[109] The Gemara (there) explains that the one who holds that the *megillah* was given [lit., said] to be written down [derives it] from a written verse (Exod. 14:14), "[Write this] as a remembrance in a book," and explains "in a book" to refer to the reading of the *megillah*…and this verse refers to the eradication of Amalek. [*Sefer*] *Haḥinnukh* (#603) wrote that women are not included in the *mitsvah* of remembering and eradicating Amalek because they are not members of [the group tasked with] conquering. Therefore, women, who do not have a support [from] this verse, were told to read through *ruaḥ hakodesh,* meaning via *divrei kabbalah* (a received tradition),[110] but reading from a written text is only [a] rabbinic [commandment].

והכל חייבין בקריאתה אנשים ונשים וכו׳. הנה בה״ג פסק דנשים מוציאות מינן אבל לא שאינן מינן... ונדחקו רבים להבין טעמא. ונראה פשוט דלזכר הנס מחויבים לקרות המגילה אבל מצי לקרותה בעל פה לא מן הכתב.... ומפרש הגמרא (שם) דמאן דסבר נאמרה לכתוב הוא מקרא דכתוב (שמות י״ד:י״ד) זאת זכרון בספר, דדריש בספר על מקרא מגילה... וקרא זה נאמר גבי מחיית עמלק. והחינוך (מצוה תר״ג) כתב דנשים אינן במצות זכירת ומחיית עמלק דלאו בני כיבוש נינהו. א״כ בנשים דליכא אסמכתא מקרא זה, בהם נאמרה לקרות ברוח הקודש היינו מדברי קבלה, אבל לקרות מתוך הכתב אין זה אלא מדרבנן.

109. He cites B.T. *Meg.* 7a; and *Tosafot* ad loc., s.v. *ne'emrah.*
110. Various commentaries understand this term differently. It most likely refers here to

Therefore, with regard to women, when a woman reads, and a man is obligated via *divrei kabbalah* to hear from a written text while a woman is not obligated [to hear from a written text], it is as if the man is reading by heart because he is not hearing the text from one who is obligated via *ruaḥ hakodesh* to write [it], but only from a rabbinic source. And our rabbi [Rambam] thinks according to the simple reading of the statement in *Arakhin* that "all are eligible to read the *megillah*, even women," meaning to discharge the obligation of men. Understand this.	וא"כ בנשים כשהאשה קוראה והאיש מחויב לשמוע מתוך הכתב מדברי קבלה והאשה אינה חייבת, הוי כקורא האיש בעל פה, דעל הכתב אינו שומע ממי שמצווה לכתוב ברוח הקודש אלא מדבריהם ודו"ק. ורבינו סבר כפשטא דשמועה דערכין דהכל כשירים לקרות המגילה אפילו נשים, ומשמע להוציא אנשים והבן.

Both men and women are obligated through *ruaḥ hakodesh* to read *megillah*; however, according to *Or Same'aḥ*, only a man has a *ruaḥ hakodesh* obligation to read from a written text, whereas a woman's obligation to do so is solely rabbinic and may be fulfilled by reciting the *megillah* by heart. The requirement to read from a written text derives from Exodus 14:14, which contains the *mitsvah* to remember Amalek. As noted above, *Sefer Haḥinnukh* rules that women are not obligated in this biblical commandment. Therefore, were a woman to read *megillah* on behalf of a man, it would be as though he had heard the *megillah* recited by heart, and therefore the reading does not actually fulfill his obligation.

Once again it is worth noting that, like the other Aḥaronim cited in this section, *Or Same'aḥ* does not raise any other concerns about a woman reading on behalf of men, such as the issue of *kevod hatsibbur*. His sole concern is for the various levels of obligation of the reader and the listener. He is focused on the question of whether a woman may read for men and does not even address explicitly the question of a woman

---

a tradition received through Moshe from Sinai. See *Encyclopedia Talmudit* (Hebrew; ed. Rabbi Shlomo Yosef Zevin; 34 vols.; Jerusalem: Yad Harav Herzog, 1942–2014), s.v. *divrei kabbalah*, Vol. 7.

reading for other women. Presumably, according to his logic, this would be permissible, since women share the same level of obligation.

Each of these Aḥaronim finds a unique way to explain why women may not read *megillah* on behalf of men even though both are obligated to read. Each source explains why there is, in fact, a fundamental, qualitative difference between the sources and levels of the obligations of men and women. This endeavor is compelling because all of the texts reject the solution offered by Behag as being difficult to understand. The idea that men and women are obligated in essentially different acts – to read versus to hear – is based on an understanding of the Tosefta that openly contradicts the Mishnah and Gemara, which Behag attempts to harmonize. The Aḥaronim reject Behag's reasoning but still desire to preserve his conclusion and so they must be creative to preserve the idea that women are essentially obligated to read *megillah* while explaining why they may not fulfill the obligation for men. Their work produces completely new understandings of a woman's obligation.

Aḥaronim #3: Women May Not Read at All and Must Hear Only from Men

A third group of Aḥaronim argue that women should not read *Megillat Ester* at all, but rather may only fulfill the *mitsvah* by hearing a man read. This minority position is not suggested by any of the Rishonim, and it is difficult to reconcile with many earlier sources, including the Mishnah and Talmud, which explicitly entertain and endorse the idea of a woman reading for others. Both of the two main sources in this group, *Magen Avraham* and *Korban Netanel,* base their unusal understandings on seemingly erroneous readings of earlier texts.

Magen Avraham and *Midrash Hane'elam*

Magen Avraham, an influential Ashkenazic commentary on *Shulḥan Arukh,* rules that women may not read *megillah* even on behalf of other women:[111]

111. See also *Ba'er Heitev, O.Ḥ.* 689:3; and *Mishnah Berurah* 689 (source #35, below).

29. ***Magen Avraham***
Oraḥ Ḥayyim #689

מגן אברהם
אורח חיים סימן תרפט

R. Avraham Halevi Gombiner, Lithuania and Poland (1637–1683)

1) **And women [are obligated].** Therefore he must read it in his house before the young women.

א) ונשים. ולכן צריך לקרותו בביתו לפני הבתולות:

5) **They may not fulfill.** And it is not comparable to Ḥanukkah candles [where women may light for men], for *megillah* is different, as it is like Torah reading (*Semag*), meaning they [women] are unfit because of the honor of the congregation, and therefore they may not even discharge the obligation of an individual [male] because we do not make distinctions [in the general law] (Re'em).[112] See what I wrote in section #271 [regarding *kiddush*].

ה) אינם מוציאות. ול"ד לנ"ח דשאני מגיל' דהוי כמו קריאת התור' (סמ"ג) פי' ופסול' מפני כבוד הצבור ולכן אפי' ליחיד אין מוציא' דלא פלוג (רא"ם) עמ"ש סי' ער"א:

6) **If a woman reads.** And in *Midrash Hane'elam* to Ruth it is written that she should not read for herself, but should only hear from men.

ו) אם האשה קורא'. ובמדרש הנעלם רות כ' דלא תקרא לעצמ' רק תשמע מהאנשים:

Shulḥan Arukh begins with the statement that women, like men, are obligated in the reading of *Megillat Ester*. *Magen Avraham* comments that for this reason men must read the *megillah* at home to ensure that the women in their families hear it read.[113] This echoes the story of

---

112. See *Responsa Benei Banim* 2:10 (quoted in n52, above), in which R. Henkin argues that this is not a valid application of the rule of *lo pelug*.

113. This comment probably reflects the reality that women did not necessarily go to synagogue to hear *megillah*. See *Mishnah Berurah* 689 (source #35, below), who comments that it would be unlikely that women would be able to hear properly from the women's section, and therefore they would not be able to fulfill their obligation in this way.

R. Yehoshua b. Levi in the Jerusalem Talmud (source #4), who read for the women of his household.

Magen Avraham goes on to explain the second opinion presented by *Shulḥan Arukh*, the *yesh omerim*, which claims that women may not discharge the obligation of *megillah* reading for men. This is not because women are less obligated than men, for both men and women are obligated to read *megillah*; rather, it is out of concern for *kevod hatsibbur*. *Magen Avraham* then goes a step further and says that this restriction would apply even if there were no *tsibbur* present; that is, a woman should not read even for an individual man. This restriction is due to the halakhic dictum of *lo pelug* (lit., no argument), the desire to limit unnecessary exceptions to general halakhic principles.[114]

R. Moshe Isserles (Rema), in his gloss on *Shulḥan Arukh*, mentions the possibility of a woman reading *megillah* for herself.[115] *Magen Avraham*, commenting on Rema's words, cites *Midrash Hane'elam* to Ruth, one of the mystical works that comprise the *Zohar*,[116] as saying that women should not read for themselves but rather should hear *megillah* from men.[117] No explanation is given for this entirely new and difficult ruling.

The statement in *Magen Avraham* is difficult to understand for two reasons, one based on the general principles of *halakhah* and the other specific to the case of *megillah*. First, it is universally agreed that all women share the same obligation in *megillah*, whether that is to read or to hear and whether it originates from the rabbis, *ruaḥ hakodesh*, or

114. See, for example, B.T. *Yev.* 107a; B.T. *Ketub.* 52b; and B.T. *B. Mets.* 43b.

115. The position of Rema is treated in greater detail below (see source #66).

116. The *Zohar* is actually a compilation of works, mostly dating from thirteenth-century Spain. *Midrash Hane'elam* is one element of this collection. For further reading on the *Zohar* in general, and on the relationship of *Midrash Hane'elam* to the rest of the corpus in particular, see Gershom Scholem, *Major Trends in Jewish Mysticism* (Jerusalem: Schocken, 1941); Isaiah Tishby, *Mishnat Hazohar* (Hebrew; 2 vols.; Jerusalem: Mosad Bialik, 1949–1960); and Yehuda Liebes, *Studies in the Zohar* (New York: SUNY Press, 1993).

117. For a discussion on the use of the *Zohar*, and kabbalistic material more generally, in *halakhah*, see Meir Sendor, "The Rule for the Admissibility of Kabbalah in Halakhah." The rule that he quotes states that material from the *Zohar* is halakhically binding only if it does not directly contradict material from the Talmud, which in this case it most certainly does.

divrei kabbalah. Based on the normative halakhic rule that anyone obligated in an act may perform it for others who share the same obligation, there should be no obstacle to a woman reading for herself or for other women. Second, even those sources that give precedence to the Tosefta over the straightforward reading of the Mishnah and Gemara understand that one cannot completely disregard the Talmud outright. As a result, they all offer an interpretation that enables women to read *megillah* in some circumstance or capacity.[118] The suggestion in *Magen Avraham* that women may not read at all completely disregards the Gemara in *Arakhin* (source #3) and its reading of the Mishnah.[119]

It is important to note that the comment in *Magen Avraham* is not a direct quote of *Midrash Hane'elam*. The actual text reads as follows:

30. ***Zohar Ḥadash***
Vol. 2 (Megillot)
Book of Ruth 47b

זוהר חדש
כרך ב (מגילות)
מגילת רות מז:

Attributed to Moses de Léon, based on earlier sources, Spain (late thirteenth century)

Women, slaves, and minors are obligated in Grace after Meals,[120] but they do not bless, for behold we learned (B.T. *Ber.* 20b): "Woe is to a man whose wife and sons bless on his behalf."

נשים ועבדים וקטנים חייבין בברכת המזון אבל הם אינן מברכין דהא תנינן אוי לו לאדם שאשתו ובניו מברכין לו.

---

118. See specifically Rosh (source #19, above), who suggests that the Gemara specifically means to teach this exact point: one might have thought that women should only hear *megillah* from men, but that is not the case; women may read for other women:
וצריך לתרץ לפי ה"ג ותוספתא הא דאמר בערכין הכל כשרין לקרות לאתויי נשים לא שיוציאו אנשים בקריאתן אלא דוקא נשים דלא תימא אף נשים אינן יוצאות אלא בקריאה חשובה של אנשים קא משמע לן שהאשה מוציאה חבירתה.

119. See *Responsa Bemareh Habbazak* 7:52 n2, which states that one does not rely on this ruling as it is derived from a kabbalistic source with no other basis:
המגן אברהם הביא מקור קבלי שעל פיו אשה לא תקרא לעצמה. הקרבן נתנאל, שהובא בשער הציון, קבע שאשה אינה מוציא ידי חובה ציבור של נשים. אכן, אין חובה לחשוש לדברי קבלה כאשר אין להם בסיס בפוסקים.

120. See above n43.

And R. Abba said: Women are obligated in the reading of *megillah*, but they do not read for others. But they [women] are obligated to hear the blessing from the mouth of the one [male] who blesses.

ואמר רבי אבא נשים חייבות במקרא מגילה אבל הם אינן קוראות לאחרים. אבל חייבות לשמוע הברכה מפי המברך.

As such, a woman is obligated to hear the blessing [Grace after Meals] from the mouth of her husband, and her husband is obligated to wait for her at the table so as [for her] to hear from the mouth of the one who blesses. (My father my teacher my elder found a different version and it is as follows: If all of the people at the meal were women, and there is no man among them, they call for one [a man] to bless for them, and they answer, "Amen." And the one who blesses for them, if he is alone, he does not say, "Let us bless," as women do not join in the *zimmun*.[121] Rather, he blesses as an individual does without a *zimmun*, as the essence of Grace after Meals is for a man, etc.)[122] ... and not for a woman, but they [women] are obligated to hear Grace after Meals and are obligated in the reading of *megillah* to hear [it] from the mouth of the reader.

כעין זה חייבת האשה לשמוע הברכה מפי בעלה וחייב בעלה להמתין לה על השולחן כדי לשמוע מפי המברך (אמ"ז מ"כ נ"א וז"ל אם היו כולן נשים בסעודה ואין ביניהן איש קוראים למי שמברך להן ועונות אמן. והמברך לנשים אם הוא לבדו אינו מזכיר נברך שנשים אינן מצטרפות לזימון אלא מברך כמו שמברך יחיד בלא זימון דעיקר ברכת המזון בזכר כו')... הוא ולא בנקבה אבל מחויבות לשמוע ברכת המזון. ומחויבות במקרא מגילה לשמוע מפי הקורא.

It is difficult to comprehend the full meaning of *Midrash Hane'elam*. The two statements concerning *megillah* reading appear awkwardly placed

121. A discussion of women and *zimmun* is beyond the scope of this chapter. See B.T *Ber.* 45b; B.T. *Arakh.* 3a; and Rishonim and commentaries ad loc.

122. The alternate version that appears in the text states a similar idea with slightly different wording:

אין שם זכר קוראים למי שמברך להם. היו נשים הרבה המברך עליהן אינו מברך בשם דתנינן נשים אינן מצטרפות לזימון והואיל ואנן /ואינן/ מצטרפות לזימון אין מברכין עליהם בשם דעיקר ברכת המזון בזכר.

within a narrative about a woman's obligation in Grace after Meals. R. Abba's statement that women are obligated to read *megillah* but may not do so for others seems at first glance to reflect exactly the view of the second group of Rishonim above,[123] as well as the *yesh omerim* in the *Shulḥan Arukh* (source #22). Though *aḥerim* (others) here is not gender-specific, this is usually understood to mean that women may not discharge the obligation of men.[124] It would be quite atypical to argue that this means that women may not read for other women. In the *midrash* itself, R. Abba's statement comes directly after the quote from the Gemara that a wife may not recite *birkat hamazon* for her husband. The text thus seems at first to support the reading that *aḥerim* refers to other men but does not necessarily exclude other women. However, the continuation of the *midrash* makes its intended meaning uncertain. R. Abba adds that women must hear the blessing over the *megillah* from the one who recites it, presumably a man, given the immediate comparison to *birkat hamazon*. The exact meaning and intention of this statement is extremely difficult to understand, as is its connection to the previous statement that women may not read for others. The text's lack of clarity is compounded by the final sentence that women are obligated to hear *megillah* from the mouth of the reader.

Although it is not necessarily the most logical and straightforward understanding of "Woe is to a man whose wife and sons bless on his behalf," *Midrash Hane'elam* clearly understands this expression to mean that women should never recite Grace after Meals for themselves. Rather, they should always fulfill their obligation in *birkat hamazon* by hearing a man recite it, even in the case of women eating alone with other women.[125] It is possible that this is also the intended meaning of the

123. Interestingly, many of those texts also link *megillah* reading and Grace after Meals although in those instances the connection is clear.

124. See, for example, Ritva to B.T. *Meg.* 4a (source #16, above); and *Tosafot* to B.T. *Meg.* 4a (source #18, above), who use the term *aḥerim* in clear reference to men.

125. *Teshuvot Hage'onim, Sha'arei Teshuvah* 345 makes a similar comparison between *birkat hamazon* and *megillah* reading but concludes that if there is no alternative, a woman should recite Grace after Meals for herself.

רבנו החסיד ז״ל אשה לא תברך ברכ׳ המזון להוציא אחרים ידי חובתן אע״פי שהיא מחוייבת ובמקום שאין בעלה יודע כמקום הדחק דמי ותבוא עליו מארה. אשה מחוייבת

statements made about women and *megillah*. If so, *Midrash Hane'elam* is in fact suggesting that women must hear the *megillah* read by a man,[126] despite the difficulties noted above regarding the position of *Magen Avraham*.[127]

However, the Vilna Ga'on, in a note on *Shulḥan Arukh, Oraḥ Ḥayyim* #689, reads *Midrash Hane'elam* in a completely different way. He only quotes the beginning of the source:

31. *Be'ur Hagera to Shulḥan Arukh Oraḥ Ḥayyim #689 s.v. ein motsi'ot*

R. Eliyahu Kramer, Lithuania (1720–1797)

ביאור הגר"א
אורח חיים סימן תרפט
ד"ה אין מוציאות

[The source of this is the] Tosefta cited above, "And they [women] may not discharge," etc., as is noted above. That

תוספתא הנ"ל ואין מוציאות כו' כנ"ל ומ"ש בערכין הכל כשרין כו' לאתויי נשים ר"ל להוציא

במקרא מגילה אבל לא תוציא את הרבים כך בברכת המזון וכ"ש דעיקר חיובה שצריך לכלול המברך הברית עם התורה והיאך תברך על בריתך שחתמת בבשרנו ועל תורתך שלמדתנו אבל לעצמה מחויבת כשאין שם אחר שיודע להוציא לה וכשתברך תדלג הברית והתורה.

126. Interestingly, all the subsequent sources, such as *Ḥayyei Adam* (source #32, below) and *Mishnah Berurah* (source #35, below), think that *Magen Avraham* has misquoted and misunderstood *Midrash Hane'elam*. In their opinion, the *midrash* does not actually state that women must hear *megillah* from a man. It is possible that they themselves did not see a full, direct quote of *Midrash Hane'elam* but rather relied on the one sentence that is cited in *Be'ur Hagera* (source #31, below), which does not bring the full context but quotes the statement of R. Abba without the conclusion of the text.

127. All subsequent authorities understand *Magen Avraham* to mean that women must hear *megillah* only when read by a man, and that is the straightforward meaning of his words when read on their own. However, it is possible that his intent was otherwise and that he was misunderstood due to the brevity of his comment and his word choice. The full ruling of Rema upon which *Magen Avraham* is commenting states that when reading for herself a woman should make the blessing *lishmo'a megillah* (to hear the *megillah*). This ruling of Rema contradicts *Midrash Hane'elam*, which states that a woman must hear the blessing from a man. Perhaps what troubles *Magen Avraham* is the question of what blessing a woman should recite in the view of those who are uncertain as to her precise obligation rather than the actual reading itself.

which is written in *Arakhin*, "All are eligible, etc. to include women," he wanted to say [women are included] to discharge the obligation of [other] women. So it is written in *Zohar Ḥadash* to Ruth 68b:[128] "R. Abba said: Women are obligated in the reading of *megillah*, but they do not read for others. But they [women] are obligated to hear [the blessing] from the mouth of the one who blesses," etc.	נשים וכ"כ בז"ח רות ס"ח ב' ואמר רבי אבא נשים חייבות במקרא מגילה אבל הן אינן קוראות לאחרים אבל חייבות לשמוע מפי המברך כו':

The Vilna Ga'on understands R. Caro's statement that women may not discharge men's obligation to be a reflection of the view of the Tosefta. The Gemara in *Arakhin*, therefore, must be understood to refer to the eligibility of women reading *megillah* for other women. To bring support for the idea that they may do so, he states: "So it is written in *Zohar Ḥadash* to Ruth." Although he does not elaborate how exactly this is a support, it is clear that in the Vilna Ga'on's eyes *Midrash Hane'elam* is a prooftext for the position that women may read for other women, even though they may not read for men.[129]

R. Avraham Danzig, in his halakhic work *Ḥayyei Adam*, clearly gives precedence to the position of *Magen Avraham*, even as he acknowledges that the text of *Midrash Hane'elam* might be understood otherwise, as per the Vilna Ga'on:

128. It appears on 47b.

129. See R. Yehuda Henkin, "Women and Megillah Reading," in *Equality Lost*, 64 n22:

> The last phrase of the *Zohar Ḥadash* is unclear, and the connecting phrase used by the Gera "and such is also written" (*vekhen katuv*) indicates that he brings the *Zohar Ḥadash* in *support* of his preceding statement that "'to include women' means to enable [other] women to fulfill their obligation" and not in contradiction.

32. *Ḥayyei Adam*
Vol. 2–3, Kelal 155

חיי אדם
חלק ב–ג כלל קנה

R. Avraham Danzig, Danzig and Vilna (1748–1820)

11) All are obligated in the reading of the *megillah*, both men and women.... Similarly women, though they are obligated, nevertheless they are not obligated to read but rather to hear as a woman is obligated to hear from a man. She may not read even for herself, but rather a man should read it for her. (This [exact] language, which *Magen Avraham* wrote...is not found in *Zohar Ḥadash* to Ruth. Gera quotes its [the *Zohar*'s] language, but it is not clear whether it means to say that she may not read for others but may read for herself. This requires [further] study.) Nonetheless, it seems to me that if she has no one to read for her, she should read herself from a kosher *megillah* and bless "that He has sanctified us with His *mitsvot* and commanded us to hear the reading of the *megillah*."[130]

יא) הכל חייבין בקריאת המגילה, אחד אנשים ואחד נשים.... וכן נשים אף על פי שמחוייבות, מכל מקום אין עליהן חובת קריאה אלא חובת שמיעה, שמחויבת לשמוע מאיש, ואפילו לעצמה לא תקרא, אלא שיקרא לפניה איש (לשון זה שכתב המ"א... לא נמצא בזוהר חדש רות והגר"א הביא לשונו ואינו מוכרח אם רוצה לומר אינה קוראת לאחרים אבל לעצמה קוראה וצ"ע). ומכל מקום נראה לי דאם אין לה מי שיקרא לפניה, תקרא היא בעצמה במגילה כשרה ומברכת אשר קידשנו במצותיו וצונו לשמוע מקרא מגילה.

R. Danzig follows the position of Behag and rules that women are only obligated to hear the *megillah*. R. Danzig further expounds that a woman must hear from a man and may not even read *megillah* for herself. This ruling is based on the statement in *Magen Avraham*, which was based in turn on the *Zohar*. R. Danzig acknowledges that the words in *Magen Avraham* do not accord with the text of the *Zohar* as quoted by the Vilna Ga'on. Indeed, it is unclear to R. Danzig whether the restriction applies only to a woman's reading for others, or whether women should not

130. See section "Women and Blessings" below, for a full discussion of which blessing women should recite when reading *megillah*.

read even for themselves. Perhaps because of this ambiguity, R. Danzig rules that if a woman has no one else to read *megillah* for her, she should make the blessing and read it herself to fulfill her obligation.[131] With this last statement, R. Danzig reveals that he does not think that it is legally impermissible for a woman to read for other women. They can fulfill their obligation in this manner, and thus R. Danzig's ruling that only a man can read for women must be based on other factors, which he does not explain.

Korban Netanel

Korban Netanel, a commentary on the work of R. Asher ben Yeḥiel (Rosh), the thirteenth-century halakhist, does suggest a reason why women should not read for many other women even though it is legally permissible. *Korban Netanel* comments on the words of Rosh (source #19, above) and relies on a quote from *Tosafot* to modify Rosh's ruling that women may fulfill the obligation for one another because all women share the obligation to hear the reading of the *megillah*:

33. ***Korban Netanel***	**קרבן נתנאל**
Megillah 4a (in Rosh)	**מסכת מגילה ד.**
Chapter 1:4	**(בדפי הרא"ש) פרק א:ד**
R. Netanel ben Naftali Tsevi Hirsch Weil, Bohemia and Germany (1687–1769)	

40) And their [men's] hearing it from a woman is not as significant as if they read it themselves: Because when it comes to reading in order to discharge the obligation of men, they [women] are like one who is not obligated in the matter, since women are only commanded to hear [*megillah*], and one who is not obligated in the matter cannot discharge the obligation of the many.... And what *Tosafot* wrote in

מ) ואין שמיעתן מנשים חשובה כאלו הן עצמן קורין. דלענין קריאה להוציא אנשים הוי כאינו מחויב בדבר דהנשים אינם מצווים אלא לשמוע וכל שאינו מחויב בדבר אין מוציאין רבים ידי חובתן.... ומ"ש תוספות בסוכה דף ל"ח אי נמי משום דרבים זילא בהו מלתא דהרי המגילה דנשים

131. *Mishnah Berurah* (source #35, below) adopts this position as well.

Sukkah 38: "Alternatively, because for the masses *zila behu milleta* (it is beneath their dignity), for behold women are obligated in *megillah*, and Behag [nonetheless] explains that they may not discharge the obligation of the many in *megillah*." That is, a woman may not discharge the obligation of many *women*, because it is beneath their dignity. However, even without this reason she would not be eligible to discharge the obligation of men – even a woman for one man – because they [women] are not obligated in the matter....[132]	חייבות בה ופי' בה"ג דאין נשים מוציאות את הרבים ידי חובתן במגילה ע"כ. היינו שאין אשה מוציאה נשים רבות ידי חובתן משים דזילא בהו מלתא. אבל להוציא אנשים בלאו הכי אין מוציאין אפילו אשה לאיש אחד דאין מחויבין בדבר הוי'....
60) For a woman may discharge the obligation of another woman: But a woman may not discharge the obligation for many women, because it is beneath their dignity, as *Tosafot* wrote in *Sukkah* 38. See there, as I explained [above].	ס) **שהאשה מוציאה חברתה.** אבל נשים רבות אין אשה מוציאן דזילא בהו מלתא וכמו שכתבו תוס' בסוכה דף ל"ח ע"ש וכדפירשתי.

According to *Korban Netanel*, because women have a lesser obligation in *megillah* reading – to hear but not to read – if a woman were to read for even one man, let alone many, it would be as if someone who is not obligated in the *mitsvah* in any way had done so. As a result, the man's obligation would not be fulfilled. Quoting *Tosafot*, he goes on to explain that according to Behag the reason why women cannot read *megillah* publicly is because it is beneath their dignity (*zila behu milleta*). *Korban Netanel* argues that since it is obvious that women cannot read for men, because their obligations in this *mitsvah* differ, the "many" here must actually refer to a group of women. The constraint of *zila milleta* applies specifically to the case of a woman reading for a large group of

132. He goes on to say that this is not for the reason given by *Magen Avraham*, that the principle of *lo pelug* applies to the rule of *kevod hatsibbur*.

women.[133] However, he concludes, when Rosh says, "A woman may fulfill the obligation on behalf of another woman," this teaches us that reading for just one other woman does not have the problem of *zila milleta,* as it is not done in public.

Korban Netanel's interpretation of *Tosafot* in *Sukkah* (source #15 above), namely, that it is undignified for women to read for other women, is a difficult one. Up to this point, all commentaries understood the text of *Tosafot* to refer to the reason why women may not read for men despite sharing a similar obligation to read *megillah.*[134] In fact, *Tosefot Harosh* on Tractate *Sukkah* – the text of *Tosafot* that Rosh used – explicitly specifies that *zila milleta* applies when women read for men.[135] The "many" for whom *zila milleta* is a problem are male, not female. However, *Korban Netanel* did not have this text of the *Tosafot* in front of him and simply read *rabbim* (many), as appears in the version of *Tosafot* in the printed edition of the Talmud (source #15 above), without specifying whether they are men. Even though the straightforward reading of that text implies that it is talking about men, *Korban Netanel* uses the ambiguity of the word "many" to fit his understanding that women should not read for other women. His view is based on the different levels of obligation for a man and a woman in opposition to *Tosafot*'s view that men and women share the same obligation to read.

---

133. Presumably the issue is, as *Korban Netanel* explained, that women are not considered truly obligated at all vis-à-vis men. As a result, there is something undignified about a woman reading publicly, given her lower status, even for other women.

134. See the discussion following this *Tosafot* in source #15, above.

135. See *Tosefot Harosh* to B.T. *Suk.* 38a:

אי נמי זילא בהו מלתא באנשים שיוציאום נשים מידי דהוה אמגילה דנשים חייבות בה וקאמר בהלכות גדולות דאין נשים מוציאות את הרבים ידי חובתן במגילה.

Responsa Benei Banim 2:10 points out this discrepancy and states that if *Korban Netanel* had known this fact, he would never have written as he did:

ומפורש שלא כדבריו בתוספות הרא"ש למסכת סוכה שם שכתב אי נמי זילא בהו מילתא באנשים שיוציאום נשים מידי דהוי אמגילה דנשים חייבות בה וקאמר בה"ג דאין נשים מוציאות את הרבים ידי חובתן במגילה עכ"ל הרי שמיירי בצבור אנשים ולא בצבור נשים, ותוספות הרא"ש בנויות על דברי התוספות כידוע ואילו היו לעיני הקרבן נתנאל לא היה כותב דבריו.

Ben Ish Ḥai and Mishnah Berurah

R. Yosef Ḥayyim of Baghdad, author of the Sephardic work *Ben Ish Ḥai*, also rules that women may not read. Although he cites no textual proof and does not refer to any of the rationales presented above, he cites the custom in the city of Jerusalem as evidence that this is the correct way to fulfill the *mitsvah*:

34. *Ben Ish Ḥai*
Parashat Tetsavveh
Laws of Purim
R. Yosef Ḥayyim of Baghdad, Iraq (1834–1909)

בן איש חי
פרשת תצוה
הלכות פורים

1) All are obligated in the reading of the *megillah*, men and women. However, women, even if they know how to read, should hear from men. And this is the custom in the holy city, may it be rebuilt and reestablished speedily in our days, that it has never been heard of that a woman reads *megillah*. Therefore, every man, even though he reads the *megillah* at synagogue, should read it at home for his wife who did not hear it at synagogue and for the young girls and the rest of the women and servants who are in the house.[136]

א) הכל חיבין במקרא מגלה, אנשים ונשים. אך הנשים אף על פי שיודעין לקרות ישמעו מן האנשים. וכן המנהג בעיר הקדש תוב"ב שמעולם לא נשמע שהאשה קראת מגלה ולכן כל אדם אף על פי שקרא המגלה בבית הכנסת יקראנה בביתו בשביל אשתו שלא שמעה בבית הכנסת ובשביל הבתולות ושאר נשים ומשרתים שבבית.

Although both men and women are obligated in the reading of *megillah*, a woman should hear *megillah* from a man even if she knows how to read it herself. He does not cite a source for this ruling though it sounds as if he is relying on *Midrash Hane'elam*. For this reason, argues *Ben Ish Ḥai*, it is unheard of in the holy city of Jerusalem for a woman

136. He goes on to say:

ואם קראה בבית הכנסת וחוזר וקורא לנשים לא יברך בשבילם וגם הם לא יברכו.

R. Yosef responds to those who say that one should read for women without a blessing. See source #72, below, and n299.

to read *megillah*. Rather, men must be careful to provide a reading for their wives in the home.[137]

Mishnah Berurah, an influential twentieth-century commentary on the first section of *Shulḥan Arukh*, presents a summary of the restrictive positions found in the Aḥaronim. He explains the different opinions and concludes that women should ideally read *megillah* only in dire circumstances.

35. *Mishnah Berurah #689* **משנה ברורה סימן תרפט**

R. Yisra'el Meir (Hakohen) Kagan, Poland (1838–1933)

1) **And women.** Although the reading is time-caused, nonetheless they are obligated, for they too were part of the same miracle, for from the start the decree was against them as well, as is written in the Bible. Therefore, a man must read it in his house for the young women and the servants. And in a few places, the custom is that they [the women] go to the synagogue, to the women's section, to hear the reading. Indeed, it requires further study how the women there fulfill their obligation, since it is impossible to hear properly....

א) **ונשים.** ואף דהקריאה היא דבר שהזמן גרמא מ"מ חייבות שאף הן היו באותו הנס דמתחלה היתה הגזירה גם עליהם כדכתיב בקרא. ולכן צריך האיש לקרותה בביתו לפני הבתולות והמשרתות ובקצת מקומות נוהגין שהם הולכות לביהכ"נ לעזרת נשים לשמוע הקריאה אכן צ"ע איך יוצאין שם נשים דא"א לשמוע שם כדין....

3) **The minors.** That is, those who have reached the age when they are obligated to be educated.... And since women are also obligated, it is obvious that minor girls must also be educated....

ג) **את הקטנים.** היינו מי שהגיע למצות חינוך.... וכיון דגם נשים חייבות פשוט דגם בקטנות יש בהן משום מצות חינוך....

137. It is interesting to note that he does not raise the possibility of women's attending synagogue to hear *Megillat Ester*. Presumably this was not the custom for women in this community. The statements of earlier authorities concerning the difficulty of women hearing every word from the women's section could also be a factor. See *Mishnah Berurah*, source #35, below.

7) **And there are those who say that women may not fulfill, etc.** This is not like lighting Ḥanukkah candles.[138] *Megillah* is different because it is like Torah reading, and she is not fit because of the honor of the congregation. Thus, she may not discharge the obligation even of an individual [man] because we do not make distinctions [in the general law], and also because it is possible that a woman is not obligated to read but only to hear, as it says below. So, she is considered as one who is not obligated in the matter as compared to a man, but a woman does discharge the obligation of another woman.	ז) **וי״א שהנשים אינם מוציאות וכו׳.** ולא דמי לנר חנוכה דשאני מגילה דהוי כמו קריאת התורה ופסולה מפני כבוד הצבור ולכן אפילו ליחיד אינה מוציאה משום לא פלוג וגם דאפשר דאשה אינה חייבת בקריאה רק לשמוע וכדלקמיה ומקרי שאינה מחוייבת בדבר לגבי איש אבל אשה מוציאה את חברתה.
8) **If a woman reads, etc.** See Magen Avraham, who is inclined to say that she may not read for herself at all but should only hear it from men. And all of this is [in a case where] she has someone from whom to hear it, but if she does not have anyone to read it for her, she may read for herself from a kosher *megillah.*	ח) **אם האשה קראה וכו׳.** ועיין במ״א שמצדד דלא תקרא לעצמה כלל רק תשמע מהאנשים. וכ״ז ביש לה ממי לשמוע אבל אם אין לה מי שיקרא לפניה תקרא היא לעצמה במגילה כשרה.

Mishnah Berurah comments on *Shulḥan Arukh*'s ruling that women are obligated in *megillah* and explains that women are included because they too were part of the miracle despite the fact that this is a positive, time-caused *mitsvah.* This obligation has several ramifications. First, women must hear the *megillah.* Like *Magen Avraham, Mishnah Berurah* mentions the requirement for a man to read *megillah* in his home to

138. *Kaf Haḥayyim* 689:13 offers another reason why Ḥanukkah candles are different:
ואר״ח כחב בשם בעל הדברות הטעם דאין הנשים מוציאות האנשים משום דקול באשה ערוה ואע״ג דמדליקות נ״ח ומברכות ל״ד לפי שא״צ שיהיו שס האנשים בעת הדלקה יעו״ש.

ensure that the women of the house all hear it. He also describes a custom practiced "in a few places" for women to attend synagogue to hear the reading. However, he questions the efficacy of this practice due to the reality that women might not hear clearly from the women's section. Furthermore, when *Shulḥan Arukh* says that minors should be educated to hear the *megillah,* this includes girls as well as boys. Little girls must be brought to the reading to fulfill the obligation of educating children to observe *mitsvot.*[139]

Mishnah Berurah then explains the second position recorded in *Shulḥan Arukh,* those who say that women may not fulfill the obligation on behalf of men. He gives two possible reasons for this position. First, he suggests, like *Magen Avraham,* that women may be prohibited from reading for men because of *kevod hatsibbur*. Second, it may be that a woman actually has a different obligation than a man: to hear *megillah* but not to read it.[140] However, a woman may discharge the obligation of another woman, presumably because in either case they share the same obligation.[141] *Mishnah Berurah* does not explicitly address the case of a woman reading for large groups of women, and it is unclear from his words here what his view would be in that case.[142]

---

139. *Mishnah Berurah* carefully emphasizes that the *mitsvah* of bringing one's children to hear the reading of *Megillat Ester* extends even to ensuring that children actually hear the *megillah*. They may not simply spend their time making noise to drown out the name of Haman:

    לשמוע וכו׳ - ועכשיו בעו״ה נהפוך הוא שלבד שאינם שומעים אלא הם מבלבלים שגם הגדולים אינם יכולים לשמוע וכל ביאתם הוא רק להכות את המן ובזה אין האב מקיים מצות חינוך כלל ובאמת מצד מצות חינוך צריך כל אב להחזיק בניו הקטנים אצלו ולהשגיח עליהם שישמעו הקריאה וכשיגיע הקורא לזכור שם המן האגגי רשאי הקטן להכותו כמנהגו אבל לא שיהיה זה עיקר הבאת הקטן לביה״מ.

140. R. Shemuel Avigdor Tosfa'a, the nineteenth-century author of *Minḥat Bikkurim,* also rules – in his comment on B.T. *Meg.* 4a – that a woman may not read on behalf of men. He does not specify which line of reasoning he follows.

141. See *Be'ur Halakhah, O.Ḥ.* 689, s.v. *venashim,* where *Mishnah Berurah* says that once a woman has fulfilled her obligation, she may not read again for another woman as women are not included in the principle of *arevut*. This statement is difficult to understand as in *Mishnah Berurah, O.Ḥ.* 271:5, in the case of *kiddush,* he rules that women function in the same manner as men when it comes to *arevut.*

142. In *Sha'ar Hatsiyyun* 689:15, he states:

    אבל לנשים רבות אין האשה מוציאן, דזילא בהו מלתא [קרבן נתנאל בשם התוספות].

Although *Mishnah Berurah* cites *Magen Avraham*'s ruling that a woman should not read *megillah* even for herself, he clarifies that this is only if there is someone else on hand to read for her. If she has no other option, even according to this relatively restrictive position, she should read *megillah* for herself. In his additional notes to his own commentary, *Mishnah Berurah* clarifies his view on why it is permissible for a woman to read for herself in that situation.

36. *Sha'ar Hatsiyyun* 689:16 — **שער הציון סימן תרפט סעיף קטן טז**

R. Yisra'el Meir (Hakohen) Kagan, Poland (1838–1933)

And logically this makes sense. First, according to the first opinion [in *Shulḥan Arukh*], which is primary, women are obligated to read. Even if we rule that they may not discharge the obligation of men, nevertheless they are obligated in reading, as *Peri Ḥadash* ruled.[143] Even if we rule like the *yesh omerim*, surely it is still proven that a woman can read for herself and even that she blesses, "on the hearing of *megillah*." And what *Magen Avraham* brought from *Midrash Hane'elam* to Ruth, that she should not read for herself, see *Ḥayyei Adam* where this formulation is not found, [but rather] only the formulation that the Gera brought in the name of *Zohar*	והדין עמו, אחד, דלהדעה ראשונה דהיא העיקרית הנשים חייבות בקריאה, ואף אם נפסק שאינן מוציאות לאנשים, על כל פנים בקריאה חייבות, וכמו שפסק הפרי חדש, ואף אם נפסק כהיש אומרים הלא גם כן מוכח שתוכל לקרוא לעצמה ואך שמברכת לשמוע מגילה. ומה שהביא המגן אברהם ממדרש הנעלם רות דלא תקרא לעצמה, עיין בחיי אדם דלא נמצא זה הלשון שם, רק הלשון שהובא בהגר"א בשם הזוהר חדש, ואינו מוכרח דלא תוכל לקרוא בעצמה, ובפרט

In response, R. Henkin, *Responsa Benei Banim* 2:10, after pointing out the difficulties with *Korban Netanel*'s position (see n135, above), writes:

גם לפלא על ספר משנה ברורה שהעתיק דעה יחידאה זו של הקרבן נתנאל נגד סתימת כל הראשונים שנשים מוציאות נשים אחרות ולא חלקו בין אחת להרבה נשים.

R. Lau, "*Keriat megillah lenashim*," writes:

אמנם המשנה ברורה ציטט בשער הציון את הקרבן נתנאל אך ניתן לומר שאילו היה רואֶה את דברי התוספות רא"ש בודאי היה קורא את התוספות כשאר האחרונים.

143. See *Peri Ḥadash, O.Ḥ.* 689:1–2.

Ḥadash. [The argument] that a woman cannot read for herself is not compelling, particularly if there is nobody else who can read for her, then surely she can read for herself. So is proven in *Peri Megadim* and the Gera.[144]

אם אין לה מי שיקרא לפניה בודאי תוכל לקרוא בעצמה, וכן מוכח בפרי מגדים והגר"א:

Mishnah Berurah explains that the logical outcome of both views presented in *Shulḥan Arukh* is that a woman may read for herself and, although not explicitly stated, by extension for other women. According to the first and primary opinion, women are obligated to read *megillah*, and so, of course, they may read for themselves. Even according to the *yesh omerim,* a woman may read and recite the blessing.[145] *Mishnah Berurah* critiques *Magen Avraham* for incorrectly quoting *Midrash Hane'elam* to Ruth. He also argues that the very idea that a woman may never read for herself is not persuasive, particularly in a case where a man is not present to read. If a woman must fulfill her obligation, then clearly she should read for herself.

Both *Ḥayyei Adam* (source #32) and *Mishnah Berurah* (source #35) respect *Magen Avraham*'s ruling (source #29) enough to quote it but do not accept his premise completely, and state that a woman may indeed read *megillah* for herself. *Korban Netanel* (source #33), who follows a different logic, also thinks that a woman may read for herself or another, although not for a large group. However, hearing a man read remained the dominant and preferred way for women to fulfill their obligation in some communities, as *Ben Ish Ḥai* noted. Contemporary sources that reflect this position are discussed below.

In summary, the Aḥaronim tend to be more restrictive than the earlier sources in defining the situations in which it is permissible for a woman to read *Megillat Ester*. Although a few do say that women can read for men, the majority seem focused on defining the obligation of

144. See *Eshel Avraham, O.Ḥ.* 689:2 and source #31, above.

145. *Mishnah Berurah* does not specify why this is the case. Perhaps the fact that Rema (source #66) explicitly states that a woman may read and bless is proof enough for *Mishnah Berurah.*

a woman, as different from that of a man. A handful of Aḥaronim, often drawing on incorrect quotations of earlier sources, conclude that women should not read *megillah* at all. This is a difficult position to understand in light of the Talmudic sources and the Rishonim, who, at the very least, allow women to read for other women, if not also for men. The next section of this chapter shows how contemporary rabbinic authorities have evaluated these later rulings in light of both the earlier source material and the increasing desire of Modern Orthodox women for ritual participation.

CONTEMPORARY SOURCES

As Jewish education for women has become more prevalent and greater numbers of women have felt empowered to take on ritual responsibilities, many halakhic decisors from the twentieth and twenty-first centuries have been called upon to address the permissibility of a woman reading *Megillat Ester*. To come to a decision, these authorities focus on the parameters of a woman's obligation in *megillah* as defined by the Rishonim and interpreted by later authorities. Some permit women to read on behalf of men, whereas others prohibit women from reading altogether, even for other women; others reject those positions and rule that women may read but only on behalf of other women.

Contemporary Sources #1: Women May Read *Megillah*, Even for Men

Some contemporary, Orthodox halakhic sources consider the possibility that women may read *megillah* for men, and a few go so far as to endorse it explicitly.[146] Some sources discuss the possibility of a woman reading for men in any situation, while other decisors are open to adopting the suggestion of *Marḥeshet* (sources #24 and 25, above) that women

146. R. Aryeh Frimer, "Women's *Megilla* Reading" (n4), cites a number of other modern authorities who suggest that it may be permissible for women to read for men, based on the formulation of *Marḥeshet* or similar ideas.

be permitted to read *megillah* for a mixed congregation but only at the nighttime reading of *Megillat Ester*.[147]

R. Tsevi Pesaḥ Frank, in his halakhic compendium on the laws of Purim, presents this latter possibility, that women may read *megillah* for men during the nighttime reading:

37. *Mikra'ei Kodesh #29* **מקראי קודש סימן כט**

R. Tsevi Pesaḥ Frank, Lithuania and Jerusalem (1873–1960)

בקריאת המגילה של לילה אשה יכולה להוציא את האנשים ועפי"ז העלה שם במרחשת שאפילו לדעת הבה"ג אין זה אלא בקריאת היום, אבל בקריאת המגילה בלילה שאז אין חיוב קריאת הלל... וקריאת המגילה בלילה אינה אלא משום פרסומי ניסא, בזה הנשים מוציאות אנשים שחיובן אז שוה.

In the nighttime *megillah* reading, a woman may discharge the obligation of men. *Marḥeshet* raised the point there that even according to the opinion of Behag [that women may not read for men] this is only with regard to the reading during the day, but with regard to the nighttime reading, when there is no obligation to recite *hallel*... the nighttime *megillah* reading is only for the sake of of *pirsumei nissa* – in this, women may discharge the obligation of men because at that point their obligations are equal.

והלכה זו שבקריאת המגילה בלילה אשה מוציאה לאיש אפילו לשיטת הבה"ג, אנו למדים גם מדברי האור שמח שנתן טעם אחר לשיטת הבה"ג כדלהן....

We also learn this law, that a woman may discharge the obligation of a man at the nighttime *megillah* reading, even according to the position of Behag, from the words of *Or Same'aḥ*, who gave a different explanation of Behag's position....

---

147. Those who oppose this practice suggest that *Marḥeshet* was not writing *halakhah lema'aseh* but rather a conceptual framework for understanding Behag. See, for example, R. Aryeh Frimer, "Women's *Megilla* Reading," and David Brofsky, *Hilkhot Mo'adim: Understanding the Laws of the Festivals* (Jerusalem: Maggid Books, 2013). R. Aaron Cohen, "Women Reading *Megillah* for Men: A Rejoinder," *Torah U-Madda Journal* 9 (2000): 248–63, argues strongly for such a reading of *Marḥeshet* and claims that no one has ever actually permitted women to read *megillah* for men in practice.

And *Ḥinnukh* wrote that women are not included in the *mitsvah* of remembering and eradicating Amalek, since they are not members of [the group tasked with] conquering. Therefore, with regard to women, who have no connection to this verse, they are instructed to read based on divine inspiration (that is, received wisdom) but it is only [a] rabbinic [obligation for them] to read from a written text.... According to his words, it also emerges regarding the nighttime *megillah* reading, which is not from *divrei kabbalah* (received words) but rather rabbinic, as is explained in *Turei Even (Megillah* 4[a], s.v. *kegon)* and in *Noda Biyehudah* [*Mahadurah*] *Kamma* (*O.Ḥ.* 11), that women discharge the obligation of men, since their obligations at that time are equal, for both of them are only rabbinically obligated.

והחנוך כתב דנשים אינן במצות זכירת ומחיית עמלק דלאו בני כיבוש נינהו, א״כ בנשים דליכא אסמכתא מקרא זה בהם נאמרה לקרות ברוה״ק היינו מדברי קבלה אבל לקרות מתוך הכתב אין זה אלא מדרבנן.... ולפי דבריו יוצא ג״כ שבקריאת המגילה בלילה, שאינה מדברי קבלה אלא מדבריהם כמבואר בטורי אבן (מגילה דף ד׳ ד״ה כגון) ובנוב״י קמא (או״ח סימן י״א) נשים מוציאות אנשים, שחיובן אז שוה, דשניהם אינם אלא מדבריהם.

And in *Turei Even* to *Megillah* (4a, s.v. *nashim*) he wrote to explain the words of Behag that [it is] because the primary obligation of women in *megillah* reading is due to the fact that they too were part of the same miracle, which is only rabbinic.... For behold from the principle of *ruaḥ hakodesh* [a woman] is not obligated in the matter, and it is impossible for them to discharge the obligation of men, who are obligated from the principle of *ruaḥ hakodesh*. According to his words, it also emerges that during the *megillah* reading at night women may discharge the obligation of men. So it appears to me.

ובספר טורי אבן מגילה (דף ד׳ ע״א ד״ה נשים) כתב לפרש דברי בה״ג משום דעיקר חיובם של הנשים במקרא מגילה הוא משום דאף הם היו באותו הנס שאינו אלא מדרבנן.... דהא מעיקר חיוב של רוה״ק אינה מחויבת בדבר וא״א להן להוציא אנשים המחויבים מעיקר רוה״ק, ולפי דבריו גם כן יוצא שבקריאת המגילה של לילה נשים מוציאות אנשים וכנ״ל.

R. Frank quotes three Aḥaronim in support of the idea that women may read *megillah* on behalf of men on Purim night. *Marḥeshet* (sources #24 and 25, above) explicitly argues that Behag's position that men and women have different obligations in *megillah* reading applies only to the daytime reading. Men and women are equally obligated to read at night, and thus women may read for men at that time.[148]

R. Frank then refers to *Or Same'aḥ* (source #28, above) and *Turei Even* (source #27, above), two of the Aḥaronim who explain how a woman's obligation in *megillah* reading stems from a different source than a man's. Both suggest that the *mitsvah* for men to read *megillah* is divinely inspired (*ruaḥ hakodesh*), whereas women have only a rabbinic obligation. However, argues R. Frank, both men and women have only a rabbinic obligation to read *megillah* at night.[149] Therefore, he rules that a woman may read on behalf of a man on Purim night.[150]

In contrast, R. Ovadiah Yosef, former Sephardic chief rabbi of

148. However, R. Frank questions *Marḥeshet*'s assertion that *hallel* is an obligation only during the day (see n96, above) and argues that in the case of Purim and *Erev* Pesaḥ, there may be a different type of *hallel* that is relevant at night, as well. See *Mikra'ei Kodesh*, p. 132 note 2. See also R. Zevulun Zaks, "*Keriat Hamegillah Al Yedei Nashim*," who explores in greater depth the question of whether *hallel* is obligatory on *Erev* Purim or not. He concludes that there is a difference of opinion and that it might be the case that women and men do not fully share the same set of obligations on *Erev* Purim because men may be obligated in *hallel* of *yom tov* and the *hallel* prompted by a miracle, whereas women are obligated only in the latter. In his view, women can only be said to have an equal obligation according to those who argue that the obligation in *hallel*, or lack thereof, is the same at night. However, *Marḥeshet* only raised the subject of *hallel* to buttress his original argument: that the commandment to remember and eradicate Amalek, in which women are not obligated, does not exist at night, since one does not wage war at night. As a result, women may read for men at night regardless of the issue of *hallel*.

149. Not all authorities agree that this is the case, but it is the dominant position. See B.T. *Meg.* 4a and *Tosafot* ad loc., s.v. *ḥayyav adam*, as well as *Arukh Hashulḥan, O.Ḥ.* 687:2, and *Noda Biyehudah, Mahadura Kamma, O.Ḥ.* 41.

150. R. Frank also notes that according to *Turei Even*, it is possible to argue that women may read for men during the day when Purim falls on Shabbat, in which case the *megillah* is read on Friday. This echoes the argument above: if a reading is only rabbinically mandated, then one can argue that men and women share the same obligation in those readings. R. Moshe Shternbuch, *Mo'adim Uzmanim*, Addendum to section 2, chapter 171, also makes this distinction between the daytime reading

Israel, accepts the position that women and men share an equal obligation in *megillah* reading regardless of the timing of the reading.

38. ***Responsa Yeḥavveh Da'at* *Vol. 3, #51***
R. Ovadiah Yosef, Israel (1920–2013)

שו"ת יחוה דעת
חלק ג סימן נא

In truth, we understand that the law is that with regard to *megillah* reading, too, women discharge the obligation of the men, in accordance with the opinion of Rambam (beginning of *Hilhkot Megillah*), Rashi in *Arakhin* (top of 3a), and *Or Zarua* (Vol. 2, #368). So too wrote Ra'avyah himself (#843, p. 580), and so agreed Me'iri (*Megillah* 4a). So is the view of Rif, and so wrote *Sefer Ha'eshkol* (Vol. 2, p. 30) and Rashba and Ritva in their commentaries to *Megillah* (4a). So ruled our rabbi, *Shulḥan Arukh* (*O.Ḥ.* 689:1), in the unattributed [statement], but afterward he concluded: "There are those who say that women do not discharge the obligation of men." It is a well-known rule that if there is an unattributed [statement] and a *yesh* [*omerim*], the law is like the unattributed [statement].

ובאמת שאנו תופסים להלכה שאף במקרא מגילה הנשים מוציאות את האנשים ידי חובתם, כדעת הרמב"ם (בריש הלכות מגילה), ורש"י בערכין (ג' רע"א), והאור זרוע חלק ב' (סימן שס"ח). וכן כתב הראבי"ה עצמו (בסימן תתמ"ג עמוד תק"פ). וכן הסכים המאירי (מגילה ד' ע"א). וכן דעת הרי"ף, וכמו שכתב בספר האשכול חלק ב' (עמוד ל'). וכן כתבו הרשב"א והריטב"א בחידושיהם למגילה (ד' ע"א). וכן פסק מרן השלחן ערוך /א"ח/ (סימן תרפ"ט סעיף א') בסתם, אלא שסיים אחר כך: ויש אומרים שהנשים אין מוציאות את האנשים. וידוע הכלל שסתם ויש הלכה כסתם.

R. Yosef is responding to a question about whether or not a man may appoint his wife as his messenger to light Ḥanukkah candles on his behalf.[151] In the course of his answer, he discusses the parallels between

---

and the nighttime reading. He says that according to these explanations of Behag's position, a woman would be permitted to read *megillah* on a man's behalf on the night of Purim; however: רק משום כבוד הציבור לא עבדינן הכי.

151. In that case he rules as follows:

a woman's obligation to light candles and her obligation to read *Megillat Ester*. After reviewing the positions of earlier authorities on this issue and citing a long chain of Rishonim who think that women may read for men, R. Yosef rules that a woman may discharge a man's obligation to read *megillah*. According to R. Yosef, *Shulḥan Arukh* also rules this way, despite the fact that some scholars find *Shulḥan Arukh*'s language ambiguous. R. Yosef thinks that there is a clear general rule in all cases, not just here, that when *Shulḥan Arukh* offers two views, one stated without attribution (*setam*) and one prefaced by *yesh omerim*, that he personally rules according to the unattributed position. In this case, a woman may read *megillah* and discharge the obligation of a man since they are both equally obligated. R. Yosef follows in R. Caro's footsteps by permitting women to read on behalf of men.

Unlike R. Frank, R. Yosef does not rely on the position of *Marḥeshet* and thus does not limit his ruling to the nighttime reading of *Megillat Ester*. His position emerges directly from a straightforward reading of the earlier sources, and he is not constrained by the Aḥaronim who understand those sources differently. However, it is important to note that R. Yosef articulated a slightly different perspective in the last few years of his life. In a public statement at a Saturday night lecture in 2009, R. Yosef said that a woman may read *megillah* for a man but only in a situation where there is no alternative.[152] For example, in a small

---

בסיכום: כשבעל הבית נאלץ להיעדר מביתו בזמן הדלקת נרות חנוכה, עד לשעה מאוחרת בלילה, ראוי ונכון שימנה את אשתו שתהיה שלוחו להדליק נרות חנוכה עם צאת הכוכבים, שהוא כרבע שעה אחר שקיעת השמש. וגם הוא יוצא ידי חובת הדלקת נרות חנוכה בהדלקה זו, ששלוחו של אדם כמותו.

152. This view is also stated on R. Yosef's *Halacha Yomit* website in an article dated March 9, 2014 (after his death); accessed October 29, 2015, http://halachayomit.co.il/QuestionDetails.aspx?ID=1414:

האם אשה הקוראת מגילה מוציאה מידי חובה את שאר הנשים השומעות? תשובה: אשה מוציאה נשים ידי חובתן. ובשעת הדחק, היא מוציאה גם את האנשים. (חזון עובדיה פורים עמוד נט).

It is clear from this ruling that R. Yosef understands the *yesh omerim* in *Sh. Ar., O.Ḥ.* 689:1 as being concerned with appropriate societal behavior rather than the question of whether women have a different obligation from men in *megillah* reading. In *Yalkut Yosef Mo'adim, Hilkh. Mikra Megillah* 12, R. Yosef's son R. Yitsḥak Yosef rules that although it is in fact the case that a woman could discharge a man's obligation,

community where there is no man who knows how to read *megillah*, R. Yosef would permit a woman to read for men. *Haaretz*, one of the major Israeli daily newspapers, reported his words: "'It is permissible for a woman to fulfill this obligation on behalf of men,' he said, because the obligation to hear the *megillah* falls equally on men and women."[153] R. Yosef emphasized, as he does in his responsa, that the concern of *kol ishah* does not apply in this case and is therefore not a reason to prohibit women from reading *megillah*.[154]

There is ample halakhic logic and precedent to support a woman fulfilling a man's obligation in reading *megillah*, both based on a straight-

---

it is appropriate to accommodate the more stringent position as well. As a result, women should not read *megillah* on behalf of men, except in a situation where there is no other option:

> י"א שאע"פ שהנשים חייבות במקרא מגילה, אינן מוציאות את האנשים ידי חובתם. ויש חולקים ואומרים שהנשים יכולות להוציא את האנשים ידי חובה. ואף על פי שהעיקר כדעה אחרונה, נכון לחוש לסברא ראשונה, אלא אם כן בשעת הדחק. ומכל מקום אין לאסור בזה משום קול באשה ערוה.

153. Yair Ettinger, "Top Sephardi Rabbi Rules Women May Chant Scroll of Esther for Men," *Haaretz*, March 2, 2009, accessed September 7, 2015, http://www.haaretz.com/print-edition/news/top-sephardi-rabbi-rules-women-may-chant-scroll-of-esther-for-men-1.271212. Interestingly, the article also reported that "Yosef also said that women could write a kosher Scroll of Esther – another task that most rabbis say can be done only by men. He said that ancient *megillahs* written by women have been found in Yemen, and it would be permissible for women to do so today as well, 'to earn a living for their household,' since women 'were part of the miracle' that the *megillah* describes. However, he admitted wryly, it is an open question 'whether anyone would buy it.'"

154. Strangely, when R. Aharon Butbul, son-in-law of R. Yosef and the head of his Yabbia Omer Institute, transmitted the class that R. Yosef gave, he specified that a woman should not chant *Megillat Ester* but should simply "be meticulous in her pronunciation without the melody" to avoid the problem of *kol ishah*. It is not clear why his statement departs from Rav Ovadia's earlier rulings in this regard. See Yechiel Spira, *The Yeshiva World News*, March 2, 2009, accessed September 7, 2015, http://www.theyeshivaworld.com/news/general/31174/maran-rav-ovadia-shlita-when-a-woman-may-read-megilla.html. In the video of the *shiur* (available on the same webpage), R. Yosef clearly states that reading with the cantillation is not a problem. Some reader comments on the website also express discomfort with this distortion. See also *Responsa Yeḥavveh Da'at* 4:1, where R. Yosef cites the fact that women may read Torah with cantillation as proof that *kol ishah* does not exist in the synagogue. See also his son's ruling at the end of n152, above.

forward reading of sources from the Mishnah through the *Shulḥan Arukh* and based on a possible reading of Behag that allows women to read for men during the nighttime reading. Although this is not a widespread practice,[155] there are communities that have done so, based on the logic of the sources above and the recommendation of their local Orthodox rabbi.[156]

Contemporary Sources #2: Women Should Not Read At All, Even for Other Women

There are some modern halakhic authorities who prohibit women from reading at all despite the many early sources that allow it. These rabbis base their positions on the restrictive positions of certain Aḥaronim as well as other, more modern considerations.

R. Ya'akov Ḥayyim Sofer, a Sephardic scholar who wrote in the early twentieth century, compiles many of the opinions cited by earlier Aḥaronim in *Kaf Haḥayyim*, his commentary on sections of *Shulḥan Arukh*. Like R. Yosef, he explains that if a man has no alternative, he may rely on the view that a woman may read for a man; however this is not ideal and only is acceptable as a last resort. R. Sofer gives precedence to the most conservative Aḥaronim and rules that it is far better for women to hear *Megillat Ester* read by a man, if at all possible.

155. R. Avraham Weiss, "Women and the Reading of the Megillah," *Torah U-Madda Journal* 8 (1998): 309, notes: "The issue of women reading *megillah* for men is more complex. Here, even the early authorities are divided. Later authorities seem more included [*sic*] to permit this kind of reading at night rather than during the day." However, since writing that article R. Weiss has also permitted a mixed *megillah* reading at his synagogue by Minyan Shachar.

156. For example, Bnai-David Judea Congregation in Los Angeles, California, under the leadership of R. Yosef Kanefsky, offered a mixed nighttime *megillah* reading in 2013, based on the opinion of *Marḥeshet* and others. See also the article by R. Daniel Landes, former director of the Pardes Institute of Jewish Studies, in which he explains that Pardes holds a mixed *megillah* reading on Purim night based on *Marḥeshet*; R. Daniel Landes, "The Reading of the Megilla on Purim Night," February 1, 1997, accessed September 7, 2015, http://elmad.pardes.org/holidays/the-reading-of-the-megilla-on-purim-night. JOFA has a list of twenty-six communities throughout the world that held mixed readings in 2014, the majority of which are partnership *minyanim*. See http://www.jofa.org/purimdirectory.

39. ***Kaf Haḥayyim***
Oraḥ Ḥayyim #689

כף החיים
אורח חיים סימן תרפט

R. Ya'akov Ḥayyim Sofer, Baghdad and Jerusalem (1870–1939)

15) **And there are those who say women may not discharge the obligation, etc.** And in a time of pressing need, if a man does not know how to read and a woman does know [how to read] and there is no other man who can fulfill his obligation, one may rely on those who think that a woman also discharges the obligation of a man. However, if afterward another man happens to be present who knows [how to read], he [the uneducated man] should return and hear it from the [educated] man. And if the man who discharges his [the uneducated man's] obligation has already fulfilled his [own] obligation, he should not make a blessing on his reading since, according to the *yesh omerim*, he [the uneducated man] already fulfilled his obligation when he heard from the woman.

טו) **וי"א שהנשים אינם מוציאות וכו'** ובשעת הדחק אם האיש אינו יודע והאשה יודעת ואין שם איש אחר שיוציאו יש לסמוך על הסוברים דגם אשה מוציאה לאיש. ומיהו כשיזדמן לו אח"כ איש שיודע יחזור וישמענה מהאיש. ואם האיש המוציאו כבר יצא י"ח לא יברך על קריאתו כיון דלי"א יצא כבר כששמעה מהאשה.

15, b) **And there are those who say that women may not discharge, etc.** But they may discharge the obligation of other women.... But a woman should not discharge the obligation of many women because it is beneath their dignity.... [157]

טו, ב) **וי"א שהנשים אונם מוציאות וכו'** אבל מוציאות נשים אחרות י"ח.... אבל לנשים רבות אין האשה מוציאן דזילא בהו מילתא....

157. *Kaf Haḥayyim* references *Tosafot* to B.T. *Suk.* 38a (source #15, above), *Korban Netanel* (source #33, above), and *Mishnah Berurah* (sources #35 and 36, above) to support this point.

יח) הגה וי"א שאם האשה קורואה לעצמה וכו' ובמדרש הנעלם רות כתב דלא תקרא לעצמה רק תשמע מהאנשים... וכן המנהג דאף אשה שיודעת לקרות בעצמה שומעת מאיש.... והא"א אות ו' כתב דנשים אין שומעים כלל המגילה אף בעזרת נשים וא"כ אשה חכמה ראוי שיהיה לה מגילה כשרה בלה"ק ותשמע הברכה מש"צ ותקרא לעצמה בעזרת נשים ולפני הבתולות יקרא בביתו בלא ברכה רק תשמע היא עכ"ל. ור"ל מפני שאין יכולה לשמוע הקריאה מש"ץ לכן תשמע רק הברכות ותקרא היא בעצמה ומפני חששת מדרש הנעלם רות תחזור לשמוע מאיש והיינו אם א"א לשמוע בטוב מש"ץ אבל אם אפשר תכוין לצאת מש"ץ הברכות וגם הקריאה וא"צ לשמוע עוד מאיש. ומ"מ נ"ל דאם אין לה מי שיקרא לפניה תקרא היא לעצמה במגילה כשירה ומברכת אקב"ו לשמוע מקרא מגילה.

18) **Gloss [Rema]: There are those who say that if a woman reads for herself, etc.** In *Midrash Hane'elam* to Ruth it says that she should not read for herself but rather should hear from men...and this is the custom, that even a woman who knows how to read on her own hears it from a man.... And *Eshel Avraham,* paragraph six, wrote "that women cannot hear the *megillah* at all from the women's section, and if so it is appropriate that a learned woman have a kosher *megillah* in Hebrew, and she should hear the blessing from the prayer leader and read for herself in the women's section. And [a man] should read for the young women in his home without a blessing, and she should just listen." And his intent is to say that because she cannot hear the reading from the prayer leader, therefore she should only listen to the blessings and [then] read for herself. Because of the concern for [the position of] *Midrash Hane'elam* to Ruth she should go back and hear it from a man. This is the case if it is impossible to hear it well from the prayer leader, but if it is possible she should have the intent to fulfill the obligation through the prayer leader, both the blessings and the reading, and she does not have to hear it again from a[nother] man. Nonetheless, it seems to me that if there is no one to read it for her she should read for herself from a

kosher *megillah* and recite the blessing,
"to hear the reading of the *megillah*."[158]

R. Sofer comments on the second position in *Shulḥan Arukh,* the *yesh omerim,* that women may not read *Megillat Esther* on behalf of men. R. Sofer's primary halakhic position is that a man should not hear *megillah* read by a woman, although he acknowledges that if there is no other way for the man to fulfill his obligation, he may have a woman read it for him based on those opinions that permit the practice. If later on it is then possible to hear *megillah* read by a man, he should do so to be certain that he has fulfilled his obligation, although if the reader himself has already fulfilled his obligation he should not repeat the blessings lest the woman's reading was actually sufficient and the blessing would be taking God's name in vain.

R. Sofer then turns to the question of whether a woman may read *megillah* for other women. He records the position mentioned by Rosh and *Tosafot* among others that women may discharge the obligation of other women. However, he also notes the two reasons that some authorities cite to prohibit this practice: the problem of *zila milleta,* presented by *Mishnah Berurah* based on *Korban Netanel,* and the idea that women may hear *megillah* only from men, based on *Magen Avraham*'s version of *Midrash Hane'elam.* Ideally, according to R. Sofer, women, even if they are educated and able to read for themselves, would attend synagogue and fulfill their obligation through the communal reading by a male. However, he quotes earlier authorities who assume that it was unlikely a woman would be able to hear every word of *Megillat Ester* from the women's section. *Eshel Avraham* recommends that women who are able to read *megillah* for themselves be provided with a kosher *megillah,* so that they can read along for themselves after listening carefully to the blessings. To accommodate the position attributed to *Midrash Hane'elam,* R. Sofer adds that a woman should then hear *megillah* again without a blessing from a man to ensure that she has fulfilled her obli-

158. *Kaf Haḥayyim* goes on to note that there are differences of opinion with regard to the blessing, and some views hold that she should recite the same blessing as a man. This topic is discussed in full below, "Women and Blessings."

gation according to all authorities. Overall, *Kaf Haḥayyim* thinks that men and women should take care in this case to fulfill their obligation in accordance with as many halakhic opinions as possible.

R. Menashe Klein, a later contemporary figure from the *ḥaredi*, Ashkenazic community, writing in 1963, advances a similar argument. Based on *Midrash Hane'elam* and those Aḥaronim who prefer that women not read for themselves, R. Klein rules that a woman may leave her eleven-year-old son at home to babysit her other children in order to go to synagogue and hear the reading of *megillah* because he is under *bar mitsvah* age and, therefore, he does not need to be in synagogue as she does. He does not raise the concern that it is difficult to hear from the women's section. Rather, he seems confident that she may, and should, fulfill her obligation in this way.

40. *Responsa Mishneh Halakhot* Vol. 4, #82 — **שו"ת משנה הלכות חלק ד סימן פב**

R. Menashe Klein, Czechoslovakia and New York (1924–2011)

Regarding one who has a baby in his house, whether it is better to leave his minor son, eleven years old, with him [the baby], so that his wife may come to synagogue to hear the reading of *megillah*, or whether it is better for his minor son to hear [the *megillah*]....	במי שיש לו תינוק בביתו אי מוטב שיניח את בנו הקטן בן י"א שנה אצלו ותבא אשתו לביהכ"נ לשמוע קריאת המגילה או שמוטב שבנו הקטן ישמע...
And since this is the case, I say that a woman certainly has a greater obligation to hear *megillah* in the synagogue than the minor, and this is what appears in *Shulḥan Arukh*, *O.Ḥ.* 689:2, [where] Rema writes: "There are those who say that if a woman reads it [the *megillah*] for herself, she blesses, 'On hearing the *megillah*,' for she is not obligated in reading." *Magen Avraham*, there, *se'if katan* 6, quotes in the name of *Midrash*	וכיון שכן אומר אני דודאי האשה יותר מחויבת לשמוע המגילה בביהכ"נ מהקטן והוא דבש"ע או"ח סי' תרפ"ט ס"ב כתב הרמ"א ז"ל י"א שאם האשה קוראה לעצמה מברכת לשמוע מגילה שאינה חייבת בקריאה, והמג"א שם ס"ק ו' הביא בשם מדרש הנעלם וז"ל ובמדרש הנעלם כתב

Hane'elam as follows: "And in *Midrash Hane'elam* it says that she should not read for herself but should only hear it from men".... And even though the Aḥaronim, of blessed memory, wrote that in a case where it is not possible for her to hear it from men, she may read it for herself... nonetheless, it seems that everyone agrees that ideally she should not read if she can hear it from men. I have brought a little support for *Midrash Hane'elam* from the Yerushalmi,[159] that R. Yehoshua b. Levi would gather the members of his household and read before them. Seemingly [one might argue], why does he himself need to read for them rather than leaving his wife to read? But if we say that a woman does not read for herself, it makes sense. One might also say that in any case there is the opinion of the Aḥaronim, of blessed memory, in the name of the *Midrash* [*Hane'elam*], that a woman should not read for herself, but with regard to a minor there is no one who disagrees that he may read *megillah* for himself. On the contrary, it is a *mitsvah* to educate them to read it. Since this is the case, it is obvious that it is preferable for the woman to come to hear the *megillah* reading in synagogue and that the minor should be at home with the baby and afterward should read the	דלא תקרא לעצמה רק תשמע מהאנשים ע"כ.... אף שכתבו האחרונים ז"ל דבאם אי אפשר לה לשמוע מאנשים קוראה לעצמה... וכי לכתחלה נראה דכולהו מודים דלא תקרא אם יכולה לשמוע מהאנשים, וקצת הבאתי סמוכין למדרש הנעלם מירושלמי דריב"ל הוי מכניש בני ביתיה וקרי קמיהון ולכאורה למה צריך לקרא בעצמו ולא הניח לאשתו שתקרא אבל אי נימא דאשה אינה קוראת לעצמה אתי שפיר וי"ל עכ"פ אית לן שיטת האחרונים ז"ל בשם המדרש דאשה לא תקרא לעצמה אבל בקטן לית מאן דפליג דקורא לעצמו המגילה ואדרבה מצוה לחנכם לקרותה וכיון שכן פשוט דיותר טוב שתבא האשה לשמוע מקרא מגילה בביהכ"נ והקטן יהיה בבית עם התינוק ואח"כ יקרא לעצמו המגילה כנלפענ"ד בס"ד.

159. Later in the same responsum, R. Klein offers another possible proof from the language of *Sh. Ar., O.Ḥ.* 689:1, who writes that it is a "good custom" to bring minors to synagogue. The implication, argues R. Klein, is that one is not obligated to do so. They may also stay home and read for themselves.

megillah for himself. So it appears in my humble opinion, with the help of God.

The question posed to R. Klein is one of priorities: if only one other person in the household can attend *megillah* reading at synagogue, either an adult woman or an eleven-year-old boy, which of them takes halakhic precedence? After a detailed discussion (not quoted above) of whether the obligation of educating minors is incumbent on the father or on the son, R. Klein concludes that it is preferable that the woman go to synagogue to hear *megillah* read by a man. The boy is permitted to read for himself, argues R. Klein, regardless of how one rules on the question of who bears responsibility for the *mitsvah* of education. In contrast, there are some Aḥaronim, such as *Magen Avraham*, who do not think that a woman is permitted to read on her own behalf. Other sources, such as *Mishnah Berurah*, allow a woman to read *megillah* for herself but only if there is no man present to read it for her.[160] R. Klein goes so far as to say that all are in agreement with this understanding.[161] He offers the story in the Jerusalem Talmud as proof that *Magen Avraham* is correct: R. Yehoshua b. Levi read *megillah* on behalf of his household; if a woman may read, why did his wife not do so? The implication, according to

---

160. In *Mishneh Halakhot* 11:550, R. Klein rules explicitly against women gathering so that one may read on behalf of the others. He thinks the reading requires a *minyan* and that women may not constitute such a quorum. (This topic is discussed in full below, "Women as Part of a Quorum.")

ובדבר אשר שאל היות כי נשים חייבות בקריאת מגילה כאנשים א"כ בפורים שקשה לנשים שיש להם ילדים לבא בביהכ"נ עם בעליהם ולכן סִדרו שיעשו הנשים מנין לעצמן ואשה אחת תקרא במגילה להוציא את כולן. ולפענ"ד פשוט דאין לעשות כן כי הגם דמגילה נקראת ביחיד ולא צריך עשרה אם אין לו מ"מ לעשות מנין כזה גרע ואם לא יוכלו לבא לביהכ"נ בשעת קריאה יקרא הבעל להם כשיבא הביתה או תלך אצל שכן ולא יעשו מנין דממילא לא מהני דבכל מקום דבעי עשרה לא מהני ונשים לא מצטרפי לדבר שבקדושה כמ"ש התוס' ברכות והארכתי כבר בזה במקום אחר.... ובאמת כי קשה לי מאד לכתוּב מענין זה שדוקא נשים כשרות נכנסו בפרצות דחוקות ורוצות ליכנס לדברים חדשים שהם נגד התורה אשר לא שערום אבותינו ואמותינו הטהורות ומעולם לא שמענו דבר כזה ובירושלמי מבואר דכשבאו מן הביהמ"ד כנס את בני ביתו אשתו ובנותיו וקרא לפניהם המגילה אבל שהנשים לעצמן יעשו מנין לא שמענו ישתקע הדבר ולא יכנסו להיות מנשים ההולכות לפי רוח הזמן רק כאמותינו הקדושות.

161. Based on the many sources presented in this chapter, this claim is clearly not an accurate portrayal of the facts.

R. Klein, is that a man must read *megillah* on behalf of a woman. Therefore, in this case, R. Klein rules that the woman should go to synagogue and hear the *megillah* read by a man.[162]

R. Hershel Schachter, one of the *rashei yeshivah* at Rabbi Isaac Elchanan Theological Seminary at Yeshiva University, also rejects the idea of a woman reading *megillah.* However, he presents a very different argument and approach in a ruling from the mid-1980s signed by a number of his fellow *rashei yeshivah.*[163] Interestingly, this responsum does not rely on the rulings of the Aḥaronim at all but rather argues that the practice of a woman reading *megillah* is an irreverent departure from *minhag* (custom), which lessens, rather than enhances, the fulfillment of the *mitsvah* in its most perfect form. R. Schachter says that at best it is a mockery of Torah, while at worst it borders on idol worship. R. Schachter is addressing the broader question of women's *tefillah* groups,[164] women who gather to read Torah, convene *hakkafot* for Simḥat Torah, read *megillah,* and pray together as a group.[165] In his seventeen-page paper, he presents at least twelve reasons why all of these practices are forbidden. Without going into detail, the concerns R. Schachter raises are as follows: when women perform ritual in this way, the *mitsvot* are not performed in a complete manner; these practices are a forgery of Torah;[166] they do not comply with the ideal of

---

162. See *Ḥelkat Ya'akov, O.Ḥ.* 232, who addresses a similar question and comes to the opposite conclusion. See n242.

163. R. Nisson Alpert, R. Mordechai Willig, R. Abba Bronspiegel, and R. Yehuda Parnes.

164. Throughout his paper, R. Schachter continuously refers to these groups as *minyanim,* ignoring seemingly on purpose the fact that the majority of women in these groups are trying to work within the halakhic system and do not consider themselves to be a *minyan.*

165. It is interesting that R. Schachter chooses to include *megillah* reading on this list, as it is the only one of these practices with strong and clear halakhic support. In doing so, he reveals that his main argument and concern is not directly linked to strict halakhic discourse but rather to larger public policy issues. This is also evident in the body of his argument.

166. He states:

> בכמה מקומות שהנהיגו "מנינים" כאלו, כונתן להראות לכל שאף הנשים חשובות הן כמו האנשים, ושפיר מצטרפות למנין עשרה.... דדבר זה איסור תורה הוא, וחשוב ככופר בתורת משה... ואיסור חמור יש בזה.

In general, a fundamental tenet of women's *tefillah* is that the group does not con-

"the king's glory is in the multitude of the nation," and, as such, there should only be one Holy Temple and one High Priest;[167] one should not simply create new customs for their own sake – the pillar of *minhag* is in keeping *mitsvot* as they have been performed in the past; the tradition includes rules about who should be leaders of the community, and these actions are a violation of the customs of the synagogue; and they fall under the prohibition of imitating non-Jews, in general,[168] and of imitating the manner in which non-Jews worship in particular.[169] In R. Schachter's view, these women's groups constitute a rebellion and, as such, even the smallest change should be forbidden.[170] They fall under the prohibition of building a *matsevah* (monument).

In the context of denouncing this broader group of practices, there are several places where R. Schachter gives particular attention to the phenomenon of women's *megillah* readings, in which women read on behalf of other women.

---

stitute a *minyan*; however, this specific claim is not directly relevant to the question of women gathering to read *Megillat Ester* for other women. *Megillat Ester* is not a *davar shebikdushah*, and it is possible to argue that a quorum of ten men is not required; see "Women as Part of a Quorum," below. However, this paragraph is indicative of R. Schachter's views regarding women who participate in women's prayer groups. He sees this phenomenon as encompassing the practice of women's *megillah* readings as well.

167. By definition, a reading that permits only women contains only a fraction of the community and so this, like any "breakaway" service, is less than ideal.

168. He writes:

> והנה הדבר ידוע, שהנהגות אלו לא נתחדשו בזמננו אנו מתוך החלל, אלא בתורת תוצאה מהתנועה הכללית לשחרור הנשים, אשר ענינה ותכליתה בשטח הזה הוא לשם פריצות, להשוות הנשים לאנשים בכל מאי דאפשר.

169. He writes:

> שנאסר לנו לעבוד את השם הנכבד באותו האופן שהם עובדים לע"ז שלהם. כלומר, שיש איסור מיוחד של חוקות עכו"ם בנוגע לעשיית מצוות התורה.... ונראה, דהוא הדין והוא הטעם בנד"ד. דתנועת שחרור הנשים הצליחה כבר להשפיע על מקצת מעוע"ז שישתפו את הנשים בעבודתם לאלהיהם... וכעת עברה אותה ההשפעה אף אצל מקצת מהאורטודוקסים לשתף את הנשים בהקפות ובמנינים וכו'.

170. Such as a change of even a single sandal strap. See B.T. *Sanh.* 64a.

41. ***Tse'i Lakh Be'ikvei Hatson***

R. Hershel Schachter, United States (1941–)

צאי לך בעקבי הצאן

In a minority of Orthodox synagogues they have instituted special *hakkafot* for women on Simḥat Torah, and extra *minyanim* for women for *tefillah* (prayer), Torah reading, and *megillah* reading. After study and patient consideration with a number of other head rabbis in the *yeshivah,* it seems clear that all of these practices mentioned above are forbidden for a number of reasons:

במקצת בתי כנסיות אור־טודוקסים הנהיגו הקפות מיוחדות לנשים בשמחת תורה, ומנינים מיותרים לנשים לתפילה, לקריאת התורה, ולקריאת המגילה. ואחר העיון והדיון במתינות ובחבורה עם כמה מרמ"י הישיבה, נראה ברור שכל ההנהגות הנ"ל אסורות מכמה טעמים:

The *mitsvot* are not [performed] in their complete [manner]

המצוות הן שלא בשלמותן

1) In *Shulḥan Arukh, Oraḥ Ḥayyim* 55:1, it is explained clearly that women do not count for a *minyan* of ten for any "matter of holiness" (*davar shebikdushah*).... So too for the matter of reading *megillah,* about which the Rishonim explicitly disagreed as to whether women count toward the ten for the issue of publicizing the miracle of the *megillah*.... And if so, because of [this] doubt, lest women do not count toward the ten even for *megillah,* they should not recite this blessing [*harav et rivenu*] when they make a "*minyan*" for themselves. And if they were to come to synagogue to hear the *megillah* reading with the regular *minyan,* they would gain this blessing, as well, and so it appears that even with a [women's] *minyan* for the reading of *megillah,* this *mitsvah* also is not [performed] in its complete [manner].

א) בשו"ע או"ה סי' נ"ה ס"א מבואר להדיא, שאין הנשים מצטרפות למנין עשרה לכל דבר שבקדושה.... וכן לענין קריאת המגילה, שנחלקו בדבר הראשונים להדיא אם הנשים מצטרפות לעשרה לענין פרסומי ניסא המגילה.... וא"כ מטעם ספק שמא אין הנשים מצטרפות לעשרה אף לענין מגילה אין להם לברך ברכה זו כשעושות "מנין" לעצמן, ואילו באו לביהכ"נ לשמוע קריאת המגילה יחד עם המנין הרגיל, היו מרויחות אף ברכה זו, ונמצא שאף במנין לקריאת המגילה ג"כ, המצוה היא שלא בשלמותה.

One is more commanded [to perform a *mitsvah*] oneself than via a messenger

4) See *Ḥayyei Adam* (*kelal* 68:7) who is in doubt as to the parameters of the rule that it is [preferable to perform] a *mitsvah* oneself rather than via a messenger: if the *mitsvah* will be performed in a better way by others, should we prefer that he do it himself or that the *mitsvah* be performed in a better way by others? And here, in our case of those [women] who make "*minyanim*" for themselves, surely the *mitsvot* (of Torah reading, prayer, and *megillah* reading) are not being performed in their complete manner. There are those [women] who argue that it is better for them to participate themselves, even though in this way they do not fulfill the *mitsvo*t in their complete manner.... So too with the reading of *megillah*, those who want to enhance the *mitsvah* and uphold the ideal form of the *mitsvah* – oneself rather than through a messenger – would read from their own *megillah* that was set before them. But [with regard to] having a reading especially for women, where just one woman reads the *megillah* while the others hear it from her and fulfill their obligation through her, it emerges therefore that just one woman – "the reader" – fulfills this enhancement of performing a *mitsvah* oneself rather than through a messenger. But this enhancement could also have been accomplished through her participation in the regular *minyan* in the

צוה בו יותר מבשלוחו

ד) ועי' חיי"א (כלל ס"ח ס"ז) שהסתפק בגדר הדין דמצוה בו יותר מבשלוחו, אם תהי' המצוה יותר מהודרת באופן שתיעשה ע"י אחרים, אם יש לנו להעדיף שיעשה הוא בעצמו, או שתיעשה המצוה ביותר הידור ע"י אחרים, והנה בנד"ד, בעושות "מנינים" לעצמן, בודאי אין המצוות (של קרה"ת, ותפילה וקריאת המגילה) מתקיימות בשלמותן, ויש שטוענות ואומרות שמוטב להן להשתתף בעצמן אעפ"י שע"י השתתפות זו לא יתקיימו המצוות בשלמותן.... וכן בקריאת המגילה נמי, אלו הרוצים להדר ולקים הלכתחילה של מצוה בו יותר מבשלוחו, קורים היו ממגילה שלהם המונח לפניהם. אבל לעשות קריאה מיוחדת לנשים, שרק אשה אחת תקרא את המגילה, והשאר ישמעו ממנה ויצאו בקריאתה, יוצא איפוא שרק אשה אחת - "בעלת הקריאה" - יצאה ידי חובת הידור זה של מצוה בו יותר מבשלוחו, וזה ההידור היתה יכולה לעשות גם בהשתתפותה במנין הרגיל שבביהכ"נ, ע"ז שהיתה קוראה לעצמה בלחש ממגילה הכתובה

synagogue, by reading to herself quietly from a *megillah* written on parchment set before her, just as some men who are careful in *mitsvot* [performance] enhance [their reading] without losing the simultaneous fulfillment of [the *mitsvah* of] reading with ten, according to all opinions, as we explained above (section 1). But by creating a *minyan* for themselves, they do not gain anything by it.

על הקלף המונחת לפניה, כמו שמהדרים כמה אנשים מדקדקים במצוות, ומבלי לאבד את הקיום הנוסף של קריאה בעשרה לכו"ע, כאשר ביארנו למעלה (אות א'), ובמה שעושות מנין לעצמן, אינן מרוויחות בזה כלום.

And the reason that they prefer to create a "*minyan*" for themselves is not because of the legal reason that it is [preferable to perform] a *mitsvah* oneself rather than through a messenger, but because of an emotion…and in their "*minyan*" the women have the feeling that this is "their thing," but it is certainly not appropriate to purposefully lose out on the legal fulfillments mentioned above (section 1) because of this feeling. On the contrary, it is incumbent upon us to train women who are learned and wise to regulate and adjust their emotional energies until their emotions match the concerns of *halakhah*….

ומה שמעדיפות לעשות "מנין" לעצמן הוא לא מטעם ההלכתי דמצוה בו יותר מבשלוחו, אלא מטעם הרגשת הלב... וב"מנין" שלהן יש לנשים הרגשה זו שזהו ה"דבר שלהן", אכן בודאי אינו כדאי לאבד בידים הקיומים ההלכתיים הנוספים אשר הזכרנו למעלה (אות א'), בעד ההרגשה הזאת. ואדרבא, עלינו להרגיל את הנשים המלומדות והמחוכמות שירגילו ויתקנו את כוחות הנפש שלהן, עד שיתאימו הרגשותיהן לחישובי ההלכה....

Creating new customs *lishmah* (for the sake of Heaven)

חידוש מנהגים לשמה

5) It is obvious that Jewish law is not frozen. Through many changes in circumstances, the law has needed to change…and the explanation of this issue is that one may not create new Torah or customs or new ways of behaving that are not *lishmah* – for

ה) דבר ברור הוא שההלכה היא לא קפואה. מרוב שינויי המצבים הוכרחה ההלכה להשתנות... וביאור ענין זה, שלא לחדש תורה או מנהגים או איזו הנהגות מחודשות

the sake of Heaven…. And behold it is known and publicized that two of the great scholars of our generation, whom we all turn to hear, our teacher the *ga'on* R. Yosef Dov Soloveitchik and our master, the *ga'on* R. Moshe Feinstein, both of them are very opposed to all the behaviors that have been mentioned: to *hakkafot* specifically for women, to "*minyanim*" specifically for prayer, and to Torah reading, and the reading of the *megillah*….	שלא לשמה.... והנה דבר ידוע ומפורסם הוא, אשר שני גדולי חכמי דורנו, אשר כולנו סרים למשמעתם, מורנו הגרי"ד סאלאוויטשיק, שליט"א, ומרן הגר"מ פיינשטיין, שליט"א, שניהם מתנגדים מאוד לכל ההנהגות הנ"ל להקפות המיוחדות לנשים, ול"מנינים" המיוחדים לתפילה, ולקרה"ת, ולקריאת המגילה....
The pillar of custom in the practice of *mitsvot*	**עמוד המנהג במעשי המצוות**
6) In all the congregations of Israel from which our fathers and our fathers' fathers emerged, we have never heard of or seen such a practice, that they should organize Torah reading or *megillah* reading just for women, or that they should organize *hakkafot* just for women. It is our obligation to continue in the tradition of our fathers and our fathers' fathers in the way in which we perform *mitsvot*.	ו) בכל קהילות ישראל שיצאו משם אבותינו ואבות אבותינו, מעולם לא שמענו ולא ראינו הנהגה כזו, שיסדרו קריאת התורה וקריאת המגילה לנשים לבדן, וכן שיסדרו הקפות לנשים לבדן. ועלינו מוטלת החובה להמשיך במסורת אבותינו ואבות אבותינו באופן עשית המצוות.

R. Schachter argues, first of all, that a women's reading is a lesser way to fulfill the *mitsvah* of reading *megillah* because women might not qualify as a *tsibbur*, a quorum, for this purpose and therefore might not be eligible to recite the final blessing.[171] R. Schachter, addressing the desire of women for more active participation, discusses the general principle that it is better to perform a *mitsvah* oneself than through a messenger. He contends that this ideal is not applicable in the case of women reading *megillah* as only one woman actually reads for the group. Instead, he

171. This issue is discussed at length below, "The Blessing After the *Megillah* Reading." Views opposing R. Schachter's views are presented as well.

suggests, every woman, like many seriously observant men, could read along from a kosher *megillah* scroll while listening to a man read as part of a traditional *minyan* at synagogue. In this way, women can both actively perform the *mitsvah* (by reading along) and also fulfill it in the best possible manner, including responding "Amen" to the final blessing. He goes on to say that the halakhic ideal of performing *mitsvot* oneself is not the real reason that women want to form these groups. Rather, it has to do with their personal feelings and the desire to have something of "their own." According to R. Schachter, one must teach women to control these feelings and to adjust them to conform to the law.[172]

Perhaps more importantly, R. Schachter is concerned about the problem of changing *minhagim* (traditions). Women reading *megillah*, he argues, is not an established custom within the Orthodox community and changing customs is not a matter to be taken lightly. Communities and synagogues have established *minhagim*, and only a great Torah authority can change such a custom. R. Schachter claims that both R. Moshe Feinstein[173] and R. Yosef Dov Soloveitchik[174] were

172. R. Schachter's view is surprising, considering the fact that women's personal feelings and desires are the motivating factor within the *halakhah* to enable them to perform *mitsvot* from which they are exempt. See B.T. *Ḥag.* 16b אלא כדי לעשות נחת רוח לנשים, and B.T. *Rosh Hash.* 33a with the commentaries ad loc. See also R. Lau's opposite approach in source #48.

173. Contrary to this claim, R. Aryeh Frimer, in "Women's *Megilla* Reading" (http://www.daat.ac.il/daat/english/tfila/frimer2.htm), note 72, paragraph b, states that R. Feinstein permitted women's *megillah* readings: "R. Moshe Feinstein, as reported to R. Chaim Spring by R. Mordechai Tendler, October 1985." Later, in n93, R. Frimer points out: "Note, however, that both *Arukh Hashulḥan* and R. Feinstein, like many other leading *posekim*, maintain that the *harav et rivenu* benediction can be said even in the absence of a *minyan*." Thus, according to R. Frimer's depiction of R. Feinstein's position, women could perform the *mitsvah* in its complete form in a women's reading.

174. Also in contrast to this blanket statement, R. Frimer points out in "Women's *Megilla* Reading," n105:

> R. Joseph B. Soloveitchik preferred that women not have their own *megillah* reading (Conversations with R. David Gorelik, R. Jacob J. Schacter, and R. Binyomin Walfish; see also: R. Jacob J. Schacter, "Facing the Truths of History," *The Torah U-Madda Journal* 8 [1998–1999]: note 97, pp. 260–261). Both R. Schacter and R. Walfish noted, however, that the Rav indicated that if necessary, there was room to be lenient. Consequently, R. Soloveitchik advised R. Walfish that

against the practice of women creating their own "*minyanim*." Therefore, R. Schachter posits, they also would be opposed to women gathering on their own to read *Megillat Ester* for other women. Such groups never existed in the past, and that situation should not change now.

R. Schachter is also deeply mistrustful of the motives of women who want to hold such services. It is forbidden to imitate the practices of non-Jews or to attempt to worship in the ways that non-Jews worship. Feminism and a widespread desire for gender equality are secular movements, which, in R. Schachter's view, are infiltrating Jewish practice. He is concerned that women who want to form their own groups for worship and change the customs of the past may be motivated not purely by the desire to serve God, but by the need to accommodate a more feminist worldview within Jewish ritual. This, argues R. Schachter, is strictly prohibited. Ultimately, the fact that these women are motivated by a non-Jewish movement and worldview means for R. Schachter that even relatively minor changes are indicative of a movement that will eventually "uproot" the rule of traditional *halakhah* entirely. Therefore,

---

> where the women of a particular congregation insist on having their own *megillah* reading, the rabbi should not object. Similarly, in a telephone conversation with R. Bertram Leff, R. Shmuel Goldin, and Mr. Nathan Lewin (in 1980 or 1981), the Rav permitted a women's *megillah* reading by Mr. Lewin's daughter, Alyza, for those women who were unable to attend the regular congregational, early morning, Purim *minyan*. R. Soloveitchik emphasized, however, that the women's reading should not be held in shul, that the *ba'alat keriah* could read only for women, and that this reading was not meant to replace the more preferred regular reading with a male *minyan*.

Frimer adds, ibid., n51:

> R. Yosef Adler (personal communication, March 10, 1996) recalls that R. Joseph B. Soloveitchik, the Rav, often commented on his difficulty in accepting the view of Behag. Nonetheless, the Rav acknowledged that since Rema cites *Halakhot Gedolot*'s ruling approvingly, it has become normative *halakhah*. Consequently, women could not read *megillah* for Ashkenazic men. Interestingly, though, in the Winter of 1977, our sister-in-law, Mrs. Sabina Frimer, asked the Rav whether she could read the *megillah* for her grandmother and home-bound grandfather – since no one else was available to do so. The Rav responded that it would be preferable to find a male to read for them, but if she were not successful, *bishat hadeḥak*, she could read for them herself. The Rav also suggested that the grandfather should make the *berakhot*.

R. Schachter thinks, even women whose motivations are pure are forbidden from joining such activities because they have become a symbol of rebellion against the authority of Torah.

As noted above, R. Schachter does not refer to any of the objections that the Aḥaronim raise with regard to a woman reading *megillah*. There is no mention of *zila milleta* as it would apply to women's reading for other women or to the position of *Midrash Hane'elam* as quoted by *Magen Avraham* and others.[175] Instead, his analysis gives precedence to those who rule that women cannot count toward a quorum for *megillah* reading and that therefore the *mitsvah* is not fulfilled in its best possible form. This position, combined with more philosophical arguments against instituting this practice – the desire to preserve custom against innovation, to maintain certain community affiliations and paradigms, and to resist outside influences – leads the Yeshiva University rabbis to conclude that the practice is forbidden. While not necessarily a specific violation of *hilkhot megillah*, a woman reading is more broadly problematic. A woman who attends such a reading perhaps technically fulfills her obligation but because of these larger halakhic issues and the social realities of the time, these *rashei yeshivah* forbid a woman to do so.

In summary, there are a number of contemporary authorities who prohibit women from reading *megillah* for others, or at least strongly prefer that a woman hear the reading from a man. Not all of these *posekim* recommend the same preferred practice. R. Sofer suggests that a woman should be read to at home, while R. Schachter and R. Klein discuss the imperative of hearing *megillah* in the synagogue. Nonetheless, whether because they follow *Midrash Hane'elam* and the opinions of various Aḥaronim who prefer that women hear the reading from a man or because they think that women's readings are more generally problematic, there are communities that prohibit women from reading *Megillat Ester*. The following section discusses a group of contemporary

175. This omission is interesting as it does seem as though R. Schachter raises every possible challenge he can think of to oppose these practices. Why does he not state these as well? Does the absence of these arguments attest to the fact that even R. Schachter understands that those sources are based on tenuous proofs and misreadings of non-normative texts and so do not really stand as cogent arguments? See many of the sources in the next section who think this way.

posekim who address and reject these concerns and rule that women may read for other women.

Contemporary Sources #3: Women May Read, But Only for Other Women

Most contemporary Orthodox halakhic authorities, and thus most Modern Orthodox congregations, prohibit women from reading to mixed audiences out of respect for the more conservative positions discussed above.[176] However, fewer of these authorities seem to find the arguments of the most stringent and restrictive group, which forbids women from reading at all, compelling. More and more Orthodox communities are holding *megillah* readings for and by women,[177] and they are bolstered by a straightforward reading of the Mishnah, Talmud, and Rishonim. It is important to remember that it is specifically those Rishonim who support Behag's conservative position – that women and men have different levels of obligation – who explicitly state that women may read for other women (while rejecting the idea that women might read on behalf of men). They understand the Gemara in *Arakhin* to explicitly state as such when the text says that women are fit to read. This rule is the view of many contemporary authorities, as well.

R. Ḥayyim David Halevi, who replaced R. Yosef as Sephardic

176. Interestingly, although they reject a woman reading for men as normative practice, many of them readily admit that this is a legitimate halakhic possibility when there is no other alternative. See n174, above, where even R. Soloveitchik permitted women's reading under such circumstances.

177. Throughout history there have always been second readings specifically for women. Since both women and men are obligated to attend the *megillah* reading and small children should not attend because one is obligated to hear every word, there was generally no alternative but to hold separate readings for women who could not attend the main reading in the synagogue. In modern times, as women have become more educated and are capable both of reading the *megillah* themselves and of seeing that the sources explicitly discuss and permit women to read for other women, the phenomenon of women's *megillah* readings has become an increasingly prevalent solution to this problem, as opposed to having a man read for them. JOFA lists fifty-four such readings in 2014, and its list is by no means exhaustive, as many such readings that take place in Israel are not listed.

chief rabbi of Tel Aviv-Jaffa in 1973, rules similarly to R. Yosef's final analysis (source #38, above):

42. ***Mekor Ḥayyim Livnot Yisra'el 34:6*** **מקור חיים לבנות ישראל לד:ו**

R. Ḥayyim David Halevi, Israel (1924–1998)

According to this logic a woman can read *megillah* and discharge the obligation of men, as we ruled with Ḥanukkah candles. There are those who say that women may not fulfill the obligation of men.... It is appropriate to worry about this view, and [therefore] a woman should only read to discharge the obligation of men in a pressing situation for one who has no one [male] to read for him. But it is quite obvious that she can read for other women to discharge their obligation.	לסברא זאת אשה יכולה לקרוא המגילה ולהוציא אנשים ידי חובתם כמו שנפסק בנר חנוכה. ויש אומרים שהנשים אינן מוציאות האנשים.... וראוי לחוש לדיעה זאת, ולא תקרא אשה להוציא אנשים אלא בשעת הדחק למי שאין שיקרא בפניהם. אבל פשוט ביותר שיכולה לקרוא בפני נשים אחרות להוציאם ידי חובתן.

Although women and men share the same obligation and thus women can legally discharge a man's obligation in *megillah* reading, as in the case of Ḥanukkah candles, R. Halevi still deems it appropriate to be stringent and refrain from such a practice whenever possible. Only if there is no alternative may a woman read for men.[178] However, he is clear that there is absolutely no problem with a woman reading and fulfilling the obligation of *megillah* for a group of other women.[179]

R. Shlomo Zalman Auerbach similarly rules that there is no

178. In the omitted section not cited, R. Halevi explains that the basis for the *yesh omerim* is *kevod hatsibbur*. Thus, *bediavad* a woman may read for men, as their obligations are equal. See n82 above.

179. R. Halevi shows no concern for the limitation of *Korban Netanel* (source #33, above) and sees no breach of dignity in having a woman read for a group of other women. However, in 34:9, R. Halevi states that the last blessing after *megillah* reading should not be recited at home and is only said in a *tsibbur*. Based on this statement, he presumably does not consider a group of ten women to constitute such a quorum.

problem with a woman discharging the obligation of a group of women. R. Auerbach treats this topic in *Halikhot Shelomo Mo'adim*,[180] a book compiled from his other writings. In the footnotes he discusses the ruling of *Korban Netanel* (source #33, above) that prohibits a woman from reading for other women:

43. *Halikhot Shelomo Mo'adim 2 19:3 and note 4*	**הליכות שלמה מועדים ב יט:ג והערה ד**
R. Shlomo Zalman Auerbach, Jerusalem (1910–1995)	
Women who hear the reading of *megillah* by themselves, one [woman] from among them recites the blessings and discharges the obligation of the others.	נשים השועמות קריאת המגילה לעצמן, מברכת אחת מהם הברכות ומוציאה את חברותיה.
Note: And what *Tosafot* wrote in [B.T.] *Sukkah* 38a...that a woman does not discharge the obligation of the many in the reading of *megillah* because it is undignified, that is in reference to discharging the obligation of men...but for other women she certainly discharges their obligation. And what *Korban Netanel* wrote...to explain their [*Tosafot's*] words with regard to a woman's discharging the obligation of other women, and what was brought in *Sha'ar Hatsiyyun* 689:15, this needs investigation for behold it is made clear in *Shulḥan Arukh*, [*O. Ḥ.*] 199:6, that women comprise a *zimmun* [for Grace after Meals] for themselves.... In any case, one blesses for	הערה: ומש"כ התוס' בסוכה ל"ח ע"א... שאשה לא תוציא את הרבים במקרא מגילה משום דזילא בהו מילתא, הייהו להוציא אנשים... אבל נשים אחרות שפיר מוציאה. ומש"כ הקרבן נתנאל... לפרש דבריהם לענין אשה להוציא נשים אחרות, והביאו השעה"צ ס' תרפ"ט סקט"ו, צ"ע דהרי מבואר בשו"ע ס' קצ"ט ס"ו דנשים מזמנות לעצמן.... עכ"פ אחת מברכת לכולן, וה"ה לשאר ברכות, וכן נהוג לענין קידוש, ולכן נראה דהדין עם הגרימ"ט

180. The work was collected and organized by two of his grandsons, R. Yitsḥak Terger and R. Aharon Auerbach, according to the holiday cycle.

them all, and so is the law for other blessings and also [it is] the custom with regard to *kiddush* [that one woman blesses for many others]. Therefore, it appears that the law is in accordance with the *ga'on* R. Yeḥiel Mikhl Tukachinsky *z"l*, who wrote in *Luaḥ Erets Yisra'el* that a woman certainly discharges the obligation of many women.[181]	ז"ל שכתב בלוח אר"י דשפיר מוציאה נשים רבות ידי חובתן.

R. Auerbach compares the rule codified in *Shulḥan Arukh* that a group of women may comprise a *zimmun* by themselves, with one woman reciting the *birkat hamazon* for others, to the case of a women's *megillah* reading.[182] He challenges *Korban Netanel*'s ruling that it would be problematic for a woman to read *megillah* for other women in public. R. Auerbach rules that one woman should recite the blessings over the reading and thus discharge the obligation of the rest of the group, just as one woman leads the *zimmun* for the others during Grace after Meals.[183] He states that a woman may act as an agent for a group of women in the case of other blessings, and he notes that it is the custom for a woman to recite *kiddush* on Shabbat for other women, as well. He does not under-

181. R. Tukachinsky, who lived in Israel from 1871 to 1955, was *rosh yeshivah* of Yeshivat Ets Ḥayyim and authored one of the first calendars that included a collection of all the laws of the holidays.

182. He makes this comparison explicitly in the footnote; however, the langage of *le'atsman* used to formulate the rule in the quoted text also echoes the language of *zimmun*. See B.T. *Ber.* 45b.

183. The scenario that R. Auerbach discusses in section 3 is that of a man reading for a group of women. In note 5 at the bottom of the page, the text describes how R. Auerbach's wife would recite the blessing (*lishmo'a megillah*) to discharge the obligation of the other women present, and then R. Auerbach or a member of his household would read the *megillah* for them. It is clear from R. Auerbach's analysis and language that he thinks that the question of a woman's agency to act for a large group of other women is the same whether she is reciting the blessings, leading a *zimmun*, reciting *kiddush*, or actually reading the *megillah* herself. In all of those cases the law is the same, and it is permissible. See also R. Waldenberg (source #59, below), who permits ten women to form a quorum and recite the blessings when a man reads for them.

stand how *Mishnah Berurah* rules in *Sha'ar Hatsiyyun* in accordance with *Korban Netanel.* R. Auerbach points out that the meaning of the original *Tosafot* upon which *Korban Netanel* based his ruling permitted a woman to read *megillah* for other women. He concludes by citing R. Tukachinsky, who ruled similarly that a woman may in fact fulfill the obligation of a group of other women. In R. Auerbach's view, this understanding is the law; there is nothing undignified about a woman performing *mitsvot* on behalf of other women.

One of the most vocal contemporary rabbis on this subject is R. Yehuda Henkin, who discusses women and *megillah* reading in a number of responsa and articles.[184] In his essay "Women and Megillah Reading" in *Equality Lost: Essays in Torah Commentary, Halacha and Jewish Thought,* R. Henkin articulates the arguments for permitting a woman to read *megillah* on behalf of other women.[185] The essay opens with a succinct summary of the three positions found in the Rishonim regarding a woman's obligation in *megillah* reading.[186] R. Henkin analyzes each of these arguments, quoting sources and tracing them through to the Aḥaronim. He then uses these texts to disprove the validity of the contention, found in only a few Aḥaronim, that women may not read *megillah* on behalf of other women. Similarly to R. Auerbach, R. Henkin thinks that this position is based on a misunderstanding introduced by *Korban Netanel* (source #33). Had *Korban Netanel* seen the original source, he and those who follow his interpretation "would not have written as they did."[187] Therefore, R. Henkin continues:

184. See R. Yehuda Henkin, "*Keriat Hamegillah Al Yedei Nashim: Hamaḥloket Enah Behalakhah,*" *Hatzofeh,* March 2, 1999; Henkin, "Women and Megillah Reading"; Henkin, "*Tsibbur Nashim Bikriat Hamegillah,*" *Keshot* 4 (March/April 1995): sec. 14, 8–10, repr. in *Responsa Benei Banim* 3:7 and 2:10.

185. Henkin, "Women and Megillah Reading," 54–65.

186. Here, R. Henkin explains his reason for writing that women's *megillah* readings have been an issue of some controversy. In his first footnote, he notes that in February 1997 the Vaad Harabonim of Queens, New York, prohibited such readings and that shortly afterward a women's reading was canceled by the administration of Stern College.

187. Henkin, "Women and Megillah Reading," 59.

44. *"Women and Megillah Reading," p. 59*

R. Yehuda Henkin, United States and Israel (1945–)

It can thus be stated categorically that there is no opinion in the Talmud or Rishonim that prohibits a woman from reading the *megillah* for herself or for any number of other women. Moreover, as opposed to many innovations in women's prayer groups which, even if not explicitly forbidden, are at the least not anticipated by any authority, women's *megillah* readings are a clearly implied halakhic option.

Not only are women's *megillah* readings theoretically permitted according to early sources, but R. Henkin says that they exist as a live possibility within these texts and are not, therefore, a radical innovation.

In the second part of his article, R. Henkin demonstrates that although it is still possible to argue that a *megillah* reading in the synagogue, attended by the entire congregation – and thus, by implication, read by men – may be preferable,[188] there are a number of factors that mitigate these concerns:

45. *"Women and Megillah Reading," p. 60*

R. Yehuda Henkin, United States and Israel (1945–)

All things are often not equal, however:

---

188. Ibid. These include: the preference (*hiddur*) of having as many participants as possible in one large public reading rather than fragmented into smaller ones; the initial obligation to read the *megillah* in the presence of ten men or ten women, which is often possible only at the synagogue reading; questions as to the proper blessings to be recited; and the general desirability of performing a *mitsvah* sooner rather than later.

The question of a quorum and the issue of which blessings are to be recited are discussed later in this chapter. As to the issue of smaller readings and the timing of these readings, R. Henkin's footnotes indicate that he is aware that many congregations are willing to compromise on these issues at other times, and so there is no reason to be strict with women's readings on Purim specifically.

1) It is often impossible to hear properly from the *ezrat nashim.* The inaudibility of even one word from the *megillah* reading means that the listener has not fulfilled her obligation.

2) Women, and particularly mothers, are often unable to come to the synagogue at the specified times.

R. Henkin asserts that a women's reading might improve upon certain aspects of a woman's experience, both from a halakhic and a practical perspective. In conclusion, R. Henkin states:

46. *"Women and Megillah Reading," pp. 59–60*

R. Yehuda Henkin, United States and Israel (1945–)

For these and other reasons there has emerged a widespread practice to have a second *megillah* reading for women, and in such circumstances it is entirely proper for a woman or women to read the *megillah.* Even women who have already heard the *megillah* read and have thus discharged their own obligation can read for other women in the second reading. In fact when the alternative is to have a teenage boy read the *megillah* for a group of learned women, it may be close to being *zila beho milleta* for the women not to read the *megillah* themselves.

In a situation where there is reason to argue that women's needs will not be met by the congregational *megillah* reading, R. Henkin thinks that it is "entirely proper" to have women read on behalf of other women. There is no question that women may fulfill this obligation on behalf of other women, and a woman who has already fulfilled her own obligation may even read on behalf of a woman who has not.[189] R. Henkin thinks that other concerns are overridden by the potential of such a reading to provide a high-quality, *megillah* reading experience for women. R. Henkin chooses to end his essay by turning on

189. Based on the principle of *arevut,* i.e., all of Israel is responsible for one another. See B.T. *Rosh Hash.* 29a and Rashi ad loc., s.v. *af al pi.*

its head the halakhic terminology used by *Korban Netanel* to prohibit a woman from reading for a group of women – it is *zila beho milleta* (beneath their dignity) for a group of learned women to be forced to hear *megillah* from a teenage boy rather than from a member of their own ranks. It is important that the reading be an honorable and respectful experience. Women's *megillah* readings, which are a direct manifestation of the normative halakhic literature, meet this goal by enabling women to fulfill their obligation and to have a more meaningful experience of *Megillat Ester*.

Taking the concerns of women one step further, *Responsa Bemareh Habbazak* not only does not have any concerns regarding a women's *megillah* reading but actually sees the positive spiritual benefit such a reading may bring women.[190] The question below was sent by a community rabbi in Israel in *Adar* 2009, communicating the desires of the women in his community to create a *megillah* reading for women by women:

47. *Responsa Bemareh Habbazak* *Vol. 7, Question 52*[191]	**שו"ת במראה הבזק חלק ז סימן נב**
R. Moshe Ehrenreich and R. Yosef Carmel, Israel (twentieth–twenty-first centuries)	
Question:	שאלה:
Many of the women in our community with the help of God care for young children. They are unable to come and	רבות מן הנשים ביישובנו מטופלות ב"ה בילדים קטנים. אין להן יכולת לבוא לשמוע

190. *Responsa Bemareh Habbazak* is the publication of Eretz Hemdah – Institute for Advanced Jewish Studies in Jerusalem, founded by R. Shaul Israeli *z"l*, that responds to legal questions from around the world. The initial responses are prepared by those studying in the institution with the guidance of the heads of the *kollel* R. Moshe Ehrenreich and R. Yosef Carmel, and reviewed by R. Zalman Nechemia Goldberg, R. Dr. Nachum Eliezer Rabinovitch, and R. Yisrael Rosen, under whose authority the final publication rests.

191. http://eretzhemdah.org/data/uploadedfiles/ebooks/36-sfile.pdf, accessed September 20, 2015, and, with slight variations, at http://eretzhemdah.org/newsletterArticle.asp?%20pageid=48&cat=1&newsletter=1266&article=4757, accessed September 20, 2015.

hear the *megillah* with the rest of the community. They turned to me as *rav* of the congregation and suggested that we set up a *megillah* reading for women at a later time.[192] At this reading, only women would participate, and they [the women] would also read the *megillah*. Is there a halakhic problem with this?

מגילה עם כלל הציבור. פנו אלי כרב הקהילה והציעו לקיים בשעה מאוחרת יותר קריאת מגילה לנשים. בקריאה זו ישתתפו אך ורק נשים, והן גם תקראנה במגילה. האם יש בעיה הלכתית בכך?

Answer:

תשובה:

1) A woman is obligated in the reading of the *megillah*, "since they too were part of the same miracle." The main opinion in the *halakhah* is that a woman can discharge another woman's obligation in the reading of *megillah*.[193]

א) אשה חייבת במקרא מגילה, "שאף הן היו באותו הנס". השיטה העקרית בהלכה היא שאשה יכולה להוציא ידי חובה אשה אחרת בקריאת מגילה.

2) The community reading, which includes the entire community, is preferable over any other reading, since "the king's glory is in the multitude of the nation."[194] The outlook of the Torah is that the community is one community, including men, women, and children,[195] each one in his place.[196]

ב) הקריאה הציבורית הכוללת את כל הציבור עדיפה על פני כל קריאה אחרת, ו"ברוב עם הדרת מלך". מבטה של תורה הוא שהציבור הוא ציבור אחד, הכולל גברים נשים וטף, כל אחד במקומו.

---

192. Presumably it was the women themselves who turned to the *rav* of the community and made this request.

193. On this statement appears the following footnote (n2):

שו"ע (או"ח סי' תרפט סע' ב). לדעת המחבר אשה יכולה גם להוציא גבר בקריאת מגילה. מאידך גיסא, המגן אברהם הביא מקור קבלי שעל-פיו "אשה לא תקרא לעצמה". הקרבן נתנאל, שהובא בשער הציון, קבע שאשה אינה מוציא ידי חובה ציבור של נשים. אכן, אין חובה לחשוש לדברי קבלה כאשר אין להם בסיס בפוסקים, וכן דברי הקרבן נתנאל אינם הפירוש העיקרי בדברי התוספות שאותם הביא כמקור לשיטתו. כך מפורש בתוס' רא"ש שלא כדברי הקרבן נתנאל בתוס'. לכן פסק הגרש"ז אויערבאך שלא כשער הציון הנ"ל.

194. Prov. 14:28.

195. Presumably this is a reference to the *mitsvah* of *hak'hel*. See Deut. 31:12.

196. In the version that appears as part of the newsletter, this last clause, "each one according to his place," has been deleted and replaced with:

לכן מי שיכולה להגיע לקריאה המרכזית צריכה לעשות כן.

3) The desire to perform *mitsvot* through personal involvement is appropriate and correct.[197] In many situations, women cannot perform certain *mitsvot* personally, since this option conflicts with other halakhic principles.	ג) רצון לקיום מצוות תוך מעורבות אישית הוא ראוי ונכון. בהקשרים רבים נשים אינן יכולות לקיים מצוות שונות באופן אישי, כיוון שאפשרות זו פוגעת בעקרונות הלכתיים אחרים.
4) A *megillah* reading that does not replace the community reading, but rather is designed for women who cannot participate in it, presents an opportunity to actualize this appropriate desire and is compatible with *halakhah* and its principles.	ד) קריאת מגילה שאינה באה כחלופה לקריאה הציבורית, אלא נועדה עבור נשים שלא יכלו להשתתף בה, מהווה הזדמנות לממש רצון ראוי זה, והיא תואמת את ההלכה ואת עקרונותיה.
5) In a congregation whose goal is to strengthen the community of women in their service of God, one should see this request as an additional positive route toward positive action. Every communal *rav* needs to judge the goals and the consequences of this type of request, and "the wise one has eyes in his head."[198]	ה) בקהילה שבה המגמה היא התחזקות ציבור הנשים בעבודת ה׳ יש לראות בבקשה מסוג זה אפיק חיובי נוסף לפעילות חיובית. כל רב קהילה צריך לבחון את המגמה והתוצאה של בקשה מסוג זה, והחכם עיניו בראשו.

Bemareh Habbazak clearly states that although a community reading that includes all its members is the ideal, in situations when many women

197. Unlike R. Schachter (source #41, above), this source distinguishes between women's *megillah* readings and women's prayer groups and acknowledges the risks one takes when forbidding something that is permitted. On this statement appears the following footnote (n5):

> באופן כללי, אין ליצור ציבוריות נשים נפרדת לתפילה וכד׳. עיקרון זה מוסכם על כל הפוסקים בדורנו. דעות האוסרים והמתירים קריאת נשים סובבות סביב השאלה אם ניתן לראות במסגרת זו עשייה לשם שמים, או שיש לראותה כניסיון לחיקוי של תפיסות עולם הזרות לעולמה של תורה. יש החוששים מהמדרון החלקלק - לאן נגיע. לעומת זאת, גם איסור המותר יכול להוות מדרון חלקלק, שעלול להרחיק במקום להוות גדר וסייג.

198. Eccles. 2:14.

would be excluded, women may legally discharge the obligation of other women through a separate women's reading.[199] This ruling follows the central opinion within the halakhic discourse. As in the texts cited above, the rulings of both *Magen Avraham* (source #29, above) and *Korban Netanel* (source #33, above) are rejected. Women are permitted to read both for themselves and for a group of other women. *Bemareh Habbazak* explains that personal, active involvement in performing *mitsvot* is a positive value that should be supported. Since opportunities to actively participate in communal *mitsvot* do not often occur for women, this *megillah* reading is a constructive opportunity for them to fulfill this natural, human desire. *Bemareh Habbazak* understands that such a request by women to participate in ritual can stem from a religious desire to serve God in a spiritual and meaningful way. It is not always a challenge to authority and tradition, and to the extent that it is genuine, it should be supported. Forbidding that which is permitted can lead to the negative consequence of distancing women from tradition.

To explain and support the practice in his congregation, R. Benjamin Lau published an article on women's *megillah* readings in *Adar Rishon* 5774 (February 20, 2014) that is posted in the responsa section of the website of Ramban Synagogue in Jerusalem. R. Lau explains that this practice reflects women's desire to take a more active role in Jewish life. He thinks that this practice is a positive force, one that can help "lead *halakhah* and religion to its central and relevant places in our lives, both personal and communal," and should therefore be encouraged:

---

199. In section 6 (not quoted above) the text states:

נשים מעדות המזרח הקוראות מגילה תברכנה לפני הקריאה ״על מקרא מגילה״, ואשכנזיות תברכנה ״לשמוע מקרא מגילה״.

In the version republished in the newsletter, there is an additional clause added to the responsum:

אם יש עשר נשים, הן יכולות לברך ׳הרב את ריבנו׳ לאחר הקריאה, אמנם יש לברר עם רב הקהילה, אם יש מנהג אחר בקהילה.

48. *"Megillah Reading for Women by Women"*

R. Benjamin Lau, Israel (1961–)

קריאת מגילה לנשים – על ידי נשים

We find therefore that *megillah* reading for women is beneficial for enhancing the hearing of the *megillah* and discharging the obligation of women, who have trouble hearing well from the women's section of the synagogue. Also, the claim of "the king's glory" is not correct.... First of all, while *pirsumei nissa* (publicizing the miracle) is accomplished with [a *minyan* of] ten, nonetheless, (a) one does not need hundreds of people for this, and (b) even ten women are considered a community that publicizes the miracle....

נמצא אם כן שקריאת המגילה לנשים מועילה להידור השמיעה של המגילה ויציאת ידי חובה של הנשים, שמתקשות לשמוע היטב מעזרת הנשים בבית הכנסת. גם טענת "הדרת מלך" אינה נכונה.... האחת - אמנם "פרסומי ניסא" נעשה בעשרה אך (א) לא צריך מאות איש לשם כך, (ב) גם עשר נשים נחשבות לקהל שמפרסם את הנס....

There is...a complaint against the entire awakening of women who wish to serve God in a more active way. Such opposition is heard frequently from rabbis, even in circles that identify with modern society. R. Tzvi (Herschel) Schachter outdid himself...but, in my humble opinion, this is not the way. No blessing will flourish for us by adopting the stringent approach that closes every door to the spirit of women who argue, "give [us] our share in Your Torah."[200] There is no doubt that with each wave of awakening various goals are added, and certainly one must be extremely cautious in identifying the [different] voices and their

יש... קריאת תגר על כל ההתעוררות של נשים המבקשות לעבוד את ה' בדרך אקטיבית יותר. התנגדויות מסוג זה נשמעות באופן תדיר מפי רבנים, גם בחוגים המזוהים עם החברה המודרנית. הגדיל לעשות הרב צבי (הרשל) שכטר... אולם לענ"ד לא זו הדרך. שום ברכה לא תצמח לנו מאימוץ הגישה המחמירה והסוגרת כל דלת בפני רוחן של נשים שתובעות "תן חלקנו בתורתך". אין ספק שלכל גל של התעוררות מצטרפות מגמות שונות ובוודאי יש צורך לנקוט בזהירות מירבית באיתור

200. M. *Avot* 5:20, and in the liturgy of the *shemoneh esreih*.

agendas. But to combine all the voices together and invalidate them seems to me a severe silencing. Perhaps I shall state it in more decisive manner: it is precisely women's frustration with their passive role in the synagogue that can be used as a catalyst for a spiritual awakening that will promote and lead *halakhah* and religion to its central and relevant place in our lives, both personal and communal. The question of the flexibility and adaptability of *halakhah* for changing needs is a direct result of the [personal] stake a *posek* feels in a given issue. The more the motivation grows stronger, the more the measure of *halakhah*'s flexibility is revealed, in all areas, within the limits of what is possible. There is no flexibility without limit, but the heavens (double entendre) are the limit.

הקולות ומגמתם. אך להכלילאת הקולות כולן ולפוסלן דומה בעיני לסתימת פה חמורה. אומר אולי בצורה יותר נחרצת: דווקא תסכולן של הנשים ממקומן הפסיבי בבית הכנסת יכול לשמש כזרז להתעוררות רוחנית שתקדם ותוביל את ההלכה ואת הדת למקומה המרכזי והרלוונטי בחיינו, האישיים והציבוריים. שאלת הגמישות וההסתגלות של ההלכה לצרכים המשתנים היא תוצאה ישירה של מידת המעורבות שחש הפוסק בסוגיה הנתונה. ככל שגוברת המוטיבציה כך מתגלה עוצמת הגמישות של ההלכה, בכל תחומיה, בגבולות האפשר. אין גמישות בלי גבול אך השמים (תרתי משמע) הם הגבול.

In summary: I am confident that in terms of pure *halakhah* there is no room to undermine the desire of women to organize themselves for a women's *megillah* reading. The group that leads the reading needs to practice the reading with great effort in order to discharge the obligation of all the women listening.... With regard to the location of the reading, there is nothing to prevent the reading of the *megillah* by women in the synagogue. Such was the custom in many communities where a man would read for women. However, in communities where this organizing [of a women's reading] arouses disagreement, it is correct to move

לסיכום: אני בטוח שמבחינת ההלכה הצרופה אין מקום לערער על רצונן של הנשים להתארגן לקריאת המגילה על ידי נשים. הקבוצה שמובילה את הקריאה צריכה להתאמן בעמל רב על הקריאה כדי להוציא ידי חובה את כל השומעות.... לגבי מקום הקריאה - אין מניעה מלקרוא את המגילה על ידי נשים בבית הכנסת. כך נהגו בקהילות רבות כשאיש היה קורא לנשים. אמנם בקהילות שההתארגנות הזו מעוררת מחלוקת נכון להמתין

slowly [lit., wait with the matter] and to undergo a process of learning and mutual listening until their hearts are opened and they are ready to bring peace of spirit[201] to each other and together [lit., with combined forces] to bring peace of spirit to their father in heaven.	עם הדבר ולעבור תהליך של למידה והקשבה הדדית עד שיפתחו הלבבות ויהיו מוכנים לעשות נחת רוח איש לרעהו ובכוחות משותפים לעשות נחת רוח לאביהם שבשמים.

R. Lau takes issue with the idea that it is better for women to attend the community reading, since "the king's glory is in the multitude of the nation," and that a women's reading is only a secondary option if attendance at synagogue is not possible. He challenges the basis for this argument on two counts. First, while the publicizing of the Purim miracle certainly happens when the *megillah* is read in a *minyan*, there is no requirement for hundreds of people to gather together to create the largest possible reading. Second, ten women themselves create a community that publicizes the miracle, and so by extension a women's *megillah* reading also brings glory to the king. In R. Lau's view, a women's reading is not an option of last resort, but rather something that should be embraced as a model of commitment and the desire to be actively involved in performing *mitsvot* and ritual. Indeed, he argues that this desire has the potential to reinvigorate the Jewish people as a whole. He sees no benefit to the stringent approach represented by R. Schachter, which silences the legitimate yearnings of women who long to be active participants in the synagogue by casting aspersions on the agenda of all women. R. Lau feels that it is the *posek*'s role to understand these women and that there is a great possibility of flexibility within *halakhah* when one's intentions are for God. He states emphatically that there is no halakhic problem with women's readings, only that the women should take their job seriously and practice to ensure a proper reading. R. Lau sees no reason why the reading cannot be held in the synagogue itself for that was the custom for women's readings in the past when the reader

201. R. Lau uses the term *naḥat ruaḥ*, evoking the motivation used by rabbinic tradition for enabling and expanding women's ritual performance. See n172 above.

was a man. He understands that creating such a reading could arouse conflict within a community, and he advocates dialogue and mutual listening on both sides so that the situation can ultimately be resolved for the sake of heaven.

Following the lead and legal logic of R. Halevi (source #42), R. Auerbach (source #43), R. Henkin (source #44), and R. Lau[202] (source #48), many contemporary rabbis and scholars lend support to the now widespread practice of women's *megillah* readings.[203] These authorities emphasize the consensus in earlier sources that women are obligated in *megillah* and the clear and explicit view of the Rishonim on the subject. In the words of R. Henkin: "In the opinion of all of the Rishonim, a woman may read *megillah* on behalf of a congregation of women."[204] Thus, these authorities do not deem this practice to be new or innovative in any way. They reject the views that forbid a woman to read for a group of other women, or even for herself individually, as mistaken textual readings that are not reflective of the mainstream halakhic discourse. In addition, some have argued that a woman reading *megillah* on behalf of other women is a natural outgrowth of the revolution in Torah learning that has produced so many skilled and knowledgeable women.[205] They think that this spiritual desire to be active participants in religious ritual should be embraced, supported, and encouraged.

---

202. Of course, this also includes contemporary authorities in the first group above, who permit women to read for men and would thus certainly permit them to read for other women.

203. For the locations of women's *megillah* readings, see the JOFA website at www.jofa.org. For a list of authorities who have permitted or endorsed women's *megillah* readings, both in print and verbally, see Frimer, "Women's Megillah Reading," n72, where the author provides an extensive list of such sources. In addition, R. Aharon Lichtenstein famously permitted the women at Midreshet Lindenbaum in Jerusalem to hold a women's *megillah* reading, which they do every year; and the practice has spread to many communities and women's *yeshivot* and high schools in Israel. See also *Responsa Tsits Eliezer* 13:73 (source #59, below), and others who think similarly, in the section below on whether ten women constitute a quorum for *megillah* reading.

204. R. Yehuda Henkin, *Responsa Benei Banim* 3:7.

205. See Wolowelsky, p.94 (see n4, above). On the ability of women today to read and understand, see R. Ovadiah Yosef, *Responsa Yeḥavveh Da'at* 1:88 (source #72, below), who argues that women today have a high level of understanding. The article about

In conclusion, each of the positions found in earlier sources is reflected among contemporary halakhic authorities. Despite being well-attested among Rishonim, only a small number of contemporary halakhic authorities endorse a woman reading *megillah* for men. Nonetheless, the position that women may read for men is maintained, albeit mainly for the nighttime reading, by a small number of contemporary *posekim*. On the other hand, some contemporary authorities advise women to make an effort to hear *megillah* from a man, reflecting the position introduced by some Aḥaronim that women should not read *megillah* at all. Many contemporary rabbis maintain the straightforward reading of the earlier sources. They are perhaps bolstered by the large number of contemporary women who are literate and able to read *megillah*; and they endorse women reading *megillah* for other women, a practice with ample support from Rishonim through contemporary halakhic authorities.[206]

To understand more fully the issues inherent in the question of a woman reading *Megillat Ester*, whether for other women or for men and women together, two additional halakhic topics must be explored: (1) the composition of a quorum for the purpose of a *megillah* reading and (2) the blessings recited in conjunction with reading the *megillah*.

WOMEN AS PART OF A QUORUM

A central component of the obligation to read *megillah* is *pirsumei nissa*, publicizing the miracle of Purim. As a result, it is considered ideal to read *Megillat Ester* in public, which is usually defined as in the presence of a *minyan*. This section focuses on the following questions:

R. Yosef in *Haaretz* (see n4, above) reports that he considers the possibility that there might be a place where a woman knows how to read and there are no men present who have such knowledge.

206. It is interesting to note that all of the contemporary sources cited above, those in the group that permits women to read for men and those in the group that supports women's readings, reside in Israel. On the other hand, many in the group that forbids reading by women live in the United States. This difference may be due to the pressures exerted by the practices of the other denominations of Jews, denominations that are much stronger in the United States.

- Is one obligated to read or hear the *megillah* reading in the presence of a *minyan*?
- If yes, are both men and women included in this obligation?
- Do women count toward the quorum of ten, along with men?
- Do ten women constitute a quorum for the purpose of their own *megillah* reading?

These questions have important ramifications for the questions raised earlier regarding the practice of women's *megillah* readings.[207] The answers to these questions also determine which blessings are recited when a woman reads *megillah* for other women, which is discussed in the next section of this chapter.

The Gemara in Tractate *Megillah* records a debate regarding the need for a quorum of ten when reading *Megillat Ester*:[208]

49. *Babylonian Talmud Megillah 5a*	**תלמוד בבלי מסכת מגילה ה.**
Rav said: *Megillah*, in its proper time, may be read even by an individual; not in its proper time – [only] with ten.[209] Rav Assi said: Whether in its proper time or not in its proper time, [it should be read] with ten. The matter occurred and Rav accommodated the position of Rav Assi.	אמר רב: מגילה בזמנה - קורין אותה אפילו ביחיד, שלא בזמנה - בעשרה. רב אסי אמר: בין בזמנה בין שלא בזמנה בעשרה. הוה עובדא וחש ליה רב להא דרב אסי.

The *mishnah* that precedes this passage raises the possibility of village communities reading *megillah* as many as three days before the actual

207. Of course, these questions also have ramifications for a man reading for a gathering of women or for a mixed group of women and men. All of these cases are discussed below.

208. See also B.T. *Meg.* 19a–b; and J.T. *Meg.* 1:5, 70d.

209. Throughout the sources quoted in this chapter, a number of different terms are used to denote the group needed for *megillah* reading: *asarah* (ten) is used here in the Gemara; elsewhere, the terms *tsibbur* (community) and *minyan* (ritual quorum) also appear.

date of Purim.[210] Rav and Rav Assi agree that such an early reading requires a *minyan*. However, when the *megillah* is read on Purim itself, Rav says that one may fulfill the *mitsvah* as an individual without a quorum present, while Rav Assi argues that one must read in the presence of a *minyan*. In practice, the Gemara reports, there was an occasion on which Rav accommodated the more stringent position of Rav Assi and read *megillah* with a *minyan* on Purim itself.[211]

Commentators and halakhic codifiers debate which position to follow in practice.[212] A small minority of halakhic authorities argues that a quorum of ten is required and is not merely a positive behavior.[213]

---

210. On the 11th, 12th, or 13th of *Adar*. See M. *Meg.* 1:1; and B.T. *Meg.* 2a.

211. Rashi to B.T. *Meg.* 5a, s.v. *verav assi amar*, notes that even Rav Assi would rule that if one cannot find nine others with whom to read, one should still read *megillah* as an individual:

> ורב אסי אמר בין בזמנה בין שלא בזמנה - מצוה לחזר אחר עשרה, משום פרסומי ניסא, אבל אי לא אשכח עשרה לא אמר רב אסי דלא ליקרי, שאין איסור קריאתה ביחיד, אלא מצוה לקרותה בעשרה.

212. In addition to the practical debate as to whether or not a quorum of ten is required for the reading of the *megillah*, there are also multiple opinions regarding how to understand the positions of Rav and Rav Assi. As *Beit Yosef, O.Ḥ.* 690:18, notes:

> והאי פלוגתא דרב ורב אסי איכא לפרושי דלכתחלה היא אבל בדיעבד מודה רב אסי דיצא. ואפשר לפרושי דבדיעבד פליגי אבל לכתחלה מודה רב דבעשרה. ואפשר דבתרווייהו פליגי דלרב אפילו לכתחלה ביחיד ולרב אסי בדיעבד נמי לא יצא.

As a result of these different readings, even those who accept the position of Rav Assi may think that an individual who reads the *megillah* has nonetheless fulfilled the obligation. Conversely, those who accept the position of Rav may still think that one ideally should read in the presence of a quorum of ten. It is therefore the case that whether one concurs with Rav Assi or with Rav is not what determines whether or not one thinks that a quorum of ten is required for *megillah* reading.

213. Many commentators, following *Semag, Aseih Derabbanan* 4, claim that Behag holds according to the strictest interpretation of Rav Assi's position: one who reads without a quorum has not fulfilled the obligation. However, *Sefer Halakhot Gedolot, Hilkh. Megillah* 19, p.236, simply cites the Gemara word for word. It is unclear if this means that it follows R. Assi in an absolute sense; however, this position does seem to be held by other Ge'onim. See, for example, *Seder R. Amram Ga'on* (ed. Harpanas), *Seder Purim*:

> והקורא את המגילה בזמנה אינו קורא אותה אלא בעשרה, שכך אמר רבינו נתן ראש ישיבה לענין מגילה, אמר רב מגילה בזמנה קורין אותה אפילו ביחיד ושלא בזמנה בעשרה, רב אסי אמר בין בזמנה בין שלא בזמנה בעשרה, הוה עובדא וחש לה רב להא דרב אסי וכיון דרב קא חייש להא דרב אסי הלכה כרב אסי.

Others think that reading *megillah* with ten is ideal, but if this is impossible, then one may *bediavad* (after the fact) fulfill one's obligation by reading as an individual.[214] The vast majority of halakhic sources accept the position of Rav, that one may fulfill the obligation of reading *megillah* even without the presence of a *minyan*, provided that the *megillah* is being read on Purim itself.[215] Of these, however, most agree that it is preferable to read in the presence of a quorum if possible.[216]

See also *Teshuvot Ge'onim Kadmonim* #134, which rules similarly. Ramban, *Milḥamot Hashem* 3a, also states:

> מגילה כשם שהצבור חייב כך כל יחיד ויחיד חייב ויחיד שלא קרא צריך י׳ משום פרסומי ניסא ובין שיצאו הן או שלא יצאו קורין בי׳ להוציא היחיד משא״כ בשאר כל המצות ואידחיא לה דרב אסי מדרבי יוחנן דאמר הא ביחיד יצא והיינו יחיד ממש שאילו יחיד כצבור צבור הוא שקורין וסעד לדברי רבינו שאלמלא לא היה רב אסי מחמיר אלא למצוה לאהדורי אבי י׳ על מה חשש רב להא דרב אסי כיון דלא ס״ל כוותיה אלא ודאי לדברי רב אסי דיעבד נמי לא יצא ומש״ה חש לה רב להחמיר ואלמלא כן הוו אמרי בגמ׳ מצותה בי׳ אי נמי הוי מפרשי בהדיא לא מצא י׳ קורין אותה ביחיד הלכך אידחיא לה דרב אסי לגמרי מסוגיין דלקמן כדברי רבינו וכ״כ רבינו חננאל אבל רב שמעון בעל הלכות פסק כרב אסי.

214. *Sefer Hama'or* to B.T. *Meg.* 3a points out that within Tractate *Megillah* itself, the Mishnah (M. *Meg.* 4:3) lists those ritual activities that may not take place without the presence of ten, and reading *megillah* is not among them. Furthermore, if Rav Assi is actually arguing that *megillah* can only be read with a *minyan* present, why does the Gemara fail to cite the above *mishnah* as a contradiction to Rav Assi? Rather, argues Ba'al Hama'or, it must be the case that everyone agrees that it is permissible to read *megillah* individually; however, reading in the presence of ten is considered a superior form of the *mitsvah* and a more robust accomplishment of *pirsumei nissa*:

> תדע דהא לא תנינן לה במתני׳ דתנן אין פורסין על שמע ואין עוברין לפני התיבה וכו׳ מכדי במס׳ מגילה קיימין אמאי לא חשיב מקרא מגילה בהדי הנך דאינן פחות מי׳? ואמאי לא אותביה מינה לרב אסי? אלא לודאי דכ״ע אם קראה ביחיד יצא שלא אמרו אלא **להידור מצוה ולפרסומי ניסא**. דהכין קא אמרי׳ קורין אותה בי׳ ולא אמרי׳ אין קורין אותה אלא בי׳ שמעת מינה דמצוה לכתחלה למעבד הכי ולהדורי אבי י׳ ואי עבר וקראה ביחיי דצא.

215. These include Rif to B.T. *Meg.* 3a; *Tosafot* to B.T. *Meg.* 5a, s.v. *hava uvda*; R. Ḥananel (quoted in *Sefer Hayashar, Ḥelek Haḥiddushim* 405); and Ra'avyah, *Meg.* 560. *Beit Yosef, O.Ḥ.* 690:18, records a dispute over how to understand Rif's position.

216. Among the authorities who rule that *megillah* may be read without a *minyan* but that a *minyan* is preferable, there is a broad range in the emphasis on the importance of a *minyan*. Some simply say that having a quorum is ideal for the purpose of *pirsumei nissa* or cite Prov. 14:28, *berov am hadrat melekh*. Others emphasize that one is permitted to read by oneself only if it is truly impossible to find a quorum. Authorities who follow the position that a quorum is ideal but not necessary include: Rashi to B.T. *Meg.* 5a, s.v. *verav assi amar*; Ran on Rif to B.T. *Meg.* 3a (in Rif), s.v. *hava uvdah*; *Sefer*

This last position is codified in *Shulḥan Arukh*:

50. ***Shulḥan Arukh Oraḥ Ḥayyim 690:18*** R. Yosef Caro, Spain and Israel (1488–1575)	**שולחן ערוך אורח חיים סימן תרצ סעיף יח**
[To read] *megillah* on the fourteenth and the fifteenth, one must seek out ten, and if it is impossible [to read *megillah*] with ten, it is read individually.[217]	מגילה בי"ד ובט"ו צריך לחזור אחר עשרה, ואם אי אפשר בעשרה קורים אותם ביחיד.

One should attempt to find a quorum of ten for the purposes of *megillah* reading, but if that is not possible, the obligation may be fulfilled even as an individual.[218]

R. Caro does not discuss who may constitute a *minyan* for this purpose. However, R. Moshe Isserles (Rema), in his gloss on this passage in *Shulḥan Arukh,* addresses the issue:

Hama'or to B.T. *Meg.* 3a; *Tosefot Rid* to B.T. *Meg.* 5a; *Ḥiddushei Harashba* to B.T. *Meg.* 5a; *Or Zarua*, Vol. 2, *Hilkh. Megillah* 370, who thinks this is also the view of Rambam; Ra'avad to Rambam, *Hilkh. Megillah Vaḥanukkah* 1:7, who simply rules that if *megillah* is not read on the actual date, it is necessary to read with a quorum; *Maggid Mishneh* to Rambam, *Hilkh. Megillah Vaḥanukkah* 1:7; *Tur, O.Ḥ.* 690; and *Kitsur Sh. Ar.* 141. *Sefer Hayashar, Ḥelek Haḥiddushim* 405, rules similarly but frames it differently: the *mitsvah* ideally should be performed in the presence of ten, but the absence of a *minyan* does not exempt one from the obligation to read *Megillat Ester*.

217. A few lines later, at the end of this section, Rema notes that if an individual reads in a place where *megillah* has already been read with a quorum of ten, this counts as if he or she had read with a quorum, since *pirsumei nissa* has already taken place in that location.

218. *Sh. Ar., O.Ḥ.* 689:5, specifies that even without a quorum, one person may still fulfill the obligation of reading *megillah* on behalf of others. However, if everyone present knows how to read, then all should do so for themselves.

51. *Rema* *Oraḥ Ḥayyim 690:18*	**רמ"א אורח חיים סימן תרצ סעיף יח**
Gloss [Rema]: It is unclear [lit., one should doubt] whether women count toward the ten.[219]	הגה [רמ"א]: ויש להסתפק אם נשים מצטרפות לעשרה.

Interestingly, Rema does not clarify whether women actually do count toward a *minyan* for *megillah* reading, and it seems from his words that the inclusion of women in this quorum of ten is subject to debate.[220] This uncertainty might stem from the varied views that arose from the discussions of the nature of a woman's obligation in *megillah* reading.

Scholars before and after Rema grappled with this question. Given that it is preferable to read *megillah* in the presence of a *minyan*, it is necessary to clarify whether women might be included. As there is no clear statement one way or the other in the Mishnah or Talmud, many of the sources extrapolate from one of the few places in the Talmud that does treat the question of whether women and men may join together to create one unit for the performance of a religious ritual:

219. *Haggahot Asheri, Meg.* 1:6, referenced by Rema as the source for this ruling, cites *Or Zarua*, Vol. 2. *Hilkh. Megillah* 370, who is apparently discussing minors, rather than women:

> מיהו מספקא ליה שלא בזמנה אי בעינן שיהו כולן בני מצות כמו כל הטעונין עשרה או דלמא הואיל ואינו אלא פרסומי ניסא אף על פי שאינן בני מצות איכא פרסומי טובא.

Magen Avraham 690:24 notes this fact and references the disagreement on the matter recorded in *Tur, O.Ḥ.* 689. *Maḥatsit Hashekel* ad loc. makes essentially the same point, noting that although *Tur* does not rule unequivocally whether or not women count toward a quorum, it is not a case of *safek* (doubt). *Tur* actually states:

> ופירש"י שמוציאות לאנשים ידי חובתן ובה"ג כ' אף על גב שחייבות במקרא מגילה אינן מוציאות לאנשים וב"ה ז"ל כ' מסתברא כי היכי דנשים מזמנות לעצמן ואינן מצטרפות לברכת הזימון ה"נ אינן מצטרפות לי' לכתחלה.

It seems that *Tur* presents only one view regarding whether women count in a *minyan* unless one assumes that according to Rashi, women count in a *minyan*.

220. This phrase, *yesh lehistappek* (one should doubt), is extremely uncommon in Rema's code. It appears only two other times in a similar context, where Rema is unsure of what the law should be. See Rema to *Sh. Ar., Ḥ.M.* 69:5 and 253:20.

zimmun before Grace after Meals.[221] The following is a brief sample of the three major perspectives on this topic found in the Rishonim and subsequently taken up in contemporary sources.[222]

Women May Count Toward a *Minyan* for *Megillah* Reading

Some Rishonim argue that because women share an equal obligation with men in *megillah* reading, the *minyan* may comprise men and women. Me'iri presents this argument in his commentary on *Berakhot*, where he juxtaposes *megillah* reading to women's obligation in *zimmun*:[223]

52. *Beit Habeḥirah*
Berakhot 47b
R. Menaḥem ben Shelomo Me'iri, France (1249–1315)

בית הבחירה
מסכת ברכות מז:

Even though for *megillah* reading they [women] join in the [quorum of] ten and discharge the obligation of the many, in this [*megillah*] their obligation is equal.

ואף על פי שבמקרא מגילה מצטרפות לעשרה ומוציאות את הרבים בזה חיובם שוה.

Me'iri argues that women and men have identical obligations in *megillah* reading. The eligibility of a woman to count toward a *minyan* goes hand in hand with her eligibility to discharge the obligation of others.

221. The *sugya* in B.T. *Ber.* 20b discusses whether women may recite *birkat hamazon* on behalf of men, while B.T. *Ber.* 45b states that women and slaves may not join together due to concerns about licentiousness.

222. A more in-depth analyis is beyond the scope of this chapter. This summary is intended to ensure the reader understands the important issues on this topic.

223. He raises two possible reasons why *megillah* is different from *zimmun*. First, since women do not recite *brit* (covenant, i.e., circumcision) or *Torah*, they are not obligated as men are in *birkat hamazon*. (This is based on *Tosafot* to B.T. *Ber.* 20b, s.v. *nashim bevirkat hamazon.*) Some authorities rule that women should not recite the clauses in *birkat hamazon* that do not apply to them. Rema, *O.Ḥ.* 187:3, does in fact rule accordingly, but this position is generally not followed. *Magen Avraham, O.Ḥ.* 187:3, and *Mishnah Berurah, O.Ḥ.* 187:9, both discuss rationales for allowing women to recite these parts of the liturgy. In addition, Me'iri suggests that *zimmun* is a *davar shebikdushah*, and women are not counted in that type of *minyan*.

The quorum for *megillah* reading is one in which men and women can participate fully as equals.[224]

Ritva also thinks that women may count in a *minyan* for *megillah* reading, but his argument differs slightly from that of Me'iri. In Ritva's commentary, he explains why the concerns in the Talmud about licentiousness in the case of a mixed *zimmun* do not apply to *megillah* reading:

53. *Ḥiddushei Haritva*
Megillah 4a
R. Yom Tov ben Avraham Ashvili, Spain (1250–1330)

חידושי הריטב"א
מסכת מגילה ד:

Now that we have come to this point,[225] it is the law that they count [in the quorum for *megillah* reading], (and the fact that they do not count) in a *zimmun*, that case is different because there is greater inclusion, since there is a change in *birkat hamazon* for them – to add the blessing of *zimmun* for them [i.e., the *zimmun* is only recited because they are included in the group] – and there is a concern of licentiousness. But in this case there is no change in the reading of *megillah* nor

והשתא דאתית להכי הש ה"הן מצטרפות (והא דאין מצטרפות לזימון שאני התם דאיכא צירוף רבה שיש שינוי בברכת המזון בשבילן להוסיף ברכת הזימון בשבילן ואיכא למיחש לפריצותא, אבל הכא אין שינוי במקרא מגילה ולא בברכותיה בין יחיד לעשרה ולא חשיב צירוף כולי האי דניחוש לפריצותא.... הילכך הכא (ל) [ד]עשרה אינם אלא לפרסומי

224. In his comments to B.T. *Meg.* 4a, Me'iri quotes Provençal authorities who justify the rule that women may not count toward the quorum for *megillah* reading on the basis of a comparison to Grace After Meals:

ואף חכמי פרובינצא כתבו בחבוריהם שכמו שחייבות בברכת המזון ובזמון ואין מצטרפות לשלשה כך אין מצטרפות כאן לעשרה למי שמצריך בה עשרה וכל שכן שלא להוציא את האנשים.

However, later in his commentary to *Berakhot*, Me'iri notes that the reason given for prohibiting a mixed *zimmun* is that the potential for licentiousness is greater when food is involved (ומשום דשכיח פריצותא במזון). Thus, this is less of a concern in the case of *megillah* reading and would not cause one to exclude women from counting in the *minyan*.

225. That is, now that we have determined that women are obligated in *megillah* reading, and they may legally discharge the obligation of men, but they do not read in practice because it is dishonorable for the community.

in its blessings whether [it is read] by an individual or with [a quorum of] ten, and so it is not considered inclusion to the same extent, such that we should be concerned for licentiousness....[226] Therefore, in this case, where the ten are only for [the] general [purpose of] *pirsumei nissa* and the inclusion is not so significant, since [women] are obligated in the reading of *megillah* they are included. [I heard this] from the mouth of my teacher, may God protect him and keep him alive.[227]	ניסא בעלמא ולא חשיב צירוף כולי האי כיון דחייבות במקרא מגילה מצטרפות, מפי מורי נר"ו.

The experience of Grace after Meals is noticeably different depending on whether or not the group required for *zimmun* is present. Unless there are three people who can count toward the *zimmun*, each person recites Grace after Meals individually, without the additional responsive introduction. When ten eat together, the language of the *zimmun* changes. However, according to Ritva, no parallel changes occur in the case of *megillah* reading. It is preferable to have ten people present, but "only for...*pirsumei nissa*," publicizing the miracle. A *minyan* is not integral to the reading experience, and the form of both the reading and the blessings remain the same regardless of how many people are involved.[228] The presence of women is not noticeable in the same way as in a *zimmun*, and so the concern of licentiousness is mitigated. In light of this difference, Ritva argues that women are included in the *minyan* since they are fully obligated, and there is no reason to exclude them.

Perhaps the strongest formulation of this position is in the commentary of Ran, who rejects the comparison to Grace after Meals and

226. Ritva also points out that when a *zimmun* is created by three men, women may respond, since in that case, as well, their presence is not as noticeable.

227. R. Aharon Halevi (Ra'ah), Ritva's primary teacher.

228. The issue of how the blessings are affected by the presence of a quorum is discussed in the next section of this chapter.

argues that women may be included in a quorum for *megillah* reading based on their equal obligation in the *mitsvah*:

54. ***Ran on Rif Megillah 6b (in Rif)***

ר"ן על הרי"ף מסכת מגילה ו: (בדפי הרי"ף)

R. Nissim ben Re'uven of Gerona, Spain (1320–1380)

And there are those who say that even though women discharge the obligation [of others], they do not count in the quorum of ten according to those who require ten for the reading of the *megillah*, as we find in *Berakhot* [45b] regarding Grace after Meals that even though women may create a *zimmun* for themselves, nonetheless they do not join in the quorum of three to create a *zimmun* with men because of licentiousness. And this is impossible, for in that case [Grace after Meals] they cannot discharge the obligation of men with their blessings, but here how is it possible that they may discharge men's obligation to read [*megillah*] and [yet] may not join with them in a *minyan*?! Rather, they certainly join [the *minyan*]! And if you should say: Why are we not concerned here in this case about licentiousness as we are there [in the case of Grace after Meals]? It is possible to say that this [*megillah* reading] is different, because there is no change in the formula of the blessing as a result of [women's] joining [in the quorum]. But [in the case of] *zimmun*, where there is a change in the formula of *birkat hamazon*,[229]

וי"א שאע"פ שהן מוציאות אין מצטרפות למנין עשרה למאן דמצריך עשרה במקרא מגילה כדאשכן בברכות [דף מ"ה ב'] לענין בהמ"ז דאע"ג דנשים מזמנות לעצמן אפ"ה אין מצטרפות למנין ג' לזמן עם אנשים משום פריצותא. וא"א דהתם הוא שאינן מוציאות אנשים בברכתן אבל כאן היאך אפשר שמוציאות אנשים ידי קריאה ואין מצטרפות עמהם למנין?! אלא ודאי מצטרפות! וכי תימא ואמאי לא חיישינן הכא לפריצותא כי היכי דחיישינן התם? אפשר לומר דשאני הכא דע"י צירוף אין שנוי במטבע ברכה אבל זמון דהוי שנוי במטבע ברהמ"ז

229. As well as the additional introductory phrases added with a *zimmun*, if a woman were to lead and recite Grace after Meals, the version of her text might be different than a man's. See n232, above.

since [women's] inclusion alongside men is noticeable, there is concern for licentiousness. But here, in the case of *megillah*, [women's] inclusion is not noticeable, since the nature of [*megillah*] reading is the same for an individual as for the masses. Because their inclusion is not noticeable, it is permitted, which is also the case regarding *birkat hamazon*: when there are three aside from women, we include the women with them as well, since then the women's joining with them is not noticeable at all.	וכיון שניכר צירופן עם אנשים איכא למיחש לפריצותא. אבל כאן במגילה אין צירופן ניכר שכן דרך קריאתה ליחיד כרבים וכיון דאין צירופן ניכר מותר דדכותיה נמי בבהמ"ז היכא דאיכא תלתא בר מנשים מצטרפין אף הנשים עמהן משום דהשתא אין צירופן של נשים ניכר עמהם כלל.

Ran acknowledges that there are those who hold that women do not count in the *minyan* for *megillah* reading despite their equal obligation due to concerns regarding immoral sexual conduct, as is the case with *zimmun*. Ran makes the same point as Ritva (source #53) to refute this claim: the inclusion of women in the ritual of Grace after Meals is more apparent because it impacts the liturgical formula itself and, therefore, carries the risk of inappropriate behavior.[230] In contrast, the inclusion of women in *megillah* reading is less noticeable, similar to the situation when women join and respond to an all-male *zimmun* unit. Rather, Ran rules that a woman's obligation in *megillah* necessitates her inclusion in the quorum. He is dismissive of the idea that women could be fully obligated in reading *megillah*, to the extent that they may perform the *mitsvah* on behalf of men, and yet not be counted in the quorum.[231] Since men and women are equally obligated, the entire structure of the

230. The argument that the presence of women is less obvious because there is no change in the language of the ritual, thus avoiding the problem of inappropriate sexual behavior, seems formalistic at best. It does not make sense in light of the reality of human interaction. The next source presents a slightly different argument for why *megillah* reading is different from Grace after Meals and why women are counted in the *minyan*.

231. *Bayit Ḥadash, O.Ḥ.* 689, understands Ran as holding that women may not discharge men's obligation in *birkat hamazon*. He argues, against Ran, that many authorities would in fact say that *megillah* and Grace after Meals are parallel.

ritual must include men and women equally.[232] Women are obligated to read *megillah,* and they can fulfill the obligation on behalf of men; as such surely they may join with men in creating the ten.

Like Ran, *Nimmukei Yosef* also rejects the comparison to *zimmun* and counts women along with men in a *minyan* for *megillah* reading. His reasoning is much more straightforward:

55. ***Nimmukei Yosef***
Megillah 4a
R. Yosef ibn Ḥabib, Spain (fourteenth–fifteenth centuries)

נימוקי יוסף
מסכת מגילה ד.

So too, women recite the blessing, "On the reading of the *megillah,*" and discharge the obligation of men – for all those who are obligated in a matter may discharge the obligation of others – and join the [quorum of] ten in the reading of *megillah.* Even though with regard to *zimmun* we say that women create a *zimmun* for themselves, there [the reason] is because of licentiousness, since drunkenness is common at a meal, but the reading of *megillah* is before the meal, and there is no drunkenness.

וכן נמי נשים מברכות על מקרא מגילה ומוציאות האנשים שכל המחויב בדבר מוציא אחרים ידי חובתן ומצטרפות לעשרה במקרא מגילה. ואע"ג דלגבי זימון אמרינן נשים מזמנות לעצמן התם משום פריצותא דשכיח בסעודה שכרות אבל קריאת מגילה קודם סעודה היא וליכא שכרות.

Women are obligated to read *megillah,* may discharge the obligation of men, and may count in the quorum.[233] The concern for immorality in the case of *zimmun* is due to the possibility of drunken behavior at meals

232. Elsewhere (B.T. *Meg.* 4a), Ran quotes *Sefer Ha'ittur* (source #56, below), who argues that women may not count in a quorum for *megillah* reading, just as they may not count for *zimmun.*

233. The concern over *peritsut* in the case of *zimmun* is not due to the general idea that a mixed group in a ritual setting poses a problem, but rather that the mixed meal attended by both men and women, and the frivolity that accompanies it, should be avoided. *Nimmukei Yosef* thinks that both variables must be present for *peritsut* to be a concern: a mixed group and frivolous behavior, such as drunkenness.

but since *megillah* reading takes place before the festive meal, this is not a relevant issue, and so *Nimmukei Yosef* allows women to join with men for the quorum of *megillah* reading.

In summary, authorities present two primary arguments to support the idea that women count together with men in a *minyan* for *megillah* reading. First, because women share the same obligation as men in *megillah* reading, the quorum that is assembled for this purpose may include women. Second, concerns that a mixed-gender quorum leads to licentiousness are misplaced because *megillah* reading differs substantially from Grace after Meals.

Women May Not Count Toward a *Minyan* for *Megillah* Reading

Some authorities argue that a mixed-gender quorum is not acceptable and that only a group of ten men may comprise the *minyan* for *megillah* reading.[234] Authorities who do not think that women may count toward a quorum generally rely on one or both of the following rationales: (1) a comparison with Grace after Meals; that is, just as women may form their own *zimmum* but may not join together with men due to concerns about inappropriate behavior, so, too, in the case of *megillah* reading; and (2) the definition of a *minyan* as a group of ten men; thus, by definition women cannot count toward a quorum for the purpose of *megillah* reading.[235]

Sefer Ha'ittur, a twelfth-century Provençal work, prohibits women from joining men in a quorum for *megillah* reading based on a comparison to Grace after Meals:

---

234. This is separate from the question of whether a woman may discharge a man's obligation. Even if a man is reading *megillah* for women, the reading could be considered problematic according to some authorities if he is the only man present.

235. The broader question of whether women may ever count in a quorum for the purpose of any *mitsvah* is beyond the scope of this chapter. It suffices to note that there is debate over a woman's inclusion in a quorum for a number of *mitsvot*. For example, many authorities agree that for the purposes of martyrdom and *kiddush Hashem*, women do count toward a quorum. For a discussion of this issue and source references, see R. Aryeh Frimer, "Women and Minyan," *Tradition* 23:4 (Summer 1988): 54–77.

56. ***Sefer Ha'ittur***
Aseret Hadibberot
Laws of Megillah 110a
R. Yitsḥak ben Abba Mari, Provence (1122–1193)

ספר העיטור
עשרת הדיברות
הלכות מגילה דף קי.

And R. Yehoshua b. Levi says that women are obligated in the reading of *megillah,* for they too were part of the same miracle. And it makes sense that just as women create a *zimmun* [for themselves] but do not join in [a quorum of men] for Grace after Meals, here too [in the case of *megillah*] they do not join [a group of men] *lekhatḥillah* (in the first place).

ואריב"ל נשים חייבות במקרא מגילה שאף הן היו באותו הנס. ומסתברא כי היכי דנשים מזמנות ואין מצטרפות לברהמ"ז ה"נ אין מצטרפות לכתחלה.

According to Ba'al Ha'ittur, just as women are obligated in Grace after Meals and may thus convene their own *zimmun* but cannot be counted toward a *zimmun* with men, so too in the case of *megillah* reading, women cannot count in the quorum even though they are obligated.[236] Unlike the authorities cited above, he seems to suggest that being obligated in a *mitsvah* does not necessarily correlate with counting in the accompanying ritual quorum. However, his use of the term *lekhatḥillah* implies that a *minyan* that included women would count *bediavad* (after the fact).[237] Ba'al Ha'ittur does not offer a reason why women cannot be included in

236. See *Sefer Ha'ittur, Hilkh. Megillah* 113b, where Ba'al Ha'ittur also quotes the Tosefta and Behag's explanation that women are obligated only to hear *megillah.*

237. However, *Shiltei Gibborim,* in Rif to B.T. *Megillah* 2b, quotes Ba'al Ha'ittur without the word *lekhatḥillah* (or perhaps he, too, is referring to *Sefer Hahashlamah,* as suggested in *Sefer Hamikhtam* [ed. 1904]):

וב"ה כתב כי היכי דנשים מזמנות לעצמן ואינן מצטרפות לברכת הזימון ה"נ אמרינן אינן מצטרפות לעשרה.

Possibly in his view there is a difference between a mixed-gender ten and a unit made up solely of women. However, Ran and *Tur, O.Ḥ.* 689, also quoting Ba'al Ha'ittur, include the word *lekhatḥillah.*

One does not know if Ba'al Ha'ittur intends only that one who reads with women in such a *minyan* need not repeat the reading, or that when the situation arose where the only *minyan* one could assemble included women, then it is permissible to read.

this quorum nor why this might be the case only *a priori*. Other sources, however, such as the opposing view presented above by Ran, refer to the potential for licentiousness when men and women come together in this way. If this concern underlies Ba'al Ha'ittur's ruling, it could explain why he thinks that a *minyan* including women would count retroactively.[238] Ideally, he does not want women and men to mix for religious ritual out of concern for possible sexual indiscretion; however, if such a situation did occur, the *megillah* would have been read legally in the presence of a quorum.

In contrast, *Sefer Hame'orot* suggests that licentiousness is a potential concern that may result in women not being included in a quorum. However, he ultimately rejects this idea in favor of a more straightforward approach as to why a woman is not counted.

---

238. *Baḥ, O.Ḥ.* 689:3, argues that Ba'al Ha'ittur himself thinks this way. He understands Ba'al Ha'ittur to hold that women may discharge the obligation of men, both in the case of *megillah* reading and in the case of *birkat hamazon*, but that it is not permitted for them to count *lekhatḥillah* toward the *minyan*, due to the concern of licentiousness:

> נראה מבואר דבעל העיטור סובר כרש״י דנשים מוציאות לאנשים אלא שהחמיר בצירוף ונראה דסבירא ליה לבעל העיטור כהראב״ד (בהשגותיו על המאור ברכות יב א אות א) שהביא רבינו לעיל בסימן קפ״ו (עמ׳ תסז-תסח) דנשים מוציאות לאנשים בברכת המזון ואפילו הכי קיימא לן דמזמנות לעצמן ואינן מצטרפות עם האנשים בזימון דהיינו בשני אנשים ואשה אחת ומשכחת לה דאשה מוציאה לאנשים בברכת המזון היכא דאיכא שלשה אנשים ואשה אחת דהאנשים מצטרפים לזימון והאשה יכולה להוציא לאנשים בברכת המזון דעיקר קפידא בצירוף משום פריצותא והכא נמי בקריאת המגילה אף על פי דאשה מוציאה לאנשים אפילו הכי אינן מצטרפות לעשרה לכתחלה משום פריצותא אלא בעינן עשרה אנשים בלא נשים והר״ן ז״ל השיג על דברי בעל העיטור ואמר דשאני התם שאינן מוציאות לאנשים בברכתן וכו׳ ונראה שהוא סובר עיקר כאינך גאונים דאשה אינה מוציאה לאנשים בברכת המזון ואין זו השגה כיון דיש דעות שמוציאה לאנשים כדפרישית.

See also *Peri Ḥadash* 690 (end). R. Henkin, *Responsa Benei Banim* 3:7, concurs with this reading as well and, therefore, thinks that Ba'al Ha'ittur would support an all-female quorum:

> ופרוש לכתחילה הוא שמעיקר הדין מועילות לפרסומא ניסא ולכן בדיעבד אם הצטרפו אנשים ונשים לעשרה יצאו ידי חובתם ורק מטעם פריצות אין לעשות כן ולפי זה בעשר נשים שקוראות לעצמן דליכא פריצותא מותר גם לכתחילה אטו בצרוף אנשים ונשים איכא פרסומא ניסא ובנשים לבדן ליכא פרסומא ניסא.

57. ***Sefer Hame'orot*** **ספר המאורות**
Megillah 5a **מסכת מגילה ה.**
R. Meir ben Shimon Hame'ili, France (second half of the thirteenth century)

And it seems [reasonable] to say that although a woman is fit to discharge a man's obligation in *megillah* reading, it is not proper for her to complete the [quorum of] ten. For wherever ten is needed, men specifically are needed.[239] Furthermore, there is [a concern for] licentiousness, as we say regarding *zimmun* that women and slaves may not create a *zimmun* [together]. But one may reject this.	ונראה לומר שאף על פי שאשה כשירה להוציא את האיש ממקרא מגלה, שאין ראוי להשלים בה עשרה, דהיכא דבעינן עשרה, אנשים דוקא בעינן. ועוד דמשום פריצותא איכא, כדאמרינן גבי זימון דנשים ועבדים אין מזמנין. ואפשר לדחות זה.

At the end of this comment, *Sefer Hame'orot* raises the idea that concerns over the possibility of inappropriate sexual behavior might be a reason to prohibit a mixed quorum, but he rejects this suggestion.[240] *Sefer Hame'orot* also rebuffs the idea, strongly voiced by Ran, that women's

239. See also *Sefer Kol Bo* 45 (source #17, above), which includes an almost identical statement, as well as the parallel position recorded in *Orḥot Ḥayyim, Hilkh. Megillah Ufurim* 2. See *Minḥat Yitsḥak* 3:53 for a contemporary *posek* who voices a similar view.

240. In the commentary to B.T. *Meg.* 19b, he explains:

ואפשר לומר דדוקא בעבדים ונשים אמרינן בזמון דחיישנן לפריצותא כדאמרין בעלמא דעבדים פרוצים הם אבל אנשי אחריני לא אמרין הכי והילכך אפילו במגילה מוציאות את האנשים.

Interestingly, *Sefer Hame'orot* assumes that if *peritsut* were an issue, then it should also be a factor when fulfilling the *mitsvah* on behalf of the other gender, for this act is also a halakhic joining together. In his comments to B.T. *Ber.* 45a, *Sefer Hame'orot* provides a much longer explanation of the same idea and there, too, makes the interesting statement that *peritsut* cannot be an issue as men regularly perform *mitsvot* on behalf of women:

והיכא דהוו עשרה קטנים ואחד גדול עמהם וכן נשים נראה לומר דהגדול מברך "נברך אלקינו" בשבילם דכיון שהוא אכל עמהן דחייב בברכת המזון יכול לברך בשבילם וכן יכול להציאם מברכת הזמון. וליכא משום פריצות הגדול עם הנשים דדוקא עבדים שהם פרוצים בעריות... אבל בבני חורין לא אמרינן הכי. ומעשים בכל יום שהאנשים מוציאין הנשים מקריאת מגילה ומקידוש והבדלה ומברכת המזון כשאכל עמהן.

equal obligation and their eligibility to discharge men's obligation necessarily correlates with their inclusion in the *minyan*. In this view, only men may count for the quorum, as in all other halakhic situations that call for a quorum of ten.[241] In other words, a *minyan* is by definition exclusively male, and this fact is not dependent on the nature of the obligation itself. *Sefer Hame'orot* represents a group of authorities who feel that the definition of who counts in a *minyan* does not change even in a case where women are equally obligated.[242]

Later sources, including the law codes,[243] remain divided on

---

241. The fact that this idea is voiced in *Sefer Hame'orot* is strange, for in his comments on B.T. *Ber.* 45a regarding women and *zimmun*, he states:

ומכל מקום נראה שלא למחות בידם מלזמן בשם, כיון שלא הוזכר דין זה בגמרא.

Possibly in his view there is a difference between a mixed-gender ten and a unit made up solely of women. See also n58 and n70, above, for a better understanding of *Sefer Hame'orot*.

242. These authorities simply state that women do not count in a *minyan*. They do not voice an opinion on whether women must hear the *megillah* reading in the presence of a male quorum. *Shibbolei Haleket*, a thirteenth-century Italian halakhist, in *Inyan Purim* #195, argues that women are obligated in *megillah* but certainly do not need to take part in a reading at which a *minyan* is present. The "custom in all of Israel," he states, is for men to read for their households at home:

והלא כל הנשים חייבות במקרא מגילה וכי בעשרה קורין אותה להן אלא כל אדם משמיע אותה לאנשי ביתו בכל ברכותיה ביחיד ומוציאין ידי חובתן ביום ובלילה שאף הן היו באותו הנס וחייבות במקרא מגילה אע"פ שהוא מצוות עשה שהזמן גרמא וכן מנהג בכל ישראל.

This view is echoed in contemporary sources by R. Mordekhai Ya'akov Breish, *Ḥelkat Ya'akov, O.Ḥ* 232. He addresses the question of whether women need to hear *megillah* read with a quorum and explains why they do not:

ורובם ככולם פוסקים דקריאה בציבור רק משום פרסומי ניסא ומשום רוב עם הדרת מלך ורק לכתחילה, אם כן כיון דבנשים שייך הא דכל כבודה בת מלך פנימה.... ואף דכמה נשים דילן הולכין לביהמ"ד לשמוע מקרא מגילה לא שייך לומר דשוויוהו עלייהו חובה, כמו שמבואר באחרונים לענין שופר בסימן תקפ"ט גבי אשה, והחילוק מובן מאליו. מסקנא דמילתא דאין שום עדיפותא לנשים לילך לביהמ"ד לשמוע מקרא מגילה.

R. Schachter, whose ruling that women should not read *megillah* is quoted above (source #41), also notes that women may not count toward a quorum. However, he concludes that it is best to be sure that ten men are present:

וברמ"א להל' פורים (סי' תר"צ סי"ח, ועיי"ש במג"א ס"ק כ"ד ע"ש הטור לסי' תרפ"ט) הביא הדבר הזה בתורת ספק מבלי להכריעו, ואף דקיי"ל דמגילה בזמנה נקראת אפילו ביחיד, מכ"מ לכתחילה, צריך לחזור אחר עשרה.

243. Rambam does not discuss this issue at all although it seems from *Hilkh. Megillah* 1:4

whether women may be included in a quorum for *megillah* reading. *Tur* rules in accordance with the position of *Sefer Ha'ittur*[244] (source #56). R. Yosef Caro does not rule on this matter in *Shulḥan Arukh*, but in his larger compendium *Beit Yosef*, he comments on *Tur*'s citation of *Sefer Ha'ittur*, noting the opposing view of Ran, who thinks that women must surely count in the *minyan*.[245] As quoted above, Rema is unsure whether or not women may be counted toward a quorum for this *mitsvah*.[246] *Mishnah Berurah* explains Rema's uncertainty by pointing out that the quorum is necessary "only for *pirsumei nissa*"; as a result, one might argue that women do count.[247] *Arukh Hashulḥan*, like Rema, argues that it is "doubtful" whether women are included in the *minyan*; he goes on to say that it appears to him that women should not be counted with men.[248]

Women May Form an All-Female Quorum for *Megillah* Reading

It is important to note that those Rishonim who rule that women do not count toward a quorum with men due to concern for potential impropriety are not necessarily excluding the possibility of an all-female quorum.[249] These Rishonim might permit women to constitute their own

---

that he does not think a quorum is required for anyone when the *megillah* is read in its proper time.

244. *Tur, O.Ḥ.* 689. However, as is discussed below, R. Henkin (source #60) points out that even this position implies that women technically do count in a quorum for the purpose of *pirsumei nissa*, but that the "external" concern about licentiousness or immodesty makes a mixed group unacceptable. See n219, above, for *Magen Avraham*'s understanding of *Tur*.

245. *Beit Yosef, O.Ḥ.* 689:2.

246. Although R. David Auerbach, R. Shlomo Zalman's nephew, in his book *Halikhot Beitah*, p. 69, writes that Rema surely accepted an all-women's quorum:

> ומה שנסתפק הרמ"א בס' תרצ סעי' יח אם נשים מצטרפות למנין עשרה בקריאת המגילה, ומשמע מדבריו דכל הספק הוא רק בנוגע להצטרפותן עם אנשים אבל לעצמן דינם כקורא בעשרה (הן לענין קריאה בזמנה והן לענין קריאה שלא בזמנה או בפורים המשולש).

See also *Responsa Tsits Eliezer* 13:73 (source #59, below), who reads the Rema similarly.

247. *Mishnah Berurah, O.Ḥ.* 690:63.

248. *Arukh Hashulḥan, O.Ḥ.* 690:25.

249. Clearly those Rishonim who allow a mixed quorum would also permit an all-female group to constitute the quorum, based on the same reasoning.

quorum, as long as only women are present. This view that ten women may create a quorum for *megillah* reading is voiced by a number of contemporary authorities.

Perhaps the ultimate test case for the possibility of a women's quorum for *megillah* reading is when the date of Purim falls on Shabbat and the *megillah* is not read "in its proper time."[250] In *Megillah* 5b (source #49, above), both Rav and Rav Assi agree that when *megillah* is read early, it must be read in the presence of ten.[251] A common explanation for this requirement is that a reading on a date other than Purim itself does not have the same degree of *pirsumei nissa* as when the *megillah* is read on the day the miracle actually happened. Thus, the Purim story must be heard by a significant group to ensure the proper publicizing of the miracle.[252] Halakhic decisors must contend with the question of whether a quorum of women is sufficient for this purpose or whether the additional stringency of reading *megillah* early means that the presence of ten men is required for a woman to fulfill her obligation.

R. Avraham Yeshayah Karelitz, known as *Ḥazon Ish*, addressed this issue and gave a list of reasons to be lenient and permit ten women to gather for a *megillah* reading, even when the reading occurs a day early:

250. For cities not surrounded by walls, if the fourteenth of *Adar* fell on Shabbat, then Purim was celebrated (and the *megillah* was read) on the previous day, Friday the thirteenth. (However, with the later acceptance of the standarized calendar, the fourteenth can no longer fall on Shabbat.) In Jerusalem, however, if the fifteenth falls on Shabbat, then there is a *Purim Meshullash* (three-day Purim), and the various *mitsvot* of Purim are spread over a three-day period. In this case, the *megillah* is read on Friday the fourteenth, as is the case in non-walled cities.

251. As discussed in *Ḥazon Ish* (source #58, below), it is nevertheless true that not all Rishonim rule that a quorum is required for reading *megillah*, even in this case.

252. See Rashi to B.T. *Meg.* 5a, s.v. *shelo bizmannah.*

58. *Ḥazon Ish*
Laws of Megillah 155:2

חזון איש הלכות מגילה
סימן קנה סעיף קטן ב

R. Avraham Yeshayah Karelitz, Lithuania and Israel (1878–1953)

Regarding the matter of a women's reading with ten [when the fourteenth falls on Shabbat in a walled city[253]] there are many sides [i.e., reasons] to be lenient.

לענין קריאת נשים בעשרה [למוקפין חל י"ד בשבת] יש הרבה צדדין להקל.

1) The opinion of Rashi, Ra'avad, Razah, and Rosh that the law [requiring] ten does not prevent [one from reading] even when it is not in its proper time.

א) דעת רש"י הראב"ד והרז"ה והרא"ש, שאין דין עשרה לעיכובא אפי' שלא בזמנו.

2) From the words of Rambam, [*Hilkh. Megillah*] 1:7, it is explained that "not in its time" as discussed in the Gemara means outside of the fourteenth or fifteenth. However, people [who live in a place where *megillah* is read on the] fifteenth [when] they read on the fourteenth, there is effective *pirsumei nissa,* since it is the time when most of the world reads....

ב) מדברי הר"מ פ"א ה"ז מבואר דשלא בזמנו הנאמר בגמ' אינו אלא חוץ מי"ד וט"ו, אבל בני חמיסר הקוראין בארביסר איכא פרסומא טובא כיון שהוא זמן קריאה לרוב העולם....

3) *Or Zarua* doubts whether those who are not obligated may be included in the [quorum of] ten (that is, minors), meaning that women are certainly included among the ten, since they are obligated and there is *pirsumei nissa*.... There is no justification for placing conditions on *pirsumei nissa* or for excluding women.

ג) באו"ז מסתפק בלאו בני חיובא אי הוו בכלל עשרה [והיינו קטנים] ומשמע דנשים ודאי הוו בכלל עשרה כיון דבני חיובא נינהו ואיכא פרסומא ניסא.... אין מקום לקבוע בפרסומא ניסא תנאים ולמעוטי נשים.

253. It should read "when ... the fifteenth falls on Shabbat."

4) According to what Rema wrote, that an individual who did not hear [the *megillah*] does not need [a quorum of] ten, since [the *megillah*] was already publicized in the public reading [with] ten, it appears that this is the law even "not in its time." And all that has been discussed [the problem of women's counting in a *minyan*] falls in the pit [i.e., is not a problem].[254]	ד) למש"כ הרמ"א דיחיד שלא שמע א"צ עשרה כיון דכבר נתפרסם בקריאת עשרה בציבור, נראה דגם שלא בזמנו הדין כן, ונפל בבירא כל הנידון.

R. Karelitz presents two approaches to permitting a group of ten women to read *megillah*, even when the reading is taking place a day early.[255] The first approach includes three of his four arguments that demonstrate that it is not strictly necessary to have a quorum present. According to some, the *megillah* can be read without a quorum even when it is read outside its proper time. In addition, it may be that reading in a walled city on the fourteenth instead of the fifteenth is, in fact, still considered *bizmano* (in its proper time), since this is the date on which most communities read *Megillat Ester*. If this is the case, then a quorum would not be required. Finally, he explains in section 4 that if an individual is in a community where a group has already read with a *minyan*, he or she can read individually without a *minyan*, since the miracle has already been publicized. All of these reasons support the idea that a women's reading does not need a quorum of ten no matter when it occurs. R. Karelitz closes by noting that this fourth argument, that a quorum is not required in a community where *megillah* has already been read publicly, circumvents the entire problem. As a result, one does not need to address the question of whether women count toward the quorum of ten, as a quorum is never strictly necessary if the *megillah* has already been read publicly.

254. This phrase is a play on Talmudic language. See, for instance, B.T. *Ber.* 56a; and B.T. *Shab.* 66b.

255. It is not entirely clear from the language of *Ḥazon Ish* who is reading the *megillah* to these women. Is it a man, or are the women reading for themselves? R. Henkin, *Responsa Benei Banim* 3:7, argues that they are reading for themselves:

ולא כתב קריאה לנשים בלמ"ד משמע שמיירי בקריאה של נשים לעצמן שלא כהקרבן נתנאל והמשנה ברורה הנ"ל.

His argument in section 3 presents a second approach that permits women to constitute a quorum and is quoted by later authorities. According to R. Karelitz, because women are obligated in the reading of *megillah,* they may be included in the ten required to form a quorum. The quorum is necessary specifically for the purpose of *pirsumei nissa,* and because women are included in the obligation to publicize the miracle, they must count as well. In this way R. Karelitz proves that although a quorum of ten may not be required at a reading for women, ten women are permitted to read together if a quorum is required.

R. Eliezer Waldenberg, a prominent twentieth-century halakhic decisor who lived in Jerusalem, also rules that women may constitute their own quorum for *megillah* reading even in the case of *Purim Meshullash* when the *megillah* is read a day early.[256] Whereas *Ḥazon Ish* cites several reasons why a quorum might not be necessary, R. Waldenberg assumes that a women's reading should take place in the presence of ten and demonstrates that women count for this quorum:

59. ***Responsa Tsits Eliezer 13:73*** R. Eliezer Waldenberg, Israel (1915–2006)	**שו"ת ציץ אליעזר** **חלק יג סימן עג**
9 Adar 5737 (February 27, 1977), Jerusalem.	ט' אדר תשל"ז, ירושלים.
[With regard to] what we asked: [given that] at the present moment, here in Jerusalem, we are observing *Purim Meshullash* and the *megillah* is read on Friday the fourteenth [of *Adar*], such that we need ten for reading the *megillah,* is it possible to read for women at home if there are ten of them, or do they specifically need to go to the synagogue where there are ten men in order to hear the *megillah*	מה ששאלנו בהשתא שעבדינן בפעיה"ק ת"ו פורים משולש ואת המגילה קורין ביום ועש"ק י"ד בו, שצריכים עשרה לקריאת המגילה, אם יכולים לקרוא לנשים בבית כשהן עשרה או שצריכות ללכת דוקא בביהכ"נ במקום שנמצאים עשרה גברים ולשמוע שם קריאת המגילה.

256. See n250, above.

כי קשה הדבר לעזוב את ביתן.

reading there? For it is a difficult matter [for the women] to leave their homes.

הנה לדעתי פשוט שיכולים לקרוא לפניהן כשהן עשרה, ולא צריכים שיהיו עשרה גברים, דהא גם הנה חייבות במקרא מגילה, ולכן יכולות שפיר להצטרף לעשרה בפני עצמן ולקרוא לפניהן.... דכוונת הרמ״א וכן המג״א היא רק לענין אם יכולות להצטרף לעשרה יחד עם אנשים... אבל שיקראו ויצטרפו לעצמן כו״ע מודו שיכולות דומיא דזימון שמזמנות מיהת לעצמן.... ועוד יעוין... דגם בנשים חשיב פרסום, דהרי התם טעמא דבעינן עשרה הוא משום פירסומא ניסא....

In my opinion, it is obvious that they may read for the women [at home] when they are ten, and there do not need to be ten men [present]. For the women, too, are obligated in *megillah* reading, and thus they can certainly join together on their own as [a quorum of] ten and have [the *megillah*] read to them.... For the intention of Rema and also *Magen Avraham* is just regarding whether they may join together with men to form [a quorum of] ten... but everyone agrees that they may join together by themselves and read, as in the case of *zimmun*, which they may in any case do for themselves.... See also [various sources][257]... [who argue] that even among women it is considered publicizing,

257. He cites R. Ya'akov Algazi, *Ḥug Ha'arets* 3, who rules that women are considered a quorum of ten and provides proof from a passage in B.T. *Pesaḥ.* 91a. There the Gemara discusses the rule presented in the Mishnah that the *Pesaḥ* offering is not slaughtered on behalf of an individual. The Gemara argues that it may, however, be slaughtered on behalf of a group of women, who are considered to be a legitimate group for this purpose, not merely a collection of individuals:

> ומצאתי בקונטרס הנקרא בשם חוג הארץ להמהר״י אלגזי ז״ל, שביאר ופסק בכאמור באר היטב, וז״ל באות ג: ונראה לע״ד פשוט שאם יהיה בבית י׳ נשים שנתקבצו שם לשמוע מקרא מגילה מהבעל הבית שפיר מקרי בי׳ וקורא להן מקרא מגילה בברכות, וראיה לזה מההיא דפסחים פ׳ האשה ד׳ צ״א א׳ רמי ליה רב עוקבא וכו׳ לרבא מי אר״י אין שוחטין את הפסח על היחיד ורמינהי אשה בראשון שוחטין עליה בפני עצמה ובב׳ עושים אותה טפלה לאחרים דברי ר״י, א״ל לא תימא בפני עצמה אלא אימא בפני עצמן, ומי עבדינן חבורה שכולה נשים והתנן אין עושים חבורת נשים ועבדים וקטנים מאי לאו נשים לחודייהו ועבדים לחודייהו, לא נשים ועבדים וקטנים, נשים ועבדים משום פריצותא, הנה מפורש יוצא דאע״ג דאין שוחטין הפסח על היחיד כל שהן חבורת נשים לא הוו יחיד ושוחטים והכא נמי פרסומי ניסא בעשרה מהן סגי שפיר, וזה פשוט עכ״ל.

And cites as well *Peri Ḥadash* 690 (end); and *Responsa Rav Pe'alim*, Vol. 2, *O.Ḥ.* #62.

for in that case the reason that ten are required is because of *pirsumei nissa*….

Therefore it is clear and simple as a matter of law that women, even *lekhatḥillah*, may gather [a group of] ten women in their homes in order to hear *megillah* reading and recite the blessings…. It is often the case that when one aims to be stringent in this matter, it turns out to be a stringency that leads people to be lenient; for women regretfully leave their children and little ones home alone, and if they bring them along to synagogue, even the very little ones, they disturb the masses from hearing the reading of *megillah*. Specifically [in this case], as stated [above], the issue is clear that women may, even *lekhatḥillah*, hear *megillah* reading among themselves and recite the blessings with [a quorum of] ten, without any doubt whatsoever.

על כן ברור ופשוט הדבר לדינא שיכולות הנשים אפילו לכתחילה לקבץ לעצמן עשר נשים בביתן לשמוע מקרא מגילה ולברך הברכות.... ובהרבה פעמים הבא להחמיר בזה הוא למעשה חומרא דאתי לידי קולא, דעוזבות הנשים ילדיהם הקטנים בבית לבד מתוך צער, ואם מביאות אתן גם את הקטני קטנים לביהכ"נ מפריעים את הרבים מלשמוע קריאת המגילה. ובפרט דכאמור הדבר ברור שיכולות לשמוע אפילו לכתחילה מקרא מגילה בעשרה בפני עצמן ולברך הברכות בלי כל חשש כלל ועיקר.

Even in the case of *Purim Meshullash*, when a quorum of ten is certainly required for *megillah* reading, R. Waldenberg states unequivocally that ten women may form their own quorum. While he notes that authorities such as Rema question whether women may be counted in the quorum, he explains that this applies only to a mixed group that includes men and women.[258] According to R. Waldenberg, once the concern of licentiousness is removed, everyone agrees that women may form their own quorum, as is the case with *zimmun*.[259] R. Waldenberg goes on to argue that the purpose of having ten people present for *megillah* reading is *pirsumei nissa*, which is accomplished just as well

258. See n270, below, where R. Lichtenstein disagrees with this reading of Rema.

259. He references other Aḥaronim, such as *Ḥazon Ish* (source #58, above) and R. Ḥayyim Sonnenfeld, *Responsa Shalmat Ḥayyim* 1:101, as support for this position.

with a group of women as with a group of men.[260] He even asserts that requiring women to come to synagogue to hear the *megillah* has the potential to do more harm than good, as they are then forced to choose between leaving their young children at home and bringing them to synagogue and risking the possibility that the children may disrupt the reading. Instead, he recommends convening a *megillah* reading specifically for women on *Purim Meshullash*, provided that at least ten of them are present.

R. Yehuda Henkin also addresses the question of reading *megillah* on *Purim Meshullash*, and he, too, concludes that it is permissible for ten women to convene their own quorum:

60. *Responsa Benei Banim* *Vol. 3, #7*

שו"ת בני בנים חלק ג סימן ז

R. Yehuda Henkin, United States and Israel (1945–)

In *Benei Banim* Vol. 2, #10, I showed that according to all the Rishonim it is permissible for a woman to read *megillah* for a congregation of women.... Now I have been asked about *Purim Meshullash* here in Jerusalem...which we move earlier this year to read [*megillah*] on Friday, the fourteenth of *Adar*:.... Do we specifically need men, or is a congregation of women also sufficient [for *megillah* reading]? Even according to the opinion of *Mishnah Berurah*, that a woman may not discharge the obligation of a congregation of women, it is relevant in a case where a man reads to discharge the obligation of women. Also, it is the custom in most synagogues to

בבני בנים חלק ב' סימן י' הראיתי שלדעת כל הראשונים מותר לאשה לקרוא המגילה לצבור נשים.... כעת נשאלתי אודות פורים משולש פה ירושלים... שמקדימים השנה לקרוא בערב שבת בי"ד אדר.... האם צריכים אנשים דוקא או סגי גם בצבור נשים. ואפילו לדעת המשנה ברורה שאשה לא תוציא צבור נשים משכחת לן באיש הקורא להוציא נשים וכן המנהג ברוב בתי הכנסת לערוך קריאה שניה לנשים גם בפורים משולש ולכן דין זה הוא נחוץ לרבים.

260. R. Waldenberg explains in the name of R. Sonnenfeld that the quorum of ten required to recite Grace after Meals with God's name is of a different nature. In that case, it is for the purpose of "respect for God's name" and is like all other instances in which a male *minyan* is necessary.

hold a second reading for women, even on *Purim Meshullash*, and therefore this law is necessary for many people.

I responded that [a *megillah* reading] works with ten women. The origin of the matter is in the disagreement among Rishonim about women's counting toward [the quorum of] ten for the reading of *megillah*.... However, there are those [Rishonim] who permitted women to join with men [in a quorum] to read *megillah*... while other Rishonim only forbid combining women and men for [a quorum of] ten, but when ten women read for themselves even they will admit that the reading of *megillah* is similar to *zimmun*, where only the combination [of men and women together] is prohibited, but men may create a *zimmun* for themselves and women for themselves. This is the opinion of *Sefer Ha'ittur*.... And see *Peri Ḥadash* #690 (end), who wrote that the primary [ruling] is like Ba'al Ha'ittur: the reason that they do not join together is because of licentiousness. [What is incorrect is] only what he wrote that according to Behag women do not discharge the obligation of men and all the more so[261] they do not join together [to form a quorum]. But this is not "all the more so" according to the opinion of Ran mentioned above, and indeed the sages of Provence [quoted] in Me'iri wrote that the "all the more so" is [actually] the

והשבתי שמועיל בי' נשים. תחילת דבר במחלוקת ראשונים בצרוף נשים לעשרה בקריאת המגילה.... ברם יש שהתירו צרוף נשים עם גברים לקריאת המגילה... ולעוד ראשונים לא נאסר אלא לצרף נשים עם אנשים לעשרה אבל כשעשר נשים קוראות לעצמן גם הם יודו שהרי דימו קריאת המגילה לזימון ושם רק הצרוף אסור ואילו אנשים מזמנים לעצמם ונשים לעצמן. כן היא דעת ספר העיטור.... ועיין בפרי חדש בסוף סימן תר"צ שכתב שהעיקר כבעל העיטור שהטעם שאינן מצטרפות הוא משום פריצותא, ורק מה שכתב שלדעת בה"ג שאינן מוציאות את הגברים כל שכן שאינן מצטרפות, אין זה כל שכן לפי דעת הר"ן הנ"ל והרי חכמי פרובינצא שבמאירי כתבו שהכל שכן הוא להפך. ובדעת בה"ג בודאי אין לאמר כל שכן כי נשים אינן חייבות בקריאה ולכן אינן מוציאות אנשים ומכל מקום כיון שחייבות לשמוע מצטרפות לעשרה לשמוע.

261. *Peri Ḥadash* does not actually use the language "all the more so" although it is the implied meaning. It states: שהעיקר כדברי בה"ג שאינן מוציאות אנשים י"ח שאינן מצטרפות.

opposite [i.e., since they are obligated, all the more so they should count]. In the opinion of Behag certainly one cannot say "all the more so," as women are not obligated in reading and therefore cannot discharge the obligation of men; but nonetheless, since women are obligated to hear, they join in the [quorum of] ten to hear [*megillah*]. And we find, according to a chain of Rishonim, that one should in any case permit [the reading] with ten women as one does with ten men....

ונמצא לפי חבל ראשונים יש להתיר על כל פנים בעשר נשים כמו בעשרה גברים....

In any case, as a matter of law, in my humble opinion, one should permit ten women to read *megillah* on *Purim Meshullash* like all these great [authorities]. In addition, it is permissible for a man to read for them, since they are ten without him. Indeed, it makes sense that if they are not counted in [the quorum of] ten, they are also not obligated in [reading with] ten. However, even if they count for the ten this is to discharge the obligation of men in [reading with a quorum of] ten, but women themselves are not obligated in ten. This can be understood according to the position of Behag that women are obligated in hearing the *megillah* but not in reading it. For there are two issues with *megillah* [i.e., two parts of the *mitsvah*]: one, to hear it, and that is in place of *hallel*,[262] since all were part of the same miracle; two, to read it, which is the

ומכל מקום לדינא לע"ד יש להתיר לעשר נשים לקרוא את המגילה בפורים משולש ככל הני רבוותא וכן מותר לאיש לקרוא להן כיון שהן י' בלעדיו. והנה בסברה אם אינן שייכות לעשרה גם אינן חייבות בעשרה, אמנם גם אם מצטרפות לעשרה זהו להוציא אנשים ידי חובת עשרה אבל אין הנשים בעצמן חייבות בעשרה, ויובן לפי שיטת בה"ג... שנשים חייבות בשמיעת המגילה ולא בקריאתה כי יש במגילה שני ענינים הא' לשמוע שהוא במקום הלל כיון שכולם היו באותו הנס והב' לקרוא אותה שהוא פרסום הנס להשמיעה לאחרים. ולדעת בה"ג נשים אינן חייבות להשמיע לאחרים ולכן

262. R. Henkin thinks the link between *megillah* reading and the *hallel* over the miracle obligates women to hear the reading. See n96, where R. Eigis makes the opposite

publicizing of the miracle, to make it heard to others. According to Behag, women are not obligated to make it heard to others; therefore even if they join together as ten to hear [*megillah*], nonetheless when they read to discharge their own obligation, which is not in reading but in hearing, they are not obligated to make it heard by others, and therefore they do not need ten for themselves.

אפילו אם מצטרפות לעשרה לשמוע מכל מקום כשקוראות להוציא עצמן שאין זה משום קריאה אלא משום שמיעה אינן חייבות להשמיע לאחרים, ולכן לא בעי לעצמן עשרה.

Like R. Waldenberg, R. Henkin rules that women may count toward a quorum for the purpose of *megillah* reading on *Purim Meshullash*. He notes that even according to those decisors who think that a woman may not read on behalf of other women, this ruling is still relevant, as a man may read for a quorum of ten women.[263] R. Henkin first summarizes the opposing arguments of Rishonim on this issue, including many cited previously in this chapter. Although some do not think that women count toward a quorum, there are others who do think women and men may join together. Furthermore, argues R. Henkin, even those authorities who restrict women from counting toward the quorum do so only when the group is mixed; even these sources would recognize a quorum composed entirely of women. The concern regarding a mixed group is for *peritsut* (sexual immorality), the same issue discussed in the context of a mixed *zimmun*.[264] However, a group of women is just as capable of fulfilling the core requirement of *pirsumei nissa* as a group of men. Therefore, R. Henkin thinks that once the problem of a mixed

argument and states that women are not fully obligated in the daytime reading like men because of the connection to *hallel*. Both of them are trying to explain Behag's view.

263. This ruling is discussed further in the section "Women and Blessings," below, in relation to the practical impact of a quorum on the recitation of blessings.

264. However, R. Henkin notes that he thinks these cases are different because women are fully obligated in *megillah*, which is not the case with *birkat hamazon*. See n43.

group is removed, all authorities would agree that women may constitute a quorum for *megillah* reading.[265]

R. Henkin argues that even according to the view of Behag – that women are obligated only to hear, but not to read *Megillat Ester* – women may count in the quorum of listeners. He cites *Peri Ḥadash,* who argues the opposite in the name of Behag: because women are not obligated and do not discharge the obligation of men, all the more so they do not count toward the quorum of ten for the reading.[266] However, R. Henkin thinks that the argument should be reversed. Since Behag thinks that women are obligated to hear *megillah,* they may certainly count in the quorum of listeners. A few paragraphs later, R. Henkin explicitly states that one's ruling on the question of whether women may read for others is not necessarily correlated with one's ruling on whether women may count for a quorum; the one does not always follow from the other. R. Henkin therefore rules that ten women do constitute a quorum for *megillah* reading,[267] even on *Purim Meshullash* when a *minyan* is required.

R. Ovadiah Yosef not only permits ten women to constitute a quorum, he wholeheartedly supports such a practice:

265. He brings further support for the position that ten women may constitute a quorum on *Purim Meshullash* from *Ḥazon Ish* (source #58, above). *Ḥazon Ish* lists four reasons why this is permitted; R. Henkin quotes all four but critiques some of the arguments.

266. *Peri Ḥadash* is discussed in greater detail in the next section of this chapter. See source #67, below.

267. R. Henkin does also offer an alternative read of Behag that the nature of only being obligated to hear *megillah* means that women are not obligated in publicizing the miracle. Therefore, they are not required to read with a group of ten, seemingly, even at a reading that is held not in the proper time. Also, R. Henkin does not explain clearly what he thinks about a mixed group of ten, including men and women. He seems to say that although women are not obligated to read with a quorum of ten, they can nonetheless join a quorum in order to help the men in the group, who are required to read with ten. This argument is difficult to understand halakhically.

61. *Responsa Yabbia Omer* *Vol. 8, Oraḥ Ḥayyim #56*

R. Ovadiah Yosef, Israel (1920–2013)

שו"ת יביע אומר חלק ח אורח חיים סימן נו

4) And here…I wrote…that if there are ten women who hear the reading of the *megillah* and fulfill their obligation they can also bless after [the reading] since in any case there is *pirsumei nissa* [with ten women]…. However, [only] when there are ten women without joining [together with men], for the reason the blessing afterward needs a quorum is because of *pirsumei nissa*…. Therefore whenever there are ten women there is *pirsumei nissa* [it is] good and they bless after…. For several years now, I have directed, with the help of God, many neighborhoods in Jerusalem that after the synagogue reading of the *megillah* for the men, an hour later the women come en masse to the synagogue, and the leader reads for them the *megillah* precisely and with cantillation, and blesses for them before the *megillah* and afterward…. For because of *pirsumei nissa* women are also included…. To exclude what was written in *Responsa Mishneh Halakhot*…to protest the custom of women who make a *minyan* by themselves to read the *megillah* [saying] that they should not do it, etc. see there. With apologies to the honor of his Torah his words are not clear; on the contrary, one should support this custom as long as the one who discharges their obligation in *megillah* reading is an expert in reading as

ד) והנה... כתבתי... שאם יש עשר נשים ששומעות קריאת המגילה ויוצאות ידי חובתן יכולות לברך גם לאחריה, כיון שעכ"פ יש בזה משום פרסומי ניסא.... אבל כשיש עשר נשים בלי שום צירוף, כיון שהטעם שברכה אחרונה צריכה צבור, היינו משום פרסומי ניסא,... הילכך כל שיש עשר נשים איכא פרסומי ניסא שפיר ומברכות לאחריה.... ובימים האלה זה כמה שנים הנהגתי בס"ד בשכונות רבות בירושלים שאחר קריאת המגילה בבהכ"נ לאנשים, כעבור שעה באות הנשים בהמוניהן לבהכ"נ, ושליח צבור קורא להן את המגילה בדקדוקיה וטעמיה, ומברך להן לפני המגילה ולאחריה.... שמשום פרסומי ניסא גם הנשים בכלל זה.... ולאפוקי ממ"ש בשו"ת משנה הלכות... לערער על מנהג הנשים שעושות מנין בפני עצמן לקריאת המגילה שאין לעשות כן וכו', ע"ש, ובמחכ"ת [ובמחילת כבוד תורתו] אין דבריו מחוורים, ואדרבה יש לעודד המנהג הנ"ל ובלבד שהמוציא אותן ידי חובת מקרא מגילה יהיה בקי בקריאתה

required by law. And I have written what seems [reasonable] in my humble opinion.	כהלכה. והנראה לע"ד כתבתי.

As the purpose of the quorum is solely to publicize the miracle, reading *megillah* in a group of ten women is acceptable, although R. Yosef clearly states his opposition to mixed groups of women and men. He explains that he writes this ruling to counter those who argue that ten women should not read together.[268] R. Yosef, by contrast, thinks that women's *minyanim* should be encouraged, as long as the reader is proficient.[269]

In conclusion, there are several major modern halakhic decisors who do count women in the quorum for *megillah* reading.[270] These *posekim* focus on the fact that both men and women are obligated in this *mitsvah*. R. Waldenberg and R. Yosef emphasize their shared obligation in *pirsumei nissa*, and R. Henkin notes that even if women are

268. R. Yosef is specifically addressing *Mishneh Halakhot* (source #40, above).

269. To be clear, the responsum is dealing specifically with the case of a man reading in his home for women and children. The question is whether he may recite the blessing after the *megillah* reading, which requires a *minyan*. R. Yosef does not seem to be talking about a woman reading for other women although presumably the same rule would apply, as long as the women were proficient readers.

270. Although supportive of women's *megillah* readings in general, R. Aharon Lichtenstein ruled that it was preferable not to have a women's *megillah* reading on *Purim Meshullash* (see Frimer, note 72, b). His son R. Mosheh Lichtenstein, in personal email correspondence on July 31, 2015, explained the rationale behind his father's thinking: The reading on Friday the fourteenth in Jerusalem might be considered a reading that is not *bizmannah*. Such a reading requires a quorum, even *bediavad*. But Rema (source #51) is unsure whether women may count toward a quorum for *megillah* reading. R. Lichtenstein therefore distinguishes between an ordinary Purim and *Purim Meshullash*. On an ordinary Purim, the reading is *bizmannah*, and so one fulfills one's obligation even as an individual (and Rema further rules that if there is a public reading *bizmannah* in the city, private readings are considered to be connected to the public reading). Hence, women reading as a group fulfill their obligation even if they do not comprise a quorum, and therefore R. Lichtenstein felt such women's readings were appropriate. However, on *Purim Meshullash*, when a quroum is required, women reading as a group might not fulfill their obligation because their group might not constitute a quorum. In such a year R. Lichtenstein thought it appropriate for women not to read as a group for there is too great a halakhic risk. He was worried that women might not fulfill their obligation in *megillah* reading at all.

only obligated to hear and not to read, such an obligation still enables them to count for the quorum. All seem to agree that once the obstacle of *peritsut* is removed, the comparison with *zimmun* no longer carries any weight. According to these decisors, it is therefore permissible for women to form their own group of ten to read *megillah*. As we see in the next section, the eligibility of women to comprise a quorum in their own right has important implications for the blessings a woman recites when she reads *Megillat Ester*.

WOMEN AND BLESSINGS

Four blessings are recited at the reading of *Megillat Ester*. The first is *birkat hamitsvah*, the blessing over the commandment itself. The second commemorates the miracles that God performed on behalf of the Jewish people on this date: *she'asah nissim la'avotenu bayamim hahem bazeman hazeh*. The reader then recites *sheheḥeyanu*, the blessing said upon performing a new act or reaching a momentous milestone.[271] After completing the reading of the *megillah*, the reader recites the fourth blessing, *harav et rivenu*, which praises God as the source of our salvation.

The following questions arise with regard to a reading of *Megillat Ester* by or for women:

- If a woman reads for other women, what blessing should be recited before the *megillah* is read?[272] The standard *birkat hamitsvah* is *al mikra megillah*: "Blessed are You, Lord our God, King of the universe, who has sanctified us with His *mitsvot* and commanded us regarding the reading of *megillah*." However, given that Behag and others think that a woman is obligated only to hear, but not to read *Megillat Ester*, is this an appropriate blessing for her to recite?
- May a woman recite the fourth blessing, *harav et rivenu*? Some authorities require that a quorum of ten be present to recite this

271. *Ashkenazim* recite *sheheḥeyanu* at both the evening and morning readings, whereas *Sefaradim* recite this blessing only at the evening reading.

272. These sources also discuss the protocol for a man who is reading only for women, as discussed below.

blessing, so this question hinges to a large degree on the discussion above of whether women count in a quorum. This question also applies to a case where a man is reading *Megillat Ester* for a group of women.

This section provides background material on these blessings and explores the answers to these questions. The following is a brief sample of the major perspectives on this topic.

The Talmud in Tractate *Megillah* discusses the requirement to recite blessings at the reading of *Megillat Ester*:

62. *Babylonian Talmud Megillah 21b*

תלמוד בבלי מסכת מגילה כא:

In a place where it is the custom to bless, one should bless. Abbaye said: This was taught only with regard to [the blessing] after [*megillah* reading], but before it – it is a *mitsvah* to bless. For Rav Yehudah said in the name of Shemuel: All *mitsvot* – a blessing is said prior to performing them....

מקום שנהגו לברך יברך. אמר אביי: לא שנו אלא לאחריה, אבל לפניה - מצוה לברך. דאמר רב יהודה אמר שמואל: כל המצות כולן מברך עליהן עובר לעשייתן....

Before [*megillah* reading] what does one bless? Rav Sheshet from Ketarzeya went before Rav Ashi, and blessed MN"Ḥ (*mikra, nissim, sheheḥeyanu*).[273]

לפניה מאי מברך? רב ששת מקטרזיא איקלע לקמיה דרב אשי, ובריך מנ"ח.

After [*megillah* reading] what does one bless? "Blessed are You, Lord our God, King of the universe, who espouses our quarrels, vindicates our cause, executes our vengeance, punishes our adversaries, and visits retribution on all the enemies of our soul. Blessed are You, Lord, who avenges

לאחריה מאי מברך? ברוך אתה ה' אלהינו מלך העולם (האל) הרב את ריבנו, והדן את דיננו, והנוקם את נקמתנו, והנפרע לנו מצרינו, והמשלם גמול לכל אויבי נפשנו, ברוך אתה ה' הנפרע לישראל

273. Rashi ad loc. explains that this is the meaning of the Gemara's acronym.

Israel on all their enemies." Rava said: [The concluding words are], "The God who saves." R. Pappa [said]: Therefore we should say both: "Blessed are You, Lord, who avenges Israel on all their enemies, the God who saves."	מכל צריהם. רבא אמר: האל המושיע. אמר רב פפא: הלכך נימרינהו לתרוייהו: ברוך אתה ה' הנפרע לישראל מכל צריהם האל המושיע.

The *mishnah* to which this section of Gemara refers says that one should recite blessings at the reading of the *megillah* "where it is the custom" to do so.[274] Abbaye notes the general practice of reciting a blessing before performing *mitsvot* and rules that only the recitation of the blessing after the *megillah* reading is a matter of custom. The Gemara relates a story about Rav Sheshet to demonstrate that three blessings should, in fact, be recited before reading the *megillah*: the blessing over the *mitsvah* to read the *megillah*,[275] the blessing recognizing the miracles that were performed on our behalf, and *sheheḥeyanu*. The Gemara then records the text of the final blessing, which is recited, where customary, after the *megillah* reading. Neither the Mishnah nor the Gemara bring gender into the discussion of these blessings. Since both the Mishnah and the Talmud (sources #1, 2, and 3, above) state that women are eligible to read the *megillah*, the assumption is that women would recite these same blessings.

The Blessing Before *Megillah* Reading

Like the Talmud, very few Rishonim directly discuss the blessings at the *megillah* reading in relation to women. Logic dictates that according to all Rishonim and the subsequent legal authorities who rule that women are obligated in the reading of *megillah*, women should recite the normative blessing beforehand, "on the reading of *megillah*." However, R. Eliezer ben Yo'el Halevi, a thirteenth-century authority known as Ra'avyah, suggests that since Behag redefines a woman's obligation as hearing the *megillah*, the language of the blessing should change accordingly:

274. M. *Meg.* 4:1; B.T. *Meg.* 21a.

275. The requirement of reciting *al mikra megillah* is also recorded in *Soferim* 14:1.

63. ***Sefer Ra'avyah*** ***Vol. 2, Megillah #569*** R. Eliezer ben Yo'el Halevi, Germany (1140–1225)	**ספר ראבי"ה חלק ב** **מסכת מגילה סימן תקסט**
And it seems to me that women recite the blessing, "on the hearing of *megillah*," even if they read it for themselves.	ונראה לי דנשים מברכות על משמע מגילה ואפילו אי קרו לה לעצמן.

Ra'avyah, who rules like Behag, thinks that the language of the blessing should reflect the specific nature of a woman's obligation.[276] This is true, notes Ra'avyah, even if a woman is reading the *megillah* for other women, because the reading is taking place to fulfill the *mitsvah* of hearing *Megillat Ester*.[277] Unlike Ra'avyah, other Rishonim who follow the view of Behag do not discuss the formula of the blessing. This presumably implies that they do not think that one should deviate from the formula of the blessing as stated in the Talmud. Therefore, even though women are only required to hear the *megillah*, this obligation falls under the general rubric of the *mitsvah* to read *megillah*, and so women should not change the wording of the blessing.

Nimmukei Yosef is one of the few Rishonim who supports the possibility of a woman reading for men and also explicitly mentions

276. The language here of *al mashma megillah* is slightly different from that recorded by Rema (source #66), who writes *lishmo'a megillah*. In both cases, however, the blessing is meant to reflect a woman's specific obligation, as distinct from a man's. Other halakhic decisors also record slightly different versions of the blessing designed to emphasize that a woman's obligation is different. See *Ḥayyei Adam*, Vol. 2–3, *kelal* 155:11 (source #32, above), and *Arukh Hashulḥan, O.Ḥ.* 692:7, who formulate the blessing as, "to hear the reading of *megillah*." *Mishnah Berurah* records two different versions of the blessing. In 689:8 (source #69), when discussing a case in which a woman is reading, he writes that the language of the blessing should be *lishmo'a mikra megillah*. In 692:11, when he talks about a man's reading on behalf of a woman, he records the blessing as *lishmo'a megillah*, the same formulation Rema presents. The fact that there are different versions of this blessing reflects that it is a later addition, different from those blessings clearly formulated by *Ḥazal*.

277. According to this position, the language of the blessing also may shift if a man reads *megillah* for women after he has already fulfilled his own obligation to read.

the blessing she should recite, perhaps in response to those who think differently:

64. ***Nimmukei Yosef***
Tractate Megillah 4a
R. Yosef ibn Ḥabib, Spain (fourteenth–fifteenth centuries)

נימוקי יוסף
מסכת מגילה ד.

So too, women recite the blessing, "on the reading of *megillah*," and discharge the obligation of men, since anyone who is obligated in a matter may discharge the obligation of others.

וכן נמי נשים מברכות על מקרא מגילה ומוציאות האנשים שכל המחויב בדבר מוציא אחרים ידי חובתן.

As men and women have the same obligation in *megillah* reading, women may read for men and recite the blessing "on the reading of *megillah*."

These blessings are codified in *Shulḥan Arukh*:

65. ***Shulḥan Arukh***
Oraḥ Ḥayyim 692:1
R. Yosef Caro, Spain and Israel (1488–1575)

שולחן ערוך אורח חיים
סימן תרצב סעיף א

One who reads the *megillah* recites three blessings beforehand: *al mikra megillah* ("on the reading of *megillah*"), *she'asah nissim* ("who performed miracles"), and *sheheḥeyanu* ("who sustained us").[278]

הקורא את המגילה מברך לפניה ג' ברכות: על מקרא מגילה, ושעשה נסים, ושהחיינו.

Shulḥan Arukh and Rema codify the practice of reciting these three blessings.[279] They do not mention any variation in practice based on

278. *Sh. Ar.* rules in this same section that *sheheḥeyanu* is not repeated at the daytime reading, but Rema records that "in our lands," it is the custom to recite it over both the evening and the daytime reading.

279. There is some debate over whether the blessings before *megillah* reading should be recited when reading as an individual. However, the vast majority of *posekim* agree that the blessings are recited whether or not a quorum is present. See, for example, *Responsa of Rashi* #129; *Tosafot* to B.T. *Meg.* 5a, *s.v hava uvda*; *Shibbolei*

who is reading or who is listening to the *megillah*.[280] It is clear that R. Caro, following the Sephardic *posekim* who came before him, rules that women recite the same blessings as men.[281]

However, a few chapters earlier, when *Shulḥan Arukh* discusses the question of a woman reading *megillah* on behalf of others, Rema records the position of Ra'avyah that a woman recites a different blessing when reading *megillah*:[282]

Haleket 195; *Kitsur Sh. Ar.* 141:9; and *Mishnah Berurah* 692:8. *Beit Yosef, O.Ḥ.* 690, quotes Mordekhai in the name of R. Gershom, who rules that when an individual reads *megillah*, no blessings should be recited. He rules like Rav Assi that the proper fulfillment of the obligation requires a quorum of ten; *Sefer Ha'agur* 1:47 rules similarly, as does Behag. However, *Beit Yosef* notes that Rambam and virtually all other *posekim* take the opposite position, namely, that these blessings should be recited even without a quorum:

> כתב המרדכי (סי׳ תשפב) בשם ר״ג יחיד הקורא את המגילה לא יברך לא לפניה ולא לאחריה דאמר רב אסי מגילה בעשרה וכיון דצריך עשרה יחיד לא מיחייב לקרות דהיכי מברך הא הוה ליה מוציא שם שמים לבטלה וכן כתב בארחות חיים (שם) שכן דעת מקצת גאונים ושהר״מ כתב שמברך אפילו ביחיד עכ״ל ומתוך מה שנתבאר יתבאר לך שדעת כל הפוסקים חוץ מבעל הלכות גדולות היפך דעת המרדכי הילכך נקטינן כדברי הר״מ שמברך אפילו ביחיד.

R. Caro rules accordingly in *Sh. Ar., O.Ḥ.* 690:18.

280. Likewise, neither Rambam, *Hilkh. Megillah* 1:3, nor *Tur, O.Ḥ.* 692, mention any distinction beween the blessings for men and women, and so it seems they assume that women would be reciting *al mikra megillah*.

281. R. Caro rejects completely the ruling of Behag that women are only obligated in the hearing of *megillah*. In *Sh. Ar., O.Ḥ.* 689 (source #22, above), he codifies in his *setam* position Rambam's view that women are obligated in the reading of *megillah* and so may read for men. In his *yesh omerim* position, however, he presents the view that this should not be done, presumably due to the honor of the community or issues of men's dignity.

282. Rema rules this way based on the opinion of Mordekhai to B.T. *Meg.* 4a (#779), who explicitly cites Ra'avyah.

66. *Rema*	**רמ"א**
Oraḥ Ḥayyim #689	**אורח חיים סימן תרפט**
R. Moshe Isserles, Poland (1525–1572)	
Gloss: And there are those who say that if a woman reads for herself, she recites the blessing *lishmo'a megillah* ("to hear *megillah*"), for she is not obligated in reading.	הגה: וי"א אם האשה קורא לעצמה מברכת לשמוע מגילה שאינה חייבת בקריאה.

Rema's statement here reflects Behag's position that women are obligated to hear but not to read *megillah*. He records the position that there are those who say that a woman should recite a different version of the first blessing that more accurately reflects the *mitsvah* in which a woman is obligated: *lishmo'a megillah*.[283] Although a number of later authorities rule in accordance with this opinion assuming that it reflects Rema's position,[284] the fact that Rema himself only cites it as a *yesh omerim* suggests the possibility that he agrees with the view implied by R. Caro that women should recite the normative blessing.[285]

---

283. See *Mishnah Berurah* 692:11, *Magen Avraham* 692:5, and *Peri Megadim* 692:5, all of whom mention that Rema's ruling is in effect even when a man reads for a group of women. Because the man is reading for the benefit of the women and their obligation is only to hear the *megillah* read, he should recite the blessing "to hear the reading of *megillah*."

284. See, for example *Ḥayyei Adam*, Vol. 2–3, *kelal* 155:11 (source #32, above), as well as *Kaf Haḥayyim, O.Ḥ.* 689 (source #39, above), who lists a number of other authorities who rule this way.

285. Many significant, later authorities understand this ruling of the *yesh omerim* to be the view that Rema himself espouses. However, there is still ambiguity in his language. In addition to the fact that it is recorded as a *yesh omerim*, there are other reasons to suspect that this does not reflect Rema's actual position. For example, why does he not reinforce it, as he does in many other instances, by saying that this is the custom in his location? And why does he not reiterate it when discussing the blessings (source #65 above)? The general discussion of the *kelalei pesikah* of Rema – his principles of stating law and his use of language – addresses the conventional case where R. Caro states something as *setam* and Rema brings a *yesh omerim*. The question is should that case follow the standard rule for reading Rema, namely, where he himself presents a *setam* statement and a *yesh omerim*, the law is according to the

However, there are prominent halakhic decisors who argue that the language of the blessing should not be changed, even if one follows the ruling of Behag:

67. *Peri Ḥadash*
Oraḥ Ḥayyim #689
R. Ḥizkiah da Silva, Italy (1569–1698)

פרי חדש
אורח חיים סימן תרפט

And what was written in the gloss, "And there are those who say [that if a woman reads for herself, she recites the blessing *lishmo'a megillah*], etc.," these are not substantial words that should be relied upon; rather, they should bless *al mikra megillah* like the men. This is obvious.

ומה שכתב בהגה ויש אומרים [אם האשה קוראת לעצמה מברכת לשמוע מגילה] כו'. אינן דברים של עיקר לסמוך עליהם, אלא מברכות על מקרא מגילה כמו האנשים, וזה פשוט:

Peri Ḥadash quotes Rema's opinion but dismisses his words as unreliable, most likely because he disapproves of creating new blessings not instituted by *Ḥazal*.[286] Instead, he argues, women and men should recite the same blessing over the reading of *megillah*.

For those authorities who think that both men and women are

---

setam? *Sedei Ḥemed, Kelalei Haposekim* 14:12, succinctly summarizes his view and that of *Peri Megadim* that this is indeed the case; Rema rules according to the *setam* brought by R. Caro:

> אם מביא הרמ"א שתי דעות אחת בסתם והשנית בלשון ויש אומרים אם דעתו כהסברא שהביא בסתם הנה ראיתי להרב רמ"ץ... כתב וז"ל ואף דהרמ"א כ' וי"א וכו' נראה לדעה ראשונה עיקר עכ"ל משמע שסובר שאף בסתם בדברי מרן ומחלוקת בדברי הרמ"א אמרינן הלכה כסתם... ואם כן כל שכן בסתם ואח"כ מחלוקת בדברי הרמ"א גופיה דאמרינן הלכה כסתם... שוב ראיתי בכללים בהוראת איסור והיתר של הגאון פרי מגדים שעמד בספק זה בדעה סתמית בדברי מרן ויש אומרים בדברי הרמ"א אי אמרינן דהלכה כסתם ובאר ספקו וסיים וראיתי בשו"ת מהגאון מוהר"ם זיסקינד אבד"ק לובלין... דעה א' עיקר אפילו דעה א' בהמחבר וי"א בהרב ולי צ"ע עכ"ל.

If this understanding of Rema is indeed correct, then in our case of a women's *megillah* reading, Rema also rules like R. Caro, that women are obligated to read *megillah*, not just to hear and, so, would recite the normative blessings as men do.

286. From a previous discussion in this section (see source #60), it is clear that *Peri Ḥadash* rules according to Behag and *Tosafot*. However, it is less clear how he understands

obligated in reading *megillah*, it follows that both should recite the same blessings. For example, R. Eliyahu Kramer, the Vilna Ga'on, writes:

68. ***Ma'aseh Rav***	**מעשה רב**
Laws of Purim #246	**הלכות פורים אות רמו**
R. Eliyahu Kramer, Lithuania (1720–1797)	
Women are obligated in reading *megillah*, and one blesses for them as for men.	נשים חייבות בקריאת מגילה ומברכים להם כמו לאנשים.

The Vilna Ga'on emphasizes that men and women have the same obligation and therefore should recite identical blessings.[287] He specifically refers to a case in which a man is reading for a group of women, and presumably this rule would apply even after he had already fulfilled his own obligation.[288] He states that the man may recite the normative blessings on their behalf.

Contemporary halakhic decisors remain divided on this issue. Some rule that women recite a different version of the blessing, while

---

the view of Behag. It seems he rules that women are obligated in the reading of *megillah* but cannot fulfill the obligation for men. This fact might be the reason he does not think one should change the formula of the blessing.

287. In his notes on the text of the Vilna Ga'on's writings, R. Issachar Ber (n2) indicates that he thinks that the logic of *Turei Even* also supports this ruling:

ועיין חדושי טורי אבן שהעלה בזה דברים ישרים ונעימים ראוין אליו ולסברתו לכל הדעות מברכים לנשים על מקרא מגילה כמו לאנשים.

288. *Arukh Hashulhan, O. Ḥ.* 692:7, suggests that when a man who has already fulfilled his obligation recites the blessing for women, he should recite a different version of the blessing, suggested by Rema:

וכשקורא בשביל נשים יברך לשמוע מקרא מגילה משום די"א שלא נצטוו אלא על השמיעה ולא על הקריאה... יש מי שאומר דמוטב לקרא לנשים אחד ששמעה הוא בביהכ"נ משום ברוב עם הדרת מלך [שם] ולענ"ד נראה דכיון דמגילה בזמנה קורין ביחיד כמ"ש בסי' תר"ץ מוטב יותר שיקרא ויצא גם הוא ויברך על מקרא מגילה משיצא מקודם ואח"כ קריאתו שלא לצורך עצמו.

This ruling is somewhat perplexing as *Arukh Hashulhan* rules that women are obligated in the reading of *megillah* like men (see source #23, above). Perhaps he rules this way here in order to be wary of all opinions, so as to avoid a possible *berakhah levattalah*.

others maintain that the language of "on reading *megillah*" should not be changed. *Mishnah Berurah* follows the ruling presented in Rema:

69. ***Mishnah Berurah***
689:8
R. Israel Meir (Hakohen) Kagan, Poland (1839–1933)

משנה ברורה
סימן תרפט סעיף קטן ח

"If a woman reads, etc."... But if she does not have anyone to read for her, she may read for herself from a kosher *megillah*. She blesses, "who has sanctified us with His *mitsvot* and commanded us to hear the reading of *megillah*."

אם האשה קראה וכו׳.... אבל אם אין לה מי שיקרא לפניה תקרא היא לעצמה במגילה כשרה ומברכת אקב״ו לשמוע מקרא מגילה.

Although he would prefer that a woman hear *megillah* from a man, if her only option is to read herself, then she should recite a blessing that reflects her obligation to hear the *megillah*.[289]

R. Eliezer Waldenberg also rules that women should recite a blessing on hearing the *megillah*. The question posed to R. Waldenberg is: Why would the language of the blessing be different in this case, given that women are generally permitted to recite the normative blessing over *mitsvot* that they choose to perform despite not being strictly obligated?

289. See also *Minḥat Yitsḥak* 3:53, who rules similarly regarding the blessing when men read for women. The responsum mostly deals with the question of who should recite the blessing, the man reading for the woman, or the woman herself. He concludes that the woman should recite the blessing:

אלא הטוב וישר שתאמר האשה הברכה לשמוע מקרא מגילה... ולענין שעשה נסים ושהחיינו, ודאי שהאשה תברך אותם גם כן.

R. Weiss does not think that ten women constitute a quorum. He therefore thinks there is an additional reason for women to recite the blessing: because it is not a "public" reading, each individual should make her own blessing rather than having one person bless on behalf of everyone.

70. *Responsa Tsits Eliezer Vol. 19, 67:2*

שו"ת ציץ אליעזר חלק יט סימן סז:ב

R. Eliezer Waldenberg, Israel (1915–2006)

Regarding Rema's ruling that women who read *megillah* for themselves must recite the blessing, "to hear the reading of *megillah*."[290]

אודות פסק הרמ"א שנשים הקוראות מגילה לעצמן צריכות לברך לשמוע מקרא מגילה...

Sunday, 19 Adar I, 5752 (February 23, 1992), Jerusalem.

יום א' י"ט אדר"א תשנ"ב, ירושלים.

Further, [the questioner] is unsure and asks: "Rema rules that women who read *megillah* should not recite the blessing, 'on reading *megillah*,' but rather, 'to hear [*megillah*],' because they were not commanded to read. I do not understand how this is different from all other positive, time-caused *mitsvot*, where the law is that if women nonetheless perform the *mitsvah*, they recite the blessing as usual. This requires further study."

עוד מסתפק ושואל וז"ל: הרמ"א פסק שנשים שקוראות מגילה לא יברכו על מקרא מגילה אלא לשמוע משום שלא נצטוו לקרוא, ולא הבנתי מאי שנא מכל מצוות עשה שהזמן גרמן שנפסק להלכה שאם בכל זאת מקיימות את המצוה מברכות כרגיל וצ"ע עכ"ל.

It seems this can be answered easily: this case [*megillah* reading] is different, for with all other positive, time-caused commandments there is no aspect in which women are obligated; rather, they approach it from the perspective of taking it upon themselves. [The rabbis] established a ruling [of voluntary observance] (according to those who hold that they may bless) that also from the perspective of [self-]

ונראה לתרץ בפשיטות, דכאן שאני, דבכל מ"ע שהז"ג הא ליכא בהן צד של חיוב לנשים ובאין רק מצד של קיבלו עלייהו, ותיקנו ע"ז (לסוברים שיכולות לברך) שיוכלו לברך גם מצד זה של קיבלו כמטבע הברכה אבל משא"כ כאן בקריאת מגילה, אם נאמר שחיובן של הנשים

290. As noted above, this is not actually the language used by Rema, but some authorities do present this as the correct language of the alternate blessing.

acceptance they may bless using the regular formula. However, this is not the same in our case of *megillah* reading. If we say that women are obligated only to hear, it emerges that there are two components: the element of actual obligation, which is to hear [*megillah*], and the element of reading, which is purely voluntary (to want to do it). Therefore, which is preferable: that they recite the version of the blessing that speaks to the obligatory element, namely hearing, or [the version] that speaks to the element of custom, namely reading? Indeed, she certainly must recite the version of the blessing that speaks to the obligatory element, and they recite the blessing over their obligation in this matter. For this reason, Rema ruled properly that if she reads for herself, she recites the blessing, "to hear *megillah*," since she is not obligated in reading, while she is obligated in hearing. Therefore, she must recite the blessing over the obligation, which is the hearing. This is also the case if another reads before her in order to discharge her obligation; he also recites the blessing, "to hear."[291]

הוא רק בשמיעה, נמצא דיש כאן ב׳ צדדים. צד של חיוב ממש שהוא השמיעה, וצד של קריאה שנובע רק מצד של קיבלו (להרצות בכך), וא״כ מאי עדיפא שיברכו נוסח ברכה שתשמע לצד החיוב שהיא השמיעה, או שתשמע לצד המנהגא שהיא הקריאה? הרי בודאי שצריכה לברך נוסחת ברכה שתשתמע ממנה צד חיוב ושמברכים על חיובן בזה ולכך פוסק הרמ״א שפיר דאם קוראה לעצמה דמברכת לשמוע מגילה מפני שאינה חייבת בקריאה, ובשמיעה היא חייבת, לכך צריכה לברך על החיובא שהיא השמיעה. וה״ה גם כשאחר קוראה לפניה להוציאה יד״ח מברך נמי ״לשמוע״.

291. He goes on to add in the next section:

ופסק הרמ״א הוא עפ״י המרדכי, והחולקים סוברים שהן חייבות גם בקריאה כאנשים, יעיין בביאור הגר״א בסי׳ תרפ״ט שם ס״ק ה׳ ו׳ ז׳. ובמעשה רב אות רל״ז ופעולת שכיר שם. וכה ראיתי בספר שו״ת שלמת חיים ח״א סימן צ״ט שהגרי״ח זאננפעלד ז״ל השיב לשואלו, כי הנראה מדברי הראשונים מפוסקים שלא הביאו נוסח אחר בברכה לנשים שאם יברכו על מקרא מגילה אין קפידה ע״ש, אלא דמלשונו של ״אין קפידה״ משמע דר״ל מפני שהרי מברכות גם על מ״ע שהז״ג, אבל העיקר נראה דהיינו משום דקסברי שגם הנשים חייבות במקרא מגילה כאנשים, יעוין מ״ש בזה גם הערוה״ש בסעי׳ ה׳, וכן בספר מרחשת ח״א סימן כ״ב ע״ש.

R. Waldenberg explains that there is no parallel between *megillah,* in which women are obligated in at least some form, and other positive, time-caused *mitsvot,* from which women are entirely exempt.[292] There is a major difference between women having a different type of obligation from men and their not being obligated at all. Women may choose to perform positive, time-caused *mitsvot* in which they are not obligated, and when they do so, they recite the standard blessing recited by men.[293] *Megillat Ester,* by contrast, is a *mitsvah* in which women are, in fact, obligated; however, their obligation is to hear, not to read. The blessing, rules R. Waldenberg, should reflect their obligation in this *mitsvah,* to hear *megillah,* and not the voluntary aspect of reading it.

R. Yehuda Henkin, in his essay on women and *megillah* reading, asserts that it is the norm for women to recite a different blessing: "Ashkenazic practice is indeed for women to make the blessing '*lishmo'a megillah*' (Rema and others) or '*lishmo'a mikra megillah*' (*Ḥayyei Adam* and *Mishnah Berurah*; cf. Rabbenu Ḥananel to *Megillah* 4a)."[294] Yet he questions why this should be the case when so many authorities clearly rule that the blessing should be the same for both men and women. "On

292. See n302 where R. Shternbuch believes the rules of time-caused *mitsvot* do apply.

293. This view is according to Ashkenazic *posekim* who follow the lead of R. Tam (*Tosafot* to B.T. *Rosh Hash.* 32b, s.v. *haRabbi Yehudah*), who holds that women may recite the blessing over *mitsvot* from which they are exempt. Sephardic *posekim,* following Rambam's ruling in *Hilkh. Tsitsit* 3:9, do not permit women to recite the blessings.

294. R. Henkin, "Women and Megillah Reading," 62 n10. It is hard to understand what exactly he means by this statement. Clearly it is not referring to women's *megillah* readings, as they have not been in existence until recently and are most certainly not yet considered the norm. Possibly he is referring to men's reading for women; however, here, too, it would be hard to make a claim that this practice is normative, since at many of these readings the man is presumably fulfilling his own obligation, as well. Even Rema himself did not add in his original comment that this practice was the custom in his location. Possibly R. Henkin means to say that a majority of Ashkenazic *posekim* rule this way, not that it is a prevalent practice, despite the fact that his language clearly seems to indicate otherwise. At the reading at Midreshet Lindenbaum, women recite the normative blessing over the reading of *megillah,* based on R. Lichtenstein's *pesak,* and many other women's groups operate similarly. See R. Yosef Ḥayyim Sonnenfeld (source #74, below) and R. Yosef (source #72, below), who think the customary practice in Israel is to say the blessing, "on the reading of *megillah.*"

what basis do we prefer the blessing according to Ra'avyah to the one according to Rashi and Rambam? Were it not for the established *minhag*," writes R. Henkin, "we might well rule that women should make no blessing at all, because of the *safek* (doubt) of which version to use."[295]

R. Ovadiah Yosef rules that the language of the blessing should not be changed and that a man who reads *megillah* on behalf of women should recite the standard blessing. This decision is recorded in several of his responsa:

---

295. Ibid. This statement is also somewhat confusing. To suggest that women would not recite a blessing because of doubt (*safek*) seems extreme. If women were to recite the normative blessing, it would surely also incorporate Behag's opinion. This was clearly the view of the many Rishonim who rule like Behag and yet do not suggest the radical idea of creating a new blessing. Even R. Waldenberg (source #70, above) admitted that although he personally thinks that "to hear *megillah*" would be a more accurate blessing, the normative blessing would work for women as well. Indeed, women always fulfill their obligation with the normative blessing when they attend the main reading in synagogue and answer, "Amen," to the man who recites the blessing. R. Moshe Shternbuch, *Teshuvot Vehanhagot, O.Ḥ.* #403, makes some of these same points. See n302, below. Interestingly, R. Henkin does not raise the issue that there is a *safek* in reciting Ra'avyah's blessing, for it could be a *berakhah levattalah* according to the view that women are equally obligated in *megillah* reading. Nobody questions whether a woman who adheres to the *pesak* that she is obligated in reading *megillah* would fulfill her obligation at a reading at which the blessing "to hear *megillah*" is recited, rather than the normative blessing. R. Ovadiah Yosef, *Responsa Yabbia Omer*, Vol. 1, *O.Ḥ.* #44, mentions that there was a custom among some not to recite a blessing at all when reading for women, based on different reasoning than that suggested here by R. Henkin:

> אכן דעת איזה אחרונים שאין לברך לנשים כלל, אלא יקראו המגילה בלא ברכה. וכמ"ש הכנה"ג בספר דינא דחיי ח"ב (דקכ"ח ע"ב) וז"ל: ומנהגינו עכשיו שהאנשים קוראים המגילה לנשים ואין מברכים עליה. וכ"כ בספר זכור לאברהם ח"ג (אות ב' ס"ק כג). ונתן טעם לדבר לפי שיש מחלוקת בראשונים אם היחיד קורא המגילה בברכה, והנשים נחשבות כיחיד שאין לברך להן, משום דספק ברכות להקל. ע"ש. והן אמת שגם בשלחן גבוה (ס"ס תרצ) פסק שיחיד אינו מברך, דספק ברכות להקל. ע"ש. וכן כתב בשו"ת ויען משה (חאו"ח סי' צה) בשם מהר"ן ביתן שהנשים אינן מברכות שדינן כיחיד שאינו מברך על מקרא מגילה. אלא שהרב מהר"א הכהן היה מורה ובא כדעת החיד"א במחב"ר, שהאיש המוציא י"ח את האשה יברך על מקרא מגילה. ע"כ. ובאמת שרוב הפוסקים ס"ל שאף היחיד מברך על מקרא מגילה.

71. *Responsa Yabbia Omer Vol. 1, Oraḥ Ḥayyim #44*

R. Ovadiah Yosef, Israel (1920–2013)

שו"ת יביע אומר חלק א אורח חיים סימן מד

Jerusalem, 5713 [1952]

1) I was asked about the law regarding reading *megillah* with the blessings for women. I will clarify the practical application very briefly. Our teacher wrote in *Shulḥan Arukh* (beginning of *siman* 689) that women are obligated in reading [*megillah*]... and our teacher's words imply that she blesses over the reading of *megillah*, as is the rule for men. So our teacher Ḥida wrote in *Maḥazik Berakhah* (689:4) that when a man discharges the obligation of a woman it is good and proper that he bless over the reading of the *megillah*, as our teacher ruled.... Similarly, our teacher *Beit Yosef* (end of *siman* 47) wrote that even according to the formula of the [personal] blessings on the Torah, "who has sanctified us with His *mitsvot* and commanded us to delve into the words of Torah," which refers to the the study of the oral law [from which women are exempt], women recite the blessings on the Torah, for one should not change the wording of the blessings as formulated by the rabbis. See there; and all the more so here, where one should say that the commandment upon women in reading is similar to men's. Thus the custom has spread according to the words of Ḥida in *Maḥazik Berakhah*, cited above.

ב"ה. פעה"ק ירושלים תשוב"ה (תשי"ג) לפ"ק.

(א) נשאלתי בדין קריאת המגילה בברכות לנשים. ואבאר בקיצור נמרץ למעשה. הנה מרן בש"ע (ר"ס תרפ"ט) כתב שהנשים חייבות בקריאתה... ומדברי מרן משמע שמברכת על מקרא מגילה כדין אנשים. וכ"כ מרן החיד"א במחזיק ברכה סק"ד, שהאיש שמוציא את האשה י"ח, הטוב והישר שיברך על מקרא מגילה כד' מרן.... וכיו"ב כ' מרן הב"י (ס"ס מ"ז), שאף לפי הנוסח בברכות התורה אקב"ו לעסוק בדברי תורה, דקאי על עסק תורה שבעל פה, נשים מברכות ברכות התורה, שאין לשנות ממטבע הברכות שתקנו חז"ל. ע"ש. וכ"ש כאן שי"ל שהמצוה על הנשים בקריאה כמו האנשים. וכן פשט המנהג, וכדברי החיד"א במחב"ר הנ"ל.

In his short summary, R. Yosef explains that R. Caro rules that women should recite the normative blessing as men do, and he cites Ḥida, who concurs. R. Yosef brings support for this logic from R. Caro's ruling regarding the personal blessings individuals recite each morning over Torah study. Despite the fact that women are exempt from the study of the oral law,[296] R. Caro still rules that they are obligated to recite the same blessings as men, for one should not deviate from the structure of the blessings that *Ḥazal* established. R. Yosef applies this logic to the case of *megillah* and says that all the more so here, where a woman shares an obligation equal to a man's, she should recite the blessing "on the reading of *megillah*" and not change the language of the blessing. In his view, this is the normative custom.

In another responsum, R. Yosef directly addresses the view of Rema:

72. *Responsa Yeḥavveh Da'at Vol. 1, #88* R. Ovadiah Yosef, Israel (1920–2013)	**שו"ת יחווה דעת** **חלק א סימן פח**
Question: One who reads the *megillah* in his home to discharge the obligation of the members of his household in reading *megillah,* does he need to recite all the blessings over the *megillah,* even if he already fullfilled his obligation at synagogue?	שאלה: הקורא את המגילה בביתו להוציא את בני ביתו ידי חובת מקרא מגילה, האם צריך לברך כל ברכות המגילה, אע"פ שכבר יצא ידי חובת קריאתה בבית הכנסת?
Answer: ... From the words of the *posekim* it seems that one must bless even over reading *megillah* for women, but Rema in a gloss (*O.Ḥ.* #689) wrote that women	תשובה:... ומדברי הפוסקים משמע שגם על קריאת המגילה לנשים צריך לברך, אלא שהרמ"א בהגה /א"ח/

296. On the question of a woman's obligation to study Torah, which is complex and has evolved over time, see *Sifrei Devarim* 46; M. *Sot.* 3:4; B.T. *Kid.* 29b; J.T. *Sot.* 19a; Rambam, *Hilkh. Talmud Torah* 1:1, 1:13; and *Hilkh. Yesodei Hatorah* 4:13; *Semak,* introduction; *Sh. Ar., Y.D.* 246:6; *Ḥafets Ḥayyim, Likkutei Hilkh. Sotah* 21b; and Lubavitcher Rebbe on *Parashat Emor* 5750.

recite the blessing, "to hear *megillah*," and not the traditional version, "on reading *megillah*".... However, *Peri Ḥadash* (*siman* 689) disagrees with Rema and has written that it is correct to also bless for women, "on the reading of *megillah*." This is also the opinion of the *ga'on* R. Eliyahu of Vilna....[297] However, the *ga'on* R. David Amar...(85b) wrote that one who reads for women should not bless at all, because it is impossible that they will not be distracted in the middle of *megillah* reading for [at least] a few words, and it will turn out that the blessing recited was in vain....	(סי' תרפ"ט) כתב, שהנשים מברכות לשמוע מגילה, ולא כנוסח המקובל, שהוא על מקרא מגילה.... אולם הפרי חדש (סי' תרפ"ט) חולק על הרמ"א וכתב שהעיקר לברך גם לנשים על מקרא מגילה. וכן דעת הגאון רבי אליהו מוילנא.... ואמנם הגאון רבי דוד עמאר... (דף פ"ה ע"ב) כתב שהקורא לנשים לא יברך כלל, מפני שאי אפשר שלא ישיחו דעתן באמצע קריאת המגילה מכמה תיבות, ונמצא שמברך ברכות לבטלה....
However, in reality the meaning of the Gemara in *Megillah* (19a)[298] is that one must bless upon reading it to women and to the ignorant, even if they do not understand Hebrew at all. This is the widespread custom in Jerusalem, to bless upon reading to women.... So also wrote Ḥida in *Maḥazik Berakhah* (689:4), that it is good and proper for a man who discharges the obligation of women to bless "on the reading of *megillah*...."[299]	אולם באמת משמעות הגמרא במגילה (דף י"ט ע"א) שצריך לברך על קריאתה לנשים ולעמי הארץ אף על פי שאינם מבינים לשון הקודש כלל, וכן פשט המנהג בירושלים לברך על קריאתה לנשים.... וכן כתב מרן החיד"א במחזיק ברכה (סי' תרפ"ט אות ד'), שהטוב והישר שהאיש שמוציא את הנשים יברך על מקרא מגילה....
And it is known that nearly all *posekim* agree that an individual also recites the	ונודע שהסכמת רוב ככל הפוסקים שגם היחיד מברך

297.R. Yosef lists other halakhic authorities who rule this way including *Turei Even* to B.T. *Meg.* 4a; *Matteih Yehudah* 689; and R. Ya'akov Algazi, *Ḥug Ha'arets, Hilkh. Purim*, p. 5.

298.This should read 18a.

299.R. Yosef lists other halakhic authorities who rule this way, including *Responsa Kol Ya'akov*, section 2, *O.Ḥ.* #28; *Ma'amar Mordekhai* 692:6; and *Benei Binyamin*, p. 104:3.

blessings before the *megillah* [reading], and these are: Rif, Rambam, R. Tam, R. Zeraḥiah Halevi Ba'al Hama'or, Ramban, Rashba, Ran, *Or Zarua*, and others. And this is the custom….[300] And if so, one who reads for women should also recite the blessings; even more so in our days, when women know how to read and write and understand very well all that is in *Megillat Ester*, we should not withhold from them the initial blessings, which are: *al mikra megillah*, *she'asah nissim*, and *sheheḥeyanu*.

ברכות הראשונות של המגילה, והם: הרי"ף, הרמב"ם, רבינו תם, רבי זרחיה הלוי בעל המאור, והרמב"ן, והרשב"א, והר"ן, והאור זרוע, ועוד. וכן המנהג.... ואם כן גם הקורא לנשים יש לו לברך על קריאתה, וכל שכן בזמנינו שהנשים יודעות קרוא וכתוב, ומבינות היטב כל הנאמר במגילת אסתר, שאין למנוע מהן ברכות המגילה הראשונות, שהן: על מקרא מגילה, שעשה נסים, ושהחיינו.

R. Yosef cites a number of authorities who disagree with Rema and hold that the normative blessing ("on the reading of *megillah*") is recited when reading *megillah* before a group of women. He also quotes R. David Amar, who rules that one should not recite any blessing at all when reading for women. According to his argument, women are unable to focus on the reading for its entire duration, and therefore a blessing would be in vain. However, R. Yosef rejects this idea as well as the position that the blessing "to hear *megillah*" should be recited. In contemporary times, women are educated and capable of fully understanding the *megillah*. Therefore, all three initial blessings must be recited as is the custom even when reading for an individual.

In another responsum, R. Yosef again emphasizes that the blessing over reading *megillah* is the same for men and for women:

300. Modern *posekim* who rule this way, cited by R. Yosef, include *Responsa Rosh Mashbir*, *O.Ḥ.* #31; *Responsa Yashiv Moshe* #332; and *Responsa Shalmat Ḥayyim* 1:99.

73. *Responsa Yabbia Omer* *Vol. 8, Oraḥ Ḥayyim #22*
R. Ovadiah Yosef, Israel (1920–2013)

שו"ת יביע אומר
חלק ח, אורח חיים סימן כב

27) Regarding the matter of blessings over the *megillah* for one who reads *megillah* in order to discharge the obligation of women.... In reality, the custom has already spread in Jerusalem and in Israel to recite blessings on the reading of *megillah* for women – all three blessings before the reading...and the great rabbis of Jerusalem have agreed...and all the more so now, with the improvement of the generations, when nearly all women read and speak Hebrew and listen intently and understand all that is said in the *megillah*.... And the wording of the blessing is, "on the reading of *megillah*," for women, as well. It is not like those who say that one should recite, "to hear *megillah*" for women. The ruling of the greatest Aḥaronim is that the formula is the same for women and men. This is correct.

כז) בענין ברכות המגילה למי שקורא המגילה להוציא י"ח את הנשים.... ובאמת שכעת כבר פשט המנהג בירושלים ובא"י לברך על קריאת המגילה לנשים, כל שלשת הברכות שלפני קריאתה... וכן הסכימו גאוני ירושלים... וכל שכן האידנא דאכשור דרי, וכמעט כל הנשים קוראות ומדברות בלשון הקודש ומקשיבות רב קשב ומבינות כל הנאמר במגילה.... ונוסח הברכה "על מקרא מגילה" גם לנשים, ודלא כדעת האומרים לברך לנשים "לשמוע מגילה", וכן פסקו גדולי האחרונים שהנוסח שוה לנשים כאנשים. וכן עיקר.

Here, R. Yosef again argues against the idea that at a woman's reading no blessing should be recited, citing women's increased level of education and their capacity to read, focus on, and understand *Megillat Ester*. He also states clearly that "the greatest Aḥaronim" – presumably referring to R. Caro, Ḥida, the Vilna Ga'on, and others – agree that the language of *al mikra megillah* should remain the same, regardless of whether a man's or a woman's obligation is being fulfilled.

Despite the fact that contemporary authorities are divided on this issue, it seems that R. Yosef's ruling reflects the dominant position and practice, at least in Israel. R. Yosef Ḥayyim Sonnenfeld, an early-twentieth-century halakhic authority, who served as chief rabbi of the *Edah Haḥaredit* (Ultra-Orthodox community) in Jerusalem, recommends in *Responsa Shalmat Ḥayyim* that the standard blessing be recited in all cases:

74. *Responsa Shalmat Ḥayyim* *Vol. 1, #99*

שו״ת שלמת חיים חלק א סימן צט

R. Yosef Ḥayyim Sonnenfeld, Israel (1849–1932)

It appears from the words of the Rishonim who did not bring a different version of the blessing for women that if women bless "on the reading of *megillah*," like men, there is no objection. In this [manner], they will not come to err since they recite [the blessing] as it is written in prayer books.	והנראה מדברי הראשונים הפוסקים שלא הביאו נוסח אחר בברכה לנשים, נראה שאם יברכו "על מקרא מגילה" כאנשים ג"כ אין קפידא, ובזה לא יבואו לטעות כי יאמרו כמו שכתוב בסידורים.

R. Sonnenfeld notes that there is no reason the normative blessing should not work for women just as it does for men, for such is the implicit view of the various Rishonim who did not cite a separate formula for women. This wording is also the version printed in prayer books, and, therefore, he writes that it is best not to risk making a mistake by inserting a different version.[301]

Many *megillah* readings for women, whether the *megillah* is read by a woman or by a man, follow this recommendation and preserve the standard language of *al mikra megillah*. However, there are some readings by or for women in which *lishmo'a megillah* or *lishmo'a mikra megillah* is

301. The questioner assumes that ten women constitute a *tsibbur* for *megillah:*

והנה במקום שיש עשר נשים שרוצות לשמוע מקרא מגילה אז יכול הקורא להוציאן גם בהברכה אפי׳ אם נמצאת ביניהם אשה חכמה שיודעת בעצמה לברך היטב בלי שום שגיאה כדי שלא לחלק בין ציבור לציבור אי נימא דגם הן נחשבות לצבור בענין מגילה שגם הן חייבות בזה כאנשים.

R. Sonnenfeld seems to agree.

recited instead. As demonstrated above, the normative blessing is certainly the correct text according to those who think that women and men share the same obligation to read *megillah*. This practice is also correct according to those *posekim* who think that the language of the blessing should remain the same regardless of the nature of a woman's obligation.[302]

302. R. Moshe Shternbuch, in *Teshuvot Vehanhagot*, section 1, *O.Ḥ.* #403, forcefully states both of these arguments. First, in all likelihood, women are obligated to read *megillah*, and even if one says that they are not, there is no reason why they should not say the standard blessing, just as they would upon performing any positive, time-caused commandment in which they are not obligated. He also points out that the Talmud does not mention another version of the blessing. However, R. Shternbuch focuses specifically on the case of a man reading for women and is more concerned with the case of a man reciting the blessing for a women's reading than for the case of a woman reading on her own:

> ונבאר בענין קריאת מגילה לנשים שנהגו כשאיש קורא הן מברכות, או למ"ב האיש מברך, ולע"ד ד"ז צ"ע טובא וחוששני שיש בזה מכשול וכמו שנבאר, ואף שהעולם נהגו כן נראה דרך מרווח יותר, ושורש הדברים שבמ"א בשם הב"ח מסיק בסימן תרצ"ב (ס"ק ה') שאם האיש קורא לה, הוא מברך לה לשמוע מגילה, ואני תמה שלע"ד העיקר הלכה למעשה שיברך על מקרא מגילה, אף שקורא לנשים לבד, ראשית שלרוב הפוסקים נשים כאנשים והייבין בקריאה, וכן פוסק הגר"א להלכה, וכן בשעה"ץ תרפ"ט ס"ק ט"ז שזהו דיעה העיקרית, ולדידהו כשמברכת על השמיעה חסר ברכה על הקריאה שמחוייבת, משא"כ כשמברכין על מקרא מגילה לכ"ע יוצאה שהרי בבית הכנסת יוצאת אף ששומעת ברכת על מקרא מגילה, ועוד אפילו נשים פטורות מקריאה היינו טעמא שזהו מ"ע שהזמן גרמא, ומטעם הן היו באותו הנס מחייבינן רק שמיעה, אבל כשמקיימת המצוה בקריאה לא גרע מכל מ"ע שהז"ג שפטורות ומ"מ יכולות נמי לברך כשמקיימות מצוה והיינו נמי דקריאה דשומע כעונה יכולה לברך על מקרא שמקיימת... אבל כאן שמחוייבת בברכה יכול לברך לה הברכה המעולה, ועוד אני חושש שהוא מוציאה לאחר שיצא מדין ערבות, שחייב גם לנשים במצות שחייבות, ונקרא בכך בר חיובא בהמצוה, וחיובו היינו לקרוא לה, ושפיר עבורו שייך כבר נוסח הברכה, וממילא היא יוצאה, ומה שהרמ"א (תרפ"ט ס"ק ב') פוסק דאשה מברכת לשמוע מקרא מגילה, הלוא מיירי להדיא שקוראה לעצמה, אבל כשאיש קורא לה הוא מברך צל מקרא מגילה והיא יוצאה. ואדרבה לפי הדרך הנהוג היום, שהאשה השומעת היא מברכת לעצמה על שמיעת מגילה, חסר לה ברכה על הקריאה, אף שמחוייבת בכך לרוב הפוסקים, או אפילו על קיום המצוה לדידן, ועוד יש טעם בזה שאם היא רק מברכת לעצמה הלוא הוא קורא בלי ברכה שנתחיב לקרוא לה שהיא אינה מוציאה אותו, ואפילו הוא שומע ממנה כשמברכת לשמוע, לא שייך אצלו הברכה לשמוע, שחיובו לקרוא לה. וע"כ נלע"ד הדרך המחוורת שאם הוא קורא לה יברך הוא עבורה על מקרא מגילה, ויוצאה הברכה כה"ג מן המובחר, וכן בש"ס מייתינן נוסח הברכה על מקרא מגילה (רפ"ג) ולא השמיענו שלנשים נוסח אחר, וע"כ די לנו לברך

THE BLESSING AFTER THE *MEGILLAH* READING

The concluding question that must be addressed is the recitation of *harav et rivenu,* the blessing after the *megillah* reading, which appears in Tractate *Megillah* (source #62, above). The Talmud combines Rava's and Rav Pappa's opinions to create the full text of this blessing, which praises God as our savior, for having fought on our behalf throughout the events of the Purim story.

Shulḥan Arukh refers to the recitation of this blessing as a custom, not a mandatory practice:[303]

75. ***Shulḥan Arukh***	**שולחן ערוך אורח חיים**
Orah Ḥayyim 692:1	**סימן תרצב סעיף א**
R. Yosef Caro, Spain and Israel (1488–1575) R. Moshe Isserles, Poland (1525-1572)	
And afterward it is customary to recite the blessing, "who espouses our quarrels," etc.	[רמ"א] ולאחריה נוהגים לברך הרב את ריבנו וכו'.
Gloss [Rema]: ... and one should only recite the blessing afterward in a congregation.	הגה [רמ"א]: ... ואין לברך אחריה אלא בציבור.

R. Isserles (Rema), in his gloss on *Shulḥan Arukh,* adds that this blessing should be recited only in the presence of a *tsibbur* – a congregation or quorum of ten. Quoting directly from those who came before him, R. Caro, in his commentary to *Tur,* explains what is unique about this blessing:

לשמוע כמבואר ברמ"א כשהיא קוראה לעצמה, ולא נוסיף דגם כשאיש קורא לה דבר המצוי טובא נוסח הברכה בזה משונה, ואף שבכמה אחרונים מפורש שהאיש מברך על השמיעה נראה למעשה כמ"ש עיקר עיין היטב בדברינו כאן.

303. *Mishnah Berurah* 692:4 explains why *Sh. Ar.* holds that it is customary: the Mishnah states that the blessings are based on custom whereas the Talmud (source #62, above) explains that only the blessing after the reading is dependent on custom.

76. *Beit Yosef* *Oraḥ Ḥayyim 692:1* R. Yosef Caro, Spain and Israel (1488–1575)	**בית יוסף אורח חיים סימן תרצב:א**
And Ran wrote (12a, s.v. *barukh*): "One can ask in astonishment, why does this blessing open with *barukh*? For it is connected to the blessing that comes before it, since the *megillah* is certainly not [considered] a separation [between the blessings], just as the recitation of *shema* is not an interruption between its blessings, for which reason the final blessing [after *shema*] is connected to its neighbor [the blessing immediately preceding it]. One should say [in reply] that this final blessing is not [recited] over the reading of *megillah* but is rather a blessing in and of itself, which was established over the miracle." It is written in *Orḥot Ḥayyim* ... "they only recited the blessing afterward in a congregation."	וכתב הר"ן (יב. ד"ה ברוך) יש לתמוה ברכה זו למה פותחת בברוך שהרי היא סמוכה לברכה שלפניה דהא מגילה ודאי לא מפסקא כי היכי דלא מפסיק קריאת שמע בברכותיה דמשום הכי חשבינן ברכה אחרונה שלה סמוכה לחבירתה י"ל דהאי ברכה אחרונה לאו אקריאת מגילה אלא ברכה בפני עצמה שנתקנה על הנס. כתוב בארחות חיים... לא אמרו ברכה לאחריה אלא בצבור.

Here, R. Caro records the question asked by Ran: There is a general rule that a blessing that immediately follows another blessing does not open with the usual clause beginning with the word *barukh*.[304] In this case, the blessing following *megillah* reading is considered to follow immediately after the earlier three blessings, because the *megillah* itself is not deemed an interruption. Why, then, does it begin with the word *barukh*? R. Caro suggests that in the case of *megillah* this rule does not apply because the blessing *harav et rivenu* is actually a separate blessing over the miracle of Purim, rather than a continuation of the blessings over the reading of *megillah*. Thus, it is not intrinsically linked to the reading itself or the preceding *berakhot*. He then quotes *Orḥot Ḥayyim*, a fourteenth-century Provençal work, which says that

304. See J.T. *Ber.* 3d (on M. *Ber.* 1:4). All the blessings in the middle of the *shemoneh esreih* follow this rule.

this blessing is recited only in the presence of a *tsibbur*.[305] Since the focus of this blessing is the publicizing of the miracle, it can only be recited in a public setting.[306] Although some authorities maintain that this blessing may be recited even by an individual who reads *Megillat Ester* alone,[307] the vast majority of halakhic decisors agree that *harav et rivenu* is recited at the conclusion of *megillah* reading only when a quorum is present.[308]

R. Ovadiah Yosef, in *Responsa Yeḥavveh Da'at,* strongly endorses this position and emphasizes that this is the accepted ruling in Israel today:

77. *Responsa Yeḥavveh Da'at* Vol. 1, #88

שו"ת יחווה דעת חלק א סימן פח

R. Ovadiah Yosef, Israel (1920–2013)

However, the final blessing of the *megillah,* which is the blessing *ha'el harav et rivenu,* which is fundamentally only a custom, as is explained in [B.T.] *Megillah* (21a), and is said by way of praise and thanksgiving and not included in the category of blessings over *mitsvot*.... Therefore, it appears that one should only recite it with ten, for in that case there is *pirsumei nissa*. But when one reads *megillah* for the members of his household, he should not recite this blessing.... And who would dare to

אולם ברכה אחרונה של המגילה שהיא ברכת האל הרב את ריבנו, שאין עיקרה אלא מנהג, כמבואר במגילה (כ"א ע"א), והיא נאמרת דרך שבח והודאה, ואינה בכלל ברכת המצוות.... לפיכך נראה שאין לברך אותה אלא בעשרה, שאז יש פרסומי ניסא. אבל כשקורא המגילה לפני בני ביתו, אין לברך ברכה זו... ומי ירהיב עוז לחלוק על כל

305. *Orḥot Ḥayyim* cites the Yerushalmi as its source; however, there is some controversy as to whether such a statement is made therein.

306. Ritva also raises this possibility in his commentary to B.T. *Meg.* 21b. Radbaz, section 2, #665, formulates a similar idea despite ruling that a quorum is not actually necessary for this blessing.

307. Among these are *Shibbolei Haleket, Purim* 195; Radbaz, section 2, #665; and *Arukh Hashulḥan* 690:25.

308. Among these are *Sefer Kol Bo* #45 (source #17, above); *Be'ur Halakhah* 692:1, s.v. *ella betsibbur*; *Kitsur Sh. Ar.* #141; R. Ovadiah Yosef, *Responsa Yeḥavveh Da'at* 1:88 (source #72, above); *Ben Ish Ḥai, Parashat Tetsavveh* 13; and many others.

הפוסקים הנ"ל במקומות אלו, ובפרט במקום חשש איסור ברכה לבטלה.... בסיכום: יחיד הקורא מגילה לבני ביתו, יברך לפניה כל ברכות המגילה להוציא את בני ביתו ידי חובתן, אבל לאחריה אין לברך אלא בצבור.

disagree with all of the aforementioned *posekim*, and particularly in a case where we are concerned about blessing in vain.... In summary: an individual who reads *megillah* for the members of his household should recite all the blessings before the *megillah* [reading], so as to discharge the obligation of all members of his household, but afterward one should only recite the blessing with a quorum.

Like *Beit Yosef*, R. Yosef explains that this blessing is a custom, instituted to thank and praise God for the miracles God has performed. It is intrinsically linked with *pirsumei nissa* and therefore should only be recited with a quorum. R. Yosef makes clear that the dominant practice is to recite *harav et rivenu* only in the presence of a *tsibbur*.

If no quorum is required for the recitation of the final blessing, then there seems to be no reason why it should not be recited at a women's reading. However, most authorities agree that a quorum is required to recite *harav et rivenu*. The question of whether or not it is recited at a women's reading depends entirely on whether or not one thinks that ten women constitute a quorum for the purpose of *megillah* reading. As the previous section of this chapter illustrates, many halakhic authorities consider ten women to constitute a quorum in this case, though some do not. This issue is often intertwined with the question of whether *harav et rivenu* should be recited.

The following excerpt from R. Yosef's responsum (already quoted in part in source #73) addresses the recitation of the final blessing:

78. *Responsa Yabbia Omer* *Vol. 8, Oraḥ Ḥayyim #22*

R. Ovadiah Yosef, Israel (1920–2013)

שו"ת יביע אומר חלק ח אורח חיים סימן כב

כז) בענין ברכות המגילה למי שקורא המגילה להוציא י"ח את הנשים.... ובאמת שכעת

27) Regarding the matter of blessings over the *megillah* for one who reads the *megillah* in order to discharge the obligation of

women.... In reality, the custom has already spread in Jerusalem and in Israel to recite blessings on the reading of *megillah* for women – all three blessings before the reading...and if there are ten women, they should also bless afterward.

כבר פשט המנהג בירושלים ובא"י לברך על קריאת המגילה לנשים, כל שלשת הברכות שלפני קריאתה... ואם יש עשר נשים יברכו גם לאחריה.

R. Yosef notes that in a gathering of at least ten women, the final blessing is recited, as well. He reinforces this idea in another responsum cited above (source #61) as part of a discussion of whether women can constitute a quorum for *megillah* reading. Here, R. Yosef defends the practice of ten women gathering to hear the *megillah*:

79. *Responsa Yabbia Omer*
Vol. 8, Oraḥ Ḥayyim #56
R. Ovadiah Yosef, Israel (1920–2013)

שו"ת יביע אומר
חלק ח אורח חיים סימן נו

Question: Should one who reads *megillah* in his home to his wife and children recite the last blessing, "*ha'el harav et rivenu,*" after *megillah* reading?

שאלה: הקורא את המגילה בביתו לאשתו ולבני ביתו, האם יברך ברכה אחרונה "האל הרב את ריבנו", אחר קריאת המגילה.

4) And here...I wrote...that if there are ten women who hear the reading of the *megillah* and fulfill their obligation, they may bless afterward, as well, since *pirsumei nissa* happens in any case.

ד) והנה... כתבתי... שאם יש עשר נשים ששומעות קריאת המגילה ויוצאות ידי חובתן יכולות לברך גם לאחריה, כיון שעכ"פ יש בזה משום פרסומי ניסא.

R. Yosef rules here that ten women accomplish the purpose of publicizing the miracle of Purim, and thus it is correct to recite the blessing of *harav et rivenu* when reading for a group of at least ten women. Similarly R. Eliezer Waldenberg, quoted in the previous section (source #59), rules that ten women do constitute a quorum for the purpose of a *megillah* reading, and he maintains that all blessings are recited at a women's reading:

80. ***Responsa Tsits Eliezer***
Vol. 13, #73
R. Eliezer Waldenberg, Israel (1915–2006)

שו"ת ציץ אליעזר
חלק יג סימן עג

Therefore it is clear and simple as a matter of law that women, even *lekhatḥillah*, may gather [a group of] ten women in their homes in order to hear *megillah* reading and recite the blessings.... Specifically [in this case], as stated [above], the issue is clear that woman may, even *lekhatḥillah*, hear *megillah* reading among themselves and recite the blessings with [a quorum of] ten, without any doubt whatsoever.

על כן ברור ופשוט הדבר לדינא שיכולות הנשים אפילו לכתחילה לקבץ לעצמן עשר נשים בביתן לשמוע מקרא מגילה ולברך הברכות.... ובפרט דכאמור הדבר ברור שיכולות לשמוע אפילו לכתחילה מקרא מגילה בעשרה בפני עצמן ולברך הברכות בלי כל חשש כלל ועיקר.

R. Waldenberg does not distinguish between the blessings prior to reading *megillah* and the blessing that follows. In his view, ten women qualify as a quorum even *lekhatḥillah* and therefore may recite *harav et rivenu* after the *megillah* reading. Those halakhic decisors, quoted above, who rule that ten women do not count as a quorum, would presumably advise that a reading by or for women should not include this final blessing.

In summary, major halakhic authorities conclude that ten women do indeed constitute a quorum for the purpose of reading *megillah* and that therefore a women's reading should include the recitation of *harav et rivenu*. However, those authorities who think that a quorum is by definition all male, and that a group of women cannot count as a *tsibbur*, maintain that this blessing should not be recited at a gathering of women.[309] While each community follows its own halakhic leadership, reciting *harav et rivenu* has become a common practice at many women's *megillah* readings.

---

309. Some contemporary rabbis, who maintain that women do not constitute a quorum, and therefore may not recite the final blessing, argue that this may be a reason not to hold a women's reading at all. See, for example, R. Howard Jachter, "May Women Read the Megillah?" in *Gray Matter* (Teaneck, N.J.: Rabbi Howard Jachter, 2000), 224–32; and R. Schachter in source #41, above.

CONCLUSION

The sources provided in this chapter illustrate the nature of a woman's obligation in reading *megillah* and the implications for how a woman may fulfill that obligation. Surveying the material, beginning with early rabbinic sources and continuing chronologically through contemporary halakhic authorities, the following conclusions can be drawn:

- Women are obligated in *megillah* reading, as they, too, were part of the miracle of Purim (source #2).
- According to many authorities throughout the ages, based on a straightforward reading of the Talmud (sources #1 and 3), all – both women and men – share the same obligation – to read *megillah* (see, for example, source #8).
- According to other authorities, who give precedence to Behag's (source #6) concern for the statements of the Tosefta (source #5) over the straightforward reading of the Talmud, women have a different obligation from men – to hear, rather than to read, *megillah.*
- The Rishonim all agree that a woman may read *megillah* for other women or for herself (see sources #8–20). The view that women may read for other women is the most restrictive and conservative ruling based on the text of the Talmud.
- Some Rishonim rule that a woman may read *megillah* on behalf of men because women and men are equally obligated (see sources #8–13). However, others feel that although it is legally correct that a woman may fulfill the obligation of a man, she should not do so for it is undignified or inappropriate for women to read for men (see sources #14–17).
- Aḥaronim are also split on the issue of women's reading for others. A few maintain that women may read for men (sources #23–25), while others permit women to read only on behalf of other women (sources #26–28). A more restrictive position, based on a difficult text in *Midrash Hane'elam* (source #30), is introduced during this time period, arguing that women may not read *megillah* at all and that a woman should only hear a man read for her (sources #29–32).

- Contemporary authorities reflect the diversity of opinions recorded in earlier sources. Several important contemporary halakhic decisors are quite explicit about permitting or even encouraging women to read for other women (sources #42–48). Some recommend that women attend readings by men, if possible (sources #39–41), while a few mention the possibility of a woman's reading on behalf of men (sources #37 and 38).
- There is a difference of opinion as to the formulation of the blessing over the *mitsvah* both in cases where a woman reads *megillah* for herself or other women and where a man reads for a group of women. Some Ashkenazic *posekim* argue that women recite a different blessing, reflecting their obligation to hear the *megillah* (sources #63, 66, and 69), whereas other Ashkenazic authorities (sources #68, 70, and 74) and all Sephardic *posekim* (sources #64, 65, and 71–73) argue that the blessing should remain the same for men and women, as it was formulated by *Ḥazal* – "on the reading of *megillah*."
- Some authorities rule that women may even join with men to create the ten for *megillah* reading (sources #52–55). Many authorities who would be uncomfortable with a mixed group due to a concern for sexual immorality agree that to publicize the miracle, women as a group themselves without men present may create a quorum of ten for *megillah* reading (sources #59–61). In this case, women are permitted to recite the blessing *harav et rivenu*.[310]

Communities, in consultation with appropriate halakhic authorities, must make their own decisions about which rulings are best suited to their situation and congregation. These decisions should also be guided by the reality, mentioned by both R. Henkin (source #46, above) and R. Yosef (source #72, above), that many women today are fluent in Hebrew and educated enough to chant, read, and understand *Megillat Ester*. As a result, they are able to take an active role in performing

310. As well, they are permitted to convene a women's reading when the *megillah* is read on a day other than the actual day of Purim.

this *mitsvah*. In the midst of the often rowdy celebration of Purim, it is important to ensure that both men and women have the opportunity to fulfill the obligation of the holiday in the best way possible. As R. Benjamin Lau writes (source #48, above), hopefully the desire of women to participate will lead to a spiritual awakening because the goal should be "to lead *halakhah* and religion to its central and relevant place in our lives, both personal and communal." By studying these *halakhot* and making well-informed decisions, may the Jewish people merit the fulfillment of the verse in *Megillat Ester*: והימים האלה נזכרים ונעשים בכל דור ודור, "these days are remembered and enacted in each generation" (Esth. 9:28).

Contributors

Raḥel Berkovits is a senior lecturer in Mishnah, Talmud, and *halakhah* at the Pardes Institute of Jewish Studies in Jerusalem, where she has been teaching for almost twenty years. She writes articles and lectures widely both in Israel and abroad on topics concerning women and Jewish law. Raḥel is a founding member of Congregation *Shira Hadasha,* a halakhic partnership synagogue, and she serves on their *halakhah* committee. In June 2015, Raḥel received rabbinic ordination from Rabbis Herzl Hefter and Daniel Sperber.

Jennie Rosenfeld serves as the *manhigah ruḥanit* in Efrat, appointed by Rabbi Shlomo Riskin, as she completes her studies toward her *heter hora'ah* at the Susi Bradfield Women's Institute for Halakhic Leadership at Midreshet Lindenbaum. Jennie is a graduate of Stern College, and YU's Graduate Program in Advanced Talmudic Studies for Women. She holds an MS in Jewish Education from the Azrieli Graduate School and a PhD in English from CUNY Graduate Center. Jennie has co-authored *Et Le'ehov: The Newlywed's Guide to Physical Intimacy* (Gefen, 2011; Hebrew translation, 2013).

Sara Tillinger Wolkenfeld is the director of education at Sefaria.org. She has taught Talmud and Jewish Law at the Drisha Institute, and served as JLIC educator and director of education at the Center for Jewish Life – Hillel at Princeton University. Sara holds a BA in Judaica and Comparative Literature from the University of Pennsylvania, and has studied Talmud and Jewish Law at Midreshet Lindenbaum, Drisha, Pardes, Nishmat, and Beit Morashah. Sara lives in Chicago with her husband and children.

The fonts used in this book are from the Arno family

Maggid Books
The best of contemporary Jewish thought from
Koren Publishers Jerusalem Ltd.